Palgrave Studies in Economic History

Series editor
Kent Deng
London School of Economics
London, UK

Palgrave Studies in Economic History is designed to illuminate and enrich our understanding of economies and economic phenomena of the past. The series covers a vast range of topics including financial history, labour history, development economics, commercialisation, urbanisation, industrialisation, modernisation, globalisation, and changes in world economic orders.

More information about this series at
http://www.springer.com/series/14632

Leandro Prados de la Escosura

Spanish Economic Growth, 1850–2015

Leandro Prados de la Escosura
Department of Social Sciences
Universidad Carlos III
Madrid, Spain

Palgrave Studies in Economic History
ISBN 978-3-319-58041-8   ISBN 978-3-319-58042-5   (eBook)
DOI 10.1007/978-3-319-58042-5

Library of Congress Control Number: 2017939926

© The Editor(s) (if applicable) and The Author(s) 2017. This book is an open access publication.

Open Access This book is licensed under the terms of the Creative Commons Attribution 4.0 International License (http://creativecommons.org/licenses/by/4.0/), which permits use, sharing, adaptation, distribution and reproduction in any medium or format, as long as you give appropriate credit to the original author(s) and the source, provide a link to the Creative Commons license and indicate if changes were made.

The images or other third party material in this book are included in the book's Creative Commons license, unless indicated otherwise in a credit line to the material. If material is not included in the book's Creative Commons license and your intended use is not permitted by statutory regulation or exceeds the permitted use, you will need to obtain permission directly from the copyright holder.

The use of general descriptive names, registered names, trademarks, service marks, etc. in this publication does not imply, even in the absence of a specific statement, that such names are exempt from the relevant protective laws and regulations and therefore free for general use.

The publisher, the authors and the editors are safe to assume that the advice and information in this book are believed to be true and accurate at the date of publication. Neither the publisher nor the authors or the editors give a warranty, express or implied, with respect to the material contained herein or for any errors or omissions that may have been made. The publisher remains neutral with regard to jurisdictional claims in published maps and institutional affiliations.

Cover illustration: Steve Race/Stockimo/Alamy Stock Photo

Printed on acid-free paper

This Palgrave Macmillan imprint is published by Springer Nature
The registered company is Springer International Publishing AG
The registered company address is: Gewerbestrasse 11, 6330 Cham, Switzerland

For Blanca

Acknowledgements

I am most grateful to Albert Carreras, César Molinas, Patrick O'Brien, Joan Rosés, Blanca Sánchez-Alonso, James Simpson, David Taguas† and, especially, Angus Maddison† for their advice and inspiration over the years. Nelson Álvarez, Juan Carmona, Albert Carreras, Sebastián Coll, Francisco Comín, Antonio Díaz Ballesteros, Rosario Gandoy, Antonio Gómez Mendoza, Alfonso Herranz-Loncán, Stefan Houpt, Pablo Martín-Aceña, Elena Martínez Ruíz, Vicente Pérez Moreda, David Reher, Blanca Sánchez-Alonso, María Teresa Sanchis, James Simpson, Antonio Tena and Gabriel Tortella kindly allowed me to draw on their unpublished data. Pilar Martínez Marín and Begoña Varela Merino, at the Spanish Statistical Institute, kindly help me with some technicalities of the latest national accounts. I thank Julio Alcaide†, Bart van Ark, Carlos Barciela, Francisco Comín, Antonio Díaz Ballesteros, Rafael Dobado, Toni Espasa, Ángel de la Fuente, Ángel García Sanz†, Pedro Fraile Balbín, Pablo Martín-Aceña, César Molinas, Jordi Palafox, Vicente Pérez Moreda, Carlos Rodríguez Braun, Nicolás Sánchez-Albornoz, Blanca Sánchez-Alonso and Piero Tedde de Lorca for their valuable comments. Of course, this project would have not been completed without the stimulating academic environment of the Department of

Social Sciences at Carlos III University. Lastly, I would like to express my gratitude to Kent Deng, series editor and two anonymous referees, for their useful suggestions, and especially to Laura Pacey, Economics Commissioning Editor, for her encouragement and patience. A research grant from Fundación Rafael del Pino (Cátedra Rafael del Pino) is gratefully acknowledged.

Contents

Part I Main Trends

1	GDP and Its Composition	3
2	GDP and GDP Per Head	15
3	GDP per Head and Labour Productivity	25
4	Spain's Performance in Comparative Perspective	39
5	GDP, Income Distribution, and Welfare	47

Part II Measurement

6	Measuring GDP, 1850–1958: Supply Side	63
7	Measuring GDP, 1850–1958: Demand Side	111

8	New GDP Series and Earlier Estimates for the Pre-national Accounts Era	153
9	Splicing National Accounts, 1958–2015	169
10	Population, 1850–2015	189
11	Employment, 1850–2015	193
Appendices		201
Author Index		371
Subject Index		377

List of Figures

Fig. 1.1	Real GDP at market prices, 1850–2015 (2010 = 100) (logs)	4
Fig. 1.2	Private, government and total consumption as shares of GDP, 1850–2015 (% GDP) (current prices)	5
Fig. 1.3	Capital formation as a share of GDP, 1850–2015 (%) (current prices)	5
Fig. 1.4	Fixed capital formation and its composition, 1850–2015 (% GDP) (current prices)	6
Fig. 1.5	Openness: exports and imports shares in GDP (%) (current prices)	7
Fig. 1.6	Gross fixed capital formation and imports, 1850–2015 (8% GDP) (current prices)	8
Fig. 1.7	GDP composition from the output side (%) (current prices)	9
Fig. 1.8	Employment: hours worked distribution by economic sectors, 1850–2015 (%)	10
Fig. 1.9	Relative labour productivity (GVA per hour worked), 1850–2015 (average labour productivity = 1)	11
Fig. 2.1	Real absolute and per capita GDP, 1850–2015 (2010 = 100) (logs)	16
Fig. 2.2	Real GDP growth and its breakdown over long swings, 1850–2015 (logarithmic growth rates) (%)	17
Fig. 3.1	Real per capita GDP and its components, 1850–2015 (logs)	27

List of Figures

Fig. 3.2	Real per capita GDP growth and its breakdown over long swings, 1850–2015 (logarithmic growth rates) (%)	28
Fig. 3.3	Labour productivity growth and structural change over long swings: shift-share, 1850–2015 (logarithmic growth rates) (%)	32
Fig. 3.4	Labour productivity growth and structural change over long swings: modified shift-share, 1850–2015 (logarithmic growth rates) (%)	33
Fig. 3.5	Hours per full-time equivalent worker, 1850–2015	36
Fig. 3.6	Hours worked per head growth and its breakdown over long swings, 1850–2015 logarithmic growth rates (%)	36
Fig. 4.1	Spain's comparative real per capita GDP (2011 EKS $) (logs)	40
Fig. 4.2	Spain's relative real per capita GDP (2011 EKS $) (%)	42
Fig. 4.3	Spain's comparative real per capita GDP with alternative splicing (2011 EKS $) (logs)	43
Fig. 4.4	Spain's real per capita GDP relative to France and the UK with alternative splicing (2011 EKS $)	44
Fig. 5.1	Net national disposable income ratio to GDP 1850–2015 (current prices) (%)	48
Fig. 5.2	Real per capita GDP and net national disposable income, 1850–2015 (2010 = 100) (logs)	48
Fig. 5.3	Real per capita GDP and private consumption, 1850–2015 (2010 = 100) (logs)	50
Fig. 5.4	Income inequality, 1850–2015: Gini coefficient	51
Fig. 5.5	Inequality extraction ratio 1850–2015	53
Fig. 5.6	Real per capita GDP and Sen welfare, 1850–2015 (2010 = 100) (logs)	54
Fig. 5.7	Real per capita GDP (2010 = 100) (logs) and historical index of human development [HIHD*] (excluding income dimension), 1850–2007	56
Fig. 6.1	Non-residential construction volume indices, 1850–1935: alternative estimates (1913 = 100)	80
Fig. 7.1	Private consumption paasche deflator and laspeyres consumer price index, 1850–1958 (1913 = 100) (logs)	116
Fig. 7.2	Gross investment in non-residential construction volume indices, 1850–1935: Alternative Estimates (1913 = 100)	121

Fig. 8.1	Alternative real GDP estimates, 1850–1958 (1958 = 100) (logs)	159
Fig. 8.2	Alternative real GDP estimates, 1900–1958 (1958 = 100) (logs)	160
Fig. 9.1	Ratio between hybrid linearly interpolated and retropolated nominal GDP series, 1958–2000	179
Fig. 9.2	Real GDP, 1958–2000 (2010 Euro) (logs): alternative estimates with hybrid linear interpolation and retropolation splicing (logs)	180
Fig. 9.3	Real gross value added, 1958–2015 (2010 Euro) (logs): alternative estimates with hybrid linear interpolation and mixed splicing, 1958–2015	181

List of Tables

Table 2.1	Growth of GDP and its components, 1850–2015 (%) (average yearly logarithmic rates)	16
Table 3.1	GDP per head growth and its components, 1850–2015 (%) (average yearly logarithmic rates)	26
Table 3.2	Labour productivity growth by sectors, 1850–2015 (%) (GVA per hour worked) (average yearly logarithmic rates)	29
Table 3.3	Labour productivity growth and structural change, 1850–2015 (%) (average yearly logarithmic rates)	31
Table 3.4	Hours worked per head growth and its composition, 1850–2015 (%) (average yearly logarithmic rates)	34
Table 4.1	Comparative per capita GDP growth, 1850–2015 (%) (average annual logarithmic rates)	41
Table 5.1	Real per capita GDP, NNDI, private consumption, and Sen-welfare growth, 1850–2015 (%) (average yearly logarithmic rates)	49
Table 5.2	Real per capita GDP and human development growth, 1850–2007 (%). (average yearly logarithmic rates)	57
Table 6.1	Agricultural final output: benchmark estimates, 1890–1960/64	66

xvi   List of Tables

Table 6.2	Agricultural final output at current prices, 1890–1964 (%)	69
Table 6.3	Construction of agricultural volume indices, 1850–1958	70
Table 6.4	Composition of manufacturing value added in 1958	73
Table 6.5	Breakdown of manufacturing value added, 1913–1958 (%)	75
Table 8.1	Real GDP growth in the pre-national accounts era: alternative estimates, 1850–1958 (%)	161
Table 9.1	Spain's national accounts, 1954–2015	170
Table 9.2	GDP at market prices: alternative estimates (Million Euro at current prices)	172
Table 9.3	Real GDP Growth: Alternative Splicing, 1958–2010 (annual average rates %)	178
Table A.1	Ratios of final output to total production for main crops	201
Table A.2	Conversion coefficients applied to livestock numbers to derive meat, wool and milk output, 1891–1924	202
Table A.3	Coverage of the sample of products included in the annual index for each agricultural group at benchmarks (%) (current prices)	203
Table S1	Gross domestic product and its expenditure components, 1850–2015 (million Euro)	205
Table S2	Gross domestic product, gross and net national income, 1850–2015 (million Euro)	213
Table S3	Absolute and per capita gross domestic product, gross and net domestic income, 1850–2015 (million Euro and Euro)	221
Table S4	Volume indices of absolute and per capita gross domestic product, gross and net national income, 1850–2015 (2010 = 100)	229
Table S5	Shares of expenditure components in gross domestic product, 1850–2015 (percentage)	237
Table S6	Volume indices of gross domestic product and its expenditure components, 1850–2015 (2010 = 100)	245
Table S7	Deflators of gross domestic product and its expenditure components, 1850–2015 (2010 = 100)	254

Table S8	Gross domestic fixed capital formation, 1850–2014 (million Euro)	261
Table S9	Composition of gross domestic fixed capital formation, 1850–2015 (percentages)	265
Table S10	Volume indices of gross domestic fixed capital formation, 1850–2015 (2010 = 100)	270
Table S11	Deflators of gross domestic fixed capital formation, 1850–2015 (2000 =100)	274
Table S12	Gross domestic product and its output components, 1850–2015 (million Euro)	278
Table S13	Absolute and per capita gross value added and gross domestic product at market prices, 1850–2015 (million Euro and Euro)	286
Table S14	Volume indices of absolute and per capita gross domestic product at market prices and gross value added, 1850–2015 (2010 = 100)	291
Table S15	Shares of output components in gross value added, 1850–2015 (percentage)	296
Table S16	Volume indices of gross value added and its output components, 1850–2015 (2010 = 100)	301
Table S17	Deflators of gross value added and its output components, 1850–2015 (2010 = 100)	306
Table S18	Employment (full-time equivalent), 1850–2015 (million)	311
Table S19	Sector shares in employment (full-time equivalent), 1850–2015 (percentage)	316
Table S20	Relative sector labour productivity (full-time equivalent employment), 1850–2015 (Average productivity = 1)	321
Table S21	Labour productivity indices (gross value added per full-time equivalent occupied), 1850–2015 (2010 = 100)	326
Table S22	Hours worked, 1850–2015 (million)	331
Table S23	Sector shares in worked hours, 1850–2015 (percentage)	336
Table S24	Relative sector labour productivity (hours), 1850–2015	341
Table S25	Labour productivity levels (per worked hour), 1850–2015 (2010 = 100)	346
Table S26	Hours worked per full-time equivalent occupied/year, 1850–2015	351

List of Tables

Table S27 Real per capita gross domestic product, 1850–2015
(EKS $2011) 356

Table S28 Real per capita gross domestic product, 1850–2015
(Geary-Khamis $1990) 363

Introduction

What does GDP really mean? Is it a measure of material welfare or simply a measure of output? In its report to President Sarkozy of France, the Commission on the Measurement of Economic Performance and Social Progress claimed 'GDP is an inadequate metric to gauge well-being over time particularly in its economic, environmental, and social dimensions' (Stiglitz et al. 2009: 8). A wave of critical publications (Coyle 2014; Masood 2016; Philipsen 2015, among others) followed rejecting any pretence for GDP to capture anything other than market economic activity.

Calls have been made to broaden the narrow focus of GDP with a more comprehensive measure of quality of life that includes health, education, non-market activities, the environment, political voice and personal security (Stiglitz et al. 2009; OECD 2011). This approach does stress capabilities, that is, the ability of individuals to choose among different functionings. It is actually with this perspective that the United Nations Development Programme (UNDP) introduced the concept of human development, defined as 'a process of enlarging people's choices'(UNDP 1990: 10) and has published an index, the HDI, that fails, though, to incorporate agency—that is, the ability to pursue and realize goals a person has reasons to value—and freedom (Ivanov and Peleah 2010).

The novelty of these claims is arguable since the depiction of GDP as a crude measure of economic progress and an even poorer measure of welfare—because it does not take into consideration informal and non-market activities, leisure and human capital investment, while ignores environmental costs and income distribution—has been shared among economists from the inception of national accounts (Beckerman 1976; Engerman 1997; Nordhaus 2000; Syrquin 2016). More than four decades have passed since William Nordhaus and James Tobin (1972: 4) wrote in a classical paper, 'GNP is not a measure of economic welfare … An obvious shortcoming of GNP is that it is an index of production, not consumption. The goal of economic activity, after all, is consumption'.

Moreover, it has long been acknowledged that, in defining GDP, the concerns of public economists during World War II and its aftermath played a decisive role, a fact that its critics now emphasise (Coyle 2014; Syrquin 2016). It is worth noting, for example, the inclusion of government services as part of GDP, a criterion of the US Department of Commerce which Simon Kuznets rejected, as he saw them as intermediate, not final goods (Higgs 2015). The problem of measuring non-market services, such as health or education, often provided by the government, is largely its legacy.

Interestingly, those who claim that GDP is a flawed measure of economic welfare tend to accept that GDP per head is highly correlated with non-monetary dimensions of well-being (Oulton 2012). In a recent contribution, Jones and Klenow (2016), after claiming that GDP is a flawed measure of economic welfare and putting forward an alternative comprehensive measure of welfare which combines data on consumption, life expectancy at birth, leisure and income inequality, come to the conclusion that per capita GDP 'is an informative indicator of welfare' as it presents a 0.98 correlation with their consumption-equivalent welfare index for a sample of 13 countries.

Such conclusion lends support to Kuznets' depiction of GDP as a measure of economic welfare from a long run perspective (Syrquin 2016). It is also provides grounds for mainstream economists to argue that GDP provides a measure of material prosperity (Broadberry et al. 2014; Mankiw 2016).

Can we, then, rely on historical estimates of GDP to assess output and material welfare in the long run? In the early days of modern economic quantification, Kuznets (1952: 16–17) noticed the 'tendency to shrink from long-term estimates' due to 'the increasing inadequacy of the data as one goes back in time and to the increasing discontinuity in social and economic conditions'. Cautious historians recommend to restrict the use of GDP to societies that had efficient recording mechanisms, relatively centralized economic activities, and a small subsistence sector (Hudson 2016; Deng and O'Brien 2016). But should not the adequacy of data be 'judged in terms of the uses of the results' (Kuznets 1952: 17)?

It is in this context that a new set of historical national accounts for Spain, with GDP estimates from the demand and supply sides, is presented and used to draw the main trends in Spanish modern economic growth.

The new set of historical national accounts revises and expands the estimates in Prados de la Escosura (2003). Firstly, historical output and expenditure series are reconstructed for the century prior to the introduction of modern national accounts. Then, available national accounts are spliced through *interpolation*, as an alternative to conventional *retropolation*, to derive new continuous series for 1958–2015. Later, the series for the 'pre-statistical era' are linked to the spliced national accounts providing yearly series for GDP and its components over 1850–2015.

All reservations about national accounts in currently developing countries do apply to pre-1958 Spain.[1] In fact, Kuznets' (1952: 9) sceptical words are most relevant, 'Consistent and fully articulated sets of estimates of income, … and its components, for periods long enough to reveal the level and structure of the nation's economic growth, are not available … The estimates … are an amalgam of basic data, plausible inferences, and fortified guesses'. Thus, despite the collective efforts underlying the historical output and expenditure series offered here, the numbers for the 'pre-statistical era' have inevitably large margins of error.[2] This warning to the user is worth because as Charles Feinstein (1988: 264) wrote, 'once long runs of estimates are systematically arrayed in neat tables they convey a wholly spurious air of precision'.

Nonetheless, the new series represent an improvement upon earlier estimates, as they are constructed from highly disaggregated data grounded on the detailed, painstaking research on Spain carried out by economic historians. A systematic attempt has been made to reconcile the existing knowledge on the performance of individual industries, including services (largely neglected in earlier estimates), with an aggregate view of the economy.

The book is organized in two parts. The first one offers an overview of Spain's long-run aggregate performance, on the basis of the new GDP, population and employment series. Thus, GDP per head is derived, decomposed into labour productivity and the amount of work per person and placed into international perspective. Later, the extent to which GDP captures welfare is discussed. Part II addresses measurement and provides a detailed discussion about how GDP estimates are constructed. Thus, it includes two sections on the 'pre-statistical era' (1850–1958) describing the procedures and sources used to derive annual series of nominal and real GDP for both the supply (section I) and the demand (section II). Then, in section III, the new results are compared to earlier estimates for pre-national accounts years. Lastly, in section IV, the different sets of national accounts available for 1958–2015 are spliced through interpolation, and the resulting series compared to those obtained through alternative splicing procedures and, then, linked to the pre-1958 historical estimates in order to obtain yearly GDP series for 1850–2015. Additionally, details are provided on the estimates of population and employment.

Notes

1. Cf. Srinivasan (1994), Heston (1994), and Jerven (2013) on national accounts in developing countries.
2. Spanish historical statistics edited by Carreras and Tafunell (2005) provide a comprehensive survey of the achievements in quantitative research during the last four decades.

References

Beckerman, W. 1976. *An Introduction to National Income Analysis*, 2nd ed. London: Weidenfeld and Nicholson.

Carreras, A., and X. Tafunell (eds.). 2005. *Estadísticas Históricas de España*, vol. 3. Bilbao: Fundación BBVA.

Coyle, D. 2014. *GDP: A Brief but Affectionate History*, Princeton: Princeton University Press.

Deng, K., and P. O'brien. 2016. China's GDP Per Capita from the Han Dynasty to Communist Times. *World Economics* 17 (2): 79–123.

Engerman, S.L. 1997. The Standard of Living Debate in International Perspective: Measure and Indicators. In *Health and Welfare during Industrialization*, ed. R.H. Steckel and R. Floud, 17–45. University of Chicago Press/NBER.

Feinstein, C.H. 1988. Sources and Methods of Estimation for Domestic Reproducible Fixed Assets, Stocks and Works in Progress, Overseas Assets, and Land. In *Studies in Capital Formation in the United Kingdom 1750–1920*, ed. C.H. Feinstein and S. Pollard, 257–471. Oxford: Clarendon Press.

Heston, A. 1994. A Brief Review of Some Problems in Using National Accounts Data in Level of Output Comparisons and Growth Studies. *Journal of Development Economics* 44: 29–52.

Higgs, R. 2015. Gross Domestic Product—An Index of Economic Welfare or a Meaningless Metric? *The Independent Review* 20 (1): 153–157.

Hudson, P. 2016. GDP Per Capita: From Measurement Tool to Ideological Construct. *LSE Business Review*.

Ivanov, A., and M. Peleah. 2010. *From Centrally Planned Development to Human Development*. UNDP Human Development Reports Research Paper 2010/38.

Jerven, M. 2013. *Poor Numbers. How We Are Misled by African Development Statistics and What to Do about It*. Ithaca: Cornell University Press.

Jones, C.I., and P.J. Klenow. 2016. Beyond GDP? Welfare across Countries and Time. *American Economic Review* 106 (9): 2426–2457.

Kuznets, S. 1952. Income and Wealth of the United States. Trends and Structure, Income and Wealth Series II. Cambridge: Bowes and Bowes.

Masood, E. 2016. *The Great Invention: The Story of GDP and the Making (and Unmaking) of the Modern World*. Pegasus.

Nordhaus, W.D., and J. Tobin. 1972. Is Growth Obsolete? In *Economic Research: Retrospect and Prospect.* V. *Economic Growth,* ed. W.D. Nordhaus and J. Tobin, 1–80. New York: NBER/Columbia University Press.

Nordhaus, W. 2000. New Directions in National Economic Accounting. *American Economic Review Papers and Proceedings* 90 (2): 259–263.

OECD. 2011. *How's Life. Measuring Wellbeing.* Paris: OECD Publishing. http://dx.doi.org/10.1787/9789264121164-en.

Oulton, N. 2012. Hooray for GDP! Centre for Economic Performance Occasional Paper 30 (August).

Philipsen, D. 2015. *The Little Big Number: How GDP Came to Rule the World and What to Do about It.* Princeton: Princeton University Press.

Prados de la Escosura, L. 2003. *El progreso económico de España, 1850–2000.* Bilbao: Fundación BBVA.

Srinivasan, T.N. 1994. Data Base for Development Analysis: An Overview. *Journal of Development Economics* 44: 3–27.

Stiglitz, J.E., Sen, A., and Fitoussi, J.P. 2009. Report by the Commission on the Measurement of Economic Performance and Social Progress. http://ec.europa.eu/eurostat/documents/118025/118123/Fitoussi+Commission+report.

Syrquin, M. 2016. A Review Essay on GDP: A Brief but Affectionate History by Diane Coyle. *Journal of Economic Literature* 254 (2): 573–588.

United Nations Development Program [UNDP]. 1990–2011. Human Development Report. New York: Oxford University Press.

Part I

Main Trends

1

GDP and Its Composition

Aggregate economic activity multiplied fifty times between 1850 and 2015, at an average cumulative growth rate of 2.4% per year (Fig. 1.1). Four main phases may be established: 1850–1950 (with a shift to a lower level during the Civil War, 1936–1939), 1950–1974, 1974–2007 and 2007–2015, in which the growth trend varied significantly (Table 2.1).[1] Thus, in the phase of fastest growth, the *Golden Age* (1950–1974), GDP grew at 6.3% annually, four and a half times faster than during the previous hundred years and twice faster than over 1974–2007, while the Great Recession represented a fall in real GDP between 2007 and 2013 (8%), and the 2007 level had not been recovered by 2015. Gross Domestic Income (GDI), that is, income accruing to those living in Spain, as opposed to output produced in Spain, shadows closely GDP evolution.

A look at the evolution of output and expenditure components of GDP provides valuable information about its determinants. Changes in the composition of demand are highly revealing of the deep transformation experienced by Spain's economy over the last two centuries.

Fig. 1.1 Real GDP at market prices, 1850–2015 (2010 = 100) (logs)

The share of total consumption in GDP remained stable at a high level up to the late 1880s, followed by a decline that reached beyond World War I (Fig. 1.2). Then, it recovered in the early 1920s, helped by the rise in government consumption (Fig. 1.2, right scale), stabilizing up to mid-1930s. The Civil War (1936–1939) and World War II (even if Spain was a non-belligerent country) accounted for the contraction in private consumption and the sudden and dramatic increase in government consumption shares in GDP. The share of total consumption only fell below 85% of GDP after 1953, when a long-run decline was initiated reaching a trough (at three-fourths of GDP) by the mid-2000s. Such a decline in the GDP share of total consumption conceals an intense decline in private consumption (which contracted from 75% of GDP in 1965 to a historical trough, 56%, in 2009) paralleled by a sustained rise in government consumption (which jumped from a 7.5% trough in the mid-1960s to a 20% peak in 2009–2010) that resulted from the expansion of the welfare state and the transformation of a highly centralized state into a de facto federal state (Comín 1992, 1994).

Investment oscillated around 5% of GDP in the second half of the nineteenth century except during the late 1850s and early 1860s railways construction boom, when it doubled (Fig. 1.3). From the turn of the

1 GDP and Its Composition 5

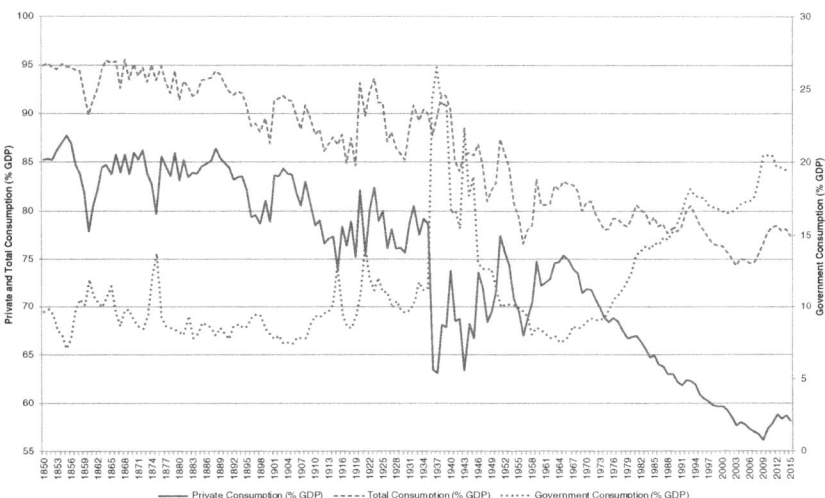

Fig. 1.2 Private, government and total consumption as shares of GDP, 1850–2015 (% GDP) (current prices)

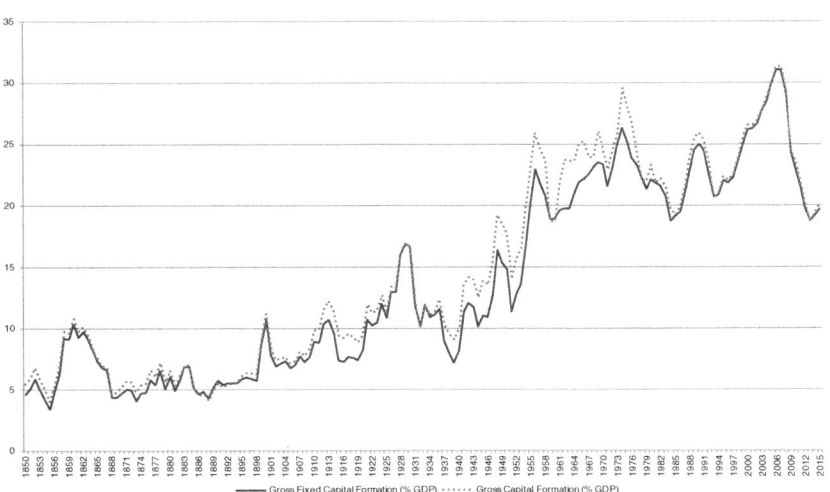

Fig. 1.3 Capital formation as a share of GDP, 1850–2015 (%) (current prices)

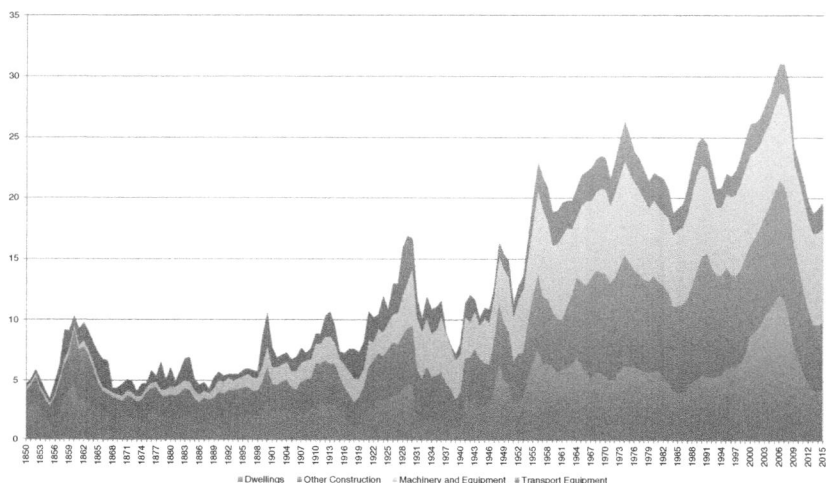

Fig. 1.4 Fixed capital formation and its composition, 1850–2015 (% GDP) (current prices)

century, a long-term increase took place with the relative level of capital formation increasing from around 5 to above 30% of GDP in 2006. Phases of investment acceleration appear to be associated with those of faster growth in aggregate economic activity, namely the late-1850s and early 1860s, the 1920s, from the mid-1950s to the early 1970s, and between Spain's accession to the European Union (EU) (1985) and 2007. Nonetheless, the long-run increase was punctuated by reversals during the World Wars and the Spanish Civil War, the transition to democracy (1975–1985), which coincided with the oil shocks, and the Great Recession (2008–2013).

The breakdown of gross domestic fixed capital formation shows the prevalence of residential and non-residential construction as its main components over time, with a gradual rise of the share of more productive assets (machinery and transport equipment) during the twentieth century up to 1974 that stabilized thereafter (Fig. 1.4). The urbanization and industrialization push in the 1920s and between 1950 and the early 1970s reflects clearly across different types of assets. It is worth noting the increase in the share of infrastructure after Spain's accession to the EU

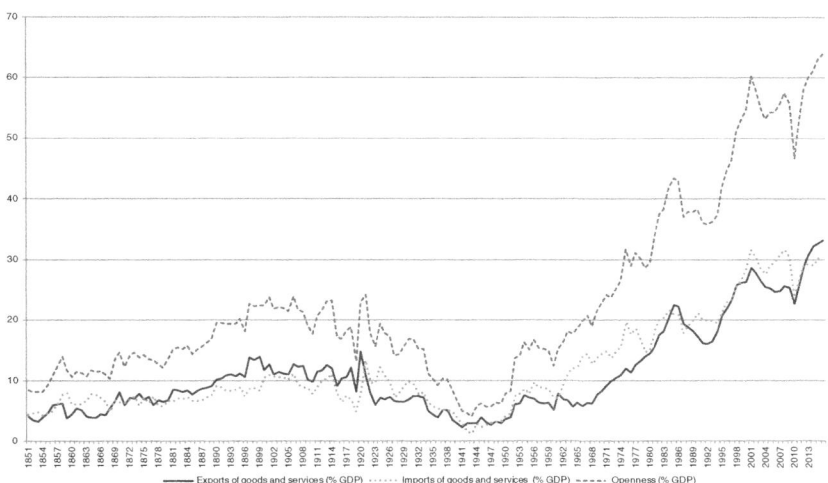

Fig. 1.5 Openness: exports and imports shares in GDP (%) (current prices)

and the residential construction bubble between the late 1990s and 2007.

The exposition of Spain to the international economy also increased but following a non-monotonic pattern, with three main phases: a gradual rise in openness (that is, exports plus imports as a share of GDP) during the second half of the nineteenth century that at the beginning of the twentieth century stabilized at a high plateau up to 1914; this was followed by a sharp decline from the early 1920s to mid-century that reach a trough during World War II (Fig. 1.5). A cautious but steady process of integration in the international economy took place since the 1950s, facilitated by the reforms associated with the 1959 Stabilization and Liberalization Plan.

How gradual was the post-1950 recovery is shown by the fact that only in 1955 the level of openness of 1929 was reached and that the historical maximum of the pre-World War I years was overcome in 1970. It took longer for exports than for imports to recover pre-World War I relative size (only in 1980 that of the 1910s was overcome). Spain's increasing openness during the last four decades suffered, nonetheless,

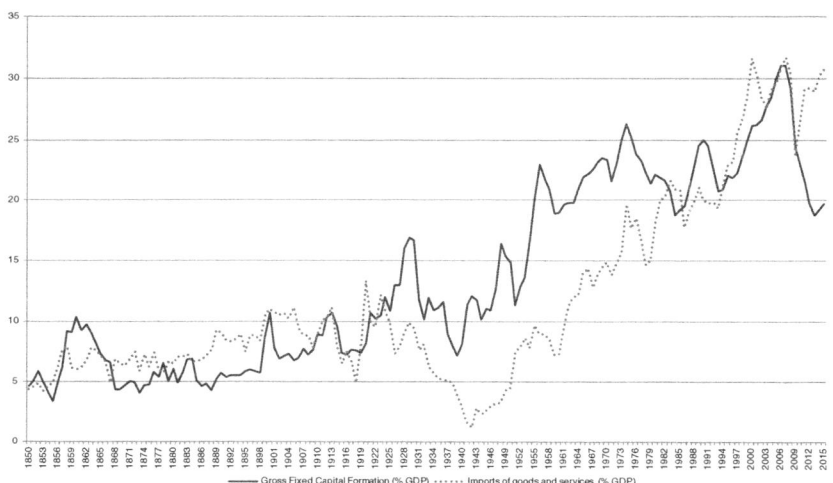

Fig. 1.6 Gross fixed capital formation and imports, 1850–2015 (8% GDP) (current prices)

reversals in the second half of the 1980s and, again, in the 2000s as a result of a contraction in exports.

It is worth mentioning the concordance observed between investment and imports, which suggests a connection between economic growth and exposure to international competition (Fig. 1.6). Furthermore, phases of more intense imports and investment are also those of deficit in the balance of goods and services, which suggests an inflow of capital and a link between the external sector and capital formation.

The composition of GDP by sectors of economic activity between 1850 and 2015 highlights the transformations associated with modern economic growth (Fig. 1.7).

Agriculture's share underwent a sustained contraction over time, but for the autarkic reversal of the 1940s, which intensified during the late 1880s and early 1890s, the 1920s and over 1950–1980. Industry, including manufacturing, extractive industries and utilities, followed an inverse U, expanding its relative size up to the late 1920s and, after the 1930s and 1940s backlash, resumed its relative increase to stabilize at a high plateau (around 30% of GDP). Since the mid-1980s, the share of

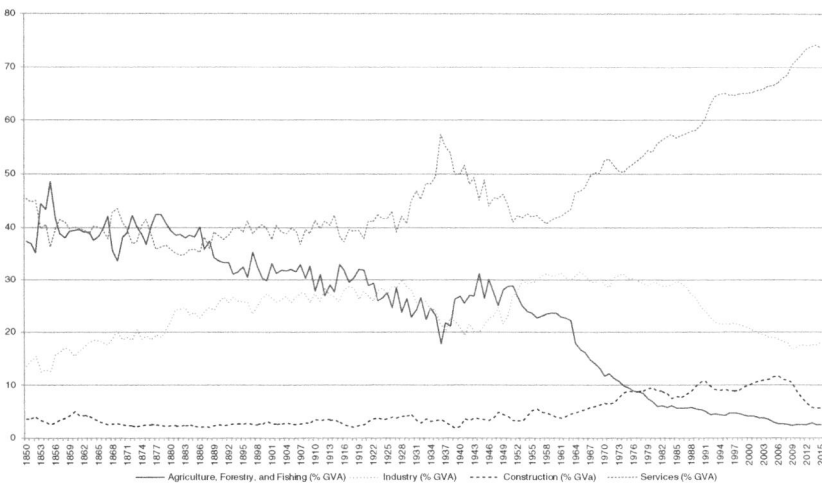

Fig. 1.7 GDP composition from the output side (%) (current prices)

industry dropped sharply, as sheltered and uncompetitive industries collapsed due to liberalization and opening up after EU accession. By 2010, the relative size of industry had shrunk to practically one-half of its peak in the early 1960s. Construction industry remained stable below 5% of GDP until mid-twentieth century (but for expansionary phases in the late 1850s and early 1860s, 1920s and 1950s), exhibiting a sustained increase since the early 1960s that peaked during the mid-2000s, more than doubling its relative size. The end of the construction bubble during the Great Recession implied a return to the mid-1960s relative size.

Services made a high and stable contribution to GDP, fluctuating around 40%, between mid-nineteenth and mid-twentieth century, but for the 1930–1940s parenthesis of depression, civil war and autarky, and expanded from less than one-half to three-fourths of GDP between the early 1960s and 2015.

The evolution of services as a share of GDP in Spain, with a high share of GDP in early stages of development (around 40%), conflicts with the literature on structural change, which suggests a growing contribution of services to GDP as per capita income increases (Chenery and Syrquin 1975; Prados de la Escosura 2007a). A path dependency explanation

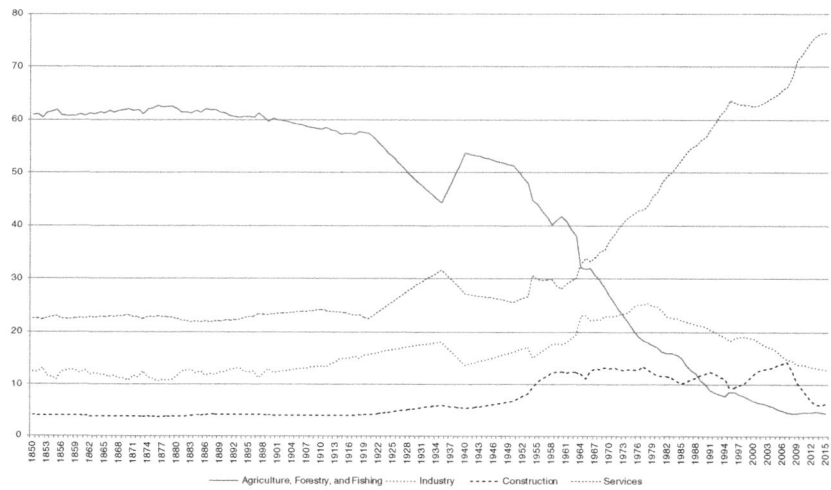

Fig. 1.8 Employment: hours worked distribution by economic sectors, 1850–2015 (%)

could be hypothesized as the arrival of American silver remittances in the early modern era (sixteenth and eighteenth centuries), altered the relative prices of tradable and non-tradable goods, in an early experience of 'Dutch disease', shifting domestic resources towards non-tradable production (Forsyth and Nicholas 1983; Drelichman 2005).[2]

Comparing the sectoral composition of GDP to that of labour can be illuminating. Figure 1.8 presents the composition of employment in terms of hours worked across industries.

Agriculture's share exhibits a long-run decline from above three-fifths to less than 5% since 2006. It fell more gradually up to 1950—but for the sharp contraction of the 1920s and early 1930s—reverted during the Civil War (1936–1939) and its autarkic aftermath, and accelerated over 1950–1990, when it shrank from half the labour force to one-tenth. Even though its numbers might be over-exaggerated prior to mid-twentieth century due to peasants' economic activities outside agriculture, agriculture provides the largest contribution to employment up to 1964, when it still represented one-third of total hours worked. The evolution of the relative size of services, whose figures may be underestimated before 1950, for the same reasons of agriculture's over-exaggeration, presents a mirror image of agriculture, taking over as the largest industry from 1965 onwards and reaching three-fourths of total hours worked by 2015. Industry's steady expansion, but for the Civil War reversal, overcame agriculture's share by 1973 and peaked by the late 1970s reaching one-fourth of employment to initiate a gradual contraction that has cut its relative size by almost half by 2015. Construction, in turn, more than trebled its initial share by 2007, sharply contracting as the sector's bubble ended during the Great Recession.

As already observed in GDP composition, an initial phase of structural change, in which the agricultural sector contracted and that of industry expanded—only broken by the post-war falling behind—was followed by a second phase since 1980, in which the relative decline involved, in addition to agriculture, the industrial sector, while employment in services accelerated its escalation.

Comparing the sectoral distribution of GDP and employment allows us to establish labour productivity (measured as Gross Value Added [GVA] per hour worked) by industry relative to the economy's average (Fig. 1.9). Several features stand out. Relative industrial productivity

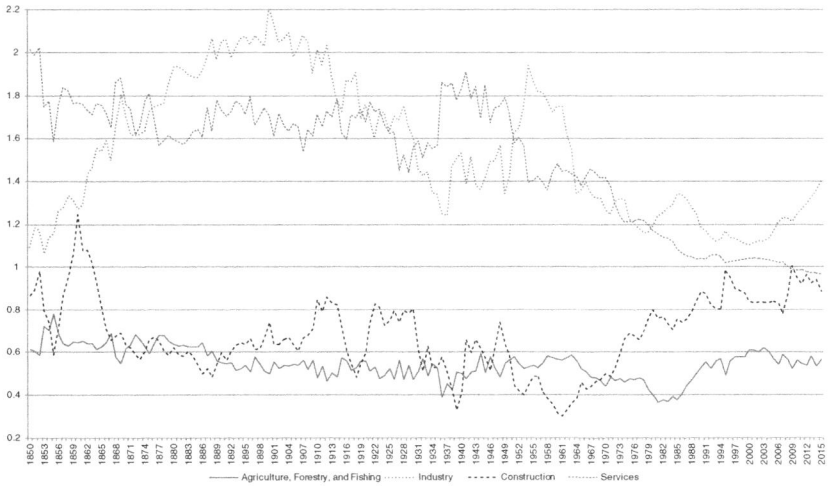

Fig. 1.9 Relative labour productivity (GVA per hour worked), 1850–2015 (average labour productivity = 1)

increased to reach a plateau over the late 1880s and World War I in which it doubled it. Episodes of intensified industrialization and urbanization in the 1920s and, to a larger extent, between the mid-1950s and mid-1970s, were accompanied by the expansion of industrial employment, which underlies the decline in the relative productivity of industry and services.

Agricultural labour productivity fluctuated between one-half and two-third of the economy's average (exceptional peaks and troughs aside) and tended to be rather stable. Such stability between 1890 and 1960, hardly affected by the gradual contraction of agricultural share in employment, shows the moderate and gradual structural transformation of the Spanish economy. In the 1960s accelerated industrialization, upheld by capital intensification and the incorporation of new technologies, and industrial restructuring in the late 1970s explain the sharp drop in the relative productivity of the agricultural sector. In turn, the recovery of agriculture's relative productivity in the late 1980s and early 1990s is attributable to the destruction of agricultural employment that cut its share by half.

The gradual reduction in productivity differences across sectors during the last half a century suggests moderate convergence in factor proportions and could be interpreted as a result of improved resource allocation.[3]

Notes

1. Main phases defined as deviations from segmented trend estimates with exogenous structural breaks in Prados de la Escosura (2003, 2007b) have been kept here. A change of trend indicates a break in the long-term rate of growth. A change in level, as the drop in economic activity during the Civil War, does not alter the established growth rate.
2. As the rise of the metropolis' price level favoured the importation of tradable goods and provoked the dissolution of local industry, while the price increase stimulated the production of goods that were not traded internationally.
3. Still, the high relative labour productivity of services during the hundred years spanning 1850–1950 calls for a revision of the sectoral distribution of employment and could be ventured that a more rigorous calculation

would reveal a lesser proportion of employment in agriculture and a greater one in services, with consequent repercussions on the relative productivity of labour in each sector.

References

Chenery, H.B., and M. Syrquin. 1975. *Patterns of Development,* 1950–1970. Oxford: Oxford University Press.

Comín, F. 1992. Una reconstrucción diferente en la España de la postguerra. *Estudis d'Historia Económica* 2: 63–78.

Comín, F. 1994. El papel del presupuesto en el crecimiento económico español: una visión a largo plazo. *Revista de Historia Económica* 12: 283–314.

Drelichman, M. 2005. The curse of Moctezuma: American Silver and the Dutch Disease. *Explorations in Economic History* 42: 349–380.

Forsyth, P.J., and S.J. Nicholas. 1983. The Decline of Spanish Industry and the Price Revolution: A Neoclassical Analysis. *Journal of European Economic History* 12 (3): 601–610.

Prados de la Escosura. L. 2003. *El progreso económico de España*, 1850–2000. Bilbao: Fundación BBVA.

Prados de la Escosura, L. 2007a. European Patterns of Development in Historical Perspective. *Scandinavian Economic History Review* 55 (3): 187–221.

Prados de la Escosura, L. 2007b. Growth and Structural Change in Spain, 1850–2000: A European Perspective. *Revista de Historia Económica/Journal of Iberian and Latin American Economic History* 25 (1): 147–181.

Open Access This chapter is licensed under the terms of the Creative Commons Attribution 4.0 International License (http://creativecommons.org/licenses/by/4.0/), which permits use, sharing, adaptation, distribution and reproduction in any medium or format, as long as you give appropriate credit to the original author(s) and the source, provide a link to the Creative Commons license and indicate if changes were made.

The images or other third party material in this chapter are included in the chapter's Creative Commons license, unless indicated otherwise in a credit line to the material. If material is not included in the chapter's Creative Commons license and your intended use is not permitted by statutory regulation or exceeds the permitted use, you will need to obtain permission directly from the copyright holder.

2

GDP and GDP Per Head

Modern economic growth is defined by the sustained improvement in GDP per head. From 1850 to 2015 while population trebled, real GDP per head in Spain experienced nearly a 16-fold increase, growing at an annual rate of 1.7% (Fig. 2.1 and Table 2.1). GDP growth was intensive, that is, driven by the advance in GDP per person, but for exceptional periods of Civil War, Depression, and Recession (Fig. 2.2). Such an improvement took place at an uneven pace. Per capita GDP grew at 0.7% over 1850–1950, doubling its initial level. During the next quarter of a century, the Golden Age, its pace accelerated more than sevenfold so, by 1974, per capita income was 3.6 times higher than in 1950. Although the economy decelerated from 1974 onwards, and its rate of growth per head shrank to one-half that of the Golden Age, per capita GDP more than doubled between 1974 and 2007. The Great Recession (2008–2013) shrank per capita income by 11%, but, by 2015, its level was still 83% higher than at the time of Spain's EU accession (1985).

Different long swings can be distinguished in which growth rates deviate from the long-run trend as a result of economic policies, access to international markets, and technological change. Growth rates, measured as average annual logarithmic rates of variation, are provided in Table 2.1

Fig. 2.1 Real absolute and per capita GDP, 1850–2015 (2010 = 100) (logs)

Table 2.1 Growth of GDP and its components, 1850–2015 (%) (average yearly logarithmic rates)

	GDP	Per Capita GDP	Population
1850–2015	2.4	1.7	0.7
Panel A			
1850–1950	1.3	0.7	0.6
1950–1974	6.3	5.3	1.0
1974–2007	3.3	2.5	0.7
2007–2015	−0.5	−0.8	0.3
Panel B			
1850–1883	1.7	1.3	0.5
1883–1920	1.2	0.6	0.6
1920–1929	3.8	2.8	1.0
1929–1950	0.0	−0.9	0.9
1950–1958	5.8	5.0	0.8
1958–1974	6.5	5.5	1.1
1974–1984	2.2	1.4	0.8
1984–1992	4.5	4.2	0.3
1992–2007	3.3	2.4	1.0
2007–2013	−1.4	−1.9	0.5
2013–2015	2.4	2.6	−0.2

(continued)

Table 2.1 (continued)

	GDP	Per Capita GDP	Population
Panel C			
1850–1855	2.6	2.1	0.6
1855–1866	1.0	0.4	0.6
1866–1873	3.2	2.9	0.2
1873–1883	1.1	0.6	0.5
1883–1892	0.8	0.6	0.3
1892–1901	1.3	0.7	0.6
1901–1913	1.2	0.5	0.7
1913–1918	0.3	−0.6	0.9
1918–1929	3.9	3.1	0.9
1929–1935	0.0	−1.5	1.5
1935–1939	−6.6	−6.9	0.4
1939–1944	4.9	4.8	0.1
1944–1950	0.2	−1.0	1.2

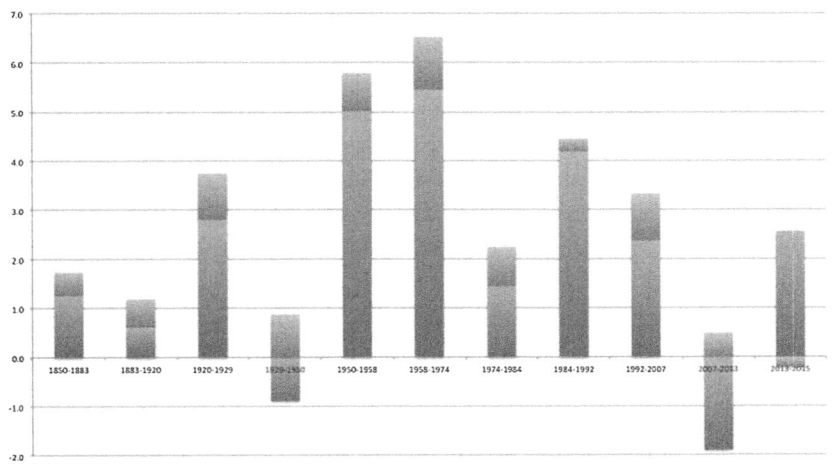

Fig. 2.2 Real GDP growth and its breakdown over long swings, 1850–2015 (logarithmic growth rates) (%). *Note* Real GDP growth results from adding up the growth rates of GDP per person and population

for main phases of economic performance (Panel A) and long swings (Panel B). A further breakdown into short cycles is presented for 1850–1950 (Panel C).

During the first long swing, 1850–1883, the rate of growth of product per person was well above the 1850–1950 average. Institutional reforms that brought higher economic freedom seem to lie beneath the significant growth experienced during these three decades (Prados de la Escosura 2016). Opening up to international trade and foreign capital made it possible to break the close connection between investment and savings and contributed to the economic growth (Prados de la Escosura 2010). It is worth stressing that, contrary to common economic wisdom, robust economic performance took place in a context of persistent political instability which included the 1854 liberal uprising and the 1868 Glorious Revolution. This suggests that an improved definition and enforcement of property rights and openness to goods and ideas contributed to offset political turmoil and social unrest.

Growth slowed down between the early 1880s and 1920s. Restrictions on both domestic and external competition help explain sluggish growth during the *Restauración* (1875–1923), despite the fact that institutional stability should have provided a favourable environment for investment and growth (Fraile Balbín 1991, 1998). Increasing tariff protection (Tena Junguito 1999), together with exclusion from the prevailing international monetary system, the gold standard, may have represented a major obstacle to Spain's integration in the international economy (Martín-Aceña 1993; Bordo and Rockoff 1996). The Cuban War of Independence, despite the already weakened economic links between the metropolis and its colony, caused significant macroeconomic instability that brought forward the fall of the peseta and increased Spain's economic isolation (Prados de la Escosura 2010). Macroeconomic instability, together with a 'sudden stop', reduced capital inflows leading to the depreciation of the peseta (Martín-Aceña 1993; Prados de la Escosura 2010) that, in turn, increased migration costs and reduced the outward flow of labour (Sánchez-Alonso 2000). Cuban independence had little direct economic impact on Spain's economy but a deep indirect one, as the intensification of protectionist and isolationist tendencies in the early twentieth century seem to be its political outcome (Fraile Balbín and Escribano 1998). World War I hardly brought any economic progress and GDP per head shrank, a result in stark contradiction with the conventional stress on the war stimulating effects on growth.[1]

The 1920s represented the period of most intense growth prior to 1950. The hypothesis that Government intervention, through trade protectionism, regulation, and investment in infrastructure, was a driver of growth has been widely accepted (Velarde 1969). The emphasis on tariff protectionism tends to neglect, however, that Spain opened up to international capital during the 1920s, which allowed the purchase of capital goods and raw materials and, hence, contributed to growth acceleration.

A fourth long swing took place between 1929 and 1950, which includes the Great Depression, the Civil War, and post-war autarkic policies, is defined by economic stagnation and shrinking GDP per head. The impact of the Depression, measured by the contraction in real GDP per head, extended in Spain, as in the USA, until 1933, with a 12% fall (against 31% in the USA), lasting longer than in the UK (where it ended in 1931 and real per capita GDP per head shrank by 7%) and Germany (1932 and 17% decline, respectively), but less than in Italy (1934 and 9% contraction) and France (1935 and 13% fall). Thus, the Depression, with GDP per head falling at −3.1% annually (−1.5% for absolute GDP), was milder than in the USA but similar in intensity to Western Europe's average (Maddison Project 2013), a finding that challenges the view of a weaker impact due to Spain's relative international isolation and backwardness. The Civil War (1936–1939) prevented Spain from joining the post-Depression recovery and resulted in a severe contraction of economic activity (31% drop in real per capita income between levels in 1935 and the 1938 trough) that, nonetheless, did not reach the magnitude of World War II impact on main belligerent countries of continental Western Europe (in Austria, the Netherlands, France, and Italy per capita income shrank by half and in Germany by two-thirds) (Maddison Project 2013).[2]

The weak recovery of the post-World War years stands out in the international context. Spain's economy did not reach its pre-war GDP per head peak level (1929) until 1954 (1950 in absolute terms) and that of private consumption per head until 1956. In contrast, it only took an average of 6 years to return to the pre-war levels in Western Europe (1951).[3] It is true that warring countries surrounded post-Civil War Spain (Velarde 1993), but the fact that its economy only grew at a rate of 0.2% yearly between 1944 and 1950 suggests a sluggish recovery after a comparatively mild contraction.

In the search for explanations, the destruction of physical capital does not appear to be a convincing one as it was about the Western European average during World War II (around 8% of the existing *stock* of capital in 1935), although its concentration on productive capital (especially transport equipment) meant that levels of destruction caused by the conflict in Spain were far from negligible (Prados de la Escosura and Rosés 2010). However, exile after the Civil War and, possibly to a larger extent, internal exile resulting from political repression of Franco's dictatorship, meant the loss of a considerable amount of Spain's limited human capital (Núñez 2003; Ortega and Silvestre 2006).[4] Thus, it can be put forward the hypothesis that the larger loss of human capital vis-à-vis physical capital contributed to the delayed reconstruction (Prados de la Escosura 2007).

The change in trend that began after 1950 ushered in an exceptional phase of rapid growth lasting until 1974. During the 1950s, though, industrialization in Spain was largely dependent on internal demand. Import volatility rendered investment risky and tended to penalize capital accumulation, while inflows of foreign capital and new technology were restricted. However, increasing confidence in the viability of Franco's dictatorship after the US—Spain military and technological cooperation agreements (1953), together with the regime's moderate economic reforms, favoured investment and innovation contributing to accelerated economic growth (Calvo-González 2007; Prados de la Escosura et al. 2012).

An institutional reform initiated with the 1959 Stabilization and Liberalization Plan, a response to the exhaustion of the inward-looking development strategy, set policies that favoured the allocation of resources along comparative advantage and allowed sustained and faster growth during the 1960s and early 1970s.[5] Without the Stabilization and Liberalization Plan, per capita GDP would have been significantly lower at the time of Franco's death, in 1975. However, without the moderate reforms of the 1950s and the subsequent economic growth, it seems unlikely the *Stabilization Plan* would have succeeded (Prados de la Escosura et al. 2012). This view challenges the widespread perception of the first two decades of Franco's dictatorship as a homogeneous autarchic era and the 1959 Stabilization and Liberalization Plan as a major discontinuity between autarky and the market economy.

The oil shocks of the 1970s happened at the time of Spain's transition from dictatorship to democracy that brought with it further opening up and economic liberalization. During the transition decade (1974–1984), GDP growth rate fell to one-third of that achieved over 1958–1974, and to one-fourth when measured in per capita terms. Was the slowdown exogenous, a result of the international crisis? Did it derive from the Francoism legacy of an economy still sheltered from international competition? Or was the outcome of the new democratic authorities' policies? Answering these questions represents a challenge to researchers. Accession to the European Union heralded more than three decades of absolute and per capita growth that came to a halt with the Great Recession. Again, the deeper contraction and weaker recovery calls for investigation on the underlying foundations of the 1985–2007 expansion.

Notes

1. Cf. Roldán and García Delgado (1973) for the established view on the impact of the Great War on Spain.
2. Actually, at the trough during the Civil War (1938) Spain's GDP per head was equal to that of 1905, while the World War II trough brought Italy, Germany, and France's back to 1880, 1886, and 1891, respectively (Maddison Project, 2013. See Bolt and van Zanden 2014, for a presentation of this collaborative project).
3. Belgium, the Netherlands, and France did so in 1949, Austria and Italy in 1950, with Germany (1954) and Greece (1956), the exceptions.
4. Regarding interior and exterior exile cf. López (1991, 1996) and Plá Brugat (1994, 1999).
5. It is worth pointing out interesting similarities between the 1959 Stabilization Plan and the Washington Consensus, including measures conducive to trade and capital account liberalization, macroeconomic policies to reduce inflation and the size of the fiscal imbalances, and other reforms to protect private property rights and to reduce the activity of the government (Williamson 1990; Fischer 2003; Schleifer 2009; Edwards 2009).

References

Bolt, J., and J.L. Van Zanden. 2014. The Maddison Project: Collaborative Research on Historical National Accounts. *Economic History Review* 67 (3): 627–651.

Bordo, M.D., and H. Rockoff 1996. The Gold Standard as a 'Good Housekeeping Seal of Approval'. *Journal of Economic History* 56: 389–428.

Calvo González, O. 2007. American Military Interests and Economic Confidence in Spain under the Franco Dictatorship. *Journal of Economic History* 67 (3): 740–767.

Edwards, S. 2009. Forty Years of Latin Americas Economic Development: From the Alliance for Progress to the Washington Consensus. NBER Working Papers 15190.

Fischer, S. 2003. Globalization and its Challenges: The Richard T. Ely Lecture. *American Economic Review* 93 (2): 1–30.

Fraile Balbín, P. 1998. *La retórica contra la competencia en España (1875–1975)*. Madrid: Fundación Argentaria/Visor.

Fraile Balbín, P., and A. Escribano. 1998. The Spanish 1898 Disaster: The Drift Toward, National-Protectionism. In *The Costs and Benefits of European Imperialism from the Conquest of Ceuta, 1415, to the Treaty of Lusaka, 1974, Revista de Historia Económica*, ed. P.K. O'Brien and L. Prados de la Escosura, 265–290. (special issue) 16.

Fraile, P. 1991. *Industrialización y grupos de presión. La economía política de la protección en España, 1900–1950*, Madrid: Alianza.

López García, S.M. 1991. La organización de la investigación científica y técnica tras la Guerra Civil: contrastes y similitudes con los logros de las primeras décadas del siglo XX. Actas del Encuentro de Historia Económica. Valencia, UIMP.

López García, S.M. 1996. La investigación científica y técnica antes y después de la Guerra Civil. In *Economía y sociedad en la España contemporánea*, ed. A. Gómez Mendoza, 265–275. Madrid: Síntesis.

Maddison Project. 2013. http://www.maddisonproject.net/.

Martin Aceña, P. 1993. Spain during the Classical Gold Standard Years, 1880–1914. In *Monetary Régimes in Transition*, ed. M.D. Bordo and F. Capie, 135–172. Cambridge, Cambridge University Press.

Núñez, C.E. 2003. El capital humano en el primer franquismo. In *Autarquía y mercado negro: El fracaso económico del primer franquismo*, ed. C. Barciela, 27–53. Crítica: Barcelona.

Ortega, J.A. and J. Silvestre. 2006. Las consecuencias demográficas. In *La economía de la Guerra Civil*, eds. P. Martín Aceña and E. Martínez Ruiz, 53–105. Madrid: Marcial Pons.

Plá Brugat, D. 1994. Características del exilio en México en 1939, Una inmigración privilegiada. In *Comerciantes, empresarios y profesionales españoles en México en los siglos XIX y XX*, ed. C.E. Lida, 218–231. Madrid: Alianza.

Plá Brugat, D. 1999. *Els exiliats catalans. Un estudio de la emigración republicana en México*. México D.F.: INAH.

Prados de la Escosura, L. 2007. Growth and Structural Change in Spain, 1850–2000: A European Perspective. *Revista de Historia Económica/Journal of Iberian and Latin American Economic History* 25 (1): 147–181.

Prados de la Escosura, L. 2010. Spain's International Position, 1850–1913. *Revista de Historia Económica-Journal of Iberian and Latin American Economic History* 28(1): 1–43.

Prados de la Escosura, L. 2016. Economic Freedom in the Long Run: Evidence from OECD Countries (1850–2007). *Economic History Review* 69 (2): 435–468.

Prados de la Escosura, L., and J.R. Rosés. 2010. Capital Accumulation in the Long-Run: The Case of Spain, 1850–2000. *Research in Economic History* 27: 93–152.

Prados de la Escosura, L., J.R. Rosés, and I. Sanz-Villarroya. 2012. Economic Reforms and Growth in Franco's Spain. *Revista de Historia Económica-Journal of Iberian and Latin American Economic History* 30 (1): 45–89.

Roldán, S. and J.L. Garcïa Delgado. 1973. *La formación de la sociedad capitalista en España*, 1914–1920, vol. 2. Madrid: Cajas de Ahorro Confederadas.

Sánchez Alonso, B. 2000. European Emigration in the Late Nineteenth Century: The Paradoxical Case of Spain. *Economic History Review* 53: 309–330.

Shleifer, A. 2009. The Age of Milton Friedman. *Journal of Economic Literature* 47 (1): 123–135.

Tena Junguito, A. 1999. Un nuevo perfil del proteccionismo español Velarde Fuertes, J. 1969. *Política económica de la Dictadura*. Madrid: Guadiana.

Velarde Fuertes, J. 1969. *Política económica de la Dictadura*. Madrid: Guadiana.

Velarde Fuertes, J. 1993. Convergencias y divergencias de la economía española: comentario a una intervención del profesor Comín. *Papeles de Economía Española* 57: 57–72.

Williamson, O. 1990. What Washington Means by Policy Reform. In *Latin American Adjustment: How Much Has Happened?*, ed. J. Williamson. Washington: Institute for International Economics.

Open Access This chapter is licensed under the terms of the Creative Commons Attribution 4.0 International License (http://creativecommons.org/licenses/by/4.0/), which permits use, sharing, adaptation, distribution and reproduction in any medium or format, as long as you give appropriate credit to the original author(s) and the source, provide a link to the Creative Commons license and indicate if changes were made.

The images or other third party material in this chapter are included in the chapter's Creative Commons license, unless indicated otherwise in a credit line to the material. If material is not included in the chapter's Creative Commons license and your intended use is not permitted by statutory regulation or exceeds the permitted use, you will need to obtain permission directly from the copyright holder.

3

GDP per Head and Labour Productivity

A breakdown of GDP per head into labour productivity and the amount of labour used per person can be made. Thus, GDP per person (GDP/N) will be expressed as GDP per hour worked (GDP/H), a measure of labour productivity, times the number of hours worked per person (H/N), a measure of effort.

$$\text{GDP}/\text{N} = \text{GDP}/\text{H} * \text{H}/\text{N} \tag{1}$$

And using lower case to denote rates of variation,

$$(\text{gdp}/\text{n}) = (\text{gdp}/\text{h}) + (\text{h}/\text{n}) \tag{2}$$

GDP per head and per hour worked evolved alongside over 1850–2015, even though labour productivity grew at a faster pace—labour productivity increased 23-fold against GDP per head 16-fold—as the amounts of hours worked per person shrank—from about 1000 h per person-year to less than 700—(Table 3.1 and Fig. 3.1). Thus, it can be claimed that gains in output per head are fully attributable to productivity gains, with phases of accelerating GDP per head, such as the 1920s

© The Author(s) 2017
L. Prados de la Escosura, *Spanish Economic Growth, 1850–2015*,
Palgrave Studies in Economic History, DOI 10.1007/978-3-319-58042-5_3

Table 3.1 GDP per head growth and its components, 1850–2015 (%) (average yearly logarithmic rates)

	Per capita GDP	GDP/hour	Hours/population
1850–2015	1.7	1.9	−0.2
Panel A			
1850–1950	0.7	0.8	−0.1
1950–1974	5.3	5.8	−0.5
1974–2007	2.5	2.7	−0.1
2007–2015	−0.8	1.3	−2.1
Panel B			
1850–1883	1.3	1.2	0.0
1883–1920	0.6	0.8	−0.2
1920–1929	2.8	3.1	−0.3
1929–1950	−0.9	−1.0	0.1
1950–1958	5.0	5.1	−0.1
1958–1974	5.5	6.1	−0.7
1974–1984	1.4	5.6	−4.1
1984–1992	4.2	2.7	1.5
1992–2007	2.4	0.7	1.7
2007–2013	−1.9	1.6	−3.5
2013–2015	2.6	0.5	2.1
Panel C			
1850–1855	2.1	2.3	−0.2
1855–1866	0.4	0.1	0.3
1866–1873	2.9	2.5	0.4
1873–1883	0.6	1.0	−0.4
1883–1892	0.6	0.9	−0.4
1892–1901	0.7	0.6	0.1
1901–1913	0.5	0.7	−0.2
1913–1918	−0.6	−0.2	−0.4
1918–1929	3.1	3.4	−0.3
1929–1935	−1.5	−1.6	0.0
1935–1939	−6.9	−5.9	−1.0
1939–1944	4.8	4.5	0.4
1944–1950	−1.0	−1.6	0.7

or the Golden Age (1950–1974), matching those of faster labour productivity growth.

A closer look at the last four decades reveals, however, significant discrepancies over long swings. In fact, a pattern can be observed

3 GDP per Head and Labour Productivity

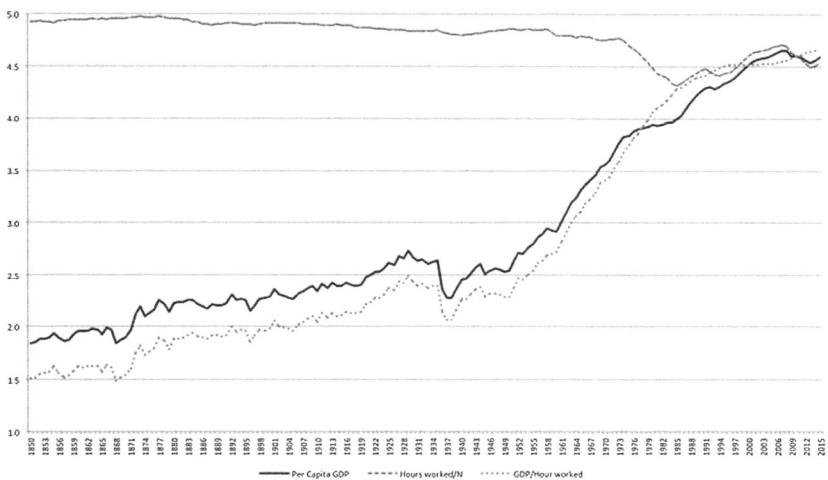

Fig. 3.1 Real per capita GDP and its components, 1850–2015 (logs)

according to which phases of acceleration in labour productivity correspond to those of GDP per person slowdown, and vice versa (Fig. 3.2). Thus, periods of sluggish (1974–1984) or negative (2007–2013) per capita GDP growth paralleled episodes of vigorous or recovering productivity growth, although only in the first case, during the 'transition to democracy' decade, labour productivity offset the sharp contraction in hours worked—resulting from unemployment—and prevented a decline in GDP per head. Conversely, the years between Spain's accession to the European Union (1985) and the eve of the Great Recession (2007), particularly since 1992, exhibited substantial per capita GDP gains, while labour productivity slowed down. Thus, during the three decades after Spain joined the EU, in which GDP per head doubled, growing at 3.0% per year, more than half was contributed by the increase in hours worked per person.

Thus, it can be concluded that since the mid-1970s, the Spanish economy has been unable to combine employment and productivity growth, with the implication that sectors that expanded and created new jobs (mostly in construction and services) were less successful in attracting investment and technological innovation. Actually, labour

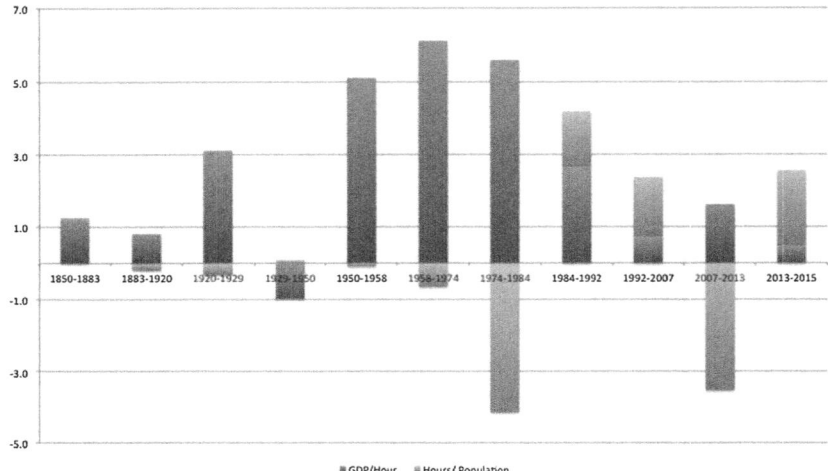

Fig. 3.2 Real per capita GDP growth and its breakdown over long swings, 1850–2015 (logarithmic growth rates) (%). *Note* per capita GDP growth results from adding up the growth rates of GDP/hour and hours per person

productivity in construction and services grew at a yearly rate of −0.2 and 0.3%, respectively, compared to 1.1% for the overall economy over 1985–2007 (Table 3.2).

Gains in aggregate labour productivity can be broken down into the contribution made by the increase in output per hour worked in each economic sector (internal productivity) and by the shift of labour from less productive to more productive sectors (structural change).[1] The level of aggregate labour productivity (A), which is obtained by dividing gross value added (GVA) by the number of hours worked (H) for the economy as a whole in the year t, can be expressed as the result of adding up labour productivity (GVA_i/H_i) for each economic sector i (i = 1, 2, ..., n), weighted by each sector's contribution to total hours worked (H_i/H).[2]

$$A_t = (GVA/H)_t = \Sigma(GVA_i/H_i)_t(H_i/H)_t = \Sigma(A_{it}U_{it}) \quad (3)$$

where A_i is gross value added per hour worked in sector i, and U_i is the contribution of sector i to total hours worked.

Table 3.2 Labour productivity growth by sectors, 1850–2015 (%) (GVA per hour worked) (average yearly logarithmic rates)

	Agriculture	Industry	Construction	Services	Total
1850–2015	2.3	2.5	1.8	1.4	1.9
Panel A					
1850–1950	0.2	1.4	0.7	0.9	0.8
1950–1974	6.2	6.4	5.5	3.4	6.0
1974–2007	6.1	3.4	1.6	1.4	2.5
2007–2015	1.8	2.2	4.8	0.7	1.4
Panel B					
1850–1883	0.6	3.2	2.1	1.1	1.2
1883–1920	0.7	0.4	0.4	1.1	0.8
1920–1929	2.6	3.4	3.2	1.3	2.9
1929–1950	−2.2	−0.7	−2.1	0.3	−1.0
1950–1958	6.0	6.7	−2.9	2.5	5.0
1958–1974	6.3	6.2	9.7	3.8	6.5
1974–1984	8.0	6.5	5.7	3.8	5.6
1984–1992	9.3	2.1	2.2	0.4	2.1
1992–2007	3.2	2.1	−1.5	0.3	0.6
2007–2013	3.1	2.0	7.4	1.0	1.8
2013–2015	−2.1	2.9	−3.0	−0.2	0.1
Panel C					
1850–1855	3.4	4.7	2.0	0.5	2.7
1855–1866	−0.7	2.0	2.1	0.2	0.0
1866–1873	2.6	4.0	−0.8	2.3	2.6
1873–1883	−0.6	3.3	4.0	1.4	0.8
1883–1892	0.7	1.4	0.1	0.7	0.9
1892–1901	0.6	0.9	0.9	0.0	0.5
1901–1913	0.0	−0.2	2.7	1.4	0.7
1913–1918	1.5	−0.6	−11.2	0.9	0.3
1918–1929	2.7	2.6	5.5	2.3	3.1
1929–1935	0.4	−3.9	−8.8	−1.8	−1.4
1935–1939	−9.7	−1.0	−15.8	−1.7	−5.8
1939–1944	2.0	4.3	17.4	4.8	3.9
1944–1950	−3.4	−1.3	−2.5	−0.3	−1.5

Using lower case letters to represent rates of change,

$$a_t = \Sigma\, a_{it}\, U_{it} + \Sigma\, A_{it}\, u_{it} \qquad (4)$$

The method usually employed in this calculation, *shift-share analysis,* involves estimating, in the first place, *internal* productivity growth (the first term on the right-hand side of expression (4), that is, the result obtained by adding up the labour productivity growth of GVA per hour worked in each economic sector weighted by the initial composition of employment (expressed in hours worked). The difference between aggregate productivity and *internal* productivity will then provide the contribution of structural change. Structural change would have made a positive contribution to productivity growth over 1850–1974 by shifting labour from agriculture into industry (Table 3.3, column 3 and Fig. 3.3). Conversely, since 1985, structural change, represented by the shift of labour from both agriculture and industry into services, would have slowed down aggregate productivity growth. Carrying out the shift-share analysis at a high level of aggregation, that is, between main economic sectors, precludes a more nuanced picture, as within industry and services there were shifts from sectors of lower productivity levels or growth rates to others of higher productivity levels or more intense growth.

Nonetheless, the shift-share analysis is based on the assumption that, in the absence of labour shift between sectors, each sector's productivity would have been identical to the actual ones. This is an unrealistic assumption when labour is rapidly absorbed by industry and services and productivity tends to stagnate or even decline in these sectors. This seems to be the case in Spain.[3] It would appear more plausible to assume that agricultural productivity partly improved, say, between 1950 and 1975, due to the reduction in the number of hours worked in the sector. Furthermore, during the 'transition to democracy' (1975–1985) GVA per hour worked in industry would have grown more slowly had employment not fallen in the sector, a result of industrial restructuring that shrank or eliminated less competitive branches. Thus, the result for the contribution of structural change to productivity growth obtained

Table 3.3 Labour productivity growth and structural change, 1850–2015 (%) (average yearly logarithmic rates)

	GVA/hour worked	Internal productivity (shift-share)	Structural change (lower bound)	Internal productivity (modified shift-share)	Structural change (upper bound)
1850–2015	1.9	2.1	−0.2	1.2	0.7
Panel A					
1850–1950	0.8	0.5	0.2	0.4	0.3
1950–1974	6.0	5.4	0.6	3.6	2.4
1974–2007	2.5	2.9	−0.4	1.6	0.9
2007–2015	1.4	1.5	−0.1	−0.2	1.6
Panel B					
1850–1883	1.2	1.1	0.1	1.1	0.1
1883–1920	0.8	0.7	0.1	0.6	0.2
1920–1929	2.9	2.5	0.5	1.5	1.5
1929–1950	−1.0	−1.2	0.3	−1.4	0.4
1950–1958	5.0	4.6	0.4	3.0	2.0
1958–1974	6.5	5.9	0.6	4.4	2.1
1974–1984	5.6	5.6	0.0	4.5	1.1
1984–1992	2.1	2.3	−0.3	0.8	1.3
1992–2007	0.6	0.7	−0.1	0.0	0.7
2007–2013	1.8	2.1	−0.3	−0.1	2.0
2013–2015	0.1	−0.1	0.1	−0.3	0.4
Panel C					
1850–1855	2.7	2.8	−0.2	2.5	0.1
1855–1866	0.0	−0.1	0.1	−0.1	0.1
1866–1873	2.6	2.6	0.1	2.4	0.3
1873–1883	0.8	0.5	0.3	0.4	0.4
1883–1892	0.9	0.8	0.1	0.7	0.2
1892–1901	0.5	0.5	0.0	0.4	0.1
1901–1913	0.7	0.4	0.3	0.2	0.5
1913–1918	0.3	0.5	−0.2	0.4	−0.1
1918–1929	3.1	2.7	0.4	1.8	1.2
1929–1935	−1.4	−1.4	0.0	−2.3	0.8
1935–1939	−5.8	−5.9	0.2	−8.0	2.2
1939–1944	3.9	4.0	−0.1	3.7	0.2
1944–1950	−1.5	−2.2	0.8	−2.7	1.2

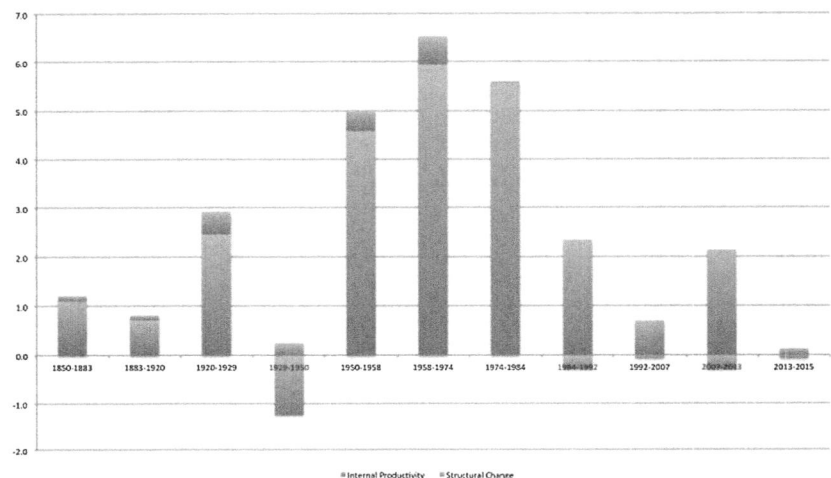

Fig. 3.3 Labour productivity growth and structural change over long swings: shift-share, 1850–2015 (logarithmic growth rates) (%)

using the conventional *shift-share analysis* (Table 3.3) would arguably represent a *lower* bound.

Alternatively, an *upper* bound can be derived using Broadberry's modified version of the *shift-share analysis*.[4] The contribution of structural change is derived by subtracting from aggregate productivity the figure that would result by weighting output per hour worked growth in each sector according to its contribution to total employment in the initial year, but with an exception for those sectors whose contribution to employment falls (e.g. agriculture over the entire time span considered and industry since 1975). In such a case, the differential between the rate of variation in hours worked for the economy as a whole and for the relevant sector would be subtracted from the latter's productivity growth.[5] As Table 3.3 shows, the difference between upper and lower bounds can be significant for some periods.

Structural change, derived with the modified *shift-share* approach, would account for 38% of the aggregate productivity growth achieved over the last 166 years. This figure is not far below from Broadberry's own findings for Germany and the USA.[6] Over 1850–1950, its

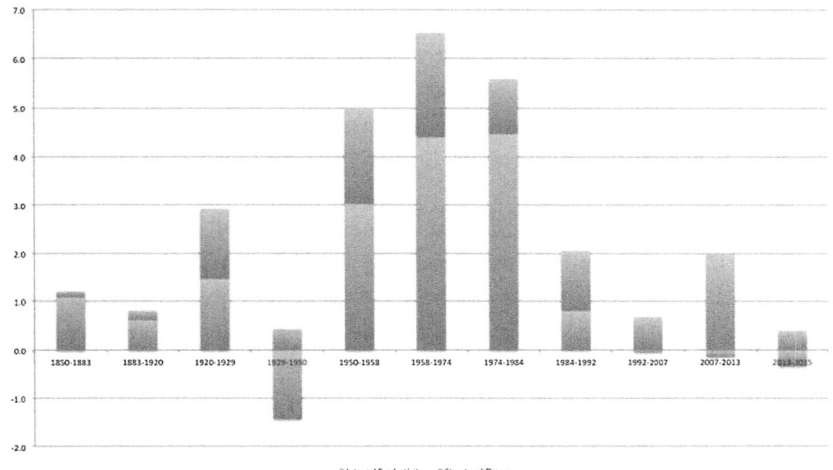

Fig. 3.4 Labour productivity growth and structural change over long swings: modified shift-share, 1850–2015 (logarithmic growth rates) (%)

contribution would reach two-fifths of labour productivity growth, against the one-fourth suggested by the conventional *shift-share* approach. A closer look indicates that structural transformation made a larger contribution to productivity growth between the 1870s and 1929, with decade 1874–1883, the long decade before World War I, and the 1920s as the most intense episodes (Fig. 3.4).

According to the modified *shift-share analysis*, it is in the Golden Age (1950–1974) when structural change would have made the larger and more sustained contribution to productivity growth.

Since 1975 and up to the eve of the Great Recession (2007), structural change accounted for more than one-third of the increase in aggregate labour productivity and avoided an even deeper productivity deceleration after 1984. This result is at odds with the negative contribution of structural change to productivity advance suggested by the conventional *shift-share* analysis. In this phase, the transfer of labour away from agriculture (which still absorbed one-fifth of the total number of hours worked in 1975 and, since then, hours worked in agriculture declined at yearly rate of −4% to 2007) was accompanied by a sustained destruction of employment in less competitive manufacturing industries, which intensified during the 'transition to democracy' decade (−3.8% yearly decline of hours worked in industry during 1974–1984). Since 2007, structural change prevented labour productivity from stalling contributing a moderate increase in output per hour worked during the Great Recession.

A clearer picture of the evolution of the number of hours worked per person, (H/N), is obtained by breaking it down into its components (Table 3.4). Thus, (H/N) equals hours worked per full-time equivalent worker, L, (H/L), times the participation rate—that is, the ratio of L, to the working age population, WAN-, (L/WAN), times the share of WAN in total population, N, (WAN/N),

$$(H/N) = (H/L) * (L/WAN) * (WAN/N) \qquad (5)$$

Table 3.4 Hours worked per head growth and its composition, 1850–2015 (%) (average yearly logarithmic rates)

	Hours worked/N	Hours/FTE worker	FTE worker/WAN	WAN/N
1850–2015	−0.2	−0.3	0.0	0.0
Panel A				
1850–1950	−0.1	−0.1	0.0	0.1
1950–1974	−0.5	−0.5	0.3	−0.3
1974–2007	−0.1	−0.6	0.2	0.3
2007–2015	−2.1	0.2	−1.8	−0.5
Panel B				
1850–1883	0.0	0.0	0.0	0.0
1883–1920	−0.2	−0.1	−0.1	0.0
1920–1929	−0.3	−0.5	0.0	0.1
1929–1950	0.1	−0.1	−0.1	0.3
1950–1958	−0.1	−0.3	0.6	−0.3
1958–1974	−0.7	−0.6	0.2	−0.2
1974–1984	−4.1	−1.7	−2.8	0.3
1984–1992	1.5	−0.4	1.3	0.6
1992–2007	1.7	0.0	1.5	0.2
2007–2013	−3.5	0.3	−3.3	−0.5
2013–2015	2.1	−0.1	2.7	−0.5

(continued)

Table 3.4 (continued)

	Hours worked/N	Hours/FTE worker	FTE worker/WAN	WAN/N
Panel C				
1850–1855	−0.2	−0.3	0.0	0.1
1855–1866	0.3	0.1	0.0	0.2
1866–1873	0.4	0.2	0.3	−0.1
1873–1883	−0.4	−0.1	−0.2	−0.1
1883–1892	−0.4	−0.1	−0.2	−0.1
1892–1901	0.1	−0.1	0.1	0.0
1901–1913	−0.2	−0.1	0.0	−0.1
1913–1918	−0.4	−0.3	−0.3	0.1
1918–1929	−0.3	−0.4	0.0	0.1
1929–1935	0.0	−0.4	0.2	0.2
1935–1939	−1.0	0.0	−1.3	0.2
1939–1944	0.4	0.0	−0.1	0.4
1944–1950	0.7	0.0	0.2	0.5

That in rates of change (lower case letters) can be expressed as:

$$(h/l) = (h/l) + (l/\mathrm{wan}) + (\mathrm{wan}/n) \qquad (6)$$

The change in hours per full-time equivalent worker-year (H/L), which fell from 2800 by mid-nineteenth century to less than 1900 at the beginning of the twenty-first century, represents the main driver of the amount of work per person, especially in periods of industrialization and urbanization such as the 1920s (to which the gradual adoption of the 8 h per day standard also contributed) and the Golden Age (1950–1974) (Fig. 3.5).

Changes in the participation rate (L/WAN) also made a contribution (Fig. 3.6). For example, in the Golden Age (1950–1974), it mitigated the decline in hours worked per person. However, it is since 1975 when the participation rate becomes the main determinant of changes in the amount of hours worked per person. Thus, (L/WAN) accounts for two-thirds of its contraction during the 'transition to democracy' decade (1975–1984). Such a decline was due to a dramatic surge in unemployment, largely resulting from the impact of the oil shocks and the exposure to international competition on traditionally sheltered industrial sectors, plus the return of migrants from Europe. The higher bargaining power of trade unions and industrial restructuring made the rest. Another surge in

Fig. 3.5 Hours per full-time equivalent worker, 1850–2015

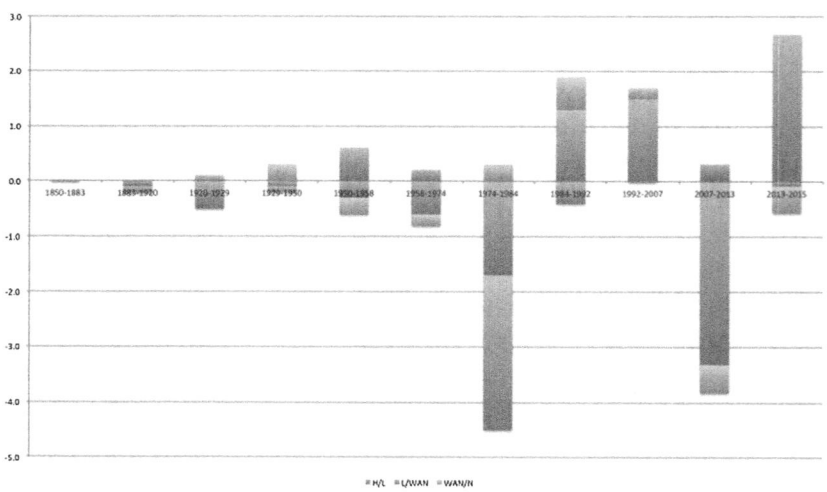

Fig. 3.6 Hours worked per head growth and its breakdown over long swings, 1850–2015 logarithmic growth rates (%)

unemployment made the participation rate accountable for most of the reduction in hours worked per person during the Great Recession (2008–2013).

Conversely, between Spain's EU accession and the Great Recession (1985–2007), the increase in (L/WAN) was the main contributor to the increase in the number of hours worked per person, helped by increasing female participation and the post-1990 inflow of migrants. Again, the rise in the participation rate, as unemployment has gradually declined, is a main actor in the post-2013 recovery in hours worked per person. Lastly, a demographic gift, as the dependency rate fell increasing the share of potentially active over total population, prevented a further decline of hours worked per person during the 1930s, contributed to its recovery in the 1940s and helped the surge in employment over 1985–2007.

Notes

1. As correctly pointed out by Matthews et al. (1982: 248–254), structural change is not really exogenous as it is caused by the interaction between the supply and demand of resources. Hence, any attempt to establish causal relationships between structural change and growth is flawed. From a historical point of view, however, perfect factor mobility does not exist and, consequently differences of marginal productivity between sectors tend to exist, as the movement of resources from one sector to another does not take place automatically. For this reason, improvements in resource allocation will contribute to growth during a given period of time. It is also the case that even when marginal productivity is the same in different industries, they will not all grow at the same rate. Growth will depend on their use of technological innovation and the existence of increasing returns.
2. I draw on Broadberry (1998) in the subsequent paragraphs.
3. Broadberry (1998) puts forward the idea that if we accept, as proposed by Kindleberger (1967), that labour moving from agriculture to industry and services is surplus labour, then it must be assumed that the hypothetical return of this labour to the agricultural sector would have a negative effect on productivity.
4. It provides an upper bound because it does not take into account differences in levels of physical and human capital per worker across economic sectors. Ideally, the contribution of structural change should be calculated.

5. In this case, internal productivity would be calculated as $\Sigma\ a'_{it}\ U_{it}$, where $a'_{it} = a_{it} - (h_t - h_{it})$, if $U_{it} < 0$ (h representing hours worked) (Broadberry 1998).
6. Broadberry (1998: 390) finds that, over 1870–1990, structural change would account for up to 45.7 and 50.3% of productivity growth in Germany (1.75%) and the USA (1.4%), respectively.

References

Broadberry, S.N. 1998. How Did the United States and Germany Overtake Britain? A Sectoral Analysis of Comparative Productivity Levels. *Journal of Economic History* 58: 375–407.
Kindleberger, C.P. 1967. *European Postwar Growth: The Role of Labor Supply*. National Bureau of Economic Research: Princeton.
Matthews, R.C.O., C.H. Feinstein, J.C. Odling-Smee. 1982. *British Economic Growth 1856–1973*. Oxford: Clarendon Press.

Open Access This chapter is licensed under the terms of the Creative Commons Attribution 4.0 International License (http://creativecommons.org/licenses/by/4.0/), which permits use, sharing, adaptation, distribution and reproduction in any medium or format, as long as you give appropriate credit to the original author(s) and the source, provide a link to the Creative Commons license and indicate if changes were made.

The images or other third party material in this chapter are included in the chapter's Creative Commons license, unless indicated otherwise in a credit line to the material. If material is not included in the chapter's Creative Commons license and your intended use is not permitted by statutory regulation or exceeds the permitted use, you will need to obtain permission directly from the copyright holder.

4

Spain's Performance in Comparative Perspective

A long-run view of Spain's economic performance cannot be completed without placing it in comparative perspective. In Fig. 4.1, Spain's real GDP per head is presented along estimates for other large Western European countries: Italy, France, the UK, and Germany, plus the USA, the economic leader that represents the technological frontier, all expressed in purchasing power parity-adjusted 2011 dollars to allow for countries' differences in price levels (Fig. 4.1).[1] A caveat is needed about this kind of exercise. Per capita income levels obtained through backward projection of PPP-adjusted GDP levels for a given benchmark year (2011, in this case, or 1990 in Maddison's estimates) with volume indices derived at domestic relative prices from historical national accounts provide a convenient way of comparing of countries' income levels over time, as it is easy to compute and does not alter national growth rates. However, it also presents a huge index number problem that gets bigger as the time span considered widens, rendering comparisons less significant. This is so because this computation procedure implicitly assumes that the basket of goods and services and the structure of relative prices for the benchmark year remain unaltered over time, something definitively misleading as long-run growth is about change in

© The Author(s) 2017
L. Prados de la Escosura, *Spanish Economic Growth, 1850–2015*,
Palgrave Studies in Economic History, DOI 10.1007/978-3-319-58042-5_4

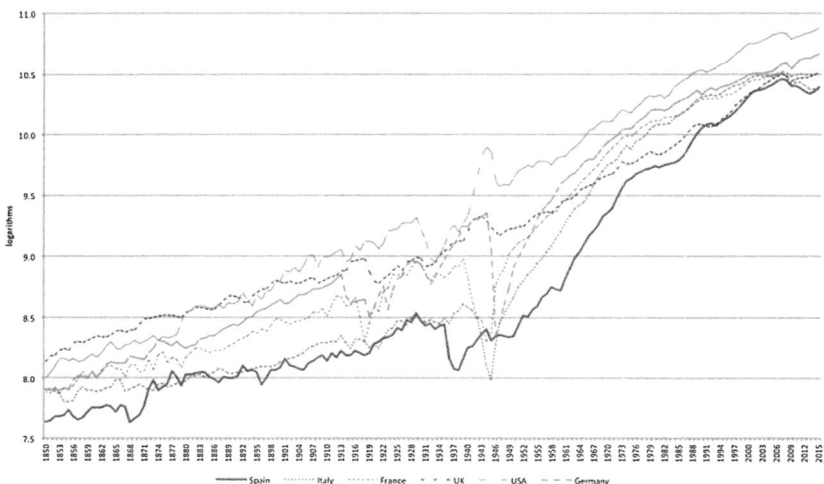

Fig. 4.1 Spain's comparative real per capita GDP (2011 EKS $) (logs)

relative prices (Prados de la Escosura 2000). As a matter of fact, this type of series only provides an effective comparison between the level of the benchmark year (2011 here) and that of any other year at the former's relative prices.

Several findings emerge from Fig. 4.1. Firstly, Spain's long-term growth appears to be similar to that of Western nations.[2] Secondly, Spain's level of GDP per head is systematically lower than those of other large Western European countries. Lastly, the improvement in Spain's GDP per head did not follow a monotonic pattern, a feature that shares with Italy and Germany, but differs from the steady progress experienced by the UK and the USA and, to less extent, with France.

The first two results would lend support to the view that the roots of most of today's difference in GDP per person between Spain and advanced countries should be searched for in the pre-1850 era.[3] However, the fact that Spain's initial level was lower would suggest—within a neoclassical framework—a potential for growth that would have not been exploited.

A closer look reveals that long-run growth before 1950 was clearly lower in Spain (as in Italy) than in the advanced countries (Table 4.1).

Table 4.1 Comparative per capita GDP growth, 1850–2015 (%) (average annual logarithmic rates)

	Spain	Italy	France	UK	USA	Germany
1850–2015	1.7	1.5	1.6	1.4	1.7	1.7
Panel A						
1850–1913	0.9	0.7	1.2	1.2	1.7	1.5
1913–1950	0.3	0.9	1.1	0.9	1.6	0.2
1950–1973	5.3	5.2	3.9	2.4	2.4	4.9
1973–2007	2.6	1.9	1.6	2.2	1.9	1.6
2007–2015	−0.8	−1.6	−0.2	0.2	0.4	1.1
Panel B						
1850–1883	1.3	0.4	1.1	1.4	1.8	1.2
1883–1913	0.6	1.1	1.4	1.0	1.5	1.8
1913–1918	−0.6	−1.0	−7.5	2.1	1.3	−4.0
1918–1929	3.1	2.2	6.1	0.1	1.8	2.8
1929–1939	−3.7	0.7	0.2	1.3	−0.5	2.9
1939–1950	1.7	0.6	0.7	0.9	3.4	−3.0
1950–1960	3.7	5.4	3.6	2.2	1.7	6.9
1960–1973	6.4	5.0	4.2	2.5	3.0	3.4
1973–1992	2.9	2.5	1.7	1.5	1.8	1.8
1992–2007	2.4	1.2	1.4	2.9	2.0	1.3

Source Spain, see the text; rest of countries, Maddison Project

Sluggish growth over 1883–1913 and not taking advantage of its World War I neutrality to catch up, partly account for it. Furthermore, the progress achieved in the 1920s was outweighed by Spain's short-lived recovery from the depression, brought to a halt by the Civil War (1936–1939), and by a long-lasting and weak post-war reconstruction. In fact, although less destructive than World War II, and despite being Spain non-belligerent in World War II, post-Civil War's recovery in Spain was longer and less intense than in the warring Western European countries after 1945.

Thus, Spain fell behind between 1850 and 1950 (Fig. 4.2). The second half of the nineteenth century and the early twentieth century witnessed sustained per capita GDP growth, while paradoxically the gap with the industrialized countries widened over 1883–1913. Moreover, the gap deepened during the first half of the twentieth century.

The situation reverted from 1950 to 2007. The Golden Age (1950–1973), especially, the period since 1960 (a common feature of countries in the European periphery: Greece, Portugal, Ireland) stands out as years

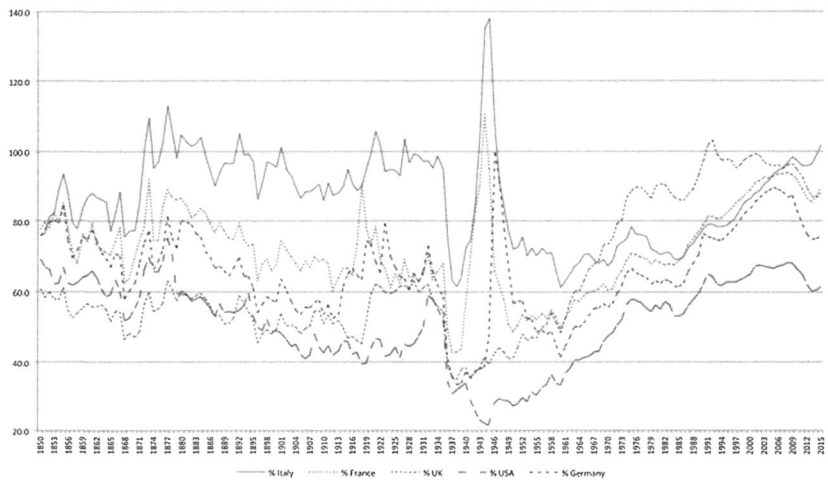

Fig. 4.2 Spain's relative real per capita GDP (2011 EKS $) (%)

of outstanding performance and catching up to the advanced nations. Steady, although slower, growth after the transition to democracy years (1974–1984) allowed Spain to keep catching up until 2007. The Great Recession reversed the trend, although it is too soon to determine whether it has opened a new phase of falling behind.

To sum up, the liberal regime of the *Restauración* (1875–1923), which provided political stability, but largely failed to offer incentives for accelerated growth; the 1930s and 1940s, with the Civil War and its slow and autarkic recovery; the 'transition to democracy' decade after General Franco's death (1975); and the Great Recession (2008–2013) stand out as those phases responsible for Spain's falling behind Western Europe. Conversely, over 1950–2007, especially during the Golden Age, Spain outperformed the advanced nations improving her relative position.

On the whole, Spain's relative position to Western countries has evolved along a wide U-shape, deteriorating to 1950 (except for the 1870s and 1920s) and recovering thereafter (but for the episodes of the transition to democracy and the Great Recession). Thus, at the beginning of the twentieth-first century, Spanish real GDP per head represented a similar proportion of USA and Germany's income to the one back in mid-nineteenth century, although had significantly improved with respect to the UK and kept a similar position to that of the 1870s with regard to France. Lastly, compared to Italy, Spain has reached parity, as had been the case in the late nineteenth century and, again, in the 1920s.

A final reminder: the choice of splicing procedure for the modern national accounts can result in far from negligible differences in the relative position of a country over the long run. Moreover, the difference between the resulting series of interpolation and retropolation procedures appears much more dramatic when placed in a long-run perspective, that is, when the spliced national accounts are projected backwards into the nineteenth century with volume indices taken from historical national accounts. This is due to the fact that most countries, including Spain, grew at a slower pace before 1950, so the level of per capita GDP level by mid-twentieth century largely determines its relative position in country rankings in earlier periods.

In order to illustrate this point, I have constructed long-run estimates of real GDP per head for Spain using the retropolated series for 1958–2015 and compared them to the series obtained through interpolation (Fig. 4.3).[4] The retropolation approach is the one conventionally used

Fig. 4.3 Spain's comparative real per capita GDP with alternative splicing (2011 EKS $) (logs)

(as discussed in Part II, Chap. 9) and has been employed, for example, in the Penn Table 9.0 ($RGDP^{NA}$ series).[5] It can be observed that when adopting the retropolated series, Spain overcomes Italy in terms of GDP per head over 1850–1950 (but for the Civil War years), matching France and Germany in the early 1880s.

Moreover, I have computed Spain's position relative to France and the UK (Fig. 4.4). The choice of yardstick countries obeys to the purpose of comparing a country of fast growth and deep structural change in the second half of the twentieth century, such as Spain, with others more mature and in which economic growth proceeded at steadier pace. The reason is that it is fast growth and deep structural transformation what produces the large disparities between new and old benchmark national accounts series for the overlapping year. In most countries, national accounts have been spliced through retropolation. However, in the yardstick countries, the method of splicing national accounts is not a relevant issue because, as their structural transformation was largely completed before the modern national accounts era (post-World War), differences between new and old national accounts estimates are small at the overlapping year.

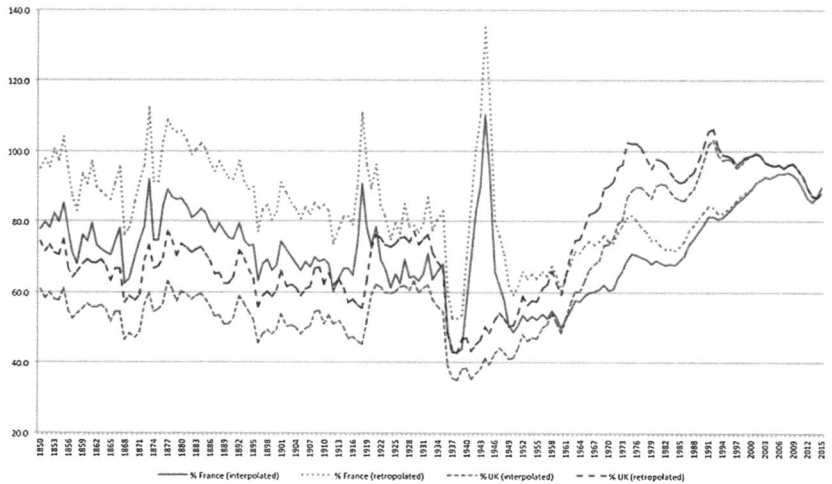

Fig. 4.4 Spain's real per capita GDP relative to France and the UK with alternative splicing (2011 EKS $)

4 Spain's Performance in Comparative Perspective 45

According to the figures derived from using the retropolation splicing procedure, during the second half of the nineteenth century, real per capita GDP in Spain would have matched that of France in the mid-1850s and, again, between the mid-1870s and mid-1880s. Furthermore, when its retropolated series are considered, Spain would have practically matched British per capita income during the last quarter of the twentieth century with a *sorpasso* in 1974 and, again, at the beginning of the 1990s. These results are in stark contrast with those derived by splicing national accounts through interpolation. Thus, Spanish GDP per head would have represented above four-fifths of the French over 1973–1984 and would have represented less than 90% of the British with a brief takeover during 1990–1993. It can be, then, concluded that whatever the measurement error embodied in the interpolation procedure may be, its results appear far more plausible than those resulting from the conventional retropolation approach.

Notes

1. GDP levels in 2011, converted into 'international' dollars using EKS purchasing power parity (PPP) exchange rates (World Bank 2013) http://siteresources.worldbank.org/ICPEXT/Resources/ICP_2011.html, have been projected backwards with per capita GDP volume series that, in the case of Spain, correspond to the new historical estimates with post-1958 hybrid linear interpolation. For the rest of countries, volume series from the Maddison Project (2013), http://www.ggdc.net/maddison/maddison-project/home.htm, completed with data from Conference Board http://www.conference-board.org/data/economydatabase/.
2. Alternatively, I have carried out the exercise with the 1990 ICP benchmark estimate favoured by Maddison (and so far, by the Maddison Project) with rather similar results.
3. A new assessment of pre-1850 Spain is provided by Álvarez-Nogal and Prados de la Escosura (2013).
4. It is worth noting that national accounts series for pre-1970 Italy have been spliced through linear interpolation (Baffigi 2013).
5. http://www.rug.nl/ggdc/productivity/pwt/.

References

Álvarez-Nogal, C., and L. Prados de la Escosura. 2013. The Rise and Fall of Spain, 1270–1850. *Economic History Review* 66 (1): 1–37.

Baffigi, A. 2013. National Accounts, 1861-2011. In *The Oxford Handbook of the Italian Economy since Unification*, ed. G. Toniolo, 157–186. Oxford: Oxford University Press.

Maddison Project. 2013. http://www.maddisonproject.net/.

Prados De La Escosura, L. 2000. International Comparisons of Real Product, 1820-1990: An Alternative Data Set. *Explorations in Economic History* 37 (1): 1–41.

World Bank. 2013. *Measuring the Real Size of the World Economy. The Framework, Methodology, and Results of the International Comparisons Programme.* Washington DC: The World Bank. Data set available at http://siteresources.worldbank.org/ICPEXT/Resources/ICP_2011.html.

Open Access This chapter is licensed under the terms of the Creative Commons Attribution 4.0 International License (http://creativecommons.org/licenses/by/4.0/), which permits use, sharing, adaptation, distribution and reproduction in any medium or format, as long as you give appropriate credit to the original author(s) and the source, provide a link to the Creative Commons license and indicate if changes were made.

The images or other third party material in this chapter are included in the chapter's Creative Commons license, unless indicated otherwise in a credit line to the material. If material is not included in the chapter's Creative Commons license and your intended use is not permitted by statutory regulation or exceeds the permitted use, you will need to obtain permission directly from the copyright holder.

5

GDP, Income Distribution, and Welfare

But how did GDP per head gains affect economic well-being? Within the existing national accounts framework, Sitglitz et al. (2009: 23–25) recommend to look at net rather than gross measures, in order to take into account the depreciation of capital goods. Net National Disposable Income (NNDI) measures income accruing to Spanish nationals, rather than production in Spain, and also accounts for capital consumption. NNDI provides, therefore, a more accurate measure of the impact of economic growth on average incomes than GDP.

In Fig. 5.1, a long-term decline in the NNDI share of GDP is observed. The reason is that as the stock of capital gets larger and its composition shifts from assets with long lives but low returns (i.e. residential construction) to shorter life assets but with higher returns (i.e. machinery), capital consumption increases. The integration of Spain into the global economy since the last quarter of the twentieth century accentuated this process.

Nonetheless, it can be noticed that per capita NNDI grows in parallel with GDP per head, although at a slower pace from 1960 onwards, that resulted in its 13-fold increase over 1850–2015, against 16-fold for per capita GDP (Fig. 5.2 and Table 5.1).

Fig. 5.1 Net national disposable income ratio to GDP 1850–2015 (current prices) (%)

Fig. 5.2 Real per capita GDP and net national disposable income, 1850–2015 (2010 = 100) (logs)

5 GDP, Income Distribution, and Welfare 49

Table 5.1 Real per capita GDP, NNDI, private consumption, and Sen-welfare growth, 1850–2015 (%) (average yearly logarithmic rates)

	Per capita GDP	Per capita NNDI	Per capita private consumption	Sen welfare
1850–2015	1.7	1.5	1.4	1.6
Panel A				
1850–1950	0.7	0.7	0.5	0.5
1950–1974	5.3	5.3	5.2	6.2
1974–2007	2.5	2.2	2.1	2.3
2007–2015	−0.8	−1.6	−1.4	−1.6
Panel B				
1850–1883	1.3	1.2	1.0	1.0
1883–1920	0.6	0.6	0.5	0.1
1920–1929	2.8	2.8	2.9	3.6
1929–1950	−0.9	−1.0	−1.2	−1.0
1950–1958	5.0	5.3	5.3	8.0
1958–1974	5.5	5.2	5.1	5.2
1974–1984	1.4	1.0	0.9	1.5
1984–1992	4.2	4.0	3.9	4.0
1992–2007	2.4	2.0	1.9	1.9
2007–2013	−1.9	−2.4	−2.7	−2.9
2013–2015	2.6	1.1	2.4	2.4
Panel C				
1850–1855	2.1	2.1	1.9	3.8
1855–1866	0.4	0.3	0.4	0.7
1866–1873	2.9	2.8	2.5	2.8
1873–1883	0.6	0.6	0.0	−1.2
1883–1892	0.6	0.6	0.7	2.0
1892–1901	0.7	0.6	0.8	−0.6
1901–1913	0.5	0.5	−0.7	−1.0
1913–1918	−0.6	−0.7	0.6	−2.6
1918–1929	3.1	3.1	3.2	4.4
1929–1935	−1.5	−1.8	−1.0	0.4
1935–1939	−6.9	−6.9	−10.4	−7.8
1939–1944	4.8	4.9	5.1	5.2
1944–1950	−1.0	−1.1	−0.4	−3.2

In their Report, Sitglitz et al. (2009) also advise focusing on household consumption, rather than on total consumption, to capture the effect of growth on material welfare. This way, government consumption that

Fig. 5.3 Real per capita GDP and private consumption, 1850–2015 (2010 = 100) (logs)

could be deemed, in Nordhaus and Tobin (1972) words, 'defensive' expenditures—namely services that represent inputs for activities that may yield utility—would be excluded.

A look at the behaviour of real private consumption per person shows a narrow parallelism with that of GDP per head, but with a lower rate of growth (Fig. 5.3), as reflected by its declining contribution to GDP (Fig. 1.1), and that implied, nonetheless, multiplying 10 times its initial level over 1850–2015. Solely during the long decade preceding World War I, the Civil War (1936–1939), and the Great Recession (2008–2013) did private consumption growth fall ostensibly behind that of GDP (Table 5.1). In short, it can be suggested that the fruits of growth were passed on to the population, so present consumption was not sacrificed to greater future consumption and, hence, no parallelism can be drawn with the post-1950 experience of former socialist countries in Europe or East Asian countries (Krugman 1994; Young 1995).

Another major objection to GDP per head is that it takes no account of income distribution. In fact, the conviction that averages fail to give 'indication of how the available resources are distributed across persons or

5 GDP, Income Distribution, and Welfare   51

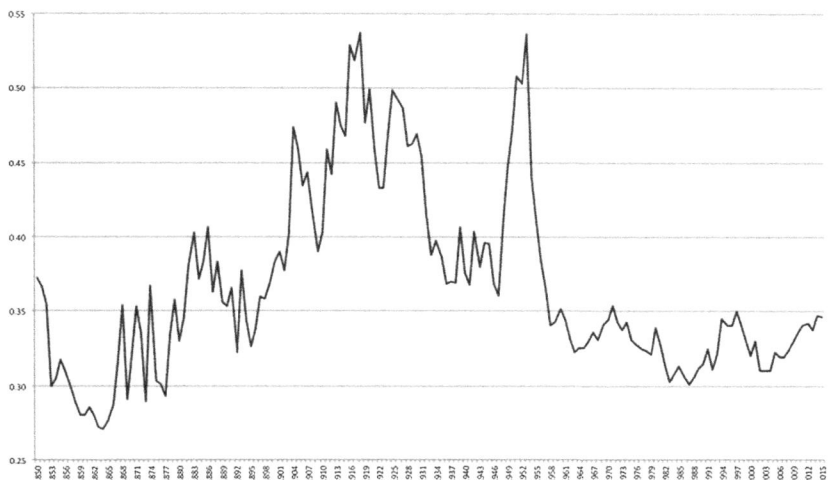

Fig. 5.4 Income inequality, 1850–2015: Gini coefficient. *Source* Prados de la Escosura (2008), 1850–1994; Eurostat 1995–2015

households' (Stiglitz et al. 2009: 32) recommends that average income should be accompanied by measures of its distribution.

How have the fruits of growth been distributed in Spain? Trends in income distribution measured by the Gini coefficient are presented in Fig. 5.4.[1] Its evolution has not followed a monotonic pattern and different phases can be observed. A long-term rise inequality is noticeable between mid-nineteenth century and World War I reaching a peak in 1918. Then, a sustained inequality reduction took place during the 1920s and early 1930s, stabilizing in the years of the Civil War (1936–1939) and World War II. A sharp reversal was experienced during the late 1940s and early 1950s, with an inequality peak by 1953, similar in size to that of 1918. Then, a dramatic fall in inequality occurred in the late 1950s and early 1960s. Henceforth, income distribution stabilized fluctuating within a narrow 0.30–0.35 Gini range.

A comparison of the evolution of real per capita NNDI and income distribution (Figs. 5.2 and 5.3) shows no trade-off between inequality and growth, by which higher living standards resulting economic growth compensate for higher inequality and vice versa, seems to exist.

Moreover, there is no clear association between them over time. Thus, in the most dynamic phases of economic performance, inequality declined (the 1920s, the Golden Age, 1950–1974), but it also increased (1850–1883); while in years of sluggish performance, inequality deepened (1880–1920, the post-Civil War autarchy), although it shrank too (during the II Republic, 1931–1936, and the transition to democracy, 1975–1984).

But how severe has been inequality in terms of well-being? Branko Milanovic et al. (2011) proposed the concept of Inequality Extraction Ratio, defined as the ratio between the actual Gini [G] and the maximum feasible Gini (G*), which is obtained as

$$G^* = (\alpha - 1)/\alpha \qquad (5.1)$$

Where α = average incomes, expressed in terms of subsistence (1.9 2011 EKS dollars a day).

Thus, the Inequality Extraction Ratio (IER) measures the actual level of inequality as a proportion of its potential maximum. The closer a country is to the maximum potential inequality, the stronger the negative impact of inequality on welfare.

The negative effect of inequality on welfare, as measured by the IER, increased during the early twentieth century peaking at two-thirds of its potential maximum by the end of World War I and, then, declined until the mid-1980s, but for a dramatic reversal at the end of the autarchic period, fluctuating thereafter around one-third of its potential maximum (Fig. 5.5).

It is worth noticing that, in Spain, similar levels of inequality are significantly different in terms of its impact on well-being. For example, although exhibiting similar levels of inequality (around 0.35 Gini), during 1850–1883, actual inequality oscillates around one-half of its potential maximum, while over 1960–2015 it fluctuates around one-third.

But can the effect of changes in income distribution on welfare be quantified? Amartya Sen's (1973) proposed to adjust the level of net national disposable income for the evolution of income distribution. Thus, I have computed the so-called Sen Welfare,

5 GDP, Income Distribution, and Welfare

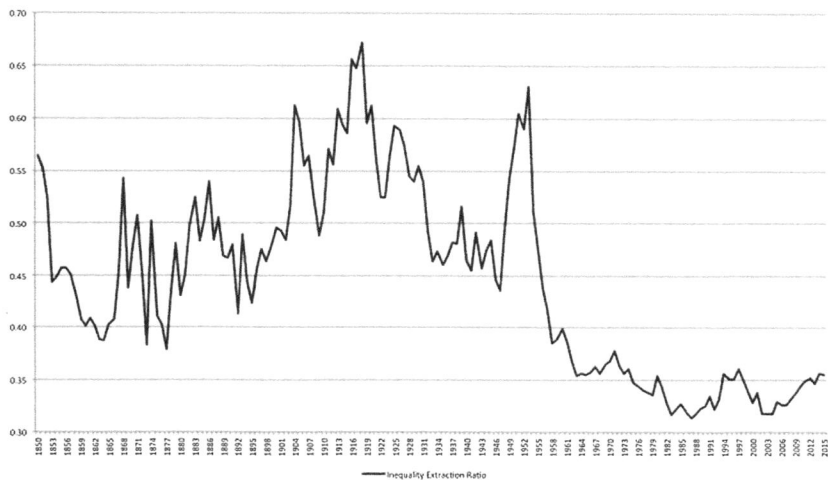

Fig. 5.5 Inequality extraction ratio 1850–2015 *Note* Actual Gini as a proportion of the maximum potential Gini

$$\text{Sen Welfare} = \text{Real Per capita NNDI} \times (1 - \text{Gini}) \quad (5.2)$$

Figure 5.6 compares GDP per head with the Sen-Welfare measure. It can be observed that except for the early twentieth century—especially in the 1910s and 1920s and in the late 1940s and early mid-1950s—when Sen-Welfare level fell behind per capita GDP, both measures exhibit similar long-run performance.

During the 1920s and, especially, the 1950s, Sen Welfare improved faster than real GDP per person, while this situation reversed from the end of the nineteenth century to the end of World War I. Moreover, in phases of income contractions such as the Civil War and its autarchic aftermath, and the Great Recession (2008–2013), welfare worsened more intensively than GDP per head. On the whole, Sen Welfare increased 13-fold over 1850–2015.

To sum up, net disposable income and private consumption exhibit similar trends to GDP but with less steep acceleration since mid-twentieth century, while the negative impact of inequality on

Fig. 5.6 Real per capita GDP and Sen welfare, 1850–2015 (2010 = 100) (logs)

economic welfare was softened from 1960 onwards and inequality decline made significant contributions to well-being in the 1920s and the 1950s. Thus, it can be concluded that in modern Spain long-run economic growth was accompanied by a substantial improvement in material welfare.

A substantive objection to GDP per head is that it fails to incorporate non-income dimensions of well-being. Human welfare is widely viewed as a multidimensional phenomenon, in which per capita income (and its distribution) is only one facet. Critics of GDP as a measure of welfare have signalled the Human Development Index as a better alternative (Coyle 2014). Human development has been defined as 'a process of enlarging people's choices'(UNDP 1990: 10), namely enjoying a healthy life, acquiring knowledge and achieving a decent standard of living, that allow them to leading 'lives they have reasons to value' (Sen 1997).

The Human Development Index (HDI), published by the United Nations Development Programme (UNDP), has three dimensions: a healthy life, access to knowledge and other aspects of well-being. It uses reduced forms of these dimensions, namely life expectancy at birth as a proxy for a healthy life, education measures (literacy, schooling) as a short cut for access to knowledge, and discounted per capita income (its log) as a surrogate for other aspects of well-being (Anand and Sen 2000; UNDP 2001). These are combined into a synthetic measure using a geometric average (UNDP 2010). Since all dimensions are considered indispensable they are assigned equal weights.

It matters how progress in the dimensions of human development is measured. Often social variables (life expectancy, height or literacy) are used, either raw (Acemoglu and Johnson 2007; Becker et al. 2005; Soares; Lindert 2004) or linearly transformed (UNDP 2010). This causes measurement problems when a social variable has asymptotic limits. An example would be life expectancy. Consider two improvements, one from 30 to 40 years and another from 70 to 80 years. These increases are identical in absolute terms, but the second is smaller in proportion to the initial starting level. When original (or linearly transformed, as happens in the case of the UNDP's HDI) values are employed, identical changes in absolute terms result in a smaller measured improvement for the country with the higher starting point, favouring the country with the lower initial level (Sen 1981; Kakwani 1993).

The limitations of linear measures become more evident when quality is taken into account. Life expectancy at birth and literacy and schooling rates are just crude proxies for the actual goals of human development: a long and healthy life and access to knowledge. Research over the last two decades concludes that healthy life expectancy increases in line with total life expectancy, and as life expectancy rises, disability for the same age-cohort falls (Salomon et al. 2012). Similarly, the quality of education, measured in terms of cognitive skills, grows as the quantity of education increases (Hanushek and Kimko 2000; Altinok et al. 2014). The bottom line is that more years of life and education imply higher quality of health and education during childhood and adolescence in both the time series and the cross section.

My alternative to the UNDP's conventional HDI is a historical index of human development (HIHD) in which non-income variables are transformed nonlinearly, rather than linearly as in the HDI, in order to allow for two main facts: (1) increases of the same absolute size represent greater achievements the higher the level at which they take place, and

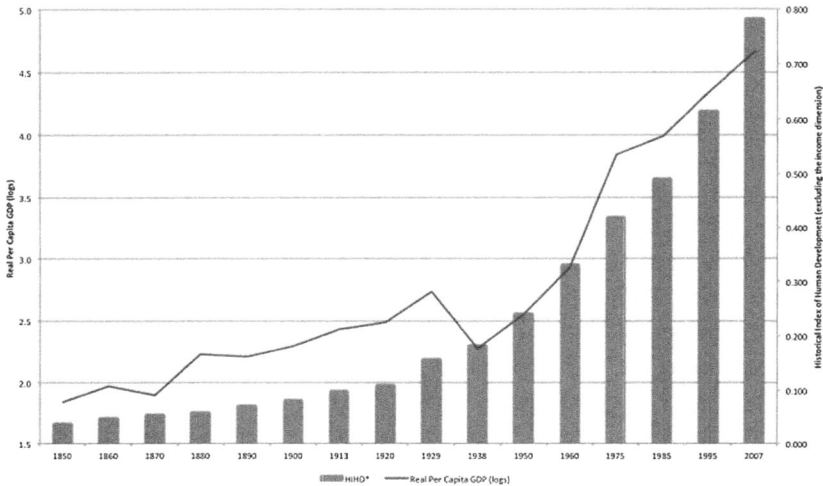

Fig. 5.7 Real per capita GDP (2010 = 100) (logs) and historical index of human development [HIHD*] (excluding income dimension), 1850–2007. *Source* Real per capita GDP, see the text; human development, Prados de la Escosura (2015) and http://espacioinvestiga.org/home-hihd/countries-hihd/hihd-esp-eng/?lang=en#

(2) quality improvements are associated with increases in quantity (see Prados de la Escosura 2015).

When per capita GDP and Human Development (in which the income dimension has been excluded) are compared, they exhibit similar long-term trends (Fig. 5.7), although improvements in the Historical Index of Human Development are more intense between 1880 and 1950 and slower thereafter (Table 5.2). A major discrepancy is observed for the 1930s and 1940s, when human development thrived, driven by improving life expectancy at birth—a result of the epidemiological transition related to the diffusion of the germ theory of disease—and broadening primary education, while GDP per head contracted as consequence of the Depression and the Civil War and its autarchic aftermath.

Table 5.2 Real per capita GDP and human development growth, 1850–2007 (%). (average yearly logarithmic rates)

	GDP per head	HIHD*
1850–2007	1.8	1.9
Panel A		
1850–1950	0.7	1.8
1950–1975	5.2	2.2
1975–2007	2.6	1.9
Panel B		
1850–1880	1.3	1.4
1880–1920	0.6	1.6
1920–1929	2.8	3.9
1929–1950	−0.9	2.0
1950–1960	3.7	3.1
1960–1975	6.1	1.6
1975–1985	1.5	1.6
1985–1995	3.4	2.3
1995–2007	2.7	2.0

Source Real per capita GDP, see the text; Human Development (excluding income dimension), Prados de la Escosura (2015) and http://espacioinvestiga.org/home-hihd/countries-hihd/hihd-esp-eng/?lang=en#

All in all, it can be concluded that GDP per head captures long-run trends in welfare in Spain, but fails to do it in the short and medium term.

Note

1. The Gini coefficient measures the extent to which the distribution of income (or consumption expenditure) among individuals or households within an economy deviates from a perfectly equal distribution. A Gini of 0 represents perfect equality, while an index of 1 (100) implies perfect inequality. This paragraph draws on Prados de la Escosura (2008).

References

Acemoglu, D., and S. Johnson. 2007. Disease and Development: The Effects of Life Expectancy on Economic Growth. *Journal of Political Economy* 115: 925–985.

Altinok, N., C. Diebolt, and J.L. Demeulemeester. 2014. A New International Dataset on Education Quality, 1965–2010. *Applied Economics* 46 (11): 1212–1247.

Anand, S., and A.K. Sen. 2000. The Income Component of the Human Development Index. *Journal of Human Development* 1: 83–106.

Becker, G.S., T.J. Philipson, and R.R. Soares. 2005. The Quantity and Quality of Life and the Evolution of World Inequality. *American Economic Review* 95: 277–291.

Coyle, D. 2014. *GDP: A Brief But Affectionate History*. Princeton: Princeton University Press.

Hanushek, E.A., and D.D. Kimko. (2000). Schooling, Labor-Force Quality, and the Growth of Nations. *American Economic Review* 90 (5): 1184–1208.

Kakwani, N. 1993. Performance in Living Standards. An International Comparison. *Journal of Development Economics* 41: 307–336.

Krugman, P. 1994. The Myth of Asia's Miracle. *Foreign Affairs* 73 (6): 62–78.

Lindert, P.H. 2004. *Growing Public. Social Spending and Economic Growth Since the Eighteenth Century*, 2 vols. Cambridge University Press.

Milanovic, B., P.H. Lindert, and J.G. Williamson. 2011. Ancient Inequality. *Economic Journal* 121: 255–272.

Nordhaus, W.D., and J. Tobin. 1972. Is Growth Obsolete? In *Economic Research: Retrospect and Prospect. V. Economic Growth*, ed. W.D. Nordhaus and J. Tobin, 1–80. New York: NBER/Columbia University Press.

Prados de la Escosura, L. 2008. Inequality, Poverty, and the Kuznets Curve in Spain, 1850–2000. *European Review of Economic History* 12 (3): 287–324.

Prados de la Escosura, L. 2015. World Human Development, 1870–2007. *Review of Income and Wealth* 61 (2): 220–247.

Salomon, J.A., H. Wang, M.K. Freeman, T. Vos, A.D. Flaxman, A.D. Lopez, and C.J.L. Murray. 2012. Healthy Life Expectancy for 187 Countries, 1990–2010: A Systematic Analysis for the Global Burden Disease Study 2010. *Lancet* 380: 2144–2162.

Sen, A.K. 1973. *On Economic Inequality*. Oxford: Clarendon Press.

Sen, A.K. 1981. Public Action and the quality of life in developing countries. *Oxford Bulletin of Economics and Statistics* 43: 287–319.

Sen, A.K. 1997. Human Capital and Human Capability. *World Development* 25: 1959–1961.

Stiglitz, J.E., Sen, A., Fitoussi, J.P. 2009. Report by the Commission on the Measurement of Economic Performance and Social Progress. http://ec.europa.eu/eurostat/documents/118025/118123/Fitoussi+Commission+report.

United Nations Development Program [UNDP]. (1990–2011). *Human Development Report.* New York: Oxford University Press.

Young, A. 1995. The Tyranny of Numbers: Confronting the Statistical Realities of the East Asian Growth Experience. *Quarterly Journal of Economics* 90 (2): 641–680.

Open Access This chapter is licensed under the terms of the Creative Commons Attribution 4.0 International License (http://creativecommons.org/licenses/by/4.0/), which permits use, sharing, adaptation, distribution and reproduction in any medium or format, as long as you give appropriate credit to the original author(s) and the source, provide a link to the Creative Commons license and indicate if changes were made.

The images or other third party material in this chapter are included in the chapter's Creative Commons license, unless indicated otherwise in a credit line to the material. If material is not included in the chapter's Creative Commons license and your intended use is not permitted by statutory regulation or exceeds the permitted use, you will need to obtain permission directly from the copyright holder.

Part II
Measurement

6

Measuring GDP, 1850–1958: Supply Side

In historical national accounts, as for most developing countries, the most reliable and easiest to estimate GDP figures are those obtained through the production approach.[1] As for most developing countries, real product has been computed from physical indicators rather than as a residual obtained from independently deflated output and inputs. The components' method has prevailed over the indicators' method as much as the data permitted it, and both direct and indirect estimating procedures have been employed.[2]

Estimating constant gross value added series involved several steps. In the first place, Laspeyres quantity indices were built up for each major component of output using 1913, 1929 and 1958 value added as alternative weights. Value added for 1913 and 1929 benchmarks was computed through either direct estimate or, more often, gross value added levels for 1958, taken from the input–output table (TIOE58) and the national accounts (CNE58) were projected backwards to 1913 and 1929 (with quantity and price indices expressed as 1958 = 1). Then, in an attempt to allow for changes in relative prices, these volume indices were spliced into a single series. The estimates with 1913 weights have been accepted for 1850–1913, while variable weighted geometric averages of the indices obtained with 1913 and 1929 (1929 and 1958) weights have been adopted for 1913–1929 (1929–1958), a procedure that allocates a higher weighting to the closer benchmark. Lastly, a volume index of real gross value added (GVA) for 1850–1958 was constructed by weighting output chain volume Laspeyres indices for each major branch of economic activity with their shares in total gross value added for 1958.

An effort to construct price indices was carried out from a wide range of price series of uneven quality and coverage.[3] Chain Paasche price indices for agriculture, industry and services were built up.[4] In fact, since volume indices are of Laspeyres type, that is,

$$Q^L = \sum q_i p_o / \sum q_o p_o, \qquad (6.1)$$

Paasche price indices,

$$P^P = \sum q_i p_i / \sum q_i p_o, \qquad (6.2)$$

are, then, required to derive current values,

$$V = Q^L * P^P = \sum q_i p_i / \sum q_o p_o \qquad (6.3)$$

where q and p are quantities and prices at the base year o or any other year i.

Yearly series of gross value added at current prices were derived for each branch of economic activity by projecting backwards its level at the 1958 benchmark, provided by official national accounts (CNE58), with its Laspeyres quantity and Paasche price indices, expressed with reference to 1958 = 1.[5] Total gross value added at current prices was derived by aggregation of sectoral value added. An implicit Paasche GVA deflator was calculated by dividing current and constant price series. Adding indirect taxes (net of subsidies) to total current GVA provided nominal GDP at market prices. Real GDP at market prices was obtained by deflating nominal GDP with the GVA deflator.

Four major branches of economic activity are taken into account: (a) agriculture, forestry and fishing; (b) manufacturing, extractive industries and utilities; (c) construction; and (d) services.

6.1 Agriculture, Forestry and Fishing

6.1.1 Agriculture

Two steps were followed in computing agricultural value added.[6] Firstly, final output, that is, total production less seed and animal feed, was constructed. Then, gross value added was derived by subtracting purchases of industrial and services inputs, from final output.

Unfortunately, annual data on crops and livestock output are incomplete and their coverage uneven over time. Nonetheless, available data allowed me:

(a) To compute agricultural final output at different benchmarks: *circa* 1890, 1898/1902, 1909/1913, 1929/1933, 1950 and 1960/1964 by valuing physical output for each product at farm-gate prices.[7]

(b) And, then, to derive, Laspeyres real output (Q^L) for each benchmark (bk) by deflating current values (V) with a Paasche chain price index built on a large sample of agricultural goods (q and p are quantities and prices at the base year o or any other year i).[8] That is,

$$Q^L_{bk} = V_{bk} / P^P_{bk} bk = 1890, 1898/1902, 1909/13, 1929/33, 1950, 1960 \tag{6.4}$$

being P^P_{bk} a chain Paasche, $P^P_{bk} = \sum p_{ip} q_{ip} / \sum p_{ip-1} q_{ip}$

The lack of quantitative evidence on low acreage, high-value crops such as fruits and vegetables that increase its importance at higher income levels and urbanization, makes the deflation of current value estimates a preferable alternative to the construction of volume indices on reduced quantitative information.[9] Actually, prices tend to move together within closer bounds than quantities.[10]

(c) Next, real final agricultural output series was derived splicing each pair of adjacent benchmarks with a yearly index of final output built on reduced information.[11] The procedure was to project each benchmark with a quantity index constructed at its relative prices and to compute, then, a weighted geometric average of the series resulting from each pair of adjacent benchmarks, in which the closer benchmark to each particular year was allocated a higher weighting,

$$Q_t^L = \left(Q_{bko}^L * O_t^L\right)^{(n-t)/(n-o)} * \left(Q_{bkn}^L * O_t^L\right)^{(t-o)/(n-o)}$$
$$= O_t^L * \left(Q_{bko}^L\right)^{(n-t)/(n-o)} \left(Q_{bkn}^L\right)^{(t-o)/(n-o)} \quad (6.5)$$

where Q is Laspeyres real final output index, O is a Laspeyres quantity index (built on reduced information) for year t, bk represents each benchmark estimate, and o and n are the initial and final years within each period.[12]

(d) Lastly, agricultural final output at current prices was obtained by extrapolating the 1958 level of final output (CEN58) backwards with the real final output index and a Paasche price index.[13] The Paasche price index was constructed by interpolating each pair of adjacent chain price benchmarks (Table 6.1, column 2) with a yearly Paasche price index derived on reduced information.[14] The linkage procedure for each pair of adjacent benchmarks was projecting each benchmark price level with the

Table 6.1 Agricultural final output: benchmark estimates, 1890–1960/64

	(1)	(2)	(3)
	Current value	Paasche price	Laspeyres volume
	(Million Pta)	Chain index	Chain index
c. 1890	2795	89.63	80.76
1898/1902	3190	95.22	86.77
1909/1913	3861	100.00	100.00
1929/1933	8919	173.76	132.96
1950	52,018	1173.27	114.84
1960/1964	156,526[a]	2158.34[b]	187.85[c]

Notes [a]value at 1960 prices. [b]1960 price level. [c]1960 prices
Incomplete coverage led to assumptions about the production of several crops in 1890 and 1900. Total output for major groups (vegetables, raw materials, fruits and nuts, meat, and poultry and eggs) was inferred on the basis of observed sample-to-total output ratios for 1909/1913
Source Quantities, prices and values derive from GEHR (1991), Simpson (1994) (unpublished data set), and the original sources quoted there, and Ministerio de Agricultura (1979a)
Ratios of final output to total production for each crop are shown in the Appendix, Table A.1. Coefficients to transform livestock output into quantities of meat, wool and milk are presented in the Appendix, Table A.2

variations of the annual price index and, then, computing a variable geometric mean in which the closer benchmark to a particular year received the higher weighting.[15]

The Construction of Annual Quantity and Price Indices on Reduced Information

The annual quantity and price indices constructed on a sample of agricultural produce, and employed to interpolate adjacent benchmark estimates of real final output, deserve some comments. A two-stage procedure was followed to build the quantity index in order to prevent undesired over-representation of particular crops in aggregate output. Ten groups of products were firstly defined, for which independent indices were constructed. This procedure did not prevent adding guesses to the data since it was assumed that, within each group, those products not included in the sample moved exactly like those that were part of it. However, the more homogeneous the group of goods is, the less strong the implicit assumptions of this method are. In any case, when output is directly estimated from a sample of products, the implicit assumptions are stronger than in my proposed two-stage calculation procedure.[16] Thus, index numbers were built for major groups of products: cereals, legumes, vegetables, raw materials, fruits and nuts, must, unrefined olive oil, meat, poultry and eggs, and milk and honey.[17]

Incomplete production data constitute a major obstacle to the construction of an agricultural output index for nineteenth-century Spain. Assumptions and conjectures are required, then, to establish trends in agricultural output and to fill in the missing data. Estimating output trends under information constraints can be approached through (a) the volume produced, in which most is made of the scattered evidence available; (b) the commercialization of crops deflated by the (expanding) length of the transportation network (road and rail) in order to prevent an upward bias in the rate of growth of agricultural production, as mercantilization evolved faster than production in the early stages of development; and (c) the demand approach, in which output is deducted from an estimate of consumption derived from a demand equation calibrated with levels of disposable income (real wages) and relative prices for food, together with their relevant elasticities.[18] The volume and commercialization approaches are used here to derive output levels.

Data coverage of crop output is much lower prior to 1891 than thereafter, and it is practically non-existent for the period 1850–1881.[19] Output for major agricultural groups had to be derived from scattered information on the production of wheat, barley, must, raw olive oil and sugar cane and beet, plus fruit export data for the period 1882–1890, whose data coverage represents 64% of final production (excluding livestock) in 1890.[20] Up to 1882, non-livestock agricultural output was proxied by trading series for major crops using evidence from maritime and rail transportation (the latter previously deflated by the network's length).[21] The commercialization series included cereals, legumes, wine, olive oil, fruits and nuts, and raw materials (raw silk, sugar cane).[22] Accepting traded crops as proxies for crops output implies the arguable assumption of a highly commercialized agriculture in which both distribution and production show a similar profile.[23] If trade in agricultural products rose faster than output, the resulting index would incorporate an upward bias.[24]

Estimates are even weaker for the years 1850–1865, when only maritime transportation data were available (coastal transport since 1857), and in the cases of wheat and legumes, output had to be derived from consumption estimates (by arbitrarily assuming a constant consumption per head times population) adjusted for net imports.[25]

Once quantity series were established for the main commodity groups, the calculation procedure used for the post-1865 estimates was applied to compute output.[26]

Evidence on livestock prior to 1905 is only available for 1865 and 1891.[27] Meat and milk outputs were obtained by applying conversion coefficients to livestock numbers for 1865, 1891 and 1905/1909 and valued at 1891 prices.[28] Annual figures for livestock output were derived through log-linear interpolation, both for 1865–1891 and for 1891–1905. The case for accepting such a crude procedure is to reach a wider coverage for agricultural production by including livestock output, which apparently had an opposite trend to that of crops output over the late nineteenth century.[29] However, it is worth noticing that a decline in livestock numbers does not necessarily mean that livestock output fell as an increased turnover of animals took place stimulated by the rise in the demand for meat and dairy products associated with urbanisation.[30] For the earlier years 1850–1864, output was obtained under the assumption that per caput consumption remained constant and equivalent to that of 1865.[31]

Then, a second step was estimating the aggregate index as a weighted average of output indices for major agricultural groups with their shares in the benchmark's agricultural final output as weights (Table 6.2). Volume indices were computed for different time spans valuing quantities of each product at the farm-gate prices for each benchmark (Table 6.3).

To construct a yearly price index, single series for a sample of goods within each agricultural subsector were gathered from a wide range of sources.[32] Individual price series were assembled for cereals (wheat, barley, rice), legumes (chick peas), vegetables (potatoes), fruits and nuts

Table 6.2 Agricultural final output at current prices, 1890–1964 (%)

	c.1890	1898/1902	1909/1913	1929/1933	1950	1960/1964[a]
Cereals	27.8	34.4	31.3	25.4	25.6	16.2
Pulses	3.7	3.1	3.3	3.2	3.0	2.0
Vegetables	13.2	13.3	13.1	16.5	17.2	16.4
Raw materials	2.9	3.7	3.3	3.7	3.9	6.8
Fruits and nuts	2.1	7.1	8.3	11.0	11.0	12.7
Wine must	18.5	11.2	6.8	6.3	6.4	4.1
Crude olive oil	7.9	5.8	6.0	5.9	2.6	4.9
Meat	12.4	11.1	13.9	15.5	11.1	14.7
Poultry and eggs	6.3	5.6	7.0	7.1	11.0	8.0
Non-animal	74.7	77.4	70.7	71.2	68.4	62.3
Animal	25.3	22.6	29.3	28.8	31.6	37.7

Note [a]1960/1964 final output computed at 1960 prices
Source Quantities are derived mostly from GEHR (1989, 1991), completed with Comín (1985a), Simpson (1986, 1994) (unpublished data set) and Carreras (1983) for the pre-Civil War years; and Barciela (1989) and Ministerio de Agricultura (1974, 1979a) for the 1940–1964 period. Prices are taken from GEHR (1989), Simpson (1994) (unpublished data set) and Ministerio de Agricultura (1974, 1979a).

Table 6.3 Construction of agricultural volume indices, 1850–1958

Periods	Benchmark year	Coverage at benchmark (%)
1850–1909	1891/1893	77.5
1890–1929	1909/1913	86.4
1913–1950	1929/1933	86.1
1929–1958	1950	86.5
1950–1958	1960	85.1

Sources Appendix, Table A.3

(oranges and almonds), must, unrefined olive oil, raw materials (sugar beet, wool), meat (beef, veal, pig and lamb), eggs and milk. Laspeyres price indices were constructed, then, for each group of goods with benchmarks' weights. An aggregate price index was, in turn, obtained as the average of subsectoral Laspeyres price indices weighted by their annual quantity indices.[33]

Gross Value Added

Nominal gross value added was obtained by deducting purchases outside the agricultural sector from final output at current prices. Real gross value added was derived, in turn, by subtracting industrial and services inputs at constant prices from real final output. An implicit deflator was derived from nominal and real gross value added series. Purchases outside the agricultural sector were proxied by the consumption of mineral fertilizers, and the level of non-agricultural inputs for 1958 was backcasted with the annual rate of variation of mineral fertilizers consumed in agriculture.[34]

6.1.2 Forestry

Evidence for forestry is only available since 1901 and quantities of wood, firewood, resin, cork and esparto grass were valued at 1912/1913, 1929/1933 and 1960 prices and added up into single values from which a chain quantity index was derived.[35] Output at current prices is available since 1901.[36] Gross value added at current prices was computed through backward projection of the 1958 level in national accounts (CNE-58) with the value index.[37] An implicit deflator was derived from the current value and volume indices.

6.1.3 Fishing

For fishing, quantity and current value series are available from 1904 onwards, but only scattered information exists for 1878, 1883 and 1888–1892 (and no data at all for 1935–1939).[38] The quantity of fresh fish captured is available but, since no allowances can be made for composition changes, the alternative of deflating the current value of fish captures was preferred on the grounds that, within a given industry, price variance is lower than quantity variance. Gross value added at current prices was obtained through backward extrapolation of the 1958 level (CNE58) with the rate of variation of the total value of captures.[39] When current values of total production were missing (1850–1903), gross value added was extrapolated backwards on the basis of output (computed under the assumption of constant per capita consumption times the population and adjusted for net exports) and a price index for cod.[40] An implicit deflator was derived from the current value and volume indices.

6.1.4 Value Added for Agriculture, Forestry and Fishing

Value added at current prices for agriculture, forestry and fishing was reached by adding up each subsector's estimates. Aggregate volume indices for agriculture, forestry and fishing output were derived as an average of the subsector indices with their share in its aggregate gross value added for 1913, 1929 and 1958 as weights, respectively.[41] Then, a single quantity index was computed as a variable weighted geometric average of the three indices.[42] The composition of the aggregate index is as follows: for 1850–1913, 1913 weights were accepted; for 1913–1929, a weighted geometric average of 1913 and 1929 weighted indices; for 1929–1958, a weighted geometric average of 1929 and 1958 weighted indices. An implicit deflator was obtained from current and constant price value added.

6.2 Industry

New series of industrial output and its main components, in nominal and real terms, are constructed in this section. The pathbreaking research carried out by Albert Carreras supplied the basis from which new series for extractive industries, utilities and manufacturing output were built up.[43]

The difficulties faced by historical attempts to produce hard empirical evidence on industrial performance can be illustrated by assessing Carreras' seminal contribution.[44] His index of industrial production used a fixed weighting system with alternative base years (1913, 1929, 1958, and 1975) that were, in turn, spliced into a single series using end years. For the period under study here, the 1958 input–output table (TIOE58) supplied the unit value added used as weights that were, then, extrapolated backwards to 1929 and 1913 with industrial prices, under the assumption that they approximated the trends in unit value added.[45] Unfortunately, the author was unable to establish earlier base years for the nineteenth century, and as no regard was paid to changes in relative prices, the further back in time we move from 1913, the less representative of industrial performance his index becomes. In addition to the use of fixed weights, limited coverage is usually a major liability for any industrial index. Carreras' index reaches an acceptable coverage, 65% in 1958 and approximately 50 and 70% for 1929 and 1913.[46]

The main objection to Carreras' index is its weighting scheme. At each benchmark (1913, 1929, 1958 and 1975), annual physical output for every product was weighted by its unit value added to compose an aggregate series that was, then, spliced into a single chain index using end years.[47] The final series approximates well overall industrial performance insofar the sample of goods from which the industrial output index is derived remains 'representative' for the whole industry. Unfortunately, the coverage of different sectors is asymmetrical in Carreras' index, and as one moves backwards in time, it declines and becomes more uneven, increasing the risk of undesired over-representation of particular products since a mere fraction of a subsector may eventually dominate the overall index.[48]

6 Measuring GDP, 1850–1958: Supply Side

Table 6.4 Composition of manufacturing value added in 1958

	(1) Carreras simple (%)	(2) CNE58 (%)	(3) Deviation[a] (%)
Food, beverages and tobacco	18.1	17.0	6
Textile and clothing	17.1	21.2	−21
Timber, cork and furniture	0.4	7.1	−288
Paper and printing	1.9	4.4	−84
Chemical	4.2	10.2	−89
Stone, clay, glass and cement	1.5	4.4	−108
Metal, basic	12.7	6.2	72
Metal, transformation	35.3	17.3	71
Transport equipment	5.4	7.6	−34
Other	3.4	4.6	−32

Note [a] $[100 * \ln((1)/(2))]$
Source Carreras (1983) and Spanish National Accounts Base 1958 (CNE58)

An illustration of this argument is provided by the coverage of Carreras' index at the 1958 benchmark. A glance at Table 6.4 shows the extent to which its coverage is asymmetrical. Metal industries (basic and transformation), for instance, are clearly over-represented conditioning the aggregate industrial index when it is computed directly, as in Carreras' case. Industrial growth might suffer, then, from an upward bias as a result of over-weighting capital goods, whose growth rate is usually higher than the industry's average.[49] In the construction of quantity indices for manufacturing industry, an attempt will be made to prevent some of the shortcomings in Carreras' industrial production index.

6.2.1 Manufacturing

Lack of information prevented the computation of total production and inputs, at current and constant prices, separately, from which nominal and real value added would be derived. In turn, changes in real value added are represented by variations in quantity indices constructed from production evidence for each manufacturing sector, as it is usually done in historical national accounts and occasionally in developing countries.[50]

In order to construct an index for manufacturing output, Laspeyres indices for each branch ($Q_{j,t}$) were, firstly, computed, and then, the aggregate index (Q_t^*) was obtained as their average, using each branch's share in total manufacturing value added at the benchmark year as weights ($P_{i,o}$).[51] That is,

$$Q_{i,t} = \sum q_{jt}^i p_{jo}^i / \sum q_{jo}^i p_{jo}^i \qquad (6.6)$$

and then,

$$Q_t^* = \sum Q_{i,t} P_{i,o} / \sum Q_{i,o} P_{i,o} \qquad (6.7)$$

where

$$P_{i,o} = \sum q_{jo}^i p_{jo}^i / \sum q_{jo} p_{jo} \qquad (6.8)$$

Here q and p represent quantities and prices; subscripts o and t are the benchmark year and any other year, respectively; j = 1,... n are goods, and i = 1, ... s are sectors; superscript i denotes quantities and prices of goods included in sector i. Goods in sector i are not included in any other sector.

Using this approach, the problem of lack of representativeness will be less acute than in the case of Carreras index, since the assumptions that (a) total output evolves as its main components, and (b) its coverage remains unchanged over a given period, are more easily acceptable at branch level than for the industry as a whole.

For manufacturing, eleven branches have been distinguished (Table 6.5). Basic series of physical quantities were taken from Carreras (1983, 1989), supplemented with production data on wine, alcohol, brandy, beer, meat slaughtering and timber.[52] Thus, most data employed in the construction of the manufacturing output index correspond to intermediate and primary inputs that would lead, in turn, to underestimating industrial growth, as efficiency gains in the use of inputs are not allowed for. In order to offset this shortcoming, I arbitrarily assumed a yearly 0.5% efficiency increase in the use of inputs for engineering industry and incorporated quality adjustments in the transport equipment industry.[53]

Table 6.5 Breakdown of manufacturing value added, 1913–1958 (%)

	(1) 1913	(2) 1929	(3) 1958
Food, beverages and tobacco	38.4	29.6	17.0
Textile	18.8	14.4	14.5
Clothing and shoemaking	10.1	7.0	6.7
Timber, cork and furniture	7.6	11.3	7.1
Paper and printing	2.2	1.7	4.4
Chemical	2.5	4.3	10.2
Stone, clay, glass and cement	0.7	4.4	4.4
Metal, basic	6.0	6.6	6.2
Metal, transformation	6.3	12.7	17.3
Transport equipment	5.0	6.6	7.6
Other	2.4	1.4	4.6

Source CNE58 for 1958; for 1913 and 1929, see text

In the construction of a Laspeyres quantity index for manufacturing production, a two-stage procedure was followed.

(a) *Quantity indices for each manufacturing branch.* Unit value added for each product in 1958 was backward extrapolated to 1929, 1913, 1890 and 1870 with its own price indices under the arbitrary assumption that the value added/total production ratio remained stable over time.[54] Whenever possible, direct estimates of unit value added were applied.[55] Also, adjustments by Morellá on Carreras' unit value added estimates for 1958 were accepted.[56] Then, for each branch of manufacturing, Laspeyres quantity indices were constructed with each benchmark's unit value added estimates as weights.[57]

(b) *Quantity index for aggregate manufacturing.* A Laspeyres quantity index for total manufacturing was obtained by adding up all *branch* indices with their benchmark shares in 1913, 1929 and 1958 current value added as weights (Table 6.5) that were obtained by extrapolation of 1958 levels (CNE58) with each branch's Laspeyres quantity and Paasche price indices. The resulting three indices were, then, spliced using a variable weighted geometric mean, in which the closer to a given year t, the larger the weight allocated to a particular benchmark.[58]

Paasche price indices for each *branch* of manufacturing industry were constructed by dividing, for a given *sample* of goods, its current value (expressed in index form) by a Laspeyres quantity index.[59] Current values for the sample of goods were obtained by multiplying quantities by prices that were, then, added up. An important caveat is that manufacturing price indices were constructed on very scant price data, strongly skewed towards raw materials and intermediate goods that, in turn, would tend to bias upward current manufacturing value added.[60] Later, an implicit Paasche deflator was obtained for aggregate manufacturing by dividing total current value added (in index form) by the Laspeyres quantity index.

6.2.2 Extractive Industries

As regards extractive industries, mining and quarrying were considered, with the latter usually representing less than 10% of sectoral value added. The construction procedure of quantity and price indices and of nominal and real value added levels was identical to the case of manufacturing.[61]

6.2.3 Utilities

Only gas and electricity output series were available on yearly basis, and an aggregate chain index was obtained by weighting gas and electricity output with their contributions to sectoral value added for 1913, 1929 and 1958, in which gas was allocated a larger share to include water supply.[62] Nominal gross value added was reached through the backward extrapolation of 1958 levels with Laspeyres quantity and Paasche price indices. Quantity indices were spliced into a single index following the same procedure used for manufacturing and extractive industries. In turn, the same construction method of price indices applied to manufacturing and extractive industries was adopted.

6.2.4 Value Added for Manufacturing, Extractive Industries and Utilities

Finally, an aggregate quantity index for industry (excluding construction) was derived as an average of manufacturing, extractive industries and utilities indices using their 1913, 1929 and 1958 sectoral shares in industrial gross value added as weights. Then, to obtain a single Laspeyres chain index of industrial gross value added, the three indices were spliced through a variable weighted geometric mean in which weighting varied according to the distance from the considered year (as in (12)). Current price estimates were obtained by adding up each industry's value added. An implicit deflator was derived from current and constant price estimates.

6.3 Construction

Five subsectors were distinguished in the construction industry, residential and commercial, railway, road building, hydraulic infrastructure and other public works.

6.3.1 Residential and Commercial Construction

I started from the available information on the stock of urban and rural dwellings and derived the number built in each inter-censal period by adding a rough estimate of the number of houses demolished in the period to the *net* increase in the stock.[63] Also, size and quality changes in housing were taken into consideration and overall improvements were arbitrarily assumed to take place at 0.5% annually.[64] Demolition rates were obtained through alternative methods that cast very close results. One procedure, adopted from the British case, was to derive decadal rates for demolition by assuming that 85% of the new homes built a century earlier would be demolished while the surviving 15% would disappear steadily over the next century (Feinstein 1988: 388). An alternative was the demolition rates computed for Spain by Bonhome and Bustinza that I accepted up to 1940.[65] For the years 1940–1958, I derived them from existing sources (Nomenclators and Censuses of dwellings).[66] The resulting demolition annual rates were 1861–1910, 0.21; 1911–1940, 0.28; 1940s, 0.36; and 1950s, 0.26.

To sum up, the change in the quality-adjusted stock of dwellings includes the net increase in stock plus the replacement of demolished dwellings, that is, the increase in gross stock, to which a yearly 0.5% quality improvement was applied. In order to distribute the inter-censal increase in the gross stock annually, available figures for the consumption of cement and timber were used for 1850–1944, while the annual number of new dwellings (mostly subsidized construction) was taken for 1944–1958.[67] To obtain yearly output figures, repairments and maintenance expenses were added to the quality-adjusted increase in gross stock. Repairments and maintenance were assumed to represent 1% of the current stock (which was obtained through log-linear interpolation between pairs of adjacent censal benchmarks). Finally, urban and rural construction indices were combined into a single index using their respective shares in the total value of dwellings.[68] A specific deflator was, in turn, built up that combined construction materials costs and mason wages with 1958 input–output weights (TIOE58).[69] Annual current value added for the residential and commercial construction industry was obtained by projecting the level of gross value added for 1958 backwards with the quantity and price indices.[70]

6.3.2 Non-Residential Construction

Railways

Expenditure on investment and maintenance in railways at 1990 prices computed by Cucarella (1999) is the basis of my estimates. He relied on decadal averages of nominal expenditure on investment and maintenance in railways estimated by Gómez Mendoza (1991) that were distributed annually over 1850–1920 using the number of kilometres under construction, for investment, and those under exploitation, for maintenance, and that he completed for the late 1920s and early 1930s with his own estimates (Cucarella 1999: 84–85). In addition, government's and Spanish national railways company's (RENFE) investment and maintenance expenditures in railways estimates by Muñoz Rubio (1995) were employed from 1940 onwards. Cucarella (1999: 78–80) deflated his current value estimates with a wholesale price index. I converted Cucarella's constant price estimates into nominal values using his own deflator and deflated the series again with a specific railway construction price index that combines the costs of railway materials and mason wages with 1958 input–output weights (TIOE58).[71]

Roads

Investment, repairs and maintenance expenditures on roads at current prices are available since 1897 (Uriol Salcedo 1992). Nominal road expenditure was backcasted to 1850 with the rate of variation of public expenditure on roads (Comín 1985b). The resulting yearly figures for 1850–1935 were adjusted to match the decennial estimates by Gómez Mendoza (1991). Finally, current expenditure estimates were deflated with a specific price index computed by combining materials costs and mason wages with 1958 input–output weights (TIOE58).[72]

Hydraulic Infrastructure and Other Public Works

Investment, maintenance and repairs expenditures on hydraulic infrastructure and maritime and harbour expenditure by the central government were deflated with a specific price index including construction materials and wages.[73]

Indices of non-residential construction were built up combining railway and road construction, hydraulic infrastructure and other public works with their 1913, 1929 and 1958 shares in the sector's value added.[74] A compromise, single quantity index for the whole period 1850–1958 was built up as a variable weighted geometric average of each pair of adjacent benchmark's indices (as in the case of manufacturing).

It is worth mentioning that Alfonso Herranz-Loncán (2004) estimated output in infrastructure for 1860–1935 at a more disaggregated level than the one presented here. His results are coincidental with mine but show higher volatility, due to the fact that only investment is considered while maintenance is neglected (Fig. 6.1). For this reason, I have not incorporated Herranz-Loncán estimates here.

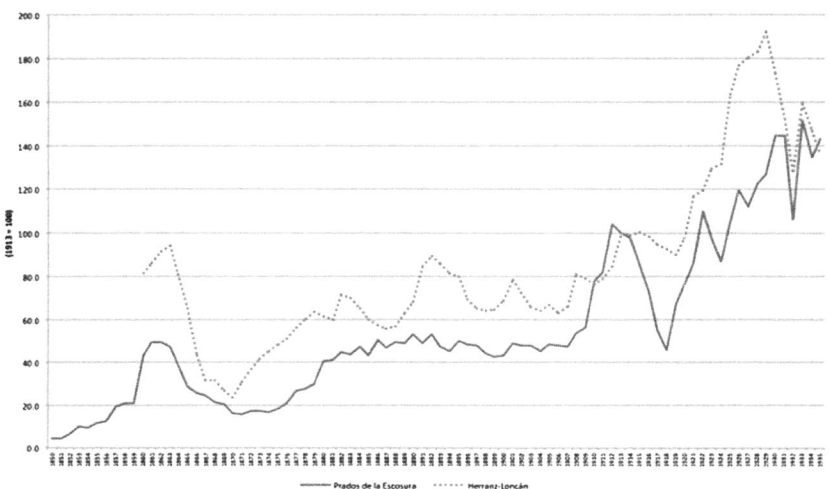

Fig. 6.1 Non-residential construction volume indices, 1850–1935: alternative estimates (1913 = 100). *Source* Prados de la Escosura, see the text; Herranz-Loncán (2004)

Current value series for each branch of non-residential construction was obtained by linking the level of gross value added for 1958 to its Laspeyres quantity and price indices and, then, added up to represent total value added in non-residential construction. An implicit deflator was computed.

6.3.3 Value Added in Residential and Non-Residential Construction

Residential and non-residential construction output was, then, combined into a single index for the construction industry with their 1913, 1929 and 1958 shares in the sector's value added, from which a spliced volume index was derived using a variable weighted geometric average.

Nominal gross value added for the entire construction industry was obtained by adding up residential and non-residential construction value added at current prices. An implicit (semi-Paasche) deflator was derived from current value (in index form) and the aggregate volume index.[75]

6.4 Services

Estimating value added in services represents the main obstacle in the construction of historical national accounts, especially in the case of those services for which no market prices exist, and also an unsurmountable problem in international comparisons.[76] In the present estimate, the use of employment data has been avoided and output indicators used instead.[77] When the output of services is derived using labour input data, productivity cannot be estimated since by construction it is implicitly assumed that output per worker remains stagnant. Major subsectors considered here are transport and communications, trade (wholesale and retail), banking and insurance, ownership of dwellings, public administration, education and health, and other services including restaurants, hotels and leisure, household services and liberal professions. Several steps were taken to produce annual quantity and price indices for the different branches of the service sector.

6.4.1 Transport and Communications

Transportation and communication services include water (coastal and international), road, urban, air and rail transport plus postal, telegraph and telephone services.

For transportation by rail, merchandise and passenger output series are available for the period 1868–1958 and were backcasted to 1859 with the volume of merchandise and passengers transported.[78] A spliced index of total rail transport output was obtained with rates per passenger-kilometre and ton-kilometre for 1913, 1929 and 1958 as weights over 1859–1964 that was extrapolated back to 1850 with the rate of variation of railway tracks. Thus, 1913 weights were applied for the period 1868–1913, while variable weighted geometric averages of 1913 and 1929 (1929 and 1958) weighted indices were accepted for 1913–1929 (1929–1958). Prices, that is, average output per passenger-kilometre and ton-kilometre (in pesetas), were taken from Gómez Mendoza (1989) and Muñoz Rubio (1995). Value added at current prices in rail transport was obtained by linking the 1958 level (CNE58) to quantity and price indices (average prices per passenger-kilometre and ton-kilometre).

For maritime transport, coastal and international transport services were distinguished. For coastal transport, merchandise output (expressed in tons-kilometre), available since 1950, was projected backwards to 1857 with tons of merchandise transported, while only the number of passengers transported was available from 1928 onwards. An unweighted average of the quantity indices of passenger and merchandise coastal transport was computed for 1928–1958 that was, then, spliced with the merchandise index in order to cover the period 1857–1958.[79] International transport services for 1942–1958 were measured by the total value of passenger and merchandise freights received by Spanish ships and, then, deflated by their respective freight indices.[80] For 1850–1942, merchandise transport was computed by applying a freight factor to the total value of exports and imports carried under Spanish flag that was, then, deflated by a freight index.[81] An index for international sea transport was computed using 1958 passenger and merchandise freight rates as weights for 1942–1958 and, then, projected backwards with the merchandise index to 1850. Finally, value added for maritime transport at current and constant prices was derived projecting value added for 1958 (CNE58) backwards with freight and quantity indices for coastal and international transport.[82]

For road transport, merchandise and passenger outputs are available since 1950 and were backward projected to 1940 with the number of tons and passenger transported.[83] A road transport output index was computed as an average of merchandise and passenger output for 1940–1958 and backward projected to 1850 with the road length that, to allow for its use, was weighted by the stock of motor vehicles over 1900–1940.[84] Value added at current prices in road transport was obtained by linking the 1958 level (CNE58) to the output index and a price index for gasoline.[85]

Urban transport was approximated by the number of passengers transported by tramways, trolley buses, buses and metro from 1901 onwards (Gómez Mendoza 1989). Value added at current prices was reached through backward projection of the 1958 level (CNE58) with the rates of variation of the sector's revenues.[86]

For air transport, passenger output is available since 1929 and merchandise output from 1950 onwards that was projected backwards to 1930 with the rate of variation of total merchandise transported; both series were combined into a single quantity index using with equal weights.[87] Value added was computed annually by backcasting the level for 1958 with the output index and a price index for gasoline.[88]

Finally, road, urban, water, air and rail indices weighted by their contributions to transport gross value added in 1913, 1929 and 1958 (CNE58) provided an aggregate index for transport services.[89] A spliced quantity index was constructed for 1850–1958 as a variable weighted geometric average of each pair of adjacent benchmark's indices.

Annual value added in transport services (at current prices) was reached by adding up rail, water, road, air and urban transport value added derived through linking 1958 value added levels (CNE58) to their quantity and price indices. An implicit deflator resulted of dividing current value added (in index form) by the aggregate volume index.

For communication services, postal (number of letters and parcels sent), telegraph (number of telegrams) and telephone (calls from 1924 onwards, backcasted with lines in service to 1897) indices were merged into an aggregate index using their 1913, 1929 and 1958 revenues as weights that were, then, spliced into a single index using variable weighted geometric average.[90] The current value of communications services was derived by linking the 1958 value added level (CNE58) to each subsector's yearly revenues.[91] An implicit deflator resulted from current value added (in index form) and the quantity index.

6.4.2 Wholesale and Retail Trade

Due to dearth of data on distribution, it was assumed that trade output was a linear function of physical output, and a quantity index was derived by combining, with 1958 weights, agricultural (including fishing), mining and manufacturing output plus imports of goods, from which a 2-year moving average was computed to allow for inventories.[92] Value added at current prices was obtained by linking the 1958 level to the quantity index and a price index (computed on the basis of the same trade components and 1958 shares).

6.4.3 Banking and Insurance

Value added at current prices was computed by splicing 1958 value added for banking and insurance services (CNE58) with the joint index of banking deposits and insurance premia. Deposits in commercial and savings banks and the value of insurance premia, expressed in index form (with 1958 = 1), were weighted according to their shares in the 1958 input–output table's sectoral value added (TIOE58) to derive an aggregate nominal index. Value added at current prices was deflated with a wholesale price index.[93]

6.4.4 Ownership of Dwellings

It was assumed to evolve as the quality-adjusted stock of dwellings.[94] Value added at current prices was derived splicing the 1958 level (CNE58) to the quantity index and a rent of dwellings deflator.[95]

6.4.5 Public Administration

Services output for public administration was measured by wages and salaries paid by the central government, which were deflated by a cost of living index.[96] Value added at current prices was obtained by backcasting the 1958 benchmark level with the rate of variation of wages and salaries paid by the central government.

6.4.6 Education and Health

For education services, an index of schooling weighted by deflated government expenditure on education, to allow for quality changes, was used.[97] For health, the number of hospital patients was combined with deflated public expenditure on health in order to incorporate quality improvements.[98] Value added in education and health was obtained by projecting value added in 1958 with their quantity indices and a wholesale price index.

6.4.7 Other Services

In the cases of household services and liberal professions, the usual assumption that output evolved as the labour force employed in each sector was accepted, namely that no productivity growth occurred, and yearly figures were obtained from log-linearly interpolating census data.[99] Value added was reached by linking the 1958 level to the quantity index and a wage index (household services) or the wholesale price index (liberal professions). Finally, for hotel, restaurant and leisure services were crudely approximated combining indices of room occupancy and leisure.[100] Value added was derived by splicing 1958 level with the quantity index and the cost of living.

6.4.8 Value Added in Services

Next, index numbers for the different branches of services were merged into an aggregate index, with 1913, 1929 and 1958 weights, which correspond to their contributions to total gross value added in services (Table 6.5). A compromise, single index was computed through a variable weighted geometric average, as in the cases of agriculture and industry.

Aggregate gross value added at current prices was computed by adding up all services' value added. An implicit deflator was obtained from current value (in index form) and the aggregate quantity index.

6.5 Total Gross Value Added and GDP at Market Prices

A real gross value added index was constructed for 1850–1958 by weighting output volume indices for each major branch of economic activity (agriculture, industry, construction and services) with their shares in total gross value added for 1958.[101] Nominal gross value added was obtained by adding up GVA at current prices for each major branch of economic activity. GDP at market prices resulted from adding indirect taxes less subsidies to total GVA. An implicit gross value added deflator was derived from nominal and real values expressed in index form (1958 = 1). Real GDP at market prices was derived with the GVA deflator.

Notes

1. Cf. Heston (1994) for a survey of developing countries GDP estimates.
2. By a component is meant a variable that is an element of GDP (i.e. agricultural output) and by an indicator a variable that is correlated with real output when the latter is available (i.e. tons-km transported by the railways) (Balke and Gordon 1989: 41).
3. Actually, the dearth of data on nineteenth-century prices has prevented economic historians from building price indices, and Sardá (1948) wholesale price index still remains widely used despite general complaints about its low and biased coverage. Available indices for wholesale prices in the early twentieth century have not been challenged so far (as it is also the case of the price index built by the Comisión del Patrón Oro, Gold Standard Committee, in 1929. Consumer price indices are provided in Reher and Ballesteros (1993), Ballesteros (1997), and Maluquer de Motes (2006, 2013).
4. Unfortunately, it was not always possible to derive Paasche price indices for every sub-branch of each sector of economic activity. In such a case, Laspeyres chain indices were used. This problem, resulting from defective statistics, is also common in today's national accounts (Cf. Corrales and Taguas 1991).
5. This procedure is most common in present-day developing countries (Heston 1994: 35). Official national accounts with 1958 base (Contabilidad Nacional de España 1958, CNE58) for the years 1954–1964 are presented in Instituto de Estudios Fiscales (1969).
6. The Ministry of Agriculture (Ministerio de Agricultura 1979) computed final output and value added in agriculture for the years 1950–1958. Aggregate national accounts (CNE58), however, are only available since 1954.
7. Unfortunately, since coverage was incomplete, assumptions about the production of several crops in 1890 and 1900 were made. Cf. Table 6.1. I am indebted to James Simpson for kindly allowing me access to the

unpublished agricultural quantity and price data set for 1890–1930 that underlies his own work (Simpson 1994).

8. Cf. For its coverage, cf. Appendix, Table A.3. It must be noticed that final output and value added series are constructed for the entire period 1850–1958 despite the fact that Ministry of Agriculture's (1979) figures at current prices were preferred for 1950–1958. The reason why the estimate is extended over the 1950s is to dispose of homogeneous deflators over the whole time span.

9. This is also a common feature of developing countries today, cf. Heston (1994).

10. There are differences in levels of real final agricultural output between Table 6.1 and Simpson (1994) that lead to productivity differences. The discrepancies mainly stem from the fact that, in Table 5.2, a deflator derived from the covered output (i.e. goods whose quantities and prices are available) is assumed to be representative for the entire agricultural sector, and it is, therefore, used to deflate current final output. Simpson (1994), in turn, assumed that the quantity index that results from the covered output is representative of agriculture as a whole. There is a long-standing debate about which approach is preferable. Cf. Maddison (1995), p. 231–232.

11. That is, on a large sample of agricultural produce, it is worth mentioning that *total* production at benchmark years over 1891–1931 has already been provided by GEHR (1983) and Simpson (1994). Also, annual quantity indices for *total* production for 1891–1935 are presented in Comín (1987) and GEHR (1987).

12. Thus, for 1890–1913, a weighted geometric average of 1891/1993 and 1909/1913 based quantity indices was taken; for 1913–1929, a weighted geometric average of 1909/1913 and 1929/1933 based quantity indices; for 1929–1950, a weighted geometric average of 1929/1933 and 1950 based quantity indices; and for 1950–1958, a weighted geometric average of 1950 and 1960 based quantity indices. For 1850–1890, in turn, an 1890-based Laspeyres agricultural quantity index was accepted.

13. The level of agricultural final output derives from Ministerio de Agricultura (1979b: 155).

14. That is, on the basis of the same variable sample of produce on which the index of final output was constructed.

15. Thus, for 1890–1913, a weighted geometric average of 1891/1893 and 1909/1913 based price indices was taken; for 1913–1929, a weighted geometric average of 1909/1913 and 1929/1933 based price indices; for 1929–1950, a weighted geometric average of 1929/1933 and 1950 based price indices; and for 1950–1958, a weighted geometric average of 1950 and 1960 based price indices. For 1850–1890, in turn, 1890-based Laspeyres agricultural price index was accepted.
16. Cf. Fenoaltea (1988). Table A.3 in the Appendix presents, for every benchmark year, the coverage of each group in the annual quantity index. For a more formal description of the method, see the section on industry.
17. In order to derive each subsectoral index, physical quantities of final output within each group of goods were valued at their benchmark year prices and the aggregated value expressed in index form. Quantities are derived mostly from GEHR (1989, 1991), completed with Comín (1985a), Simpson (1986, 1994 unpublished data set) and Carreras (1983) for the pre-Civil War years; and Barciela (1989) and Ministerio de Agricultura (1974, 1979a) for 1940–1950. For the Civil War, scant information, only for cereals, is provided in Barciela (1983, 1989) and Almarcha (1975).
18. Simpson (1994, 1995) followed option (a), while Prados de la Escosura (1988) used both (a) and (c).
19. Partial evidence for 1857–1860 is collected in Prados de la Escosura (1988).
20. Output was interpolated for missing years in the cases of wheat (1887) and olive oil (1887 and 1889).
21. The reason to adjust the traded volume by the length of the network is that this a period of construction of roads and railways that clearly reduced transportation cost and, hence, incentivize commercialization. I am indebted to Albert Carreras for the suggestion.
22. Specific commercialization series used were transportation by rail (metric tons/km) for cereals (wheat and rice) and wine, and by sea (including coastal and export trade) for wine, olive oil, sugar cane and beet, fruits and nuts. Information (except for fruits and nuts that come from Gallego and Pinilla (1996) and *Estadística(s) del Comercio Exterior*) was derived from Carreras (1983, i, 386–502). Raw wool output was taken from Parejo (1989).

23. Cf. Simpson (Simpson 1992, 1994, 1995) for objections to this point of view, but cf. Federico (1986) for the wide diffusion of the market economy in another nineteenth-century Mediterranean agriculture, Italy. Domínguez (1994) research on northern Spain shows that peasants had regular access to the market by mid-nineteenth century.
24. It is not clear that the relationship between total output and commercialised output was stable over time and it seems reasonable to presume that the gap would decline as the economy developed.
25. The level of per capita consumption for 1865–1869 was arbitrarily assumed to remain stable over 1850–1865. That is, $D = c * N = (1 - s) * Q + (X - M)$, where D is the demand for wheat (legumes), c is its consumption per caput, N is the total population, Q is output, s is the proportion of seed and animal feed, X is exports, and M is imports. Thus, total wheat (legumes) output will be obtained as $Q = (c * N - (X - M))/(1 - s)$. Implicit in this calculation is the assumption that disposable per capita income and agricultural relative prices did not experience significant alterations over these 15 years and represent a particular case of a demand function.
26. That is, 1891/1893 prices were applied to physical output of each crop and the resulting annual values added up for the previously defined groups of products and expressed in index number form, from which a quantity agricultural index was obtained by weighting them with their shares in the 1890 benchmark.
27. Less reliable estimates for livestock numbers are available for 1859 and 1888. Cf. Mitchell (1992) for data and GEHR (1978/1979, 1991) for a critique of the sources.
28. Since it has been argued that livestock numbers are underestimated for the 1891–1916 period, conversion coefficients from 1929 and 1933 livestock censuses were adopted (Simpson 1994; GEHR 1978/1979, 1991). Animal produce for 1865 was derived from livestock numbers by applying the turnover of animals in García Sanz's (1994). It is noticeable that the percentage of livestock slaughtered changed over the late nineteenth century, in particular, for sheep and cattle (Cf. García Sanz 1994; GEHR 1983; and Simpson 1994). Constant average weights per animal in 1920, derived in Flores de Lemus (1926), were accepted in Simpson (1994) and GEHR (1978/1979) and maintained in my estimates since no alternative estimates were available. Coefficients applied are presented in Appendix, Table A.2.

29. The cautious estimating procedure would, nevertheless, offset the claimed upward bias in growth rates stemming from approximating crops output from traded crops. An additional reason to choose such a rough procedure is that livestock output could be arguably seen as less volatile than crops output, and by its inclusion in the estimate of agricultural output, excess volatility would have been reduced.
30. Agrarian historians coincide in pointing to a decline in livestock output simultaneous to a rise in crops output over the late nineteenth century (GEHR 1978/1979, 1983, 1989). The literature does not address, however, the issue of over time change in animals' weight (most authors keep using weights per unit taken from the 1920 census by Flores de Lemus (1926)) and, more significantly, the increased turnover of animals. García Sanz (1994) shows the share of livestock slaughtered in 1865, and its differences with similar estimates for 1900 or 1930 (much closer among themselves) are striking, in particular, for cattle (the proportion in 1865 is, at least, 1–3 with respect those of 1904 or 1929), a feature consistent with the rise in urbanization within the period that brought a rise in beef consumption. Mutton consumption rose, in turn, (as sheep became increasingly less oriented towards wool production) and goats' meat experienced a marked decline.
31. The same procedure used for crops output was applied here. Alternatively, the 1858 livestock census could be used, but its noticeable underestimation of livestock numbers prevented me from doing it.
32. Sources used for yearly agricultural prices were Arenales (1976), Barciela (1983, 1989), Carreras (1989), Comín (1985a, c), *Estadística(s) de Comercio Exterior* (various years), GEHR (1981a, b, 1989), Gómez Mendoza and Simpson (1988), Martín Rodríguez (1982), Ministerio de Agricultura (1974, 1979a), Ministerio de Trabajo (1942), *Anuarios Estadísticos de España* (various years), Paris Eguilaz (1943), Piqueras (1978), Reher and Ballesteros (1993), Sánchez-Albornoz (1975, 1979, 1981) and Simpson (1994, unpublished data set).
33. Actually, since quantity indices are of Laspeyres type, price indices should be of Paasche type to derive current values (see expressions (I), (II) and (III) above). It is worth noticing that a hybrid of Laspeyres and Paasche price indices, which stems from defective statistics, is still common in today's national accounts (Cf. Corrales and Taguas 1991).
34. Fortunately, the small share of agricultural final output represented by purchases outside agriculture keeps the size of the bias introduced by

such crude proxies within reasonable limits. The source for the 1958 benchmark was Ministerio de Agricultura (1979b: 155). The $N + P_2O_5 + K_2O$ content of mineral fertilizers in Gallego (1986) and Barciela (1989) provides a homogeneous annual indicator for the years 1892–1958 that was backcasted with fertilizer imports to 1850. Missing values for the content of mineral fertilizers in 1935–1939 and 1945–1950 were log-linearly interpolated from available data for 1935, 1945 and 1950. For 1940–1944, it was assumed the same value as for 1945. For mineral fertilizers, prices were taken from Pujol (1998), Carreras (1989) and *Anuario(s) Estadístico(s)*. Quantities and prices for fertilizer imports were derived from *Estadística(s) del Comercio Exterior*.

35. The index was derived from splicing four sub-indices: 1901–1913, values at 1912/1913 prices; 1913–1929, geometric average of values at 1912/1913 and 1929/1933 prices; 1929–1940, values at 1929/1933 prices; 1940–1958, values at 1960 prices. Splicing the subseries was done using ratios for overlapping years. Sources used were GEHR (1989, 1991), Barciela (1989) and Ministerio de Agricultura (1979a, b).
36. Reseña Estadística (1952) for the current value of total output, 1901–1950. Current values of total and final output are provided in Ministerio de Agricultura (1979) for 1950–1958.
37. It was arbitrarily assumed that variations in value added at current prices corresponded to those in total output in nominal terms.
38. Sources used are Giráldez (1991) for 1883–1934, completed with unpublished data obtained by Gómez Mendoza (1983) for 1878, 1888–1892 and 1904–1907; and Barciela (1989) for 1940–1958.
39. The value of total production is considered to provide an acceptable proxy for value added. Cf. Hemberg (1955) and Giráldez (1991), pp. 520–521.
40. Cod prices in Arenales (1976).
41. Gross value added for 1958 comes from 1958-based national accounts, CNE58 I.E.F. (1969). The shares for 1958 were: agriculture, 0.8963; forestry, 0.0722; fishing, 0.0315. For the period 1850–1900 when forestry data are missing, agriculture's share was increased correspondingly. For the Civil War years (1936–1939), when no data exist for forestry and fishing I assumed these two sectors evolved as agriculture.
42. In the compromise single index, each benchmark's index gets a larger weight the closer it is to each particular year (the formula used is (12)).

43. Cf. Carreras (1983, 1984, 1990, 1992). Most of the annual data and the weighting system used for this section were derived from Carreras (1983).
44. An alternative estimate can be found in Prados de la Escosura (1988), Chap. 4, in which Fisher indices were computed for 1860, 1890 and 1910 benchmarks using 1856, 1900 and 1920 weights.
45. The actual procedure followed by Carreras (1983, 1984) to derive unit value added for 1913 and 1929 was applying the ratio of gross *value added* at factor cost to *total value* for 1958 to industrial prices in 1913 and 1929, assuming implicitly that such a ratio was stable over time.
46. Industrial gross value added used to obtain these percentages derived from contemporary estimates by Vandellòs (1925) for 1913 and de Miguel (1935) for 1927. The coverage of Carreras' industrial production index is still lower than the one by Lewis (1978) for the UK, which covered 91% of manufacturing and mining value added in 1907.
47. In Carreras (1987, 1990), the final index results from linking the series for 1831–1913 (built using the 1913 benchmark) with the series for 1913–1935 (1929 benchmark), the series for 1935–1958 (1958 benchmark) and the series 1958–1981 (1975 benchmark).
48. Cf. Harley (1982) and Fremdling (1988) for a critique of analogous problems in British and German industrial production indices built by Hoffmann (1955). A debate on industrial growth in early nineteenth-century Spain along these lines can be found in Prados de la Escosura (1988), Chap. 4 and Carreras (1990), Chap. 3 (*addenda*). Cf. Rosés (2003) for a re-assessment.
49. However, as Morellá (1992) suggests, the Gerschenkron effect, that is, the downward bias in the growth rate introduced by end-year weighting may offset it.
50. Cf. Holtfrerich (1983) and Fenoaltea (2003, 2005), for German and Italian historical accounts, and Heston (1994: 35, 47), for present-day developing countries. Cf. Gandoy (1988) for a critique of the use of production indices instead of real value added derived as a residual of double deflated output and inputs and David (1962) and Fenoaltea (1976) for support of single deflation.
51. As it has been shown above, the same method was applied to the construction of the agricultural final output series.

52. Almarcha et al. (1975), Coll (1985, 1986) and Comín (1985a), together with the reference provided in the section on agriculture above, provide complementary sources.
53. Lewis (1978) made the same assumption for the UK Quality indices for shipbuilding and locomotive production have been applied the tons constructed. For shipbuilding, Feinstein (1988) quality index has been adjusted to the Spanish case. Thus, for 1850–1869, no adjustment has been made; a 0.35% annual increase was applied to 1870–1885 that rose to 0.7% for 1885–1900 and to 0.83% over 1901–1936, while no increase was assumed for 1937–1949. Finally, a 1% quality improvement was accepted for 1950–1958. For the production of locomotives, a quality adjustment has been derived from Cordero and Menéndez (1978) evidence on the increase in power per type of locomotive (including electric and diesel engines).
54. This is the procedure followed by Carreras (1983) for 1913 and 1929.
55. Historical estimates for unit value added in mining, cement and metal and engineering industries derived from Coll (1985, 1986), Escudero (1989) and Gómez Mendoza (1985a, b) were employed.
56. Cf. Morellá (1992).
57. Thus, each branch or sectoral index was built using 1870 benchmark's unit value added for 1850–1870; indices with 1870 and 1890 unit value added weights for 1870–1890; and 1890 and 1913 unit value added weights for 1890–1913. Then, a geometric mean was calculated for each sub-period, and a single sectoral index was reached for 1850–1913 splicing the three segments 1850–1870, 1870–1890 and 1890–1913 on the basis of overlapping years. For the post-1913 period, branch indices were derived with 1913 and 1929 unit value added for 1913–1929 and with 1929 and 1958 unit value added weights for 1929–1958. I did not follow the common practice in historical industrial accounts of smoothing the resulting series with some sort of moving average in order to allow for stocks (Cf. Batista et al. 1997; Maluquer de Motes 1994) since I did not have any knowledge about the size and evolution of industrial stocks.
58. Thus, 1913 weighted indices were used for 1850–1913 and variable geometrical averages of 1913 and 1929 based indices, for the years 1913–1929, and of 1929 and 1958 based indices, for 1929–1958.
59. This implies that goods whose prices were not available were assumed to have the same price behaviour as those within the sample. For

manufacturing, price indices for different subsectors (food, textile, shoemaking, metal, chemical, cement, timber, paper) were constructed from a wide variety of sources. Thus, for food industry, its price index was based on price series for wine, brandy, beer, olive oil, flour, rice, sugar, coffee, cocoa and tobacco. Prices for yarn and semi-manufactures of cotton, silk, wool, hemp and jute were, in turn, the basic ingredients of the textile price index. Again, for metal industries, both basic and transforming, iron ingots, steel and cast iron, tin, lead, copper, blister, zinc, tin, silver and mercury, that is, inputs prices, were the almost exclusive ingredients of their price indices. Prices for shoes, corks, common and Portland cement and paper were the available information for shoemaking, cork, cement, paper and printing industries. For the chemical industries, a wider coverage was achieved. In any case, price coverage was uneven and the sources quite heterogeneous. The main sources for industrial prices used, including mining, utilities and construction, were Arenales (1976), Barciela (1989), Carreras (1989), Coll (1985, 1986), Martín Rodríguez (1982), Ministerio de Trabajo (1942), Paris Eguilaz (1943) and Prados de la Escosura (1981).

60. This is so because as efficiency increases, intermediate consumption is reduced rendering, hence, a lower increase (or a sharper decline) for the value added deflator than for inputs prices or for the deflator of total production.

61. No data were available for quarrying before 1920 and extractive industries' output was backcasted till 1850 with mining output. The sources for quantities and prices were Carreras (1983, 1989), Coll (1985) and Escudero (1998). Coal, iron ore, lead ore and pyrites are the main components of the price index for mining (see note 98).

62. For water supply, no national aggregate figures were found and only scattered data are available for a few capital cities (Madrid (Rueda Laffond 1994), Barcelona, Bilbao (Antolín 1991) and Pamplona (Garrués 1998)). For utilities, gas and electricity prices were available (see note 98). Data for gross value added come from 1958 national accounts (CNE58) distributed by branches with the 1958 input–output table (IOT58). In allocating a higher weight to gas, to compensate for the lack of data on water supply, I followed a suggestion by Fenoaltea (1982: 627).

63. No distinction can be made between residential and commercial use of dwellings. However, Tafunell (1989b) points out that in 1890s

Barcelona non-residential dwellings did not reach 5% of total dwellings, with the ground floor of residential buildings being commonly allocated to industrial and services' activities. The sources are *Nomenclators* and *Censos de viviendas*. Residential construction indices are available for several cities, including Madrid and Barcelona for the late nineteenth and early twentieth century, i.e. Tafunell (1989b); Gómez Mendoza (1986). Data on the stock of urban dwellings are available in Tafunell (1989a).

64. The assumed annual increase in size and quality is similar to the one estimated by Cairncross (1953) for the UK and was also accepted by Lewis (1978).
65. Cf. Bonhome and Bustinza (1969). The extent to which the results from each estimate are similar is provided by the percentage of houses built in 1850 that still survived a century later (under the assumption that the demolished houses are always the oldest):

	1950	1960
Bonhome and Bustinza method	64.5	60.1
Feinstein method	64.6	59.4

66. Before 1860, the stock of dwellings was backcasted with the rate of population growth and a demolition yearly rate of 0.2% was assumed.
67. Input consumption was derived from Carreras (1983). A 2-year moving average was computed to allow for stocks. Consumption of timber and cement was combined into a single index with 1958 input–output (TIOE58) weights. Evidence on new dwellings comes from *Anuario(s) Estadístico(s)*.
68. The value of urban and rural dwellings (the cost of the average rural (urban) dwelling times its number) over the following periods, prior to 1860, 1861–1911, 1911–1940 and 1961–1960, was computed from data in Bonhome and Bustinza (1969) for dwellings built in these periods and still existing in 1965. The resulting shares for urban dwellings were 0.3448 (1850–1860), 0.5289 (1861–1910), 0.8623 (1911–1940) and 0.8663 (1941–1960).
69. The residential construction deflator included construction materials representing 49% (0.32, timber; 0.30, cement; 0.38, iron and steel) and mason wages, 51%.

70. The 1958 Input–output table (TIOE58) provided the shares for residential and commercial (0.7756) that was used to derive each sector value added from official national accounts (CNE58).
71. For 1936–1939, only the expenditure per kilometre of line by the major railway companies, Norte and MZA, on the nationalist side was available (no data are available on the republican side during the Spanish Civil War). Lacking line length and expenditure per kilometre of line on the whole of Spain, no attempt was made to compute total expenditure and I accepted expenditure per line kilometre in the Francoist side as a proxy for changes in railway construction during the war years, 1936–1939. The deflator for railways construction was obtained by allocating 65.6% to materials costs (0.13, timber; 0.23, cement; 0.64, rails) and 34.4% to mason wages.
72. 73.In the road construction deflator construction materials represented 55% (0.69, cement; 0.31, iron) and mason wages, 45%.
73. Data on government expenditure on hydraulic infrastructure are provided in Fundación BBV (1992) and public expenditure on maritime works and harbours in Comín (1985b). The deflator used was constructed from prices for public works materials and wages, weighted according to 1958 input–output table (TIOE58). Thus, 57.4% was allocated to public works materials (0.08, timber; 0.24, iron; 0.68, cement) and 42.6%, to mason wages.
74. The 1958 input–output table (TIOE58) offers the shares of each non-residential construction branch in its total value added provided by 1958 national accounts (CNE58). The shares for 1913 and 1929 were derived from the current value estimates described in the text. For 1936–1939, given the dearth of data, an index was built up on the basis of railways construction and spliced with the main index using 1935 as the link year. Also, an index including 1940 was constructed on reduced information as maritime, and harbour expenditure was missing and spliced with the main index with 1941 as the link year.
75. The 1958 Input–output table (TIOE58) provided the shares for residential and commercial (0.7756) and non-residential construction (0.2244) that were used to derive each sector value added from official national accounts (CNE58).
76. See Maddison (1983) and Krantz (1994). Cf. Melvin (1995) for the evolution of the concept of services.
77. The exception is household services.

78. Actually, while merchandise output, measured in metric tons-kilometre, is available since 1868, passenger output, measured in passenger-kilometre, is only available for the two main railway companies, Norte and MZA, before 1913. I linked MZA and Norte's passenger output over the years 1867–1913 to total passenger output for 1913–1958. The sources are Gómez Mendoza (1989) and Muñoz Rubio (1995). For the Civil War (1936–1939), the output series were interpolated with evidence on merchandise and passenger transported by Norte and MZA on the nationalist side, cf. Muñoz Rubio (1995), pp. 282 and 287.
79. The source for merchandise output since 1950 is Instituto de Estudios de Transportes y Comunicaciones (1984). Merchandise and passenger transported are provided in Frax (1981) and Gómez Mendoza (1989) for 1850–1950.
80. Data from Estadística de fletes y seguros (1942–1956) and Ministerio de Hacienda, Dirección General de Aduanas (1957–1958) kindly supplied by Elena Martínez Ruíz.
81. The freight factor series is used, that is, the ratio of freight costs to total traded value, and the total value of Spanish international trade is derived from Sect. 6.4. The freight indices correspond to iron ore, for exports, and a weighted average of wheat and coal freights, for imports. The sources for freights are Coll and Sudrià (1987), Isserlis (1938), North (1965) and Prados de la Escosura (1984). The share of tonnage transported under Spanish flag is derived from Valdaliso (1991) for 1850–1935 and from Anuario(s) Estadístico(s), thereafter.
82. Coastal freights per ton were computed for 1932–1958 from Valdaliso (1997). For 1857–1932, it was assumed that coastal freights evolved as freights in international trade (on freights see Sect. 6.4). Shares of coastal (0.6) and international transportation (0.4) in 1958 value added were derived using freight rates and tons and passenger transported.
83. Road output (both passenger and merchandise) is provided in Muñoz Rubio (1995) from 1950 onwards. Tons and passenger transported for 1940–1950 are derived from Anuario(s) Estadístico(s).
84. The stock of motor vehicles is provided in López Carrillo (1998). For the road length, the sources are Gómez Mendoza (1982, 1989) and López Carrillo (1998).
85. The price of gasoline is available since 1913 in Anuario(s) Estadístico(s) and was backward projected to 1901 with the price of petroleum in

Carreras (1989). For the late nineteenth century, it was assumed that road transport prices fluctuate along rail transport prices.

86. Actually, CNE58 only provides value added for 'other transport' that was distributed between urban and air transport using the 1958 input–output table (TIOE58).
87. The sources are Gómez Mendoza (1989) and Anuario(s) Estadístico(s).
88. This price index is the same used in the case of road transportation.
89. Weights were 0.44 for road transport; 0.1148, urban; 0.16, water; 0.0266, air; and 0.2586, rail, derived from CNE58 and TIOE58. For years in which information was incomplete, indices were built on partial evidence and spliced with the main index. That was the case for 1936–1939, when only air, road and sea transport indices were available, and for 1850–1856 when just rail and sea transport indices existed.
90. Only figures for mail services go back to 1850; telegraph services are recorded for 1855 and, then, annually from 1860, and telephone services from 1886 (number of telephones, but calls only from 1924). The sources are Calvo (1998), Gómez Mendoza (1989) and Mitchell (1992). 1958 weights were 0.6198, telephone; 0.2955, post; 0.0847, telegraph. The spliced index was constructed as in the case of transportation.
91. Revenues for telegraph services are only available from 1896 (Gómez Mendoza 1989) onwards and for telephone services since 1925 (kindly provided by Nelson Alvarez).
92. This short cut has been used before by Lewis (1978), van der Eng (1992), Cortés Conde (1994, 1997), Batista et al. (1997) and Smits et al. (2000) in historical estimates for Britain, Indonesia, Argentina, Portugal and the Netherlands, respectively. Similar methods were applied to Denmark, Sweden and Germany (cf. Krantz 1994). In the Spanish case, this procedure was accepted in both contemporary and historical estimates (Vandellòs 1925; Schwartz 1977). 1958 shares in gross value added (CNE58), except for imports where total value was accepted (see next section), were the weights used for computing the trading quantity index. The shares used were: agriculture, 0.3953; manufacturing, 0.4575; mining, 0.0339; imports, 0.1133. Krantz (1994: 26) assertion that 'some form of association exists between commodity production and trade but a priori a total correlation cannot be expected' led me to prefer a 2-year moving average alternative of the form, $Y_t = 0.5 X_{t-1} + 0.5 X_t$, where Y represents distribution and X the combination of physical output plus imports in year t.

6 Measuring GDP, 1850–1958: Supply Side 99

93. 1958 input–output table shares (TIOE58) were 0.7946 for banking and 0.2054 for insurance services. Data for insurance premia are only available from 1909 onwards, and evidence on banking deposits was accepted as a good proxy for banking and financial services beforehand. When information was incomplete, as it was the case during the Civil War, indices were built on partial evidence and spliced with the main index. The sources for banking deposits are Tortella (1974, 1985), for 1856–1899, and Martín Aceña (1985, 1988), from 1900 onwards. Insurance data are derived from Frax and Matilla (1996) for 1909–1937 and *Anuario(s) Estadístico(s)*, thereafter.
94. Estimates at census dates were log-linearly interpolated to derive annual figures (see section on construction industry above).
95. The average price of urban dwellings that times the mortgage interest rate offered by Banco Hipotecario (kindly supplied by Juan Carmona) provides the implicit rent of dwellings for 1864–1865 and 1904–1934, while Ojeda (1988) presents a deflator for dwelling rents for 1936, 1939–1958. The rent of dwellings deflator was interpolated with the rate of variation of the construction industry deflator.
96. No allowance for government's rents (and depreciation) from buildings was made. Wages and salaries paid by the government are taken from Comín (1985b). The cost of living index is derived from Ojeda (1988) for 1909–58, and it was backcasted to 1850 with Reher and Ballesteros (1993) price index. This option has been preferred to the alternative of deflating government's wages and salaries by a wages index. The latter would imply that no labour productivity increase takes place at all, since total wages and salaries paid by the government, that is, employment numbers times wages, are deflated by a wage index (Krantz 1994). This only holds, of course, under the assumption that wages in the public sector and in the economy as a whole evolve the same. In the favoured alternative, if wages and salaries rise faster than prices, a productivity increase will be attributed to government (Heston 1994: 46).
97. A geometric average was computed with indices of education enrolment (primary, secondary and tertiary education log-linearly interpolated) from Almarcha (1975), Anuario(s) Estadístico(s); Núñez (1993), Mitchell (1992) and government expenditure on education (Comín (1985b) deflated by a wholesale price index (Sardá 1948; Ojeda 1988). An alternative measure using Núñez (2005) data on education enrolment hardly alters the overall index so I have kept the initial estimates.

98. A geometric mean of the number of patients and public expenditure on health deflated with a wholesale price index, expressed in index form, was computed. The sources are Almarcha (1975) and Anuario(s) Estadístico(s). Before 1909, it was assumed that health services evolved as education services.
99. The sources are Spain's population census. Alternatively, it could have been assumed steady labour productivity improvement over time as Lewis (1978: 264) did for late nineteenth-century Britain.
100. Evidence on room occupancy was only available since 1941. Over 1901–1941, the index of leisure was employed only. This leisure index was an average (with TIOE58 weights) of theatre and cinema (from 1940 onwards) and bullfighting (since 1901) attendance. For the late nineteenth century, it was assumed that the index fluctuates along the retail and wholesale trade index.
101. Alternatively, independent indices have been built for 1850–1913, 1913–1929 and 1929–1958 and, then, spliced using variable weighted geometric averages of the three indices. Differences between the chain index and the single 1958-weighted index are practically negligible due to the fact that chain indices have been previously computed for each main sector of economic activity. Therefore, I have preferred the aggregate GVA series that results from single 1958 weighting, so additivity of the aggregate index's components is maintained throughout 1850–1958. In the alternative approach, additivity would only hold for each period, but not for the aggregate, single GVA index.

References

Almarcha, A., et al. 1975. *Estadísticas Básicas de España 1900–1970*. Madrid: CECA.
Antolín, F. 1991. Las empresas de servicios públicos municipales. In *Historia de la empresa pública en España*, ed. F. Comín and P. Martín Aceña, 283–330. Madrid: Espasa-Calpe.
Arenales, M.C. 1976. Un indicador de precios de la economía española para el período 1850–1900. In *Datos básicos para la historia financiera de España*, 1109–1123, 2 vols. II. Madrid: Instituto de Estudios Fiscales.

Balke, N.S. and R.J. Gordon. 1989. The Estimation of Prewar Gross National Product: Methodology and New Evidence. *Journal of Political Economy* 97: 38–92.
Ballesteros, E. 1997. Una estimación del coste de la vida en España, 1861–1936. *Revista de Historia Económica* XV (2): 363–395.
Barciela, C. 1983. Producción y política cerealista durante la guerra civil española (1936–1939). In *Historia económica y pensamiento social*, ed. G. Anes, L.A. Rojo, and P. Tedde, 649–675. Madrid: Alianza.
Barciela, C. 1989. El sector agrario desde 1936. In *Estadísticas históricas de España. Siglos XIX-XX*, ed. A. Carreras, 131–167. Madrid: Fundación Banco Exterior.
Batista D., C. Martins, M. Pinheiro and J. Reis. 1997. *New Estimates of Portugal's GDP, 1910–1958*. Lisbon: Banco de Portugal.
Bonhome, L. and P. Bustinza. 1969. Valoración del patrimonio inmobiliario de España. *Boletín de Estudios Económicos*, XXIV (76): 79–92.
Cairncross, A.K. 1953. *Home and Foreign Investment, 1870–1913*. Cambridge: Cambridge University Press.
Calvo, A. 1998. El teléfono en España antes de Telefónica (1877–1924). *Revista de Historia Industrial* XIII: 59–81.
Carreras, A. 1983. La producció industrial espanyola i italiana des de mitjan segle XIX fins l'actualitat, 3 vols. Universitat Autònoma de Barcelona, unpublished Ph.D. dissertation.
Carreras, A. 1984. La producción industrial española, 1842–1981: Construcción de un índice anual. *Revista de Historia Económica*, II (1): 127–157.
Carreras, A. 1987. An Annual Index of Spanish Industrial Output. In *The Economic Modernization of Spain, 1830–1930*, ed. N. Sánchez-Albornoz, 75–89. New York: New York University Press.
Carreras, A. 1989. Industria. In *Estadísticas Históricas de España. Siglos XIX–XX*, ed. A. Carreras, 169–247. Madrid: Fundación Banco Exterior.
Carreras, A. 1990. *Industrialización española: Estudios de historia cuantitativa*. Madrid: Espasa Calpe.
Carreras, A. 1992. La producción industrial en el muy largo plazo: Una comparación entre España e Italia de 1861 a 1980. In *El desarrollo económico en la Europa del sur: España e Italia en perspectiva histórica*, ed. L. Prados de la Escosura, and V. Zamagni, 173–210. Madrid: Alianza.
Coll, S. 1985. Producción y valor añadido de los sectores minero y metalúrgico. Memoria del Banco de España (mimeo).

Coll, S. 1986. Producción y valor añadido del sector de cementos. Memoria del Banco de España (mimeo).
Coll, S., and C. Sudrià. 1987. *El carbón en España, 1770–1961. Una historia económica.* Madrid: Turner.
Comín, F. 1985a. Cálculos para la estimación de la producción agraria entre 1900 y 1950. Memoria del Banco de España (mimeo).
Comín, F. 1985b. *Fuentes cuantitativas para el estudio del sector público en España 1801–1980.* Madrid: Instituto de Estudios Fiscales, monografía no. 40.
Comín, F. 1987. Métodos indirectos para la estimación de la producción agraria en España (1891–1935). Memoria del Banco de España (mimeo).
Comín, F. 1985c. Superficie, producción y rendimientos de los cereales y leguminosas, vid y olivo entre 1891 y 1981. Memoria del Banco de España (mimeo).
Cordero, R., and F. Menéndez. 1978. El sistema ferroviario español. In *Los ferrocarriles en España, 1844–1943*, 2 vols., I, ed. M. Artola, 161–338. Madrid: Banco de España.
Corrales A., and D. Taguas. 1991. Series macroeconómicas para el período 1954–1988: Un intento de homogeneización. In *La economía española. Una perspectiva macroeconómica*, ed. C. Molinas, M. Sebastián and A. Zabalza, 583–646. Barcelona/Madrid: Antoni Bosch/Instituto de Estudios Fiscales.
Cortes-Conde, R.1994. Estimaciones del Producto Bruto Interno de Argentina, 1875–1935 (mimeo).
Cortes-Conde, R. 1997. *La economía argentina en el largo plazo (Siglos XIX y XX).* Buenos Aires: Editorial Sudamericana/Universidad de San Andrés.
Cucarella, V. 1999. El stock de capital ferroviario en España y sus provincias: 1845–1997. In *El 'stock' de capital ferroviario en España y sus provincias: 1845–1997*, ed. B.B.V. Fundación, 61–172. Fundación BBV: Bilbao.
David, P.A. 1962. The Deflation of Value Added. *Review of Economics and Statistics XLIV* 3: 148–155.
Domínguez Martín, R. 1994. La mercantilización de factores en la agricultura española, 1860–1880: Un intento de estimación de los contrastes regionales. *Revista de Historia Económica* XII (1): 85–109.
Escudero, A. 1998. *Minería e industrialización en Vizcaya.* Barcelona: Crítica/Universidad de Alicante.
Escudero, A. 1989. Valores añadidos de la minería vizcaína, 1876–1936. In *Proceedings of the IV Congreso de Historia Económica.* Universidad de Alicante.
Frax, E. and M.J. Matilla. 1996. Los seguros en España, 1830–1934. *Revista de Historia Económica* XIV (1): 183–203.

Federico, G. 1986. Mercantilizzazione s sviluppo economico in Italia (1860–1940). *Rivista di Storia Economica* III (2): 149–186.

Feinstein, C.H. 1988. Sources and Methods of Estimation for Domestic Reproducible Fixed Assets, Stocks and Works in Progress, Overseas Assets, and Land. In *Studies in Capital Formation in the United Kingdom 1750–1920*, ed. C.H. Feinstein, and S. Pollard, 257–471. Oxford: Clarendon Press.

Fenoaltea, S. 1976. Real Value Added and the Measurement of Industrial Production. *Annals of Economic and Social Measurement* 5 (1): 113–139.

Fenoaltea, S. 1982. The Growth of Utilities Industries in Italy, 1861–1913. *Journal of Economic History XLII* 3: 601–627.

Fenoaltea, S. 1988. The Extractive Industries in Italy, 1861–1913: General Methods ans Specific Estimates. *Journal of European Economic History XVII* 1: 117–125.

Fenoaltea, S. 2003. Notes on the Rate of Industrial Growth in Italy, 1861–1913. *Journal of Economic History* 63 (3): 695–735.

Fenoaltea, S. 2005. *The growth of the Italian economy, 1861–1913: Preliminary.*

Flores de Lemus, A. 1926. Sobre una dirección fundamental de la producción rural española. *El Financiero*, 5 April 1926. Reprinted in (1976), *Hacienda Pública Española* 42–43: 471–485.

Frax, E. 1981. *Puertos y comercio de cabotaje en España, 1857–1934*. Madrid: Banco de España, Estudios de Historia Económica no. 2.

Fremdling, R. 1988. German National Accounts for the 19th and Early 20th Century. A Critical Assessment. *Vierteljahrschrift für Sozial- und Wirtschaftsgeschichte* LXXV (3): 339–355.

Fundación BBV. 1992. *Series históricas de capital público en España*, Bilbao: Fundación BBV.

Gallego, D. 1986. Transformaciones técnicas de la agricultura española en el primer tercio del siglo XX. In *Historia agraria de la España contemporánea 3. El fin de la agricultura tradicional (1900–1960)*, ed. R. Garrabou, C. Barciela and J.I. Jiménez Blanco, 171–229. Barcelona: Crítica.

Gallego, D., and V. Pinilla. 1996. Del librecambio matizado al proteccionismo selectivo: El comercio exterior de productos agrarios y de alimentos en España entre 1849 y 1935. *Revista de Historia Económica* XIV (2): 371–420 and (3): 619–639.

Gandoy Juste, R. (1988). Evolución de la productividad global en la industria española. Un análisis desagregado para el período 1964–1981. Universidad Complutense de Madrid, Unpublished Ph.D. dissertation.

García Sanz, A. 1994. La ganadería española entre 1750 y 1865: Los efectos de la reforma agraria liberal. *Agricultura y Sociedad* 72: 81–119.

Garrués Irurzun, J. 1998. Servicio público de aguas y servicio privado de producción y distribución de electricidad en Pamplona, 1893–1961. Fundación Empresa Pública, Programa de Historia Económica, Documento de Trabajo 9810.

Giraldez, J. 1991. Fuentes estadísticas y producción pesquera en España (1880–1936): una primera aproximación. *Revista de Historia Económica* IX (3): 513–532.

Gomez Mendoza, A. 1982. *Ferrocarriles y cambio económico en España, 1855–1913*. Madrid: Alianza.

Gomez Mendoza, A. 1983. La industria pesquera, 1880–1935. Memoria del Banco de España (mimeo).

Gomez Mendoza, A. 1985a. La industria de construcciones navales, 1850–1935. Memoria del Banco de España (mimeo).

Gomez Mendoza, A. 1985b. La industria del material ferroviario, 1884–1935. Memoria del Banco de España (mimeo).

Gomez Mendoza, A. 1986. La industria de la construcción residencial: Madrid, 1820–1935. *Moneda y Crédito* 117: 53–81.

Gomez Mendoza, A. and J. Simpson. 1988. El consumo de carne en Madrid durante el primer tercio del siglo XX. *Moneda y Crédito* 186: 57–91.

Gomez Mendoza, A. 1989. Transportes y Comunicaciones. In *Estadísticas Históricas de España. Siglos XIX-XX*, ed. A. Carreras, 269–325. Madrid: Fundación Banco Exterior.

Gomez Mendoza, A. 1991. Las obras públicas (1850–1935). In *Historia de la empresa pública en España,* F. Comín and P. Martín Aceña, 177–204. Madrid: Espasa-Calpe.

Grupo de Estudios de Historia Rural (GEHR). 1978/1979. Contribución al análisis histórico de la ganadería española, 1865–1929. *Agricultura y Sociedad* 8: 129–182 and 10: 105–169.

Grupo de Estudios de Historia Rural (GEHR). 1981a. *Los precios del aceite de oliva en España, 1891–1916.* Madrid: Banco de España, Estudios de Historia Económica no. 4.

Grupo de Estudios de Historia Rural (GEHR). 1981b. *El vino, 1874–1907: Dificultades para reconstruir la serie de sus cotizaciones.* Madrid: Banco de España, Estudios de Historia Económica no. 6.

Grupo de Estudios de Historia Rural (GEHR). 1983. Notas sobre la producción agraria española, 1891–1931. *Revista de Historia Económica* I (2): 185–252.

Grupo de Estudios de Historia Rural (GEHR). 1987. Un índice de la producción agraria española, 1891–1935. *Hacienda Pública Española* 108/109: 411–422.
Grupo de Estudios de Historia Rural (GEHR). 1989. Sector agrario (hasta 1935). In *Estadísticas históricas de España. Siglos XIX-XX*, ed. A. Carreras, 91–129. Madrid: Fundación Banco Exterior.
Grupo de Estudios de Historia Rural (GEHR). 1991. *Estadísticas históricas de la producción agraria española, 1859–1935*. Madrid: Ministerio de Agricultura, Pesca y Alimentación.
Harley, C.K. 1982. British Industrialization before 1841: Evidence of Slower Growth during the Industrial Revolution. *Journal of Economic History* XLIII (2): 267–289.
Hemberg, P. 1955. Informe preliminar sobre la renta interior de España. *Revista de Economía Política* VI (2): 114–171. Reprinted in P. Schwartz, ed. 1977. *El Producto Nacional de España en el siglo XX*, 265–341. Madrid: Instituto de Estudios Fiscales.
Herranz-Loncán, A. (2004). *La dotación de Infraestructuras en España, 1844–1935*, Madrid: Banco de España, Estudios de Historia Económica no. 45.
Heston, A. 1994. A Brief Review of Some Problems in Using National Accounts Data in Level of Output Comparisons and Growth Studies. *Journal of Development Economics* 44: 29–52.
Hoffmann, W.G. 1955. *British Industry 1700–1950*. Oxford: Basil Blackwell.
Holtfrerich, C.L. 1983. The Growth of Net Domestic Product in Germany, 1850–1913. In *Productivity in the Economies of Europe*, ed. R. Fremdling, and P.K. O'Brien, 124–131. Stuttgart: Klett-Cotta.
Instituto de Estudios de Transportes Y Comunicaciones. 1984. *Estadísticas de Transportes. Series cronológicas (1950–1980)*. Madrid: Ministerio de Transporte, Turismo y Comunicaciones.
Instituto de Estudios Fiscales. 1969. *La Contabilidad Nacional de España. Años 1954 a 1964*. Madrid: Ministerio de Hacienda.
Isserlis, L. 1938. Tramp Shipping Cargoes and Freight 1869–1919. *Journal of the Royal Statistical Society CI* 1: 53–134.
Krantz, O. 1994. Service Production in Historical National Accounts. *Review of Income and Wealth* 40 (1): 19–41.
Laffond, J.C. 1994. *El agua en Madrid. Datos para la historia del Canal de Isabel II 1851–1930*. Fundación Empresa Pública. Programa de Historia Económica. Documento de Trabajo 9405.

Lewis, W.A. 1978. *Growth and Fluctuations, 1870–1913*. London: George Allen and Unwin.

López Carrillo, J.M. 1998. Autarquía y automoción: Evolución de la empresa nacional de autocamiones (ENASA) entre 1946 y 1958, Fundación Empresa Pública, Programa de Historia Económica, Documento de Trabajo 9809.

Maddison, A. 1995. *Explaining the Economic Performance of Nations: Essays in Time and Space*. London: Edward Elgar.

Maddison, A. 1983. A Comparison of Levels of GDP per Capita in Developed and Developing Countries, 1700–1980. *Journal of Economic History* XLIII (1): 27–41.

Maluquer de Motes, J. 1994. El índice de la producción industrial de Cataluña. Una nueva estimación (1817–1935). *Revista de Historia Industrial*, 5: 45–71.

Maluquer De Motes, J. 2006. 'la paradisíaca estabilidad de la anteguerra'. Elaboración de un índice de precios de consumo en España, 1830–1936. *Revista de Historia Económica* 24 (2): 333–382.

Maluquer de Motes, J. 2013. *La Inflación en España. Un Índice de precios de consumo, 1830–2012*. Estudios de Historia Económica 64. Madrid: Banco de España.

Martin Aceña, P. 1985. *La cantidad de dinero en España 1900–1935*. Madrid: Banco de España. Estudios de Historia Económica no. 12.

Martin Aceña, P. 1988. *Una estimación de los principales agregados monetarios en España: 1940–1962*. Banco de España. Servicio de Estudios. Documento de trabajo 8807.

Martín Rodríguez, M. 1982. *Azúcar y descolonización*, Granada: Instituto de Desarrollo Regional.

Melvin, J.R. 1995. History and Measurement in the Service Sector: A Review. *Review of Income and Wealth* 41 (4): 481–493.

Miguel, A. de. 1935. *El potencial económico de España*, Madrid: Gráfica Administrativa. Partially reprinted in P. Schwartz, ed. 1977. *El Producto Nacional de España en el siglo XX*, 171–187. Madrid: Instituto de Estudios Fiscales.

Ministerio de Agricultura. 1974. *Anuario de estadística agraria 1972*. Madrid: Secretaría General Técnica del Ministerio de Agricultura.

Ministerio de Agricultura. 1979a. *Anuario de estadística agraria 1978*. Madrid: Secretaría General Técnica del Ministerio de Agricultura.

Ministerio de Agricultura. 1979b. *Cuentas del sector agrario no 4*, Secretaría General Técnica del Ministerio de Agricultura.

Ministerio de Trabajo. 1942. Precios al por mayor y números índices, 1913 a 1941. *Boletín de Estadística*, special issue.
Mitchell, B.R. 1992. International Historical Statistics. *Europe, 1750–1988*. London: MacMillan.
Morella, E. 1992. Indices sectoriales de producción industrial de posguerra (1940–1958). *Revista de Historia Económica* X (1): 125–143.
Muñoz Rubio, M. 1995. *Renfe (1941–1991). Medio siglo de ferrocarril público*. Madrid: Ediciones Luna.
North, D.C. 1965. The Role of Transportation in the Economic Development of North America. *Les grandes voies maritimes dans le monde XVe-XIXe siècles*, 209–246. Paris: Ëditions Jean Touzot/S.E.V.P.E.N.
Núñez, C.E. 1993. *La fuente de la riqueza. Educación y desarrollo económico en la España contemporánea*. Madrid: Alianza.
Núñez, C.E. 2005. Educación. In *Estadísticas Históricas de España, siglos XIX y XX*, I. ed. A. Carreras and X. Tafunell, 155–244. Bilbao: Fundación BBVA.
Ojeda, A. de.1988. *Indices de precios en España en el período 1913-1987*. Madrid: Banco de España. Estudios de Historia Económica no. 17.
Parejo Barranco, A. 1989. Producción y consumo industrial de lana en España (1849–1900), *Revista de Historia Económica* VII (3): 589–618.
Paris Eguilaz, H. 1943. *El movimiento de precios en España. Su importancia para una política de intervención*, Madrid: Instituto Sancho de Moncada.
Piqueras, J. 1978. Los precios de la seda, el aceite y el vino. *Estudis* 7: 169–216.
Prados de la Escosura, L. 1981. Las estadísticas españolas de comercio exterior (1850–1913). El problema de las 'valoraciones. *Moneda y Crédito* 156: 43–60 (and underlying dataset).
Prados de la Escosura, L. 1984. El comercio hispano-británico en los siglos XVIII y XIX. I. Reconstrucción. *Revista de Historia Económica* II (2): 113–162.
Prados de la Escosura, L. 1988. *De imperio a nación. Crecimiento y atraso económico en España (1780–1930)*. Madrid: Alianza.
Pujol, J. 1998. La difusión de abonos minerales y químicos hasta 1936: El caso español en el contexto europeo. *Historia Agraria* 15: 143–182.
Reher, D.S. and E. Ballesteros. 1993. Precios y salarios en Castilla la Nueva: La construcción de un índice de salarios reales, 1501–1991. *Revista de Historia Económica* XI (1): 101–151.
Reseña Estadística. 1952. Madrid: Instituto Nacional de Estadística.

Rosés, J.R. 2003. Regional Industrialisation without National Growth: The Catalan Industrialization and the Growth of Spanish Economy (1830–1861). UPF Economics and Business Working Paper.

Sanchez-Albornoz, N. 1975. *Los precios agrícolas durante la segunda mitad del siglo XIX. I.* Trigo y cebada, Madrid: Tecnos.

Sanchez-Albornoz, N. 1979. *Los precios del vino en España, 1861–1890,* 2 vols. Madrid: Banco de España, Documentos de Trabajo 7903–7904.

Sanchez-Albornoz, N. (ed.). 1981. *Los precios agrícolas durante la segunda mitad del siglo XIX.* II. *Vino y aceite.* Madrid: Tecnos.

Sardá, J. 1948. *La política monetaria y las fluctuaciones de la economía española en el siglo XIX.* Madrid: Instituto Sancho de Moncada.

Schwartz (ed.). 1977. *El Producto Nacional de España en el siglo XX,* 443–592. Madrid: Instituto de Estudios Fiscales.

Simpson, J. 1986. La producción agraria en 1886–1890: un enfoque de la agricultura española en el siglo XIX, Memoria del Banco de España (mimeo).

Simpson, J. 1992. Los límites del crecimiento agrario. España, 1860–1936. In *El desarrollo económico en la Europa del sur: España e Italia en perspectiva histórica,* ed. L. Prados de la Escosura, and V. Zamagni, 103–138. Madrid: Alianza.

Simpson, J. 1994. La producción y la productividad agraria españolas, 1890–1936. *Revista de Historia Económica* XII 1: 43–84.

Simpson, J. 1995. *Spanish Agriculture: The Long Siesta, 1765–1965.* Cambridge: Cambridge University Press.

Smits, J.P., E. Horlings, and J.L. van Zanden. 2000. *Dutch GNP and Its Components, 1800–1913.* Groningen Growth and Development Centre Monograph No. 5, Groningen: University of Groningen.

Tafunell, X. 1989b. La construcción residencial barcelonesa y la economía internacional. Una interpretación sobre las fluctuaciones de la industria de la vivienda en Barcelona durante la segunda mitad del siglo XIX. *Revista de Historia Económica* VII (2): 389–437.

Tafunell, X. 1989a. Construcción. In *Estadísticas Históricas de España. Siglos XIX-XX,* ed. A. Carreras, 249–267. Madrid: Fundación Banco Exterior.

Tortella, G. 1974. Las magnitudes monetarias y sus determinantes. In *La banca española en la Restauración,* 2 vols., I, ed. G. Tortella and P. Schwartz, 457–521. Madrid: Tecnos.

Tortella, G. 1985. El Producto (Valor Añadido Bruto) del sector bancario español, 1856–1935. Una primera aproximación. Memoria del Banco de España (mimeo).

Uriol Salcedo, J.I. 1992. *Historia de los caminos de España*. Madrid: Historia de los caminos de España.

Valdaliso, J.M. 1991. *Los navieros vascos y la marina mercante en España, 1860-1935*. Una historia económica, Bilbao: Instituto Vasco de Administración Pública.

Valdaliso, J.M. 1997. *La navegación regular de cabotaje en España en los siglos XIX y XX: Guerras de fletes, conferencias y consorcios navieros*. Vitoria: Servicio Central de Publicaciones del Gobierno Vasco.

Vandellós, J.A. 1925. La richesse et le revenu de la Péninsule Ibérique. *Metron V* 4: 151–186.

Open Access This chapter is licensed under the terms of the Creative Commons Attribution 4.0 International License (http://creativecommons.org/licenses/by/4.0/), which permits use, sharing, adaptation, distribution and reproduction in any medium or format, as long as you give appropriate credit to the original author(s) and the source, provide a link to the Creative Commons license and indicate if changes were made.

The images or other third party material in this chapter are included in the chapter's Creative Commons license, unless indicated otherwise in a credit line to the material. If material is not included in the chapter's Creative Commons license and your intended use is not permitted by statutory regulation or exceeds the permitted use, you will need to obtain permission directly from the copyright holder.

7

Measuring GDP, 1850–1958: Demand Side

Measuring aggregate economic activity through the expenditure side represents adding up all final products or sales to final demand. Ideally, each expenditure component should be computed with actual data from households, firms and public administration. Unfortunately, lack of direct evidence renders such a task impossible and the so-called commodity flows approach provides a second-best alternative.[1] This method uses output figures for agriculture and industry that are adjusted to include imports and to exclude exports in order to derive estimates of consumption and investment. An implication is that the GDP output and expenditure estimates are not independent from each other.

I will succinctly describe the procedures and sources used to derive estimates for private and public consumption of goods and services, domestic investment and net exports of goods and services. In all cases, except for net exports of goods and services, the same method employed in the output approach to obtain GDP levels will be followed. That is, in order to compute annual nominal GDP, the level for each expenditure component in 1958 was backcasted with the yearly variations of Laspeyres quantity and Paasche price indices and the resulting series added up. For investment, private consumption and gross domestic

© The Author(s) 2017
L. Prados de la Escosura, *Spanish Economic Growth, 1850–2015*,
Palgrave Studies in Economic History, DOI 10.1007/978-3-319-58042-5_7

expenditure quantity indices at 1913, 1929 and 1958 relative prices were constructed and, then, a single index for each demand component was obtained by splicing the three volume indices using a variable weighted geometric average. A volume index of real GDP results from adding up its component indices with weights from 1958 national accounts.

A word of warning is necessary. GDP estimates from the expenditure and output sides are not coincidental. Since it is widely accepted that measurement errors tend to be smaller when the production approach is used, I have chosen GDP computed from output side as the 'control final', and private consumption, the largest expenditure component, was adjusted so GDP from the demand side conforms to GDP derived from the supply side.

7.1 Consumption of Goods and Services

Consumption represents the part of final output used up for its own sake. Current expenditure on goods and services by consumers (households and non-profit organizations) and by public administration (central and local government) can be distinguished. While tastes, incomes and relative prices will determine household consumption, political motives are behind public consumption (Beckerman 1976).

7.1.1 Private Consumption

To derive yearly estimates of private consumption, quantity and price indices were constructed for its major components: foodstuffs, beverages and tobacco; clothing; current housing expenses, including the rent of dwellings, heating and lighting, plus current expenses on household maintenance; household consumption of durable goods; hygiene and personal care; transport and communications; leisure; and other services including education and financial services. Most of the available evidence for private consumption's components comes from output estimates to which net imports were added. I will discuss briefly the construction of indices for each consumption component. Paasche price indices were computed for each private consumption component using, unless otherwise stated, the same method and evidence described for agriculture and industry in the previous section.[2]

Foodstuffs, Beverages and Tobacco

This was still the main component of private consumption by 1958 and includes bread and cereals, meat, fish, milk, cheese and eggs, oil and fat, potatoes, legumes, vegetables and fruit, coffee and cocoa, and sugar, plus beverages (beer, wine, brandy) and tobacco. Evidence on quantities and prices gathered to compute output in agriculture and in food industry in the previous section together with net imports has been used to produce constant and current price series of foodstuffs consumption.[3] Major consumption groups in national accounts (CNE58) were disaggregated into its individual components using the input–output table for 1958 (TIOE58). Consumption, in most cases, was estimated from final output figures, that is, total output less seed and animal feed, to which net imports were added.[4] Wheat and rice milling output were accepted as indicators for bread and cereals. Evidence on meat consumption in capital cities was used to cross check estimates of total consumption on the basis of meat output plus net imports.[5] Fish captures plus net imports were used for fish consumption. For milk, cheese and eggs, output figures were used. For oil and fat, evidence on the proportion of human consumption of olive oil and its derivatives was employed.[6] Data on final output less net exports were used for potatoes, legumes, vegetables and fruits. The consumption of sugar (both cane and beet) was obtained by adding up output and net imports.[7] Imports were accepted for the consumption of tobacco, chocolate (cocoa) and coffee.[8] Quantity indices were computed with 1870, 1890, 1913, 1929 and 1958 benchmarks and, then, spliced into a single index using variable weighted geometric averages in which the larger weight corresponds to the closer benchmark (see expression 12). Individual price series were taken from the section on output. A Paasche price index was derived from current values (in index form) and the chain Laspeyres quantity index.[9]

Clothing and Other Personal Articles

The output and price series for clothing and shoemaking were accepted and aggregated with weights from 1958 national accounts (CNE58). For clothing, a spliced index for the whole period under consideration was constructed using 1913, 1929 and 1958 weights.

Housing Current Expenses

Under this label, dwelling rents, heating and lighting, and maintenance expenses are included. For rents paid for dwellings and for those imputed when occupied by their owners, quantities and prices from the output series were accepted. For heating and lighting, figures on domestic consumption of electricity and gas are provided by Anuario(s) Estadístico(s) since 1901 and 1930, respectively. I have computed figures for the earlier years by extrapolating consumption levels with the rate of variation for electricity and gas total output. Domestic consumption of coal was also added, but lack of direct evidence led me to assume that household consumption of coal evolved as total coal consumption. Prices were taken from the output estimates. Household maintenance expenses were computed by adding up domestic services and the consumption of non-durable goods with 1958 input–output weights.[10] Output and price estimates for domestic services were employed. Non-durable goods consumption was estimated through backward projection of 1958 levels, taken from the input–output table (TIOE58), with the rates of variation of its output, under the arbitrary assumption that household consumption represented a stable proportion of its production.[11]

Household Consumption of Durable Goods

Household consumption of durables was approximated with furniture consumption. 1958 consumption levels were backcasted with rates of variation for timber and furniture output under the arbitrary assumption that the proportion allocated to private consumption was constant over time. Price indices for output were accepted.

Hygiene and Personal Care

The output and price series for health services were used to approximate the expenses on personal care.

Transport and Communications

Expenses on transport services included purchases of automobiles and transport and communications expenses. 1958 levels were projected backwards with the number of registered automobiles and the rate of variation in the number of registered cars and in transport and communications output, respectively.[12]

Leisure

The corresponding series for the output of restaurants, hotels and leisure services were accepted, while the paper industry's output was used to approximate books and periodicals consumption.[13] Weights were taken from the 1958 input–output weights (TIOE58).

Education, Financial and Other Services

The output of education services has been adopted for education and research consumption. The consumption of financial services was also approximated through its output. Liberal professions employment represented the consumption of other services. The price index for 'other household consumption services' was used back to 1939 and spliced with the cost of living index back to 1850 (de Ojeda 1988).

Nominal private expenditure on goods and services was derived by projecting the current value of each of its components in 1958 (CNE58) backwards with their quantity and price indices (expressed a 1858 = 100) and, then, adding them up.

An aggregate volume index of real private consumption was, then, computed. Quantity indices were, firstly, built up on the basis of volume

Fig. 7.1 Private consumption paasche deflator and laspeyres consumer price index, 1850–1958 (1913 = 100) (logs). *Sources* Private Consumption Deflator, see the text: CPI, Maluquer de Motes (2006)

indices for private consumption components at 1913, 1929 and 1958 relative prices and, later, spliced into a single index for 1850–1958 resulted from splicing all three segments using a variable weighted geometric average of quantity indices at 1913 and 1929 prices for 1913–1929, and at 1929 and 1958 prices for 1929–1958. An implicit deflator was calculated with current and constant price estimates. The resulting Paasche deflator of private consumption and Maluquer de Motes (2006) Laspeyres consumer price index are highly coincidental, somehow an unexpected result due to their different weighting (Fig. 7.1).

7.1.2 Public Consumption

Wages and salaries and purchases of goods and services by the central Government are both provided for the entire period 1850–1958 by Francisco Comín (1985), while no data on rents imputed to public buildings were available. Annual figures for local government consumption are only available from 1927 onwards, but scattered evidence exists for 1857–1858, 1861–1863, 1882 and 1924.[14] I have rescaled central government figures with their ratios to local and central government consumption for these years.[15] Yearly public consumption at current prices was derived through backward projection of the level for 1958 (CNE58) with the annual rate of variation of central and local government consumption estimates. Nominal public consumption was deflated with the cost of living, a wholesale price index and the rent of dwellings deflator weighted with the shares of salaries, goods purchased and rents imputed to public buildings in 1958.[16]

7.2 Gross Domestic Capital Formation

The current output of goods and services devoted to increase the nation's stock of capital and, hence, to raise the future potential income flow is called domestic investment or capital formation. Fixed capital formation and changes in inventories are the components of domestic investment.

7.2.1 Gross Domestic Fixed Capital Formation

Gross fixed capital formation can be defined as capital expenditure on domestic reproducible fixed assets (including both new investment and replacement). More frequently, it is described as the value of purchases and construction of fixed assets by residents firms and government, and all durable production goods lasting more than a year, are included. In addition, major alterations of existing assets are considered capital formation and this includes all of those affecting buildings and construction. Inventories, in turn, refer to raw materials, work in progress and stored finished goods.

Gross domestic fixed capital formation was classified in the OECD national accounts system according to three criteria: products, branches of activity and institutions (CNE58). More detailed breakdown is presented in the contemporary input–output table for 1958 (TIOE58).

Given data constraints, the products criteria will be followed to compute historical capital formation in pre-1958 Spain. As for consumption, the way of constructing current and constant price series for gross domestic capital formation was to start from the 1958 benchmark level and to extrapolate each of its individual components back to 1850 with quantity and price indices.[17]

Two alternative ways are used in capital formation estimates: the expenditure and the commodity flows approaches. The expenditure approach establishes the actual investment by firms or by the government, and it is the most rigorous and data demanding one. Its large data requirements, however, make it also the less frequent procedure in historical accounts and in present-day developing countries national accounts. In the present historical estimates, this expenditure approach was exceptionally used for private investment (only for telephone communications). The alternative commodity flows method reaches investment figures by adding net imports to domestic output of capital goods. In other words, the commodity flows approach is not independent from the output method, but it is the only feasible way to compute investment in historical cases, aside from the most recent period or from those countries with exceptionally good records (i.e. the UK and the USA).

An additional difficulty comes from the lack of evidence on prices for capital goods. With the exception of unit value data from commercial statistics from trading partners (UK, France, Germany, the USA) and occasional evidence for bulky and expensive capital goods (locomotives, ships), deflators had to be constructed on the basis of input prices, wages and raw materials, combined with input–output weights (TIOE58). This means that usually no allowances are made for productivity change in capital goods' industries.[18]

In the classification by products, fixed capital formation is distributed into dwellings, other buildings, other constructions and works, transportation material and other materials (machinery and equipment). In the following paragraphs, a brief description of the sources and procedures used to construct quantity and price indices for the main categories of fixed capital formation and for variations in stocks are provided.

Dwellings and Other Buildings

Data restrictions prevent to consider dwellings and other buildings separately.[19] Capital formation in dwellings and other buildings is represented by the output index of residential and commercial construction, excluding repairs and maintenance expenses. The output deflator was used.

Other Constructions and Works

Roads, streets, sanitation, railways, docks, tunnels, bridges, dams, harbours and airports, drainage, irrigation and land improvement, electric installations, telegraph and telephone lines are all included in this category.

For capital formation in railway and road construction, hydraulic infrastructure and other works (maritime and harbours), output (quantity and price) indices have been accepted.[20]

Land improvement was approximated, in addition to central government investment on irrigation and drainage (already included under hydraulic infrastructure), through fertilizer consumption and afforestation (after 1900).[21] Price indices were built up on the basis of input costs.[22]

Capital formation in gas and mining was computed under the arbitrary assumption that the capital–output ratio was stable over time.[23] First differences (excluding negative values) in the output series provide, hence, new capital formation to which scrapping is added to obtain gross investment figures.[24] Scrapping is computed assuming an average asset life of 50 years.[25] When evidence on scrapping, that is, new capital formation 50 years back in time, was not available, I assumed it was proportional to fixed capital formation. A price index was computed with input prices.[26]

Capital formation on electricity structures was assumed to represent 15% of total capital expenditure on electricity supply, and the level for 1958 was projected backwards with the rate of variation in installed capacity (kilowatts) to 1890, to represent new investment, while scrapping was estimated assuming 60 years average life.[27] The deflator was constructed with input prices for construction costs (0.8) and costs of plant and machinery (0.2).[28]

For communications works, private investment in telephone buildings and works was assumed to represent 15% of total investment outlays over 1925–1958.[29] A deflator computed with construction materials and wages, combined with 1958 input–output weights, was used to derive constant price estimates.[30] For the years 1903–1924, real investment was extrapolated backwards with an index of investment. On the basis of the number of telephone offices, available since 1902, and assuming an average life above 60 years, real investment was computed as first differences from which a 3 year moving average was accepted as the investment index.[31]

Once quantity and price indices were built up for each major component of capital formation on 'other constructions and works', current price series were obtained by projecting 1958 levels (derived from CNE58 and TIOE58) backwards to 1850 with quantity and price indices that were, then, added up into a single series.[32] Quantity indices for total investment on 'other constructions and works' were, then, constructed on the basis of its components' indices with 1913, 1929 and 1958 weights, and a single index was derived through variable weighted geometric mean. The comparison between my estimates and those obtained by Herranz-Loncán shows a substantial degree of coincidence, although Herranz-Loncán series exhibits higher volatility (Fig. 7.2). An implicit deflator was derived from current and constant price indices.

Transportation Material

Under this concept, all expenses on ships, vans, commercial vehicles, vehicles for public transport, airplanes and rolling stock for railways and tramways are included. Purchases of transport vehicles for private use (i.e. automobiles) are not considered as investment but as private consumption. Given the dearth of reliable data, only capital formation in railway rolling stock, ships and road vehicles will be considered here.

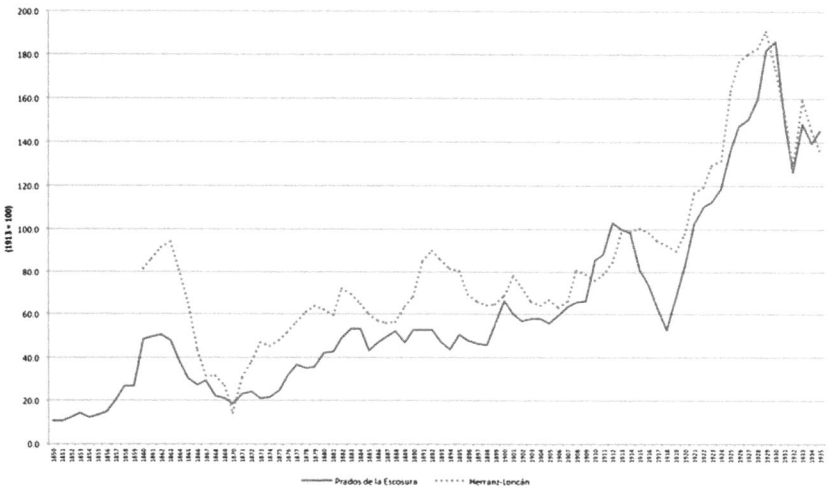

Fig. 7.2 Gross investment in non-residential construction volume indices, 1850–1935: Alternative Estimates (1913 = 100). *Sources* Prados de la Escosura, see the text: Herranz-Loncán (2004)

As for capital formation in railway rolling stock, new investment was derived as first differences from the stock of locomotives, cars and wagons to which scrapping obtained by assuming an average life for each type of asset was added.[33] Quality adjustments were introduced to allow for the locomotives' increasing power.[34] Quantity indices of investment in locomotives, cars and wagons were computed at 1913, 1929 and 1958 prices and, then, a single index was derived as a variable weighted geometric average. Current price estimates up to 1940 were obtained with quantities (unadjusted for quality) and available prices for locomotives, cars and wagons.[35] After 1940, data on current capital expenditure, available for Spanish state company, RENFE, were deflated with a price index constructed with input costs.[36] An implicit deflator was obtained from current values and the quality-adjusted quantity index.

The estimates of capital formation in merchant shipping include all sailing and steam ships.[37] No evidence on capital expenditure on shipping exists but yearly additions to tonnage can be computed through domestic production and net imports available from 1850 onwards.[38] A quantity index for investment has been obtained by adding net imports to domestic output.[39] A quality adjustment constructed for Britain, adapted to the case of Spain, was introduced in the investment series.[40] Feinstein's price index (adjusted for exchange rate fluctuations between the sterling and the peseta) was used for 1850–1920 and a deflator was built using weighted input prices for 1920–1958.[41]

For capital formation in road vehicles (excluding automobiles owned for private use which are classified as consumer goods), domestic output (since 1946) plus imports (since 1906) were added up and backcasted to 1900 with yearly registered vehicles.[42] A deflator was built up with input prices for labour and construction materials.[43]

Current price series of fixed capital formation on transportation material were obtained through backwards projection of the 1958 levels for each of its components (derived from CNE58 and TIOE58) with their quantity and price indices that were, in turn, aggregated into a single series.[44] Quantity investment indices were constructed with 1913, 1929 and 1958 weights, and a single index was obtained as a variable weighted geometric mean. An implicit deflator was computed from current and constant price indices.

Other Materials

Machinery and equipment are the main components under this category, including electrical implements, tractors, office equipment and furniture, research equipment, construction and mining materials, and school and hospital materials. Dearth of data precludes estimating capital formation except for electric and non-electric machinery and equipment.

Mains and other plant and machinery were assumed to represent 85% of total investment outlays in electricity supply.[45] As capital stock was highly correlated with installed power, first differences in kilowatts of installed capacity were, hence, accepted as a proxy for new capital formation to which scrapping was added in order to obtain total capital formation.[46] Scrapping was derived assuming an average assets life of 30 years.[47] The deflator was constructed with input prices (copper, 0.5; engineering wages, 0.5) (Feinstein 1988).

Investment on telephone equipment and plant was obtained by assuming it represented 85% of total capital outlays by Spanish telephone company for the years 1924–1958.[48] A constant price series was computed with a deflator constructed with input prices and weights from the 1958 input–output table (TIOE1958).[49] Real investment was backcasted to 1903 with an investment index built from first differences in the number of telephone lines plus scrapping under the assumption of 30 years average (Feinstein 1988: 354).

As for non-electric machinery, while quantities and values are available for imports, no historical series exists for the production of machinery.[50] I have backcasted the level for 1958 with the rate of variation of an index of input consumption in the engineering industry computed through the commodity flows method. Iron and steel output plus net imports, from which iron and steel consumption in the construction of dwellings, shipping and railway rolling stock was deducted, are the basic series available to compute the output of machinery and equipment.[51] A 3 year moving average for the iron and steel available for machinery industry's consumption was computed to allow for stocks and, then, a quality adjustment of 0.5% per year was applied.[52] A machinery output deflator was constructed by combining engineering wages and steel prices with 1958 input–output weights.[53]

As for other components of fixed capital formation, investment on 'other material' (machinery and equipment) at current prices was obtained by extrapolating 1958 levels backwards with quantity and price indices for its components that, later, were added up into a single series.[54] Real indices for investment in machinery and equipment were constructed with its components' volume indices using 1913, 1929 and 1958 weights, and a compromise index was reached through variable weighted geometric mean. An implicit deflator was derived from current and constant price series.

Gross domestic fixed capital formation at current prices was obtained by adding up its components' nominal value. Quantity indices for fixed capital formation were constructed combining its main components at 1913, 1929 and 1958 prices that were, in turn, spliced into a single index using a variable weighted geometric average. An implicit deflator was derived from current and constant price series.

In order and to keep consistency with post-1958 national accounts, fixed capital formation was distributed into four main categories: residential structures (dwellings), non-residential structures (other buildings and other constructions and works), transportation material and machinery and equipment.[55]

7.2.2 Variations in Stocks

Purchases of raw materials for further elaboration, work in progress, or partially transformed products that are not on sale unless a final transformation takes place, plus stored finished goods for future sale, are all included in this category. Variations in livestock, agriculture, trade and manufacturing also are taken into account.

Lack of historical data on inventories has frequently forced researchers to look for short-cut estimates. In their pioneer contribution on the British case, Jefferys and Walters (1955: 7) assumed that the annual variation in the stocks value was 'equal to 40% of the first difference between national income estimates in successive years'. Feinstein (1972, 1988) assumed, in turn, that the ratio of stocks to output was stable over time and, hence, the change of final expenditure corresponded to stock building. For Spain, a similar approach was followed, and I accepted the rate of variation of final demand at current prices (GDP at market prices, derived from the output approach, plus imports of goods and services) to approximate stock building and spliced it to the level of variations in stocks in 1958 (CNE58). A wholesale price index was used to deflate the series.

Lastly, variations in stocks were added to gross domestic fixed capital formation to obtain total domestic investment.

7.3 Net Exports of Goods and Services

To compute GDP from the expenditure side, the net value of goods and services supplied to the rest of the world (excluding net returns to factors of production) should be added to consumption and capital formation.

Two main categories are included under this label: net exports of goods and services and non-residents expenses in Spain (net of resident expenses abroad). Free on board (fob) value of goods exported and imported, commodity transport services provided by residents to foreigners, and by foreigners to residents, and other incomes (insurance, communications, patents' royalties) derived from non-residents, and those paid by residents, are considered under traded goods and services. Under the second label are included consumption expenses in Spain by non-residents less expenditures of residents abroad, payments by non-residents to nationals for passenger transport services net of those payments by residents to foreign passenger carriers and any other net expenses by non-residents within Spanish boundaries.

Current values of exports and imports of goods and services for 1940–1958 are from Elena Martínez Ruíz (2003).[56] For the period 1850–1939, the sources and procedures used to construct current values for the main components of exports and imports of goods and services are briefly described below.

7.3.1 Net Exports of Goods

Free on board (fob) value of goods exported and imported needs to be computed. Data from Spanish official trade statistics have been corrected for quantity underestimation and price biases through a comparison of Spanish trade with its main trading partners on the basis of foreign and Spanish trade statistics by Prados de la Escosura (1986) for 1850–1913 (who included an estimate of smuggling through Gibraltar and Portugal), Antonio Tena Junguito (1992) for 1914–1935 and Martínez Ruíz (2003, 2006) for 1936–1939. Cost, insurance and freight (cif) imports were converted into fob imports to comply with balance of payments conventions.[57] In addition, exports and imports were grossed-up to include the Canaries, while trade between these islands and the Peninsula was excluded.[58]

7.3.2 Gold and Silver

Quantities of gold and silver as recorded in trade statistics (coins, bars and paste) are considered as monetary gold and silver and, therefore, non-monetary gold and silver trade was not included in the estimates of net exports of goods and services.[59]

7.3.3 Freight and Insurance

Freight income received for exports carried in Spanish ships less freight expenses paid for imports transported in foreign vessels constitute the first item to be computed under this label. Following North and Heston, the freight-value method, or freight factor, was preferred to the earnings per ton method.[60] Total freight revenues on exports and imports were first computed by applying freight factors to the fob value of exports and imports and, then, to ascertain freight income on exports (a credit for Spain) the share of tonnage exported carried under Spanish flag was used, while the share of imported tonnage in foreign ships was employed to compute freight expenses on imports.[61] In addition, freight income from carrying trade between foreign ports was assumed, following North (1960) and Simon (1960), to represent a percentage of freight earnings and a 10% of freight income on exports was accepted.[62] Port outlays by Spanish ships in foreign ports and by foreign ships in Spain's harbours as payments for port dues, loading and unloading expenses and coal are assumed to represent a fixed share of shipping earnings and expenses.[63] Foreign ships transported more tonnage than in Spanish vessels as they exhibited, according to Valdaliso (1991: 71), a more efficient transport capacity ratio. I assumed that more fully loaded vessels made smaller outlays per ship and, hence, port outlays by Spanish ships abroad (a debit) were established at 30% of the freight income on exports, while port outlays by foreign ships in Spain (a credit) were fixed at 20% of freight expenses on imports.[64] Finally, marine insurance income and expenses were computed under the widely shared assumption that underwriting follows the flag and exports in Spanish ships were, hence, usually insured by Spanish companies, while imports in foreign vessels were insured by foreign companies.⁶⁵ I arbitrarily assumed that insurance rates were identical by Spanish and foreign companies and accepted those used by Prados de la Escosura (1986) for 1850–1913 and by Tena for 1914–1939, to which I added an extra 2% to include shipping commissions and brokerage.⁶⁶

7.3.4 Tourism, Emigrants' Funds, Passenger Services and Other Services

Yearly income from tourist services was derived on the basis of expenses per visitor (net of Spanish tourist expenses abroad) calculated by Jáinaga for 1931, times the annual number of tourists and, then, reflated with a cost of living index to obtain current price estimates.⁶⁷ Unfortunately, the total number of tourists is only known since 1929 and was backward projected to 1882 with the rate of variation of passengers arriving by sea, while no tourism was assumed to exist over 1850–1881.⁶⁸

Spain was a net emigration country over the late nineteenth and early twentieth centuries (Sánchez Alonso 1995, 2000). Emigrants carried small sums with them to cover their arrival expenses. It can be reckoned that, in 1931, emigrant funds to America represented, on average, 200 gold pesetas, that is, 400 current pesetas, including the fare and small amounts to cover arrival expenses.⁶⁹ If the fare represented around 340 current pesetas, 60 pesetas corresponded to emigrant's funds.⁷⁰ However, its author only added 'a small amount for unavoidable expenses', to the cost of the passage, and this sum is most likely an underestimate.⁷¹ I, therefore, accepted a higher estimate of 100 pesetas for those emigrating to America and one-tenth, 10 pesetas, for those to Algeria (and to France) in the eve of World War I.⁷² These average sums times the number of emigrants to America, Algeria and France cast a yearly series of emigrants' funds that were reflated with a wage index.⁷³

In addition, revenues and expenses from passenger transport have to be taken into account. Fares paid by tourists carried by Spanish ships and by immigrants returning in Spanish vessels are included on the credit side, while fares paid by emigrants to foreign shipping companies represented a debit. The number of migrants provided by Sánchez Alonso

(1995) for 1882–1930 was completed up to 1939 with Spain's official migration statistics and those from the main destination countries, plus an estimate of migration for the years 1850–1881 on the basis of scattered foreign evidence.[74] The share of arrivals and departures in Spanish and foreign ships is provided by official migration statistics from 1911 onwards, and shows a stable pattern, roughly one-third of emigrants returned home under Spanish flag and three-fourths left in foreign ships, except during World War I when the distribution pattern was reversed.[75] These shares were accepted for the nineteenth and early twentieth centuries. The fares for trips to Argentina, Cuba and Algeria are obtained from Vázquez, Llordén and official emigration statistics.[76]

Lastly, Government transactions (credits and debits) were taken from official accounts were added up (Instituto de Estudios Fiscales 1976).

Total exports and imports of goods and services at current prices were reached by adding up its components. Constant price values were obtained with price indices for commodity exports and imports.[77]

7.4 Gross Domestic Product at Market Prices

A yearly series of nominal gross domestic product at market prices was obtained by adding up individual indices for private and public consumption, capital formation and net exports of goods and services. A GDP volume index was constructed by weighting each expenditure series with their shares in nominal GDP in 1958. An implicit deflator was derived from current and constant price GDP series.

However, the resulting GDP estimates from the demand side do show discrepancies with those obtained through the supply side. As discussed before, it is widely accepted that both in present time developing countries and in historical accounts measurement errors are smaller when GDP is computed from production rather than from expenditure.[78] Hence, I have chosen GDP derived from the output approach as the control final and adjusted private consumption (at both current and constant prices), the largest expenditure component, so GDP from the expenditure side equals to GDP derived through production.[79] The consumption structure remained, however, unchanged.

7.5 Gross National Income

Net payments to foreign factors must be added to gross domestic product in order to compute gross national income. Martínez Ruiz (2003) provides the data for 1940–1958. Jáinaga's contemporary estimates of net factor incomes, converted from gold to paper pesetas, were accepted for 1931–1934.[80] Due to the dearth of data, only very crude estimates of foreign capital incomes (dividends and interest payments to private foreign capital and external debt service), on the debit side, and of Spanish labour returns abroad (wages and salaries), on the credit side, could be carried out. These are the main components of net factor payments abroad, as neither Spanish investments abroad nor foreign labour in Spain was significant over the long period considered.

Assessing returns to Spanish labour employed abroad is a complex task because labour incomes (wages and salaries), the relevant concept for GNI estimation, have to be distinguished from emigrants' remittances, a variable not included in the calculation.[81] Actually, such a distinction can only be made since 1917. For the period 1850–1913, I accepted that only 5% of those migrating to America and 60% of those migrating to Algeria returned within the year.[82] The next step was to assess the amount that, on average, was brought home by returning Spanish workers after 1 year, or less, away from home. I computed an average sum that was taken home by the temporary emigrant or sent annually by the long-term emigrant to their relatives and friends.[83] García López (1992) presents the most comprehensive estimates for the years prior to World War I, 250–300 million pesetas as an annual average over 1906–1910, that amounts to 340–400 pesetas per emigrant (either returning home or sending remittances). I accepted 400 pesetas per emigrant as a benchmark that was, then, projected backwards and forward with a nominal wage index constructed for the destination countries and adjusted for exchange rate between the peseta and each destination country's currency.[84] Finally, returns to Spanish labour abroad were obtained by multiplying the annual sum per head times the number of emigrants returning home within their first year abroad.

On the debit side, three main items can be distinguished: the external debt service, dividends and interests paid to railway shares and debentures owned by foreigners, and returns to foreign factors in mining, to which crude estimates of incomes paid to foreign capital invested in insurance, tramways and utilities, were added for the twentieth century.[85]

Service payments on the external debt have been computed by applying specific interest rates to each class of Government bonds.[86] After the debt conversion of 1882 in which existing foreign debt was given in exchange for new bonds (at 43.75% of its nominal value), and simultaneously with the abandonment of gold convertibility of Spanish currency, debt repatriation started as Spaniards found more secure to invest in bonds serviced in gold pesetas as a shelter against currency depreciation.[87] Since 1891, when the peseta's depreciation took actually place, Spanish citizens purchased external debt bonds while foreign bondholders were trying to get rid of them. A government measure intended to cut short such a trend was the introduction of the so-called affidavit in 1898, which implied that only non-resident bondholders would continue receiving their interests in gold pesetas (or francs), while the rest would be paid in current pesetas (and offered to convert their external debt bonds into internal debt). As a result, the external debt fell, in 1903, to 52.7% of its volume in 1898; in other words, it proves that Spanish residents had purchased almost half Spain's external debt between 1891 and 1898. Hence, only half of the interest paid (52.7%) on external debt should be computed as payment to foreign capital invested in external debt over 1891–1898. Moreover, in so far debt service was in gold pesetas, the amount of interests paid (obtained by applying the interest rate to foreign debt in non-residents' hands) had to be increased by the depreciation rate of the current peseta with respect to the gold peseta over 1891–1914.[88] After World War I, unlike the experience of the 1890s, Spanish foreign debt in foreign hands tended to disappear. I have computed the share of interest payments that accrued to foreign citizens on the basis of Banco Urquijo data.[89] Fortunately, for the purpose of this study, railway companies were highly concentrated, and the detailed studies by Pedro Tedde de Lorca provide enough evidence to estimate dividends on share capital and interests on debentures paid to non-residents.[90] Dividends paid to shareholders and interest payments on debentures issued by the three major railway companies are available from the mid-nineteenth century up to the Civil War.[91] Both the percentage represented by the three main companies in total capital invested in railways and the proportion of railways capital in foreign hands have to be ascertained in order to compute the returns to foreign capital invested in Spanish railways. Tedde de Lorca (1978, 1980) provides total capital shares and bonds held by the three major companies and its proportion in total investment, and, based on Broder's research, also the participation of French capital in total capital invested in 1867, at the time of network construction, and over the nineteenth century. Broder's (1976) estimates of foreign investment in railways allowed, in turn, to gross-up French railways capital to cover all foreign capital. For the interwar years, I have had access to estimates of the proportion of shares and debentures in non-resident hands.[92]

Foreign capital in mining was mainly British. On the basis of effective capital invested by British companies and cumulated total foreign investment in mining, it can be suggested that, over 1870–1913, more than half of all foreign capital in Spanish mining came from the UK, while the British share raised to three-fourths in the interwar years.[93] Decadal averages of dividend and interest payments to British companies are provided by Harvey and Taylor that were grossed-up to include all payments to foreign capital in Spanish mining for 1851–1913, assuming similar rates of return in non-British foreign investment, and using the estimated British participation in total foreign capital.[94] Estimates of foreign capital returns in mining derived through this procedure were, then, distributed annually with an index of non-retained value in Spanish mineral exports.[95] Dividend and interest payments from 1914 onwards were estimated by projecting the average level for 1911–1913 with an index of non-retained export proceeds.

Finally, crude estimates of incomes paid to foreign capital invested in tramways, electricity, gas and water supply, and insurance were carried out through backwards extrapolation of an estimate for 1931–1934 (Jáinaga) with the rates of variation of their output.[96] For foreign insurance companies, the volume of declared premia times the yield of British consols provided their yearly returns.[97]

The difference between credit and debit estimates provided the value of net payments to foreign factors abroad. To derive constant price series, the import price index was used as a way of assessing its purchasing power.[98] Gross National Income was, in turn, computed adding net factor payments abroad to gross domestic product at market prices.

7.6 Net National Income

Net National Income was obtained by subtracting capital consumption—provided in Prados de la Escosura and Rosés (2010)—from Gross National Income.

7.7 Net National Disposable Income

Net National Disposable Income was derived by adding an estimate of net transfers to the rest of the world to Net National income. Emigrants' remittances constituted its main historical component in Spain. Not all emigrants sent money home while being abroad. In historical estimates, it is usually accepted that most of those who established themselves abroad stopped sending money after 5 or 6 years either because they have already payed for their debts or because they planned to invest in the receiving country. I arbitrarily assumed that emigrants only sent money home within their first 5 years and computed emigrants' remittances by multiplying the estimated average sum per emigrant times the cumulative figure of emigrants arrived in the last 5 years, after deducting those migrants who returned home within 1 year.[99]

Notes

1. The commodity flows approach is common in present time developing countries (Heston 1994) and in historical national accounts. Cf. the pioneering work by Jefferys and Walters (1955) on the UK, extended by Deane (1968) and Feinstein (1972), and more recently, the research by

Carreras (1985) on Spain, Vitali (1992) and Baffigi (2013) on Italy, and Smits, Horlings and van Zanden (2000) on the Netherlands.
2. Unfortunately, prices are, unless otherwise stated, wholesale prices and not retail prices, as national accounts convention establishes.
3. Net imports, that is, retained imports less domestic exports, were taken from Estadística(s) del comercio exterior. Gallego and Pinilla (1996) provide agricultural trade figures at 1910 prices for main commodity groups in the years 1850–1935, and I have drawn on their figures whenever necessary.
4. The description of the construction of output figures is presented in section III of the essay.
5. Gómez Mendoza (1995) provides estimates of meat consumption for 1900–1933. Anuario(s) Estadístico(s) provide consumption figures from 1921 onwards.
6. García Barbancho (1960: 299).
7. Martín Rodríguez (1995) supplies quinquennial average estimates of sugar consumption from 1855 to 1904. I constructed annual consumption estimates for the nineteenth century on the basis of Martín Rodríguez estimates, imports of sugar and data on domestic production.
8. Alonso Alvarez (1993, 1995) provides current values of legal consumption of tobacco. Anuario(s) Estadístico(s) present evidence for 1901–1958. Estimates of smuggling through Gibraltar and Portugal for 1850–1913 are provided in Prados de la Escosura (1984).
9. Incidentally, the Paasche deflator for foodstuffs, beverages, and tobacco matches closely Maluquer de Motes (2006) Laspeyres index of foodstuffs.
10. Weights were 0.5518 for domestic services and 0.4482 for non-durables.
11. Household consumption of non-durable goods included chemicals (0.6748), construction materials (0.2225) and rubber goods (0.1027). Weights are taken from TIOE58. Prices from output estimates were employed.
12. An alternative measure would be tax revenues on land transportation, petroleum and gasoline, and on post, telegraph and telephone services. However, changes in the tax rate make impossible to employ available evidence without a previous adjustment of tax returns for changes in fiscal pressure.

13. Prices used were the cost of living index for restaurants, hotels and entertainment, and the paper industry deflator. TIOE58 weights were 0.2102, entertainment (films and theatre performances, bullfights and radio broadcasting); 0.6291, hotels and restaurants; 0.1607, books and newspapers.
14. I am indebted to Francisco Comín for kindly supplying me with his unpublished figures.
15. Fortunately, the ratio ranges from 0.63 to 0.70, in a diminishing order. I have log-linearly interpolated the ratio, and I used it to re-scaling central government's expenditure correspondingly. No data exist for the Civil War years (1936–1939). I assumed public consumption was at its peak during those years and adopted its ratio to private consumption during World War II years.
16. Weights come from TIOE58 and they are 0.6791, cost of living; 0.2995, wholesale price index; 0.0214, the rent of dwellings deflator.
17. This is a similar method to the one followed by Feinstein (1972: 184) for late nineteenth and early twentieth century Britain.
18. Cf. Feinstein (1988: 262).
19. See construction industry in section III.
20. For railway and road construction, the use of output as investment constitutes a wide definition of capital formation that includes maintenance and hence it implies a short life of assets. See the section on non-residential construction industry.
21. The sources for fertilizer consumption are Gallego (1986), Barciela (1989) and Estadística(s) del comercio exterior (see footnote 56 for details). For afforestation, the sources are GEHR (1989) and Barciela (1989).
22. For land improvements deflator, wages were allocated 0.5 and material input prices 0.5 (0.25 for construction materials and 0.25 for fertilizers). For afforestation, material input prices were approximated with the agricultural deflator. Weights were computed from the 1958 input–output table (TIOE58).
23. I follow here Feinstein (1988: 281–285, 303).
24. The sources for gas and mining output are provided in the section on the output approach.
25. Unfortunately, it was not possible to distinguish between buildings and work, on the one hand, and plant, machinery and equipment, on the other, that do have different asset lives (60 and 30 years, respectively, in

the case of Britain, according to (Feinstein 1988). Given the longer life of assets in developing countries, I assumed a 50 year average for both buildings and plants and machinery. As a consequence of this decision, capital formation in other construction and works is overexaggerated, as it also includes plant and machinery in gas and mining. However, such an upward bias is small given the size of capital formation in mining and gas.

26. Weights taken from TIOE58 were 0.49, construction materials and 0.51, mason wages.
27. The 15% share of total investment outlays and 60 years average life are taken from (Feinstein 1988: 305), for the case of Britain. The value of capital expenditure in electricity supply comes from Banco Central (1961). Installed electric power is available since 1901 in Reseña Estadística (1952) and Anuario(s) Estadístico(s). Given its high correlation with electricity output (0.95 over 1901–1913), the installed capacity was backcasted with electricity output to 1890. For electricity output, see Carreras (1983, 1989).
28. Cf. Feinstein (1988). Construction costs include wages (0.51) and construction materials (0.49). In turn, plant and machinery include steel (0.44) and wages (0.56).
29. Capital expenditure by Telefónica, at current prices, for 1925–1958 was kindly supplied to me by Nelson Álvarez. The number of telephone offices is available since 1902 and, assuming a life average above 60 years (Feinstein 1988) assumes 100 years, investment can be computed as first differences. A 3 year average ($Y_t = (X_{t-2} + X_{t-1} + X_t)/3$) was estimated to smoothing the investment series.
30. TIOE58 weights are 0.49, construction materials; 0.51, mason wages.
31. A 3 year moving average of the form, $Y_t = (X_{t-2} + X_{t-1} + X_t)/3$, was used to smooth the series. Gómez Mendoza (1989) provides data on telephone centres. It should be bear in mind that (Feinstein 1988) assumed a 100 years average life, but 60 years is enough to make my computational procedure acceptable as the period under consideration (1903–1958) is shorter and, hence, no scrapping has to be taken into account.
32. The level of capital formation on other constructions and works for 1958 provided in CNE58 was distributed among its components using TIOE58.

33. Evidence on rolling stock comes from Gómez Mendoza (1985b, 1989) and Muñoz Rubio (1995). No negative first differences were accepted. Average life of locomotives was estimated in 50 years while for cars and wagons 40 years was assumed, based on evidence presented in Cordero and Menéndez (1978: 298–299). Feinstein (1988: 313) accepted shorter lives for rolling stock in Britain (30 years). For 1850–1860, rolling stock deflated imports from Britain were used to project 1861 investment levels backwards to 1850.
34. Cf. Average power of locomotives (steam, electric and diesel engines) was used to construct a quality index. Evidence is provided in Cordero and Menéndez (1978: 292–293) and Muñoz Rubio (1995: 306).
35. The reason to excluding quality-adjusted quantities is that improvements in quality are already incorporated in locomotive prices. Prices for 1900–1935 are presented in Gómez Mendoza (1985b). Prices were backcasted to 1877 with a deflator constructed on the basis of input prices, weighted according to Gómez Mendoza's estimates and, again back to 1850, with unit values from imports of British rolling stock. Unit values for rolling stock imports from Britain were obtained from the UK Annual Statements of Trade and Navigation. The weights used are locomotives, 0.55, engineering wages; 0.45, iron; for cars, 0.35 wages; 0.41, iron; 0.27, wood; and, for wagons, 0.4 wages; 0.48, iron; 0.12, wood.
36. Muñoz Rubio (1995) provides RENFE investment expenditure at current prices. The inputs and their weights are wages (0.5), steel (0.4) and wood (0.1). Weights come from TIOE58.
37. Warships are not considered here and they are included under current public consumption expenditure, following the national accounts' convention.
38. An exception is Valdaliso (1991) for Vizcaya.
39. The years covered are 1850–1936 and 1940–1958. It was arbitrarily assumed that no investment took place over 1937–1939 (it should be remember that warships did not represent capital formation but public consumption). The sources are (Valdaliso 1991), Carreras (1989), Gómez Mendoza (1985a) and Anuario(s) Estadístico(s). Carreras' output estimates have been revised upwards with Gómez Mendoza's estimates over 1855–1914. For 1850–1854, the output level of 1855 was accepted as a crude approximation.

40. Cf. Feinstein (1988: 338–339). The position of Britain as a major shipbuilder and the fact that Spain's fleet was imported to a large extent over the studied period justifies accepting the British quality index for Spain. I adjusted it to Spain's case by extending the yearly rate of quality improvement for 1901–1913 (0.83%) up to 1936, with no change over 1936–1950, and a slight increase in the rate (to 1%) for 1950–1958.
41. Prices for 1850–1920 are presented in Feinstein (1988: 338–339, col. 5). For 1920–1958, input prices are weighted according to the 1958 input–output table (TIOE58), 0.38, engineering wages; 0.62, steel prices.
42. The sources are López Carrillo (1998), Apps. 1–7 (registered industrial vehicles, 1945–1958; imported vans, 1925–1945) and Estadística(s) de Comercio Exterior.
43. TIOE58 weights are 0.23, engineering wages; 0.77, steel prices.
44. The 1958 level of capital formation on transportation material is provided in CNE58 and was distributed among its components using TIOE58.
45. Distinguishing between buildings and plant and equipment is difficult, and I had to estimate capital formation for structures and plant and machinery from the same installed capacity series (see the section on other constructions and works). Investment expenditure is available since 1953 (Banco Central, 1961). The series of installed power cover the period 1901–1958 and the sources are Reseña Estadística and Anuario(s) Estadístico(s). Given the high correlation (0.987 over 1901–1935) between electricity output and installed power, the former was used to backcast the estimates to 1890. Electricity output comes from Carreras (1989).
46. Negative first differences were excluded. A 2 year average, $Y_t = 0.5X_{t-1} + 0.5X_t$, was computed to smoothing investment.
47. Asset life for electricity supply means and other plant and equipment are 25 and 20 years, respectively, in the British case (Feinstein, 1988: 305). I assumed a longer average life, 30 years, in the case of Spain.
48. Investment expenditure by Spanish telephone monopoly was kindly provided by Nelson Álvarez.
49. Weights, according to TIOE58, were 0.25, copper; 0.25, steel; 0.5 engineering wages.

50. Unfortunately, such difficulty is frequent in historical studies. See, for example, Cairncross (1953), Lewis (1978), and (Feinstein 1988) for the UK, and Smits et al. (2000) for the Netherlands.
51. The estimates of iron and steel consumption in rolling stock and shipbuilding were computed using conversion coefficients provided by Gómez Mendoza (1982, 1985a, b). For dwellings, Schwartz (1976) provides the iron and steel consumption per building in 1958 that has been downward adjusted for earlier years when the consumption of iron and steel was significantly smaller.
52. The form of the moving average is $Yt = (Xt - 2 + Xt - 1 + Xt)/3$. The quality adjustment or allowance, as Feinstein, put it, 'for the upward trend in the degree of fabrication' has been previously employed in Lewis (1978) and Feinstein (1972, 1988).
53. According to TIOE58, weights were 0.44, engineering wages; 0.56, steel prices. For machinery imports, the plant, machinery and equipment deflator for Britain constructed by Feinstein (1988) was adopted over 1850–1920 (adjusted for exchange rate fluctuations between the sterling and the peseta). After 1920, an input cost index was used with equal weights for engineering wages and steel plates.
54. The level of capital formation on other materials for 1958 provided in CNE58 was distributed among its components using 1958 input–output table (TIOE58).
55. Dwellings were split from 'other buildings' by projecting their benchmark levels with the same volume index for 'dwellings and other buildings' and, the resulting 'other buildings' series was, then, added to 'other constructions and works' to conform an index for non-residential structures. The investment levels for each type of capital formation in 1958 were obtained from TIOE58.
56. The author kindly supplied her data.
57. Official imports for 1850–1913 have been now corrected with a coefficient derived from a sample of Spain's main trading partners instead of with coefficients obtained from commodity and country samples for primary products and manufactures, respectively, as in Prados de la Escosura (1986). The change was introduced to maintain consistency with Tena Junguito (1992) and Martínez Ruíz (2003) estimates for 1914–1958. It must be stressed that the new results are almost identical to the earlier ones. Minor changes have also been introduced in Tena Junguito (1992) series by choosing different freight indices in the

construction of freight factors. Thus, the 1913 export freight factor (ratio of freight costs to the value of commodities traded) from Prados de la Escosura (1986) has been extrapolated with iron ore freights (from (1998), expressed in index form, as the numerator, and the export price index, as the denominator. As regards imports, Tena Junguito (1992) freight factor for 1926 has been projected over time with a freight index computed as a trade weighted average of coal and wheat freights (tons imported are the weights) and the import price index.

58. Neither Tena Junguito (1992) nor Martínez Ruiz (2003) included the Canary Islands into their Spanish trade estimates. I rescaled their revised trade series with the Spain and Canary Is. to Spain ratio. This procedure implies the arguable assumption that quantity and price biases in Peninsular Spain (and Balearic Is.) trade are similar to those in Canary Is. trade.

59. There are serious doubts about how gold and silver exports and imports were recorded in official trade statistics (Tortella 1974: 121–122). It could be argued that, since Spain never was part of the Gold Standard, trade in gold and silver should be treated as non-monetary. The fact that Spain behaved in practice as country member of the Gold Standard led me to consider gold and silver exports and imports as monetary.

60. North and Heston (1960). Cf. also Simon (1960) to whom I tried to follow as closely as the data permitted. Freight factor is the ratio of freight costs to the current value of traded commodities.

61. Freight factors are taken from Prados de la Escosura (1986) for 1850–1913 and from Tena Junguito (1992), revised according to the procedure described above, for 1914–1939. The distribution of tons exported and imported between Spanish and foreign ships for 1850–1935 comes from Valdaliso (1991). I assumed the distribution for 1940 (in Anuario Estadístico) was representative for the Civil War years.

62. Alternatively, Sudrià (1990) estimates for the period 1914–1920 are available in those cases in which the earnings per ton method were used. No substantial differences emerged from the two methods with Sudrià's showing lower levels.

63. For similar assumptions for the USA and the Netherlands, cf. Simon (1960) and Smits et al. (2000).

64. The idea that more fully loaded ships made smaller outlays is taken from (Simon 1960). These figures roughly correspond to those accepted by Smits et al. (2000).

65. This assumption is borrowed from (Simon 1960). It could, however, overexaggerate Spain's earnings from marine insurance, as it was rather common for Spanish ships to be underwritten by foreign companies.
66. Tena Junguito (1992: 39) assumed a constant 0.5% of trade value for 1914–1939. I accepted his estimate for 1920–1935 but assumed that the insurance rate evolved with the freight factor over the World War I and the Spanish Civil War years.
67. Jáinaga (1932) reprinted in Velarde (1969). Tourist numbers from 1929 onwards are taken from Fernández Fúster (1991). The implicit assumption here is that real expenses per tourist remained constant tourists over time. The implicit assumption here is that real expenses per tourist remained constant over time. The cost of living index has resulted from splicing Ojeda's (1988) index for 1909–1913 with Reher and Ballesteros (1993) for the previous years.
68. For passengers arriving by ship, cf. Nicolau (2005). The low numbers in the early 1880s allow the presumption that tourism was not economically significant by mid-nineteenth century.
69. Computed from Jáinaga (1932).
70. Vázquez (1988) provides third class fares to Cuba (325 pesetas), Argentina and Brazil (356 pesetas) in 1930 that yield an average of 340 pesetas.
71. This figure, 60 pesetas, corresponds to a lower bound estimate of the average funds brought by Italian immigrants into the USA in 1892, according to Simon (1960: 676–677).
72. The one-tenth ratio derives from comparing fares to America (Vázquez 1988) with those to Algeria (Ministerio de Trabajo 1935) in 1934. These are roughly similar to the lower bound figures produced by Marolla and Roccas (1992: 252), for Italian emigrants to America and Europe in 1911. Llordén (1988: 62), on the other hand, provides a larger sum for Spanish emigrants' funds in the 1860s, 125–200 pesetas, once the fare is deducted.
73. Agricultural wages (Anuario(s) Estadístico(s)) were used for 1913 and 1925–1939 and were linked to mason wages for the rest of the time span considered (Reher and Balleste 1993).
74. For 1850–1881, figures of Spanish inmigration in Argentina, Uruguay, Brazil, and the USA, provided by these countries' official statistics were completed with emigration to Cuba in 1860–1861 from *Anuario*(s) *Estadístico*(s) that was assumed to remain constant over the period.

Emigration to Algeria was derived from Spanish arrivals in Alger and Oran for the years 1872–1881, while the figures for 1850–1871 were estimated under the arbitrary assumption that the share of emigrants remaining in Algeria after 1 year was similar to the one over the period 1872–1881 (25%). Estimates for returned migration were computed by assuming that the average returns from America for 1869–1873 were acceptable for 1850–1868 while 92% of emigrants to Algeria returned home within the first year. A consistency check of the yearly migration data was performed using the migration balances from population censuses along the lines described in Sánchez Alonso (1995). Data for returned migration from America, 1869–1881, were taken from Yáñez (1994: 120). Data on presents the data on migration to Algeria, 1850–1881, come from Vilar (1989).

75. Ministerio de Trabajo (1934: 491) provides data for 1925–1934. Consejo Superior de Emigración (1916) offers evidence for 1911–1915. The actual percentages used were 0.354 for returned migration under Spanish flag (0.646 for World War I years) and 0.764 for emigrants in foreign ships (0.276 during World War I).

76. Cf. Llordén (1988) for fares to Havana over 1862–1876; Vázquez (1988) provides lowest fares to Cuba, Brazil and Argentina for 1880–1930 at 1913 prices that have been reflated to obtain current price fares using the same Sardá (1948) wholesale price index he employed to derive constant price fares. Missing years were interpolated (1862 fares to Cuba were accepted for 1850–1861; fares to Argentina prior 1880 were assumed to moved along fares to Cuba). I assumed that fares to Algeria moved along the fares to America and that the fares ratio Algeria/Argentina in 1934 (Ministerio de Trabajo 1935) was stable over the considered period. I also assumed that tourist fares from Europe moved along migrants' fares.

77. Export and import price indices for 1850–1913 are provided by Prados de la Escosura (1988), where a chain price index for Spanish exports to Great Britain was accepted as Spain's export price index, and an average of export price indices of Spain's main partners weighted by their shares in Spanish imports was employed as import price index. For the years 1914–1958, the export price index is taken from Anuario(s) Estadístico (s) and the import price index has been computed as an average of export price indices of Spain's main partners weighted by their shares in Spanish imports. The deflation of current values has been preferred to

the available quantity indices for 1914–1958, as the latter are built up on the basis the official trade statistics in which quantities and prices are mismeasured (Cf. Tena Junguito 1992).

78. Statistical evidence on production seems to be more reliable than on expenditure or income. Heston shows that more than 80% of developing countries use the production side GDP as their control total. Assessments of Spanish national accounts prior the mid-1960s concur with this view (Schwartz 1976: 456; Uriel and Moltó 1995: 73). Historical national accounts estimates confirm this assertion, see, for example, Baffigi (2013), van der Eng (1992: 348), and Batista et al. (1997) on the cases of Italy, Indonesia and Portugal, respectively.

79. By 'control total' is meant that 'estimates from alternative approaches are adjusted to conform to this total' Heston (1994: 33).

80. Cf. Chamorro and Morales (1976) where Jáinaga's full set of estimates were published. Velarde (1969) reprinted Jáinaga (1932) balance of payments estimates for 1931.

81. Net current transfers are needed in order to compute Net National Disposable Income.

82. Evidence on transatlantic emigrants returned after less than a year abroad is presented in Yañez (1994) for 1917–1921 and 1925–1930 and in Ministerio de Trabajo (1935: 14) for 1926–1934. It represents between 3.5 and 6.2% of total emigration to America, averaging 5%. Yáñez (1994: 225–227) provides higher shares, 7.8 and 6.6% for 1917–1921 and 1925–1930, respectively. I accepted the average for 1917–1918 for 1914–1916 and the share for 1934 was extended to 1935. For the period 1850–1913, I accepted 5% and for 1922–1924, I log-linearly interpolated the percentages for 1921 and 1925 while no return emigrants were assumed during the Civil War (1936–1939). For the share of emigrants to Algeria returning within a year, Bonmatí (1989: 135) points to 59% of total emigrants.

83. Unfortunately, no distinction can be made between short- and long-term migrants. Contemporary estimates are collected in Chamorro (1976), for 1899, 1900 and 1904; Vázquez (1988) for 1906, 1908–1913 and 1920–1922; and García López (1992), averages for 1906–1910 and 1920–1921. Lastly, those by Jáinaga for 1931–1934 were reprinted in Chamorro and Morales (1976).

84. Nominal wages for Argentina are collected in Williamson (1995). Zanetti and García (1977) provide nominal wages for Cuba from 1903

onwards. French nominal wages from Williamson (1995) are used for emigrants to France and Algeria. The trading exchange rates of the peseta against the peso, the French franc and the US dollar are computed on the basis of Cortés Conde (1979), Della Paolera (1988), and Martín Aceña and Pons (2005). I assumed that no labour returns were sent home during the Civil War years (1936–1939).

85. Muñoz et al. (1978: 209–213). Electricity alone represented 19%. Foreign capital in railways and mining reached 42% of the total. Altogether, the sectors included here constituted two-thirds of all foreign capital invested in Spain in 1923.
86. External debt and the interest rates applied are provided in Fernández Acha (1976).
87. Cf. Sardá (1948) for a detailed evaluation of Spain's external debt in the late nineteenth and early twentieth century.
88. The exchange rate of the peseta against the French franc is provided in Martín Aceña and Pons (2005).
89. Banco Urquijo (1924) provides evidence on the declining share of Government bonds in non-residents hands during the post-World War I years.
90. Cf. Tedde de Lorca (1978, 1980) for research on Norte, MZA and Andaluces, the three main railway companies. Evidence on foreign investment in railways has been gathered in Broder (1976).
91. Tedde de Lorca (1978), Appendices IV-9 and IV-18 provides the data on dividends and interests paid by Norte and MZA, while Tedde de Lorca (1980), pp. 44–45, presents the same evidence for Andaluces.
92. The information on the shares deposited in order to participate in MZA shareholders meetings (1891–1935) comes from Pedro Pablo Núñez Goicoechea who kindly provided it to me. Vidal Olivares (1999: 628–639) presents similar information for scattered years for the Norte railway company. Tedde de Lorca (1980: 31–34) offers quantitative evidence on the decline of debentures in foreign hands during the interwar years.
93. Cf. Harvey and Taylor (1987: 197), for British capital (effective share capital and debentures and mortgage bonds). Cumulated total foreign investment (excluding railways) and cumulated French investment in mining was derived from Broder (1976). When only French and British capital in mining are considered (the large majority of it), the British share ranged from 63 to 73% over 1870–1900, the mining boom era

(and only 22–41% in the earlier period 1851–1870). When, alternatively, Broder's estimates of non-railway investment from other countries are cumulated, British capital represented from 52 to 61% over 1870–1900 (22–31% in 1851–70). Evidence in Muñoz, Roldán and Serrano (1976) indicates that British capital was above 50% in the years 1900–1913 (53% on average for 1900 and 1912), while its contribution rose up to three-fourths in the interwar years (76.6% on average for 1923 and 1931).

94. The British participation in total foreign capital was assumed to be 30% in 1850–1870, 60% in 1870–1890 and 50% in 1890–1913 (see the previous footnote for justification).

95. Non-retained exports represent the value of exports receipts that accrued to foreign productive factors used in mining production and, therefore, are not kept in Spain. Non-retained values over total mineral export proceeds represent 0.35 for iron ore, 0.40 for lead, 0.49 and 0.625 for copper pyrites before and after 1896, 0.54 for mercury, according to Prados de la Escosura (1988) who took them from González Portilla (1981), Broder (1981), Harvey (1981) and Nadal (1975), respectively. Recent revisionist work by Escudero (1996) suggests that these shares should be revised upwards and Témime et al. (1982) pointed out that 70–75% of export proceeds were not retained in Spain. Escudero (1998) has estimated that the share of foreign returns in Basque iron ore mining represented 39.5% (204 million pesetas) of its total over 1876–1913, to which should be added the differential between market prices and much lower preferential prices (that foreign mining companies charged their matrix firms abroad) times the quantities sold at preferential prices, approximately 200 million pesetas, so the share of non-retained exports would be over half of total export proceeds. I have used, then, non-retained shares of 0.55 for iron ore, 0.90 for lead, and 0.73 for pyrites.

96. Tramway revenues are provided in Gómez Mendoza (1989). For utilities, see section III.

97. Frax and Matilla (1996) provide the declared value of insurance premia by foreign companies for 1907–1937 that was backasted with the number of foreign companies to 1850. The yield of British consols was taken from Mitchell (1988).

98. I follow Feinstein (1972) who suggested deflating those components of the balance of payments for which no specific deflators are available by an import price index to ascertaining their purchasing power.
99. Following Simon (1960) I have attributed double weight to the last year of each 5 year period considered. Due to lack of data, no distinction has been made between the sum brought back home by the emigrant who returned home within his/her first year abroad and the average remittances sent during the first 5 years abroad by the rest of emigrants.

References

Alonso Alvarez, L. 1993. *La modernización de la industria del tabaco en España, 1800-1935*, 9304. Documento de trabajo: Fundación Empresa Pública. Programa de Historia Económica.

Alonso Alvarez, L. 1995. Crecimiento de la demanda, insuficiencia de la producción tradicional e industrialización del sector tabaquero en España, 18001935. In *La cara oculta de la industrialización española. La modernización de los sectores no líderes*, ed. J. Nadal and J. Catalan, 163–197. Madrid: Alianza.

Baffigi, A. 2013. National Accounts, 1861-2011. In *The Oxford Handbook of the Italian Economy since Unification*, ed. G. Toniolo, 157–186. Oxford: Oxford University Press.

Banco Central. 1961. Estudio Económico 1960. Madrid: Sucesores de Rivadeneyra.

Banco Urquijo. 1924. *El progreso y la riqueza de España*. Madrid: Imprenta de Samarán y Compañía.

Barciela, C. 1989. El sector agrario desde 1936. In *Estadísticas históricas de España*, ed. A. Carreras, 131–167. Fundación Banco Exterior: Siglos XIX–XX, Madrid.

Batista D., C. Martins, M. Pinheiro, and J. Reis. 1997. *New Estimates of Portugal's GDP, 1910–1958*. Lisbon: Banco de Portugal.

Beckerman, W. 1976. *An Introduction to National Income Analysis*, 2nd ed. London: Weidenfeld and Nicholson.

Bonmatí, J.F. 1989. *La emigración alicantina a Argelia (siglo XIX y primer tercio del siglo XX)*. Alicante: Universidad de Alicante.

Broder, A. 1976. Les investissments étrangers en Espagne au siècle XIXe: Methodologie et quantification. *Revue d'Histoire Economique et Sociale, LIV* 1: 29–63.

Broder, A. 1981. Le ròle des interests étrangers dans la croissance de l'Espagne (1767–1923). Université de Paris IV-Sorbonne, Unpublished Ph.D. Dissertation.

Cairncross, A.K. 1953. *Home and Foreign Investment, 1870–1913.* Cambridge: Cambridge University Press.

Carreras, A. 1983. La producció industrial espanyola i italiana des de mitjan segle XIX fins l'actualitat. Universitat Autònoma de Barcelona, 3 vols., unpublished Ph.D. dissertation.

Carreras, A. 1985. Gasto nacional bruto y formación de capital en España, 1849–1958: Primer ensayo de estimación. In *La Nueva Historia Económica en España*, ed. P. Martín Aceña and L. Prados de la Escosura, 17–51. Madrid: Tecnos.

Carreras, A. 1989. Industria. In *Estadísticas Históricas de España. Siglos XIX-XX*, ed. A. Carreras, 169–247. Madrid: Fundación Banco Exterior.

Chamorro, S. 1976. Bosquejo histórico de la Balanza de Pagos de España. *Información Comercial Española* 517: 151–159.

Chamorro, S., R. Morales. 1976. Las balanzas de pagos de Francisco Jáinaga. *Información Comercial Española* 511: 107–118.

Comín, F. 1985. *Fuentes cuantitativas para el estudio del sector público en España 1801-1980.* Madrid: Instituto de Estudios Fiscales, monografía no. 40.

Consejo Superior de la Emigración Española. 1916. *La emigración española transoceánica, 1911–1915.*

Cordero, R., F. Menéndez. 1978. El sistema ferroviario español. In *Los ferrocarriles en España, 1844–1943*, 2 vols., ed. M. Artola, 161–338. Madrid: Banco de España. I.

Cortes-Conde, R. 1979. *El progreso argentino 1880–1914.* Buenos Aires: Editorial Sudamericana.

Deane, P. 1968. New Estimates of Gross National Product for the United Kingdom 1830-1914. *Review of Income and Wealth* 14 (2): 95–112.

Della Paolera, G. 1988. *How the Argentine Economy Performed during the International Gold Standard: A Reexamination.* Unpublished Ph. D. Dissertation, University of Chicago.

van der Eng, Pierre. 1992. The Real Domestic Product of Indonesia, 1880–1989. *Explorations in Economic History* 29 (3): 343–373.

Escudero, A. 1996. Pesimistas y optimistas ante el 'boom' minero. *Revista de Historia Industrial* 10: 69–91.

Escudero, A. 1998. *Minería e industrialización en Vizcaya*. Barcelona: Crítica/Universidad de Alicante.

Feinstein, C.H. 1972. *National Income, Expenditure, and Output of the United Kingdom, 1855–1965*. Cambridge: Cambridge University Press.

Feinstein, C.H. 1988. Sources and Methods of Estimation for Domestic Reproducible Fixed Assets, Stocks and Works in Progress, Overseas Assets, and Land. In *Studies in Capital Formation in the United Kingdom 1750–1920*, ed. C.H. Feinstein, and S. Pollard, 257–471. Oxford: Clarendon Press.

Fernández Acha. 1976. La deuda pública. In *Datos básicos para la Historia Financiera de España, 1850–1975*, 2 vols., ed. Instituto de Estudios Fiscales. Madrid: Imprenta de la Fábrica de la Moneda y Timbre. II.

Fernández Fúster, L. 1991. *Historia general del turismo de masas*. Madrid: Alianza.

Frax, E., M.J. Matilla. 1996. Los seguros en España, 1830–1934. *Revista de Historia Económica* XIV (1): 183–203.

Gallego, D. 1986. Transformaciones técnicas de la agricultura española en el primer tercio del siglo XX. In *Historia agraria de la España contemporánea 3. El fin de la agricultura tradicional (1900–1960)*, ed. R. Garrabou, C. Barciela and J.I. Jiménez Blanco, 171–229. Barcelona: Crítica.

Gallego, D., V. Pinilla. 1996. Del librecambio matizado al proteccionismo selectivo: El comercio exterior de productos agrarios y de alimentos en España entre 1849 y 1935. *Revista de Historia Económica* XIV (2): 371–420 and (3): 619–639.

Garcia Barbancho, A. 1960. Análisis de la alimentación española. *Anales de Economía* 66: 72–119 and 67: 271–367.

García López, J.R. 1992. Las remesas de emigrantes españoles en América. Siglos XIX y XX. Colombres: Ediciones Júcar.

Gomez Mendoza, A. 1982. *Ferrocarriles y cambio económico en España, 1855–1913*. Madrid: Alianza.

Gomez Mendoza, A. 1985a. La industria de construcciones navales, 1850–1935. Memoria del Banco de España (mimeo).

Gomez Mendoza, A. 1985b. La industria del material ferroviario, 1884–1935. Memoria del Banco de España (mimeo).

Gomez Mendoza, A. 1989. Transportes y Comunicaciones. In *Estadísticas Históricas de España. Siglos XIX–XX*, ed. A. Carreras, 269–325. Madrid: Fundación Banco Exterior.

Gómez Mendoza, A. 1995. Del matadero a la tenería: Producción y consumo de cueros en España (1900–1933). In *La cara oculta de la industrialización española. La modernización de los sectores no líderes*, ed. J. Nadal and J. Catalan, 267–293. Madrid: Alianza.

González Portilla, M. 1981. *La formación de la sociedad capitalista en el País Vasco (1876–1913), 2 vols*. San Sebastián: Haramburu.

Harvey, C. 1981. *The Rio Tinto Company. An Economic History of a Leading International Mining Concern, 1873–1954*. Penzance: Alison Hodge.

Harvey, C., and P. Taylor. 1987. Mineral Wealth and Economic Development: Foreign Direct Investment in Spain, 1851–1913. *Economic History Review* XL (2): 185-207.

Herranz-Loncán, A. 2004. *La dotación de Infraestructuras en España, 1844–1935*. Madrid: Banco de España, Estudios de Historia Económica no. 45.

Heston, A. 1994. A Brief Review of Some Problems in Using National Accounts Data in Level of Output Comparisons and Growth Studies. *Journal of Development Economics* 44: 29–52.

Instituto De Estudios Fiscales. 1976. Datos básicos para la Historia Financiera de España, 1850–1975, 2 vols. Madrid: Imprenta de la Fábrica de la Moneda y Timbre.

Inspección General de la Emigración. 1934. *Estadística general de la emigración española en el año de 1932*. Madrid: Ministerio de Trabajo y Previsión.

Inspección General de la Emigración. 1935. *Estadística general de la emigración española en el año de 1942*. Madrid: Ministerio de Trabajo y Previsión.

Jáinaga, F. 1932. *Balance de Pagos internacionales*. Año 1931. Madrid: Gráficas Reunidas. Reprinted in *Revista de Economía Política* VIII (2): 586–605.

Jefferys, J.B., and D. Walters. 1955. National Income and Expenditure of the United Kingdom, 1870–1952. In *Income and Wealth, Series V*, ed. S. Kuznets, 1–40. London: Bowes and Bowes.

Lewis, W.A. 1978. *Growth and Fluctuations, 1870–1913*. London: George Allen and Unwin.

Llordén, M. 1988. Los inicios de la emigración asturiana a América, 1858–1870. In *Españoles hacia América. La emigración en masa, 1880–1930*, ed. N. Sánchez-Albornoz, 53–65. Madrid: Alianza.

López Carrillo, J.M. 1998. *Autarquía y automoción: Evolución de la empresa nacional de autocamiones (ENASA) entre 1946 y 1958*, 9809. Programa de Historia Económica, Documento de Trabajo: Fundación Empresa Pública.

Maluquer de Motes, J. 2006. 'la paradisíaca estabilidad de la anteguerra'. Elaboración de un índice de precios de consumo en España, 1830–1936. *Revista de Historia Económica* 24 (2): 333–382.

Marolla, M., and M. Roccas. 1992. La riscostruzione della bilancia internazionale dei servizi I trasferimenti unilaterali dell'anno 1911. In *I conti economici dell'Italia. II. Una stima del valore aggiunto per il 1911*, ed. G.M. Rey, 241–282. Roma: Laterza.

Martín Aceña, P., and M.A. Pons. 2005. Sistema monetario financiero. In *Estadísticas Históricas de España. Siglos XIX–XX*, 3 vols., ed. A. Carreras and X. Tafunell, II, 645–706. Bilbao: Fundación BBVA.

Martín Rodríguez, M. 1995. Del trapiche a la fábrica de azúcar, 1779–1904. In *La cara oculta de la industrialización española. La modernización de los sectores no líderes*, ed. J. Nadal and J. Catalan, 43–97. Madrid: Alianza.

Martínez Ruiz, E. 2003. *El sector exterior durante la autarquía. Una reconstrucción de las balanzas de pagos de España (1940–1958)*. Madrid: Banco de España Estudios de Historia Económica no. 43.

Martínez Ruiz, E. 2006. *Guerra Civil, comercio y capital extranjero. El sector exterior de la economía española (1936–1939)*. Madrid: Banco de España Estudios de Historia Económica no. 49.

Mitchell, B.R. 1988. *British Historical Statistics*. Cambridge: Cambridge University Press.

Muñoz Rubio, M. 1995. *Renfe (1941–1991)*. Ediciones Luna: Medio siglo de ferrocarril público. Madrid.

Muñoz, J., S. Roldán, and A. Serrano. 1976. Minería y capital extranjero. *Información Comercial Española* 514: 59–89.

Muñoz, J., S. Roldán, A. Serrano. 1978. La involución nacionalista y la vertebración del capitalismo español. *Cuadernos Económicos de ICE* 5: 13–221.

Nadal, J. 1975. *El fracaso de la Revolución Industrial en España, 1814–1913*. Barcelona: Ariel.

Nicolau, R. 2005. Población, salud y actividad. In *Estadísticas Históricas de España. Siglos XIX–XX*, 3 vols., ed. A. Carreras and X. Tafunell, 77–154. Bilbao: Fundación BBVA.

North, D.C. 1960. The United States Balance of Payments, 1790-1860. In *Trends in the American Economy in the Nineteenth Century, Studies in Income and Wealth*, vol. 24, ed. W.N. Parker, 573–627. Princeton University Press: Princeton.

North, D.C., and A. Heston. 1960. The Estimation of Shipping Earnings in Historical Studies of the Balance of Payments. *Canadian Journal of Economics and Political Science* XXVI: 265–276.

de Ojeda, A. 1988. *Indices de precios en España en el período 1913–1987*, 17. Madrid: Banco de España. Estudios de Historia Económica no.

Prados de la Escosura, L. 1984. El comercio hispano-británico en los siglos XVIII y XIX. I. Reconstrucción. *Revista de Historia Económica* II (2): 113–162.

Prados de la Escosura, L. 1986. Una serie anual del comercio exterior español (1821–1913). *Revista de Historia Económica* IV (1): 103–150.

Prados de la Escosura, L. 1988. *De imperio a nación. Crecimiento y atraso económico en España (1780–1930)*. Madrid: Alianza.

Prados de la Escosura, L., J.R. Rosés. 2010. Capital Accumulation in the Long-Run: The Case of Spain, 1850–2000. *Research in Economic History* 27: 93–152.

Reher, D.S., and E. Ballesteros. 1993. Precios y salarios en Castilla la Nueva: La construcción de un índice de salarios reales, 1501–1991. *Revista de Historia Económica* XI (1): 101–151.

Reseña Estadística. 1952. Madrid: Instituto Nacional de Estadística.

Sánchez Alonso, B. 1995. *Las causas de la emigración española, 1880-1930*. Madrid: Alianza.

Sánchez Alonso, B. 2000. European Emigration in the Late Nineteenth Century: The Paradoxical Case of Spain. *Economic History Review* 53: 309–330.

Sardá, J. 1948. *La política monetaria y las fluctuaciones de la economía española en el siglo XIX*. Madrid: Instituto Sancho de Moncada.

Schwartz, P. 1976. El Producto Interior Bruto de España de 1940 a 1960. In *El Producto Nacional de España en el siglo XX*, ed. P. Schwartz, 443–592. Madrid: Instituto de Estudios Fiscales.

Simon, M. 1960. The United States Balance of Payments, 1861–1900. In *Trends in the American Economy in the Nineteenth Century, Studies in Income and Wealth*, vol. 24, ed. W.N. Parker, 629–715. Princeton University Press: Princeton.

Smits, J.P., E. Horlings, and J.L. van Zanden. 2000. *Dutch GNP and Its Components, 1800–1913, Groningen Growth and Development Centre Monograph No. 5*. Groningen: University of Groningen.

Sudrià, C. 1990. Los beneficios de España durante la Gran Guerra. Una aproximación a la balanza de pagos española, 1914–1920. *Revista de Historia Económica* 7 (2): 363–396.

Tedde de Lorca, P. 1978. Las compañías ferroviarias en España, 1855–1935. In *Los ferrocarriles en España, 1844–1943*, 2 vols., ed. M. Artola, 9–354. Madrid: Banco de España. II.

Tedde de Lorca, P. 1980. La Compañía de los Ferrocarriles Andaluces (1878–1920): Una empresa de transportes en la España de la Restauración. *Investigaciones Económicas* 12: 27–76.

Témime, E., Broder, A., and Chastagnaret, G. 1982. *Historia de la España contemporánea. Desde 1808 hasta nuestros días*. Barcelona: Ariel.

Tena Junguito, A. 1992. *Las estadísticas históricas del comercio internacional: Fiabilidad y comparabilidad*. Madrid: Banco de España, Estudios de Historia Económica no. 24.

Tortella, G. 1974. Las magnitudes monetarias y sus determinantes. In *La banca española en la Restauración*, 2 vols., ed. G. Tortella and P. Schwartz, 457–521. Madrid: Tecnos. I.

Uriel, E., M.L. Molto. 1995. *Contabilidad Nacional de España enlazada. Series 1954–1993*. Valencia: IVIE.

Valdaliso, J.M. 1991. *Los navieros vascos y la marina mercante en España, 1860-1935*. Una historia económica, Bilbao: Instituto Vasco de Administración Pública.

Vázquez, A. 1988. La emigración gallega. Migrantes, transporte y remesas. In *Españoles hacia América. La emigración en masa, 1880–1930*, ed. N. Sánchez-Albornoz, 80–104. Madrid: Alianza.

Velarde Fuertes, J. 1969. *Política económica de la Dictadura*. Madrid: Guadiana.

Vidal Olivares, J. 1999. La estructura de la propiedad, de la organización y la gestión de una gran empresa ferroviaria: la compañía de los Caminos de Hierro del Norte de España, 1858–1936. *Revista de Historia Económica XVII* (3): 623–662.

Vilar, J.B. 1989. *Los españoles en la Argelia francesa (1840–1914)*. Murcia: C.S.I. C./Universidad de Murcia.

Vitali, O. 1992. Gli impieghi del reddito nell'anno 1911. In *I conti economici dell'Italia. II. Una stima del valore aggiunto per il 1911*, ed. G.M. Rey, 283–337. Roma-Bari: Laterza.

Williamson, J.G. 1995. The Evolution of Global Labor Markets since 1830: Background Evidence and Hypotheses. *Explorations in Economic History* 32: 141–196.

Yáñez Gallardo, C. 1994. *La emigración española a América (siglos XIX y XX). Dimensión y características cuantitativas*. Colombres: Fundación Archivo de Indianos.

Zanetti, O., and A. GARCÍA. 1977. *United Fruit Company: Un caso de dominio imperialista en Cuba*. La Habana: Ediciones de Ciencias Sociales.

Open Access This chapter is licensed under the terms of the Creative Commons Attribution 4.0 International License (http://creativecommons.org/licenses/by/4.0/), which permits use, sharing, adaptation, distribution and reproduction in any medium or format, as long as you give appropriate credit to the original author(s) and the source, provide a link to the Creative Commons license and indicate if changes were made.

The images or other third party material in this chapter are included in the chapter's Creative Commons license, unless indicated otherwise in a credit line to the material. If material is not included in the chapter's Creative Commons license and your intended use is not permitted by statutory regulation or exceeds the permitted use, you will need to obtain permission directly from the copyright holder.

8

New GDP Series and Earlier Estimates for the Pre-national Accounts Era

How do the new GDP series compare to earlier estimates?[1] Let us examine them first. Unlike contemporaries who were interested in assessing national income levels, early Spanish research has been concerned with trends and fluctuations in real output and expenditure.[2] All available GDP estimates are output indices constructed with a fixed, single benchmark level whose economic significance tends to decline as one moves away from the base year.[3] Moreover, trends in real gross value added are proxied by production indices, which imply the unlikely assumption that total output and input consumption evolve in the same direction and with the same intensity.[4] Three types of yearly GDP estimates can be distinguished: official estimates by the Consejo de Economía Nacional, its revisions and extensions, and independent estimates.

8.1 Consejo de Economía Nacional Estimates

In 1944, the Consejo de Economía Nacional or National Economic Council (CEN, thereafter) was asked to estimate a set of national accounts for Spain (CEN 1945, 1965). Three were the main targets: to provide income figures for the years prior to the Civil War (1936–1939), to evaluate 1940 GDP on the available, fragile statistical basis, and to design a direct method to estimate national income for the years to come (Schwartz 1977: 460).

Dearth of data forced CEN to split output indices into two segments with 1929 as the link year. In each case, independent production indices for agriculture and industry were obtained, from which an aggregate index was derived to approximate national income. No regard was paid to services and was implicitly assumed that output in services evolved as a weighted average of agricultural and industrial production.

For the earlier period, 1906–1929, an agricultural output index was built up on the basis of eleven products, mostly dry farming crops (while no livestock output was included), representing half the value of total output. The index of industrial production included eighteen products, rendering a good coverage for mining, but insufficient for manufacturing and construction. Output indices were obtained for agriculture and industry by weighting each single product with its average price over 1913–1928, and the aggregate results were expressed by taking the average for 1906–1930 as 100.

The composition of agricultural and industrial indices changed from 1929 onwards. Thirteen new crops were added to the agricultural index, distributed into eight main groups of products, that reached up to 80% of total production, while the industrial index's coverage rose to 38 products distributed into ten different groups.[5] To derive output indices for agriculture and industry, quantities were weighted by 1929 farm-gate prices and unit value added, respectively.[6] Improvements in data coverage took place in the 1950s, but the method remained practically unaltered until 1956.

An index of total production was obtained by combining agricultural and industrial indices with fixed weights (0.6 and 0.4, respectively, over 1906–1929, and 0.5 each, thereafter). In addition, to allow for short-term fluctuations over the period 1906–1935, a de-trended nuptiality index was combined with the total production index. Nuptiality was excluded after the Civil War (1936–1939) as unsuitable for post-war cycles.

In a second stage, the total production index was linked to an estimate of national income for 1923 in order to derive national income at constant prices.[7] A further step was to obtain national income figures at current prices by reflating real income with a wholesale price index. Finally, for the years 1957–1964, CEN computed national income directly.

8.2 Revisions and Extensions of CEN Estimates

Modern national accounts constructed according to OECD rules are available in Spain since 1954. Attempts to extend them backwards led to revisions of CEN figures that, occasionally, were expanded to cover the expenditure side. Three estimates are worth mentioning.

8.2.1 Comisaría del Plan de Desarrollo

A first attempt to revise CEN's estimates was carried out by Comisaría del Plan de Desarrollo, the Development Planning Authority (CPD, thereafter), and covered the period 1942–1954 (CPD 1972).[8] CPD economists were concerned with the high volatility shown by CEN figures that they attributed to its high dependence on agricultural output and to the exclusion of services. The alternative proposed by CPD was to construct a new index of aggregate performance in which services were added to CEN's indices of agricultural and industrial output. Services output was obtained by combining series on transport and communications and banking.[9] A real product index was calculated by weighting each sectoral index with the shares of agriculture, industry and services in

1954 GDP at factor cost, as established in official national accounts (CNE58).[10] GDP at constant prices for 1942–1953 was, then, derived through backward extrapolation of the 1954 GDP level with the real product index. GDP at current prices was computed, in turn, by reflating real output with a composite index of wholesale prices (0.3) and the cost-of-living index (0.7).[11]

GDP was completed with a breakdown of its expenditure components that included direct estimates of investment, public consumption and net exports of goods and services. To approximate private non-residential fixed capital formation, a physical index of private investment was built up by combining, with 1954 weights (CNE58), steel and cement output, machinery imports, electric power and registered transport vehicles. An index of residential investment was proxied by the number of completed dwellings. Public investment, in turn, resulted from adding up investment in agriculture and public works and provincial and local public investment, deflated by a wholesale price index. Levels of each type of investment for 1954 were taken from the national accounts and projected backwards with each investment index to derive real capital formation series and, then, reflated with price indices for production goods and construction materials. Total expenditure of public administration (central, provincial and local governments) re-scaled to match national accounts was used for public consumption and, then, deflated with a wholesale price index. Net exports of goods (at current and constant prices) were used as a proxy for net exports of goods and services, except in the case of tourism, in which the number of tourists (and the cost of living index as deflator) was accepted. Private consumption was obtained as a residual from GDP at market prices (derived by adding indirect taxes net of subsidies to GDP at factor cost, obtained through the production approach) and the directly estimated components of expenditure.

8.2.2 Alcaide

A revision of CEN series was also attempted by Julio Alcaide, a pioneer of Spanish national accounts, who, concerned for its volatility and cyclical behaviour, attempted to smoothing CEN's real output (Alcaide

1976).[12] For the period 1901–1935, Alcaide derived an index of domestic production by combining, with 1906 fixed weights, CEN indices for agricultural and industrial output, and total employment in services, as a proxy for its output.[13] GDP at current prices was obtained by reflating real output with a wholesale price index.[14]

8.2.3 Naredo

An apparent inconsistency in the CEN series that would have led to underestimating national income for the post-Civil War years motivated José Manuel Naredo's revision of CEN's national accounts (Naredo 1991). The rationale for the under-registration of economic activity in official national accounts lies in the response of economic agents to systematic regulation and intervention of markets under Francoist autarchy.[15] He also noticed that CEN's implicit income-elasticity of demand for imports in the 1940s was too low. Naredo proposed, then, an alternative real GDP series for 1920–1950 based upon the revision of official national account estimates by hypothesizing higher income-elasticity of the demand for imports in the 1940s and by assuming a 10% fall in GDP resulting from the Spanish Civil War (1936–1939).

8.3 Independent Estimates

8.3.1 Información Comercial Española

The contribution by the research unit of the Ministry of Commerce and published in its journal, *Información Comercial Española* (ICE, thereafter), represented a major improvement over earlier indices of Spanish aggregate performance (ICE 1962).[16] The 'general index of total production', as its authors named it, covered 1951–1960 and represented a Laspeyres volume index in which three major sectors, agriculture and fishing, mining, manufacturing and construction, and trade and services, were combined with 1958 gross value added as weights. For each sector, a Laspeyres volume index with 1958 weights was constructed, in which four branches were included for agriculture, sixteen for industry, and six for services, the latter appearing for the first time in pre-national accounts GDP estimates.[17]

Real product series was complemented with a quantity index for investment based on construction and public works, afforestation and the consumption (production plus imports) of machinery and equipment.

8.3.2 Schwartz

A major attempt at overcoming CEN's estimates for the period 1940–1960 was carried out by Pedro Schwartz, at the Bank of Spain's research unit, where he assembled new empirical evidence and used transparent methods in which indirect methods and regression analysis were combined (Schwartz 1976). In the new series, gross value added for every major sector in the economy was obtained by regressing their value-added levels (derived from official national accounts) on a set of indicators over 1954–1960, and the resulting structural relationship was applied to the set of variables or indicators to compute sectoral value added for the earlier pre-national accounts period 1940–1953. Gross domestic product (nominal and real) was derived by aggregation.[18]

8.3.3 Carreras

The most ambitious attempt to derive historical series of real GDP was produced by Albert Carreras (1985) who built up an index from the demand side, covering a longer time span, 1849–1958.[19] Weights for the main aggregates (private and public consumption, investment, net exports) were derived from the 1958 benchmark from the national accounts, while the 1958 input–output table allowed the breakdown of each series into its main components.[20]

However, a few shortcomings can be observed in an otherwise major piece of research. For example, the consumption series only cover food, beverages and tobacco, and clothing while services are neglected.[21] Actually, it could be argued that consumption growth may be possibly biased downwards since the goods included in the series (food and clothing) are those of lower income-elasticity of demand.[22] In addition, the use of end-year (1958) fixed weights could underestimate GDP growth since relative prices for capital goods, the fastest growing component of expenditure, declined over time rendering, hence, a lower weight for investment than would have been the case if relative prices of any previous year were used.[23]

8.4 Comparing the New and Earlier GDP Estimates

How does the new GDP series compare to the earlier estimates? There is a significant agreement about performance over the long run between Carreras estimates and my new series, although significant discrepancies emerge in the short term. During the first half of the twentieth century, the new GDP series present slower growth than those by Alcaide and CEN (Fig. 8.1).

When the focus is placed on specific periods, the variance across different estimates emerges. World War I years seem to have been of fast

Fig. 8.1 Alternative real GDP estimates, 1850–1958 (1958 = 100) (logs)

growth (CEN, Alcaide and Carreras), in which the economy would have taken advantage of Spain's neutrality to cater for the needs of belligerent nations while domestic industry expanded on the basis of import substitution. This conventional depiction is challenged by the new GDP series. Then, the post-war years and especially the 1920s exhibit accelerated growth in CEN and Alcaide's. estimates while Carreras' suggest deceleration. The new GDP series provide an even more optimistic picture than Alcaide's.

The impact of Great Depression in Spain (1929–1933) varies dramatically according to different authors. Spain's economy decelerated but continued growing in Alcaide's view, stagnated in Naredo's, mildly contracted in Carreras' computations and definitely shrank in CEN's estimates. The new series side along CEN's but with a less intense decline.

Earlier estimates are discontinued between 1936 and 1939, so comparing output levels in 1935 and 1940 is the only way to assessing the impact of the Civil War (Fig. 8.2). A consensus exists about a substantial contraction in economic activity during the war years, around 6% per annum, but for Naredo's mild −2.1%. In my new estimates, the Civil War represented a milder but still deeper shrinkage than Naredo's.[24]

Fig. 8.2 Alternative real GDP estimates, 1900–1958 (1958 = 100) (logs)

Table 8.1 Real GDP growth in the pre-national accounts era: alternative estimates, 1850–1958 (%)

	CEN	CPD	Alcaide	Naredo	ICE	Schwartz	Carreras	New series
1850–1958							1.7	1.7
1901–1958	2.6		2.8				1.6	1.8
1850–1883							2.2	1.7
1883–1913							0.6	1.1
1901–1913	1.6		2.3				0.1	1.2
1913–1918	1.4		1.9				2.2	0.3
1918–1929	2.5		2.6	1.6			1.5	3.9
1929–1933	−2.1		1.0	−2.1			−0.6	−1.5
1933–1935	4.3		1.5	4.3			−1.1	3.0
1935–1940	−6.7		−6.0	−2.1			−5.9	−3.5
1940–1944	3.6	0.7	2.6	4.8		2.6	6.5	4.0
1944–1950	0.8	2.8	2.5	2.9		0.6	−1.5	0.2
1950–1958	7.2	6.2	5.8	5.8	5.1	6.0	5.0	5.8

Note 'New Series' are GDP estimates at market prices. *Sources* New Series, see the text. CEN (1945, 1965), ICE (1962), CPD (1972), Alcaide (1976), Naredo (1991), Schwartz (1976), and Carrerras (1985)

The post-war recovery was mild (but for Carreras and Naredo estimates) and short-lived (CEN, Carreras and Schwartz), and only resumed at a fast pace in the 1950s (except for Alcaide) (Table 8.1). The new GDP estimates concur with the view of a post-Civil War mild and long recovery, which makes Spanish post-war experience different from western Europe's fast return to pre-war output levels (Maddison 2010).

Notes

1. Attempts to provide historical GDP at benchmark years have been carried out by economic historians. Bairoch (1976) and Crafts (1983, 1984) included Spain in their estimates for the nineteenth century computed along Beckerman and Bacon (1966) indirect approach. Following Deane (1957), Prados de la Escosura (1982) reconstructed Mulhall (1880, 1884, 1885, 1896) figures in a consistent way and derived a set of benchmark estimates for Spanish national income for 1832–1894. In addition, GDP estimates for seven benchmarks over the period 1800–1930 from the industry of origin approach are provided in Prados de la Escosura (1988).

2. It is worth mentioning Mulhall (1880, 1884, 1885, 1896) estimates of national income for a large number of countries, including Spain, in the late nineteenth century. The main contemporary attempts to derive levels of Spain's national income have been collected in Schwartz (1977). The literature on Italy, where detailed benchmark estimates have been constructed, provides a counterpoint (Rey 1991, 1992, 2000, 2002).
3. Unfortunately, the 1958 GDP benchmark is the earliest available in Spain. New, direct GDP estimates for benchmark years prior to 1958, e.g. 1910 or 1930, years for which population censuses are available, would be required to provide a rigorous check on GDP figures derived by projecting benchmarks backwards with quantity and price indices.
4. The reader should be aware that my own estimates suffered from this bias (see Section III). Actually, only a double deflation procedure for inputs and output would provide a correct alternative. By double deflation is meant independent deflation, with their own price indices, of final production and intermediate inputs, so real value added is obtained as a residual. Cf. Cassing (1996).
5. In order to reduce the downward bias for manufacturing, CEN (1945, 1965) overweighted electricity output.
6. Mining was allocated 22.68% of total industrial output; utilities (represented by electric energy), 20.96%; and manufacturing only 56.36%. If the size of the industrial sample (2077 million pesetas) is compared to Banco Urquijo's estimate of industrial output *circa* 1924, its coverage represents 25% of total industrial value added.
7. CEN (1945) used an arithmetic average of Banco Urquijo (1924) and Vandellòs (1925) estimates assuming that were independent from each other. Assessments of CEN (1945) income figures are provided by Guerreiro (1946), Hemberg (1955) and Fuentes Quintana (1958), all reprinted in Schwartz (1977). Hemberg (1955) pioneering computation of income using a production approach showed that there were enough statistical data to carry out a direct estimate of GDP from the supply side.
8. The purpose of CPD estimates was to provide statistical background for the econometric model used in simulations during the third 'plan de desarrollo', an instrument of *planification indicatif* in the early 1970s.
9. Fixed value-added weights from 1954 National Accounts were accepted.
10. National accounts are named after the benchmark year used for its construction. Thus, CNE58 is Contabilidad Nacional de España with 1958 as the base year.

11. The weights tried to reflect the relative importance of private consumption (70%) and the rest of the demand components of GDP (30%).
12. Alcaide carried out another revision of the historical accounts for the period 1901–1985 that did not challenge, however, his earlier findings for real product in the pre-national accounts period (Banco de Bilbao 1986). Nevertheless, nominal levels were revised upwards as the historical series were linked to more recent figures from Banco de Bilbao's own GDP estimates. Alcaide (2000) revised his estimates for the early twentieth century, starting in 1898, and spliced them with Fundación BBV's GDP estimates for 1955–1998 (also Alcaide's own work). Unfortunately, Alcaide neither discusses his methods nor substantiates his arguments with empirical evidence, while no sources are provided.
13. Weights were 0.4 for agriculture, 0.25 for industry and 0.35 for services. Since historical active population figures are only available at census years, either Alcaide interpolated census data or applied participation rates, derived at census intervals, to available yearly figures for total population. Alcaide claimed to having adjusted employment in services 'to accute changes in total production' (Alcaide 1976: 1129). As stressed by Tortella (1987), using employment as a proxy for output implies the assumption of stagnant labour productivity in services.
14. Alcaide's revision of CEN figures for 1940–1954 is also far from clear. He relies on a revision of CEN's real output carried out by Tamames without providing the reference. Moreover, while in the case of GDP only the wholesale price index seems to have been used, it appears that Alcaide reflated real national income with the cost of living and wholesale price indices weighted by the shares of consumption and investment in 1954 national accounts, respectively.
15. Naredo (1991) illustrated his argument by referring to the 26% increase in agricultural output in a single year (1951), following the abolishment of food rationing, which partially liberalized the domestic market.
16. The first independent attempt to derive national income estimates on an yearly basis was carried out by José Castañeda (1945) who provided an estimate of national expenditure from a sample of indirect taxes and government's monopoly revenues, deflated by a wholesale price index, for the period 1901–1934.
17. Each of the 26 groups of goods and services, defined according to the 1958 input–output table's (TIOE58) classification of economic

activities, was constructed as a Laspeyres volume index with 1958 weighting. In ICE estimates, the coverage of output was far superior to CEN's, with 227 and 45 basic series for industry and services. For agricultural output (excluding livestock, forestry and fishing, for which 21 basic new series were used), CEN revised index was adopted. Weights applied to agriculture, industry and services to derive the "general index of total production" were 0.2693, 0.3200 and 0.4107, respectively.

18. An indicator is, according to Balke and Gordon (1989), a time-series variable that is correlated with real product in the time period when real GDP is known, i.e. the post-1954 years.
19. The only precedent of Carreras' demand approach is CPD (1972), but it did not represent an independent estimate.
20. Some objections can be raised to the use of a 1958 benchmark as it comes from an autarchic period in which prices were intervened by government regulation and protection. This is a similar case to those of Italy's 1938 (Bardini et al. 1995:123) and Germany's 1937 (Broadberry, 1997) benchmarks. It can be argued, however, that the 1958 input–output table is not only the first one available but also the most detailed Spanish one (207 sectors) to date.
21. Food and clothing represent 70% of total consumption in the benchmark year 1958 (CNE58). However, the sample of consumption goods used in the construction of the annual index only reaches a coverage of 20% up to 1928, and 41% thereafter, as measured for the 1958 benchmark (Carreras 1985: 38–39, 45). Naredo (1991: 144) claimed that Carreras reliance on García Barbancho's (1960) food consumption data led him to use out-dated, downward biased agricultural output statistics.
22. Income elasticity of demand for housing, durables, personal care, transport, recreation, etc. was significantly higher than for food and clothing in 1958 Spain (Lluch, 1969: 68, 78).
23. Two other objections could also be raised to Carreras' pathbreaking contribution. Government consumption was deflated by a wholesale price index, and not by a consumer price index, a better suited deflator, as wages and salaries constituted its main component, since no comprehensive CPI was available at the time the paper was written. In addition, the trade balance only covers commodities. Carreras used

official values for exports and imports that exaggerate commodity trade deficit for most of the period up to 1913 (see Sect. 7.3).
24. Actually, my yearly estimates indicate a sharper decline between 1935 and 1938, at −11% per year, followed by a recovery up to 1944.

References

Alcaide Inchausti, J. 1976. Una revisión urgente de la serie de renta nacional en el siglo XX. In *Datos básicos para la historia financiera de España*, 2 vols., 1126–1150. Madrid: Instituto de Estudios Fiscales.

Alcaide Inchausti, J. 1986. Series históricas de las principales macromagnitudes en España. *Banco de Bilbao. Informe Económico Anual.* Madrid: Banco de Bilbao.

Alcaide Inchausti, J. 2000. La renta nacional de españa y su distribución. Serie años 1898 a 1998. In *1900–2000 Historia de un esfuerzo colectivo*, ed. J. Velarde Fuertes, 2 vols., 375–449. Madrid: Planeta.

Bairoch, P. 1976. Europe's Gross National Product: 1800–1975. *Journal of European Economic History V* 2: 273–340.

Balke, N.S., and R.J. Gordon. 1989. The Estimation of Prewar Gross National Product: Methodology and New Evidence". *Journal of Political Economy* 97: 38–92.

Bardini, C., A. Carreras, and P. Lains. 1995. The National Accounts for Italy, Spain and Portugal. *Scandinavian Economic History Review XLIII* 1: 115–146.

Beckerman, W., and R. Bacon. 1966. International Comparisons of Income Levels: A Suggested New Measure. *Economic Journal* LXXVI: 516–536.

Broadberry, S.N. 1997. Anglo-German Productivity Differences 1870–1990: A Sectoral Analysis. *European Review of Economic History* 1 (2): 247–267.

Carreras, A. 1985. Gasto nacional bruto y formación de capital en España, 1849–1958: primer ensayo de estimación. In *La Nueva Historia Económica en España*, ed. P. Martín Aceña, and L. Prados de la Escosura, 17–51. Madrid: Tecnos.

Cassing, S. 1996. Correctly Measuring Real Value Added. *Review of Income and Wealth* 42 (2): 195–206.

Castañeda, J. 1945. El consumo de tabaco en España y sus factores. *Revista de Economía Política*, I, 1: 195–292. Partially reprinted in P. Schwartz, ed.

1977. *El Producto Nacional de España en el siglo XX*, 209–215. Madrid: Instituto de Estudios Fiscales.

Comisaria del Plan de Desarrollo Economico y Social. 1972. *Series cronológicas del modelo econométrico*, vol. II. Madrid: Presidencia del Gobierno.

Consejo de Economia Nacional. 1945. *La Renta Nacional de España, 2 vols.* Madrid: C.E.N.

Consejo de Economia Nacional. 1965. *La Renta Nacional de España, 1906–1965.* Madrid: C.E.N.

Crafts, N.F.R. 1983. Gross National Product in Europe, 1870-1910: Some New Estimates. *Explorations in Economic History* 20 (4): 387–401.

Crafts, N.F.R. 1984. Patterns of Development in Nineteenth Century Europe. *Oxford Economic Papers, XXXVI* 4: 438–458.

Deane, P. 1957. Contemporary Estimates of National Income in the Second Half of the Nineteenth Century. *Economic History Review* IX: 451–461.

Fuentes Quintana, E. 1958. Las estimaciones de la renta nacional de España. In *La contabilidad nacional de España (Cuentas y cuadros de 1954)*, ed. M. De Torres, 13–48. Madrid: Instituto Sancho de Moncada. Reprinted in P. Schwartz (ed.). 1977. El. Producto Nacional de España en el siglo XXInstituto de Estudios Fiscales Madrid 369–422.

Garcia Barbancho, A. 1960. Análisis de la alimentación española. *Anales de Economía* 66: 72–119 and 67: 271–367.

Guerreiro, A. 1946. A propósito de 'La Renta Nacional en España'. *Moneda y Crédito* 17: 3–18. Reprinted in P. Schwartz,1977 *El Producto Nacional de España en el siglo XX* Instituto de Estudios Fiscales Madrid 233–263.

Hemberg, P. 1955. Informe preliminar sobre la renta interior de España. *Revista de Economía Política* VI (2): 114–171. Reprinted in P. Schwartz, ed. (1977), *El Producto Nacional de España en el siglo XX*, 265–341. Madrid: Instituto de Estudios Fiscales.

Informacion Comercial Española. 1962. Datos y reflexiones sobre el desarrollo de la economía española. *Información Comercial Española* 341: 39–97.

Lluch, C. 1969. Elasticidades de Engel y de precios para las grandes categorías de bienes de consumo en España. *Moneda y Crédito* 108: 47–94.

Maddison, A. 2010. *Statistics on world population, GDP and per capita GDP*, 1-2008 AD, Horizontal file. http://www.ggdc.net/maddison/.

Mulhall, M.G. 1880. *The Progress of the World in Arts, Agriculture, Commerce, Manufactures, Instruction, Railways, and Public Wealth since the Beginning of the Nineteenth Century*. London: Edward Stanford.

Mulhall, M.G. 1884, 1886, 1892, 1899. *Dictionary of Statistics.* London: Routledge and Sons.
Mulhall, M.G. 1885. *History of Prices since the Year 1850.* London: Longmans, Green, and Co.
Mulhall, M.G. 1896. *Industries and Wealth of Nations.* London: Longmans, Green, and Co.
Naredo, J.M. 1991. Crítica y revisión de las series históricas de renta nacional de la postguerra. *Información Comercial Español* 698: 132–152.
Prados de la Escosura, L. 1982. *Comercio exterior y crecimiento económico en España, 1826–1913: tendencias a largo plazo*, 7. Madrid: Banco de España, Estudios de Historia Económica no.
Prados de la Escosura, L. 1988. *De imperio a nación. Crecimiento y atraso económico en España (1780–1930).* Madrid: Alianza.
Rey, G.M. (ed.). 1991. *I conti economici dell'Italia. I. Una síntesis dell fonti ufficiali 1890–1970.* Roma-Bari: Laterza.
Rey, G.M. (ed.). 1992. *I conti economici dell'Italia. II. Una stima del valore aggiunto per il 1911.* Roma-Bari: Laterza.
Rey, G.M. (ed.). 2000. *I conti economici dell'Italia. III. Il valore aggiunto per gli anni 1891, 1938, 1951.* Roma-Bari: Laterza.
Rey, G.M. (ed.). 2002. *I conti economici dell'Italia. IV. Il conto risorce e impieghi 1891(1911), 1938, 1951.* Roma-Bari: Laterza.
Schwartz, P. 1976. El Producto Interior Bruto de España de 1940 a 1960. In *(1977), El Producto Nacional de España en el siglo XX*, ed. P. Schwartz, 443–592. Madrid: Instituto de Estudios Fiscales.
Schwartz, ed. 1977. *El Producto Nacional de España en el siglo XX*, 443–592. Madrid: Instituto de Estudios Fiscales.
Tortella, G. 1987. El sector terciario en España antes de 1936: una nota de escepticismo sobre las estimaciones al uso. *Revista de Historia Económica V* 2: 587–597.
Vandellós, J.A. 1925. La richesse et le revenu de la Péninsule Ibérique. *Metron V* 4: 151–186.
Urquijo, Banco. 1924. *El progreso y la riqueza de España.* Madrid: Imprenta de Samarán y Compañía.

Open Access This chapter is licensed under the terms of the Creative Commons Attribution 4.0 International License (http://creativecommons.org/licenses/by/4.0/), which permits use, sharing, adaptation, distribution and reproduction in any medium or format, as long as you give appropriate credit to the original author(s) and the source, provide a link to the Creative Commons license and indicate if changes were made.

The images or other third party material in this chapter are included in the chapter's Creative Commons license, unless indicated otherwise in a credit line to the material. If material is not included in the chapter's Creative Commons license and your intended use is not permitted by statutory regulation or exceeds the permitted use, you will need to obtain permission directly from the copyright holder.

9

Splicing National Accounts, 1958–2015

National accounts rely on complete information on quantities and prices to compute GDP for a single benchmark year, which is, then, extrapolated forward on the basis of limited information for a sample of goods and services. To allow for changes in relative prices and, thus, to avoid that forward projections of the current benchmark become unrepresentative, national accountants periodically replace the current benchmark with a new and closer GDP benchmark. The new benchmark is constructed, in part, with different sources and computation methods.[1]

9.1 National Accounts in Spain

In Spain's national accounts, benchmarks for 1958 (CNE58) and 1964 (CNE64) were derived using OECD criteria, while the United Nations System of National Accounts (SNA) was used for all the rest (CNE70, CNE80, CNE86, CNE95, CNE00, CNE08, CNE10) (Table 9.1).[2] Detailed sets of quantities and prices (derived from the closest input-output table) were employed to compute GDP at the benchmark year (1958, 1964, 1970, 1980, 1986, 1995, 2000, 2008, 2010).[3]

Table 9.1 Spain's national accounts, 1954–2015

	Benchmark year	Coverage
CNE58	1958	1954–1964
CNE64	1964	1964–1972
CNE70	1970	1964–1982
CNE80	1980	1970–1985
CNE86	1985/86	1964–1997
CNE95	1995	1995–2004
CNE00	2000	1995–2009
CNE08	2008	1995–2013
CNE10	2010	1995–2015

Note Direct estimates only refer to years after the benchmark. *Sources* IEF (1969), INE (various years)

Differences in a new benchmark year between 'new' and 'old' national accounts stem from statistical (sources and estimation procedures) and conceptual (definitions and classifications) bases. Once a new benchmark has been introduced, newly available statistical evidence would not be taken on board to avoid a discontinuity in the existing series (Uriel 1986: 69) so the coverage of new economic activities may explain the discrepancy between the new and old series. Furthermore, discrepancies between 'new' and 'old' benchmarks for the year in which they overlap also stem from statistical (sources and estimation procedures) and conceptual (definitions and classifications) differences. As a result, the consistency between the new and old national account series breaks.

The obvious solution to this inconsistency problem would be *recompilation*, that is, computing GDP for the years covered by the old benchmark with the same sources and procedures employed in the construction of the new benchmark. However, national accountants do not follow such a painstaking option.

A simple solution, widely used by national accountants (and implicitly accepted in international comparisons), is the *retropolation* approach, in which the new series (Y^R) results from accepting the reference *level* provided by the most recent benchmark estimate (Y_T) and, then, re-scaling the earlier benchmark series (X_t) with the ratio between the new and the old series for the year (T) at which the two series overlap (Y_T/X_T).

$$Y_t^R = (Y_T/X_T) * X_t \quad \text{for} \quad 0 \leq t \leq T \tag{9.1}$$

For example, in order to obtain CNE70 estimates for 1964–1969, Spanish national accountants projected backwards (*retropolated*) the new 1970 GDP level (CNE70) with the rates of variation derived from the old benchmark series (CNE64). The *retropolation* approach was also adopted to derive series levels for the years 1964–1979 in both the 1980 and the 1986 benchmarks (CNE80 and CNE86).[4]

The choice of the *retropolation* procedure was made on the arguable assumption that growth rates originally calculated could not be improved (Corrales and Taguas 1991). Underlying this approach is the implicit assumption of an error level in the old benchmark's series whose relative size is constant over time. In other words, no error is assumed to exist in the old series' rates of variation that are, hence, retained in the spliced series Y_t^R (de la Fuente 2014). Official national accountants have favoured this procedure of linking national accounts series on the grounds that it preserves the earlier benchmark's rates of variation.[5] The *retropolation* approach pays no regard to the unpredictable but significant effects of using a set of relative prices from the old benchmark to project the level of the new benchmark backwards.

The main methodological discontinuity in Spanish national accounts occurred when the SNA substituted for the OECD method in the late 1970s. Table 9.2 provides the values of each benchmark series at base years and the ratio between each pair of adjacent 'new' and 'old' benchmark values. Substantial discrepancies are noticeable between CNE64 (constructed with OECD criteria) and CNE70 (derived with SNA criteria), benchmarks within a period of fast growth and deep structural change (Prados de la Escosura 2007).

It is worth noting that the most recent benchmark usually provides a higher GDP level for the overlapping year, as its coverage of economic activities is wider. Thus, the backward projection of the new benchmark GDP level with the available *growth rates*—computed at the previous benchmark's relative prices—implies a systematic upward revision of GDP *levels* for earlier years.[6] The evidence in Table 9.2 highlights the

172 L. Prados de la Escosura

Table 9.2 GDP at market prices: alternative estimates (Million Euro at current prices)

	[I]	[II]	[III]	[IV]	[V]	[VI]	[VII]	[VIII]	[IX]	[X]	[XI]	[XII]	[XIII]	[XIV]	[XV]
	CNE10	CNE08	CNE00	CNE95	CNE86	CNE80	CNE70	CNE64	[(I)/(II)]	[(II)/(III)]	[(III)/(IV)]	[(IV)/(V)]	[(V)/(VI)]	[(VI)/(VII)]	[(VII)/(VIII)]
1964					7265	7360	7225	**6543**					0.9871	1.0187	1.1042
1970					15806	15772	**15483**	13607					1.0021	1.0187	**1.1379**
1980					91161	**91409**	91264						0.9973	**1.0016**	
1986				175625	**194271**	192009						0.9040	**1.0118**		
1995	459337	446795	447205	**437787**	419387	413788			1.0281	0.9991	1.0215	**1.0439**	1.0135		
2000	646250	629907	**630263**	610541					1.0259	0.9994	**1.0323**				
2008	1116207	**1087788**	1088124						1.0261	**0.9997**					
2010	**1080913**	1045620							**1.0338**						

Sources IEF (1969), INE (various years)

impact of successive one-side upward revisions, which widens the gap over time. In fact, the GDP figure obtained by the cumulative re-scaling different national accounts subseries from 2010 backwards (that is, using the *retropolation* approach) is 28.4% higher for 1970 than the one computed by CNE64 (and 24.6% higher than the one directly calculated for 1964).[7]

Would it be reasonable to expect such an underestimate from a direct GDP calculation on the basis of 'complete' information about quantities and prices of the goods and services in the old benchmark? Can the direct measurement of GDP level at an early benchmark year be really improved through the backward projection of the latest benchmark year with earlier benchmarks' annual rates of variation?

The challenge is to establish the extent to which conceptual and technical innovations in the new benchmark series hint at a measurement error in the old benchmark series. In particular, whether the discrepancy in the overlapping year between the new benchmark (in which GDP is estimated with 'complete' information) and the old benchmark series (in which reduced information on quantities and prices is used to project forward the 'complete' information estimate from its initial year) results from a measurement error in the old benchmark's *initial* year estimate, or it is the cumulative result of the emergence of new goods and services not considered in the old benchmark series.

An alternative to the *retropolation* method is provided by the *interpolation* procedure that accepts the levels computed directly for each benchmark year as the *best* possible estimates—on the grounds that they have been obtained with 'complete' information on quantities and prices—and distributes the gap or difference between the 'new' and 'old' benchmark series in the overlapping year T at a constant rate over the time span in between the old and new benchmark years.[8]

$$Y_t^I = Y_t * \left[(Y_T/X_T)^{1/n}\right]^t \quad \text{for } 0 \leq t \leq T \qquad (9.2)$$

Being Y^I the linearly *interpolated* new series, Y e X the values pertaining to GDP according to the new and old benchmarks, respectively; t, the year considered; T, the overlapping year between the old and new benchmarks' series; and n, the number of years in between the old (0) and the new benchmark (T) dates.[9]

Contrary to the *retropolation* approach, the *interpolation* procedure assumes that the error is generated between the years 0 and T. Consequently, it modifies the annual rate of variation between benchmarks (usually upwards) while keeps unaltered the initial level that of the old benchmark. As a result, the initial level will be probably lower than the one derived from the *retropolation* approach.

In Spanish national accounts, a break in the linkage of GDP series through *retropolation* was introduced in CNE86, when national accounts were spliced using the *interpolation* approach and the GDP differential between CEN86 and CEN80 in 1985 was distributed at a constant rate over the years 1981–1984 (expression 16) (INE 1992). However, a new national accounts benchmark in 1995 (CNE95) did not bring along a splicing of CNE95 and CNE86 series.[10] In later benchmarks (CNE00, CNE08 and CNE10), the *interpolation* method was resumed, but only after adjusting upwards the old benchmark for methodological changes.[11] Thus, the gap between, say, CNE10 and CNE00-08, in the year 2010, was decomposed into methodological and statistical plus other differences.[12] Firstly, CNE00-08 series for 1995–2009 were adjusted upwards for methodological discrepancies with CNE10. Then, the *residual* gap, due to statistical and other differences, was distributed at a constant rate (using expression 16) over the in-between benchmark years, 2001–2009.[13] As a result, no officially spliced GDP series are available at the present for the entire national accounts era.

9.2 Splicing National Accounts Through Interpolation

A straightforward procedure would be, then, splicing the all benchmark series available by accepting the levels directly computed for each benchmark year and distributing the gap between each pair of adjacent benchmark series at their overlapping year at either a constant rate over the time span between them. This solution has the advantage of being transparent and linking different benchmarks equally.

Nonetheless, before computing and comparing alternative splicing results, pre-1980 national accounts need to be examined because, as mentioned earlier, it is during the transition between OECD and SNA methodologies when larger disparities between adjacent benchmarks series emerged in overlapping years. By examining the way OECD (CNE64) and SNA (CNE70) benchmarks were constructed, an attempt to reconcile their differences can be made.

In pre-1980 official national accounts, annual nominal series of, say, industrial value added were usually obtained through back and forth extrapolation of the benchmark year's gross value added with an index of industrial production that was, then, reflated with a price index for industrial goods. Projecting industrial real value added with an index of industrial production amounts to a single deflation of value added, in which the same price index is used for both output and inputs.[14] However, only if prices for output and intermediate inputs evolve in the same direction and with the same intensity, real value added is accurately represented by an industrial production index. In periods of rapid technological change (or external input price shocks), significant savings of intermediate inputs do take place while relative prices change dramatically, and, hence, the assumption of a parallel evolution of output and input prices does not hold.[15] This description applies well to Spain in the 1960s and 1970s, when the country opened up to foreign technology and competition and suffered the oil shocks.[16] Fortunately, alternative estimates of gross value added at constant prices derived through the Laspeyres double deflation method[17] are available for industry and construction over the years 1964–1980 (Gandoy 1988).[18] Gandoy's value added series exhibit higher real growth rates than CEN70 series since her implicit value added deflator grows less than the national accounts' deflator (biased towards raw materials and semi-manufactures).[19] This is what should be expected in a context of total factor productivity growth, such as was the case of Spain in the 1960s and early 1970s, with output prices growing less than inputs prices, as inputs savings resulted from efficiency gains (Prados de la Escosura 2009).[20]

Thus, CEN70 series for GDP have been revised for 1964–1980. Firstly, Gandoy Juste (1988) alternative value added estimates for industry and construction (GVA_i^G and GVA_c^G) were substituted for those in official national accounts (GVA_i^{cen70} and GVA_c^{cen70}).[21] CNE70 value added figures for agriculture (GVA_a^{cen70}) and services (GVA_s^{cen70}) were kept.[22] Total gross value added was reached by adding up sectors' gross value added.

$$GVA^T = GVA_a^{cen70} + GVA_i^G + GVA_c^G + GVA_s^{cen70} \quad (9.3)$$

GDP at market prices was derived, in turn, by adding taxes on products net of subsidies to total gross value added.

CEN70 GDP estimates on the expenditure side were also adjusted. While Gandoy (1988) provides alternative value added series at factor cost for industry (VA_{fci}^G) and construction (VA_{fcc}^G), Gómez Villegas (1988) presents new series for fixed domestic capital formation in industry (GCF_i^G) and construction (GCF_c^G). Thus, in order to adjust the aggregate figure for investment in CNE70 (GCF^{cen70}), I firstly computed the share of value added at market prices (VA_{mp}) allocated to investment in industry and construction, according to Gandoy (1988) and Gómez Villegas (1988), (GCF_i^G/VA_{mpi}^G and GCF_c^G/VA_{mpc}^G), which implied adjusting value added to include taxes on production and imports net of subsidies.[23] Then, I applied this share to the difference between the value added estimates at factor cost in Gandoy's (VA_{fci}^G and VA_{fcc}^G) and in CEN70 (VA_{fci}^{cen70} and VA_{fcc}^{cen70}).

$$GCF_i^{add} = \left(GCF_i^G/VA_{mpi}^G\right) * \left(VA_{fci}^G - VA_{fci}^{cen70}\right) \quad (9.4)$$

$$GCF_c^{add} = \left(GCF_c^G/VA_{mpc}^G\right) * \left(VA_{fcc}^G - VA_{fcc}^{cen70}\right) \quad (9.5)$$

So the additional investment—that is, the portion of gross capital formation not included in CNE70—was obtained. Thus,

$$GCF^{add} = GCF_i^{add} + GCF_c^{add} \quad (9.6)$$

And the revised figure for gross capital formation was derived as,

$$GCF^{1970R} = GCF^{cen70} + GCF^{add} \quad (9.7)$$

Then, I adjusted private consumption figures in CEN70 for the changes introduced in gross capital formation. That is, I assumed that the additional value added in industry and construction (derived by deducting CNE70 value added from Gandoy's estimates) *less* the additional investment (GCF^{add}) accrued to private consumption, since the values for net exports of goods and services (NX^{cen70}) and public consumption ($GOVT^{cen70}$) provided by CEN70 were obtained from a sound statistical basis.[24] That is,

$$CONS^{add} = \left(\left(VA^{G}_{fci} + VA^{G}_{fcc}\right) - \left(VA^{cen70}_{fci} + VA^{cen70}_{fcc}\right)\right) - GCF^{add} \quad (9.8)$$

And the revised figure for total private consumption was reached as,

$$CONS^{1970R} = CONS^{cen70} + CONS^{add} \quad (9.9)$$

Lastly, the new estimates of GDP at market prices were obtained as,

$$GDP^{1970R}_{mp} = CONS^{1970R} + GCF^{1970R} + GOVT^{cen70} + NX^{cen70} \quad (10.1)$$

How are interpolated, then, earlier, pre-1980, national account benchmark series? CNE70^R series have been accepted for the years 1964–1969, rather than distributing the difference in 1970 between CNE70^R and CNE64 over these years. The reason of this choice is that CNE70^R series have been mainly derived through double deflation, as opposed to CNE64 single deflation series. CNE70^R and CNE58 series were, in turn, interpolated by distributing their gap in 1964 over 1959–1963.[25] Lastly, in order to I derived a single series for GDP and its components for the pre- and post-1980 series, I distributed their gap in the overlapping year, 1980, over 1971–1979. Aggregated GDP figures result from adding up its previously spliced components.[26]

This strict *interpolation* procedure has, nonetheless, the shortcoming of deviating from official national accounts series for the years 1995–2009. The reason is that, as observed above, in post-2000 Spanish national accounts its splicing is performed in two stages: firstly, the old benchmark series are adjusted upwards for methodological changes in the new benchmark; and, then, the remaining statistical gap is distributed at a constant rate over the years between the new and the old benchmarks.

Thus, an alternative to deriving GDP series through strict *interpolation* appears, namely accepting the official *interpolation* linkage for 1995–2010 and interpolating the different benchmark (CNE58 to CNE95) series for the previous years, 1958–1995.[27]

It is worth noting, however, that, in CNE10 series, the GDP level for 1995 is higher (4.9%) than the one originally computed with complete information in CNE95 (Table 9.3). What share of this gap is attributable to methodological differences? The CNE10 linkage procedure consisted in adjusting the CNE00 series for methodological differences back to 1995 and, then, distributing the remaining, mostly statistical, gap over 2001–2009, under the assumption that no statistical error exists in 2000. Thus, the entire discrepancy in 1995 between CNE10 and CNE95 could be attributable to methodological differences.[28] Should pre-1995 series, resulting from splicing all previous benchmarks (CNE58–CNE95), be raised, then, by a fixed ratio (1.0492)? This option does not seem reasonable, as it can be conjectured that the impact of methodological changes would be larger the closer the year's estimate to CNE10 benchmark year, 2010. A compromise solution would be to distribute the entire gap over the 1954–1994 series. Therefore, I have

Table 9.3 Real GDP Growth: Alternative Splicing, 1958–2010 (annual average rates %)

	Hybrid linear interpolation	Retropolation
1958–1964	5.9	6.2
1964–1970	6.4	6.2
1970–1980	4.9	3.7
1980–1986	1.9	1.5
1986–1995	3.7	3.2
1995–2000	4.1	4.0
2000–2010	2.2	2.2

Fig. 9.1 Ratio between hybrid linearly interpolated and retropolated nominal GDP series, 1958–2000. *Sources* See the text

spliced the pre- and post-1995 series through a 'hybrid' *interpolation*, with an adjustment for methodological differences as described above.

Figure 9.1 presents the ratio between the figures for nominal GDP obtained by splicing national accounts through 'hybrid' linear *interpolation* and those derived through *extrapolation*. It can be observed how the over-exaggeration of GDP levels derived through *retropolation* cumulates as one goes back in time, reaching around one-fifth by the late 1950s.

Once GDP series at current prices were obtained, the next task was to deflate them in order to obtain GDP volume indices. Deflators for each CNE benchmark GDP series were also spliced through 'hybrid' linear *interpolation* as well as through *retropolation*. Interestingly, deflators derived through alternative splicing methods do not exhibit the far from negligible differences observed for current values.

Figure 9.2 presents the evolution of GDP at constant prices, expressed in log form, using alternatively the interpolated and retropolated series over 1958–2000. It can be observed that their differential widens

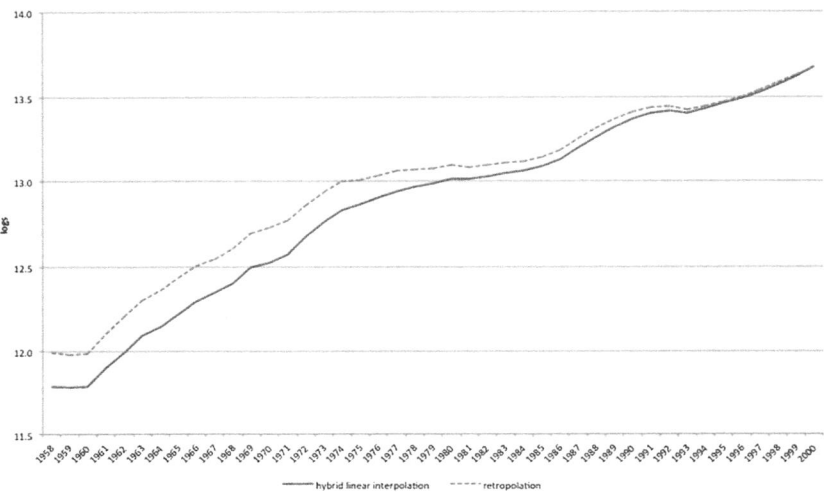

Fig. 9.2 Real GDP, 1958–2000 (2010 Euro) (logs): alternative estimates with hybrid linear interpolation and retropolation splicing (logs). *Sources* see the text

significantly over time suggesting lower levels and faster growth for GDP estimates derived through interpolation.[29]

Table 9.3 compares the resulting GDP growth rates between National Accounts benchmark years derived by splicing national accounts alternatively with 'hybrid' linear interpolation and retropolation approaches. GDP estimates derived through the interpolation procedure cast higher growth rates over the entire time span considered than those estimates resulting from the conventional retropolation method. The annual cumulative rate per person over 1958–2000 is 4.5% compared to a 4.0% for the retropolated series, respectively. The main discrepancies correspond to period 1970–1995, and particularly during the 1970s, in which the interpolated series exhibit a more than one-third faster growth rate. The implication is that, in the period of rapid expansion 1958–1974, Spain's delayed Golden Age, and, again, between Spain's accession to the European Union (1985) and the eve of the Great Recession (2007), the interpolated series grew faster that the retropolated ones. However, it is during the so-called transition to democracy period (1974–1984), when the positive growth differential between the interpolated and the retropolated series reached its peak (2.3 and 1.3%, respectively). As a result, the deceleration following the exceptional growth of Spain's delayed Golden Age was less dramatic than suggested by conventional narrative. It is worth comparing the results to another alternative to the retropolation procedure provided by the 'mixed splicing', in which Ángel de la Fuente (2014, 2016) proposes an intermediate position in which an initial error in the old series, stemming from the insufficient coverage of emerging economic sectors, grows at an increasing rate. Unfortunately, the correction to the growth rate of the original series implies an arbitrary assumption about its size (see the discussion in Prados de la Escosura 2016).

Since de la Fuente (2016) favours Gross Value Added (GVA, equivalent to GDP at basic prices), the comparison is carried out in terms of real GVA (Fig. 9.3). It can be observed that the results from 'mixed splicing' are not far apart from those I obtained through hybrid linear interpolation. Discrepancies only appear in the pre-1980 period for which de la Fuente (2016) linked his series to Uriel et al. (2000) GDP series spliced through retropolation.

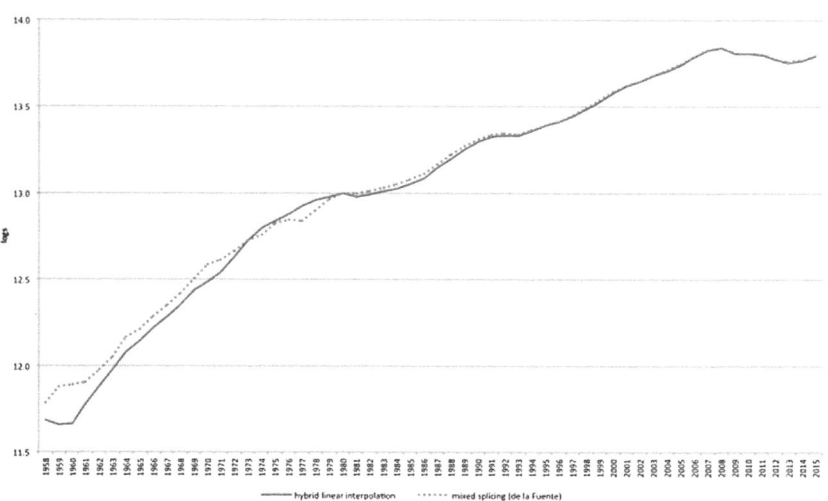

Fig. 9.3 Real gross value added, 1958–2015 (2010 Euro) (logs): alternative estimates with hybrid linear interpolation and mixed splicing, 1958–2015. *Sources* Hybrid linear interpolation, see the text; Mixed splicing, de la Fuente (2016)

Notes

1. Improving the comprehensiveness, reliability and comparability of national accounts estimates through the use of new statistical sources, the inclusion of new concepts and the adoption of new computation procedures, often due to the adoption of new or updated international standards, are the technical reasons provided by national statistical offices for their periodical revisions of national accounts' benchmarks and the resulting breaks in GDP time series.
2. At the turn of the century, the European System of Accounts (ESA) replaced the SNA, being SNA93 and ESA95 fully consistent. Series constructed with different benchmarks' prices and quantities are named after the year, e.g. CNE70, that is, *Contabilidad Nacional de España* (National Accounts of Spain) with 1970 as the base year.
3. For all these benchmark years, input-output tables are available, except for 1964 and 1986, for which the closest ones are those for 1962 and 1966, and 1985, respectively.
4. Such is the approach implicitly supported by Uriel (1986) and Uriel et al. (2000). This procedure has the advantage of being less time consuming and not altering the yearly rates of variation resulting from the 'old' benchmark series.
5. For the case of Spain, cf. Uriel (1986), Corrales and Taguas (1991), INE (1992), Uriel et al. (2000). In the Netherlands, a pioneer country in national accounts, it was only after the 1993 SNA classification that the *retropolation* method was challenged (den Bakker and van Rooijen 1999).
6. This linkage procedure helps to understand the one-sided upward revisions Boskin (2000) finds in US national accounts.
7. This percentage increase for 1970 results from successively multiplying the ratios of adjacent benchmarks at overlapping years, that is, CNE10/CNE08 in 2010, CNE08/CNE00 in 2008, CNE00/CNE95 in 2000, CNE95/CNE86 in 1995, CNE85/CNE80 in 1985, CNE80/CNE70, in 1980, and CNE70/CNE64 in 1970, [1.0338 * 0.9997 * 1.0323 * 1.0439 * 1.0118 * 1.0016 * 1.1378 = 1.2841]. If alternatively, CNE10/CNE00 in 2010 is used, the results alter slightly [1.0254 * 1.0323 * 1.0439 * 1.0118 * 1.0016 * 1.1378 = 1.2741] (see Table 9.2).

8. Maddison (1991) presented the first methodological discussion along these lines and spliced GDP series through *interpolation* for the case of Italy.
9. An alternative to the linear interpolation is a nonlinear one, in which the gap between the new and old series at the overlapping year is distributed over the old series at a growing, rather than at a constant, rate. However, there are hardly any significant discrepancies between the linearly and nonlinearly interpolated series (Prados de la Escosura 2016). Therefore, in order to keep consistency with the official national accounts from 1995 onwards and facilitate updating insuccesive years, I have chosen to use the linear interpolation.
10. The National Statistical institute (INE) never produced a new spliced series of the latest base-year CNE00 back to 1964, 1970, or 1980. The Quarterly National Accounts provided spliced series from 1980 onwards but without a detailed explanation of the splicing procedure.
11. No mention of any methodological adjustment was made in the splicing through interpolation of CNE80 and CNE86.
12. It should be noted that since there were minor methodological and statistical changes between CNE00 and CNE08, the major revision embodied in CNE10 led to a new interpolation between CNE00–CNE08 and CNE10 that was extended over the years 1995–2009.
13. The same procedure was applied to the gap between CNE00 and CNE95 in 2000, and CNE08 and CNE00 in 2008, with the statistical gap distributed over the intermediate years 1996–1999, and 2001–2007, respectively. The Spanish Statistical Institute notes, 'The [remaining] differences between both estimates [CNE00 and CNE95 in the year 2000] are due to the statistical changes, and given that information is not available regarding how and at what time they have been generated, it is assumed that this has occurred progressively over time, from the beginning of the previous base' (INE 2007: 5).
14. Cf. Cassing (1996) for a discussion of alternative deflation procedures. See, alternatively, David (1962) and Fenoaltea (1976) for a defence of single deflation as a way of avoiding negative values of real value added.
15. In the dual approach to computing total factor productivity (TFP), over time changes in TFP are measured as the differential between the rate of variation of the output price and that of weighted input prices. In other words, a faster decline (less marked increase) of output prices than of inputs prices, due to input savings, reflects TFP growth.

16. The 1950s, especially since 1953, were years of rapid growth and structural change in which double deflation would make a difference over single deflation. Unfortunately, lack of data prevents this option.
17. By double deflation is meant that real gross value added is obtained as the difference between output at constant prices and intermediate consumption at constant prices, that is, each of them independently deflated with their own price indices. For a theoretical discussion of double deflation, cf. David (1962), Sims (1969), Arrow (1974) and Hansen (1975).
18. Cf. also Gandoy and Gómez Villegas (1988). Occasionally, when strong discrepancies between output and inputs prices were observed, and data availability allowed it, CNE70 used double deflation but, in any case, never over the years 1978–1981. In the case of agriculture, real value added was properly assessed in CNE70, as the purchases of industrial and service inputs represented a small share of final output. As for services, the difficulties to produce double-deflated value added series, comparable to those for agriculture and manufacturing, persisted over time.
19. Cf. Krantz (1994).
20. Although, fortunately, from 1980 onwards, CNE80 provided industrial value added computed through the standard double deflation procedure, double-deflated value added figures for construction and services were still problematic. Cf. INE (1986) for a discussion of CNE80.
21. Also van Ark (1995) chose Gandoy (1988) series over the original national accounts. Among van Ark's reasons are the downward bias in the growth rates of industrial production indices and its failure to adjust to the emergence of new products and quality changes.
22. For the reasons to keeping original CNE70 gross value added for agriculture and services, see Chap. 11, note 2. For a discussion of the problems in measuring services' gross value added through double deflation, see Mohr (1992).
23. In practical terms, the adjusted was carried out with the ratio between GDP at market prices and factor cost.
24. Actually, $CONS^{add}$ equals the differential between the revised GDP estimates (GDP^r_{mp}) and CNE70 GDP (GDP^{cen70}_{mp}) plus the estimated additional investment (GCF^{add}).
25. There is no discrepancy between CNE58 and CNE64 estimates at their overlapping year, 1964. It is worth noting that in absence of double

deflation in CNE58, splicing through interpolation provides a correction of its series that somehow amounts to an allowance for efficiency gains.
26. It is worth mentioning that the resulting discrepancies between obtaining GDP through aggregation of its spliced components and splicing GDP directly are negligible. Thus, additive congruence has not been imposed. By additive congruence is meant that the addition of the different components of a given magnitude (output or expenditure) must be equal to its aggregate value (GDP). This is obtained by distributing, proportionally to their relative weight, the deviations of the addition of the linked components' values from the aggregate magnitude (Cf. Corrales and Taguas 1991). This is implicitly done, however, for each of the subcomponents of GDP components.
27. As mentioned above, for the years 1980–1986, CNE86 provides spliced series derived from interpolating CNE86 and CNE80.
28. Unfortunately, national accounts explanatory notes do not address this issue.
29. The following discussion applies to all estimates derived through the retropolation approach, including Uriel et al. (2000) and Maluquer de Motes (2008, 2016), who erroneously uses the CPI as an alternative to the GDP implicit deflator. See my discussion of Maluquer de Motes estimates (Prados de la Escosura 2009).

References

Ark, B. van 1995. Producción y productividad en el sector manufacturero español. Un análisis comparativo 1950–1992. *Información Comercial Española* 746: 67–77.

Arrow, K.J. 1974. The Measurement of Real Value Added. In *Nations and Households in Economic Growth. Essays in Honor of Moses Abramovitz*, eds. P. A. David and M.W. Reder, 3–19. New York: Academic Press.

Boskin, M.J. 2000. Economic Measurement: Progress and Challenges. *American Economic Review, Papers and Proceedings* 90 (2): 247–252.

Cassing, S. 1996. Correctly Measuring Real Value Added. *Review of Income and Wealth* 42 (2): 195–206.

Corrales, A., & D. Taguas. 1991. Series macroeconómicas para el período 1954–1988: un intento de homogeneización. In *La economía española*, eds.

C. Molinas, M. Sebastián, and A. Zabalza. Una perspectiva macroeconómica, Barcelona/MadridAntoni Bosch/Instituto de Estudios Fiscales, 583–646.

David, P.A. 1962. The Deflation of Value Added. *Review of Economics and Statistics XLIV* 3: 148–155.

de la Fuente, A. 2014. A Mixed Splicing Procedure for Economic Time Series. *Estadística Española* 56 (183): 107–121.

de la Fuente, A. 2016. Series enlazadas de PIB y otros agregados de ContabilidadNacional para España, 1955–2014 (RegDat_Nac versión 4.2), BBVA Research, Documentos de Trabajo 16-01 (and electronic appendix).

den Bakker, G., & R. van Rooijen. (1999). Backward Calculation of Dutch National Accounting Data Lessons from the Past: Towards a New Approach. *OECD Meeting of National Accounts Experts.* OECD: Paris STD/NA(99)39.

Fenoaltea, S. 1976. Real Value Added and the Measurement of Industrial Production. *Annals of Economic and Social Measurement* 5 (1): 113–139.

Gandoy Juste, R. 1988. Evolución de la productividad global en la industria española. Un análisis desagregado para el período 1964–1981. Unpublished PhD dissertation, Universidad Complutense de Madrid.

Gandoy, R., & J. Gómez Villegas. 1988. Evolución y modificaciones en la estructura de la industria española, Secretaría General Técnica del Mº de Industria, Comercio y Turismo, Documentos e Informes 21/88.

Hansen, B. 1975. Double Deflation and the Value Added Product: Comment. *Review of Economics and Statistics LVIII* 3: 382–383.

Instituto Nacional de Estadística [INE]. 1992. *Contabilidad Nacional de España. Serie enlazada 1964–1991. Base 1986.* Madrid: INE.

Krantz, O. 1994. Service Production in Historical National Accounts. *Review of Income and Wealth* 40 (1): 19–41.

Maddison, A. 1991. A Revised Estimate of Italian Economic Growth 1861–1989. *Banca Nazionale del Lavoro Quarterly Review* 177: 225–241.

Maluquer de Motes, J. 2008. Del caos al cosmos: Una nueva serie enlazada del Producto Interior Bruto de España entre 1850 y 2000. *Revista de Economía Aplicada* 17 (49): 5–45.

Maluquer de Motes, J. 2016. *España en la economía mundial. Series largas para la economía española (1850–2015).* Madrid: Instituto de Estudios Económicos.

Mohr, M.F. 1992. Recent and Planned Improvements in the Measurement and Deflation of Services Outputs and Inputs in BEA's Gross Product Originating Estimates. In *Output Measurement in the Services Sector*, ed. Z. Griliches, 25–68. Chicago: NBER/University of Chicago Press.

Prados de la Escosura, L. 2007. Growth and Structural Change in Spain, 1850–2000: A European Perspective. *Revista de Historia Económica/Journal of Iberian and Latin American Economic History* 25 (1): 147–181.

Prados de la Escosura, L. 2009. Del cosmos al caos: la serie del PIB de Maluquer de Motes. *Revista de Economía Aplicada* 17 (51): 5–23.

Prados de la Escosura, L. 2016. Mismeasuring Long Run Growth. The Bias from Spliced National Accounts: The Case of Spain. *Cliometrica* 10 (3): 251–275.

Sims, C.A. 1969. Theoretical Basis of a Double Deflated Index of Real Value Added. *Review of Economics and Statistics, LI* 4: 470–471.

Uriel, E. 1986. *Enlace entre los sistemas de contabilidad nacional CNE-58 y CNE-70*, 47. Madrid: Instituto de Estudios Fiscales, monografía no.

Uriel, E., M.L. Moltó and V. Cucarella. 2000. *Contabilidad Nacional de España. Series enlazadas 1954–1997 (CNEe-86)*. Madrid: Fundación BBV.

Open Access This chapter is licensed under the terms of the Creative Commons Attribution 4.0 International License (http://creativecommons.org/licenses/by/4.0/), which permits use, sharing, adaptation, distribution and reproduction in any medium or format, as long as you give appropriate credit to the original author(s) and the source, provide a link to the Creative Commons license and indicate if changes were made.

The images or other third party material in this chapter are included in the chapter's Creative Commons license, unless indicated otherwise in a credit line to the material. If material is not included in the chapter's Creative Commons license and your intended use is not permitted by statutory regulation or exceeds the permitted use, you will need to obtain permission directly from the copyright holder.

10

Population, 1850–2015

Spain's Statistical Office (Instituto Nacional de Estadística, INE) provides yearly series of 'resident' population from 1971. INE also presents annual series of 'de facto' population for 1900–1991, in which figures for census benchmark years are linearly interpolated. Roser Nicolau (2005) collected and completed the series back to 1858. More recently, Jordi Maluquer de Motes (2008) has constructed yearly estimates of 'de facto' population for 1850–1991 and spliced them with 'resident' population for 2001. In order to do so, Maluquer de Motes started from census figures at the beginning of each census year adding up annually the natural increase in population (that is, births less deaths) plus net migration (namely immigrants less emigrants). I have followed Maluquer de Motes's approach with some modifications. Thus, I have accepted census benchmark years' figures and Gustav Sündbarg (1908) estimate for 1850 and obtained the natural increase in population with Nicolau (2005) figures for births and deaths from 1858 onwards, completed for 1850–1857 with Sündbarg (1908) net estimates at decadal averages equally distributed.[1] My main departure from Maluquer de Motes approach has been with regards to net migration for which I have accepted Blanca Sánchez-Alonso (1995) estimates for 1882–1930, completed back to 1850 and forth to 1935 with statistical evidence from Spanish and main destination countries' sources (see Sect. 7.3.4). For the years of the Civil War (1936–1939) and its aftermath (1940–1944), I have accepted José Antonio Ortega and Javier Silvestre (2006) gross emigration estimates for 1936–1939, assuming no immigration during the war years, and distributing evenly an upward revision of their return migration estimates for 1940–1944, while assuming no gross emigration during World War II.[2] In order to obtain a consistent series for 1850–1970, I have spliced population estimates linearly by distributing the difference between the estimated population obtained by forward projection of the initial census benchmark figure for the year of the next census benchmark and the observed figure at the new census using expression (16). Lastly, I have linked the linearly interpolated series for 'de facto' population for 1850–1970 with the 'resident' population series from 1971 onwards to get a single series.[3] Fortunately, the difference between the 'de facto' and 'resident' series over 1971–1991 is negligible.[4]

Notes

1. Sündbarg (1908) estimates are reproduced in Maluquer de Motes (2008: 145). I have used the average birth and death rates in 1858–1860 for the years 1850–1857, except in the case of 1855–1856 for which the death rate (45 per 1000) estimated for 1855 as a consequence of cholera epidemics by Pérez Moreda (1980: 398) has been used. I have also used the average of birth and death rates in 1870 and 1878–1880 for the years 1871–1877 in which data on total births and deaths are missing.
2. Ortega and Silvestre (2006) consider the 162,000 net migration figure during 1940–1944 grossly underestimated. Pérez Moreda (1988: 418) reckoned a maximum permanent exile of no more than 190,000 people, a figure below the 200,000 provided by Tusell (1999) and much lower than a post-Civil War exile estimate (300,000) (Tamames 1973). I have accepted Pérez Moreda's conjecture.

3. Choosing 'resident' over 'de facto' population allows me to keep consistency with Spanish official national accounts, which employ 'resident' population.
4. The average ratio between the resident and de facto population over 1971–1991 is 0.9956 with a coefficient of variation of 0.0048.

References

Maluquer de Motes, J. 2008. El crecimiento moderno de la población en España de 1850 a 2001: una serie homogénea anual. *Investigaciones de Historia Económica* 10: 129–162.

Nicolau, R. 2005. Población, salud y actividad. In *Estadísticas Históricas de España, Siglos XIX–XX,* 3 vols, I, eds. A. Carreras and X. Tafunell, 77–154. Bilbao: Fundación BBVA.

Ortega, J.A. and J. Silvestre. 2006. Las consecuencias demográficas. In *La economía de la Guerra Civil*, eds. P. Martín Aceña and E. Martínez Ruiz, 53–105. Madrid: Marcial Pons.

Pérez Moreda, V. 1980. *Las crisis de mortalidad en la España interior siglos XVI–XIX*. Madrid: Siglo XXI.

Pérez Moreda, V. 1988. La población española. In *Enciclopedia de Historia de España I. Economía y sociedad*, ed. M. Artola, 345–431. Alianza: Madrid.

Sánchez Alonso, B. 1995. *Las causas de la emigración española, 1880–1930*. Madrid: Alianza.

Sündbarg, G. 1908. *Aperçus statistiques internationaux*. Stockholm: Imprimerie Royale.

Tamames, R. 1973. *La República. La era de Franco*. Madrid: Alianza.

Tusell, J. 1999. *Historia de España del siglo XX. III. La dictadura de Franco*. Madrid: Taurus.

Open Access This chapter is licensed under the terms of the Creative Commons Attribution 4.0 International License (http://creativecommons.org/licenses/by/4.0/), which permits use, sharing, adaptation, distribution and reproduction in any medium or format, as long as you give appropriate credit to the original author(s) and the source, provide a link to the Creative Commons license and indicate if changes were made.

The images or other third party material in this chapter are included in the chapter's Creative Commons license, unless indicated otherwise in a credit line to the material. If material is not included in the chapter's Creative Commons license and your intended use is not permitted by statutory regulation or exceeds the permitted use, you will need to obtain permission directly from the copyright holder.

11

Employment, 1850–2015

The latest round of national accounts (CNE10) provides data on the number of full-time equivalent (FTE) workers and hours worked and its distribution by industry from 1995 to 2015. Unfortunately, no similar data are provided in earlier rounds of national accounts that present only figures for the number of occupied back to 1980 (CNE80 and CNE86). However, the 1995-based quarterly national accounts (CNTR95) provide data on FTE workers for 1980–1995. I have, then, spliced the two sets of FTE workers through linear interpolation to get consistent estimates over 1980–2015.[1]

For the pre-1980 years, García Perea and Gómez (1994) provide estimates of employment back to 1964 that can be pushed further back to 1954 with the rate of variation of employment provided in earlier national accounts (CNE64) (Instituto de Estudios Fiscales 1969: 33–34). I have assumed that the number of FTE workers evolved alongside employment and, thus, projected its 1980 level backwards to 1954 with the employment rate of variation to derive FTE employment series for the period 1954–2015 for the economy as a whole and its main economic sectors.

The next challenge was to link the post-1954 series with the historical evidence back to 1850. Thus, on the basis of population censuses, I constructed yearly employment estimates for 1850–1954 for the four main sectors: agriculture, forestry, and fishing; industry, mining, and utilities; construction; and services. Major shortcomings appear in Spanish census data: working population is only available at benchmark years and refers to the economically active population [EAN, thereafter], with no regard of involuntary unemployment.[2] Moreover, censuses tend to only record one activity per person, the one that individuals consider to be their principal activity, and this is usually 'farmer'. However, in a developing society the division of labour is low and a single person might undertake various work tasks over the course of a year.[3] Henceforth, activities corresponding to the industrial and, particularly, service sectors end up being underestimated in population censuses.[4] In addition, figures for female EAN in agriculture seem to be inconsistent over time.[5] Therefore, I have been forced to make some choices. For example, in order to derive consistent figures over time for EAN in agriculture, I excluded the census figures for female population, while assumed that female labour represented a stable proportion of male labour force in agriculture and, hence, increased the number of days assigned to each male worker (see below).[6] Moreover, as the share of EAN in agriculture is suspiciously stable over 1797–1910, in spite of industrialization and urbanization, I corrected it by assuming that the agricultural share of EAN moved along, and could not exceed, the proportion of rural population (living in towns with less than 5,000 inhabitants) in total population.[7] Thus, I adjusted downwards the percentage of EAN employed in agriculture between 1887 and 1920 by redistributing 'excess' agricultural workers proportionally between industry, construction, and services.[8] The next step was to obtain yearly EAN figures through log-linear interpolation of benchmark observations. Since the resulting estimates do not capture yearly fluctuations in economically active population, a partial solution has been, firstly, to compute EAN share in working age population (WAN) and WAN share in total population (N), being WAN and N computed through linear interpolation (¹) between population censuses.[9] Then, these ratios have been multiplied by the new yearly population estimates (N) to derive annual figures of economically active population (EAP). Thus,

$$EAP = (EAP^i/WAN^i)(WAN^i/N^i)N \qquad (11.1)$$

Later, in order to adjust for differences in labour intensity across main economic sectors and obtain a crude measure of full-time equivalent worker by industry, the data on EAP were converted into days worked per year. I assumed that each full-time worker was employed 270 days per annum in industry, construction, and services. Such figure results from deducting Sundays and religious holidays plus an allowance for illness. This assumption is in line with contemporary testimonies and supported by the available evidence.[10] In agriculture, however, contemporary and historians' estimates point to a lower figure for the working days per occupied, as full employment among peasants only occurred during the summer and, consequently, workers were idle for up to four months every year. It can be assumed that the working load per year for the average male worker in agriculture would range, at most, between 210 and 240 days.[11] However, in order to make for the exclusion of female employment in agriculture (due to the absence of consistent data), I increased the number of days assigned to male workers employed in agriculture to match the figure used for the rest of economic sectors (270).[12]

Lastly, figures for full-time equivalent employment by economic sector for 1850–1953 were derived by assuming that their yearly changes mirrored those in economically active population and, thus, FTE employment estimates for 1954 were backwards projected with those for economically active population (EAN). Total FTE employment for 1850–1954 resulted from adding up figures for sectoral estimates. It is worth noting that, in 1954, the ratio between FTE employment and EAN for each economic sector is 1.003 (agriculture), 0.872 (industry), 1.095 (construction), and 1.069 (services), and 1.000 for the aggregate. The implication, in the case of agriculture, is that the upper bound figure for male employment (resulting from an attempt to make for missing female labour figures) matches that of full-time equivalent total employment (including female work).

The final step has been to derive hours worked in which I draw on Prados de la Escosura and Rosés (2010: 526). For mid-nineteenth-century agriculture, Caballero (1864) estimated 10 h per day and a similar average figure, 9.7 h, was found for the mid-1950s.[13] Thus, I accepted 10 h per day for 1850–1911, interpolated these two figures over 1912–1935, and retained 9.7 h for the period 1936–1954. For industry and services, I interpolated Huberman's (2005) figures for 1870–1899 to derive annual hours worked, and the number of hours worked in 1870 was accepted for 1850–1869. I adopted Domenech's (2007) estimates for different industries and services in 1910 for 1900–1910, and Silvestre's (2003) annual computations for industry for 1911–1919. As regards the interwar years, Soto Carmona (1989: 596–613) provides some construction and services figures. Data on hours worked for the early 1950s are often close to those of 1919. I accepted the number of working hours per occupied in 1954 for the years 1936–1953, and interpolated the figures for 1919 and 1936. For the post-1954 period, hours worked for each branch of economic activity derive from Sanchis (private communication) for the 1950s, Maluquer de Motes and Llonch (2005) for 1958–1963, Ministerio de Trabajo (1964–1978) for 1964–1978, and OECD (2006) for 1979–1994. From 1995 onwards, the latest round of national accounts (CNE10) provides annual figures of hours worked. The resulting estimates show that the amount of total hours worked increased moderately, multiplying by 2.1 over the 166 years considered, but falling short of the increase in population that multiplied by 3.1.

Notes

1. The CN10/CNTR95 ratio in the overlapping year, 1995, is 1.02 for total FTE workers and 0.99, 0.93, 1.00, and 1.04 for full-time equivalent workers employed in agriculture, industry, construction, and services, respectively. See Section VI.1 and, in particular, expression (16) for the linear interpolation procedure used.
2. Nevertheless, in a predominantly agricultural economy such as that of Spain up to the 1950s, modern unemployment in the modern sense of the word was quite reduced, save during exceptional crises. Still, there

was a lot of seasonal as well as hidden unemployment in the agricultural sector (labour hoarding) (Pérez Moreda 1999: 57).
3. Moreover, as the opportunity cost of allocating agricultural labour to alternative occupations during the slack season was minimal, peasants carried out additional non-agricultural activities, such as producing their own implements, clothing and providing services such as transportation and storing, and working in construction industry.
4. The time of year in which census data were collected will also affect the very definition of one's occupation. If, for example, a census is conducted during the harvest season, results for agricultural employment include all those persons temporarily employed in agriculture, despite the fact that their principal occupation during the rest of the year may be in a separate sector.
5. Female labour was not included in agricultural EAN in the 1797 and 1860 population censuses and represented a small and declining proportion of male labour, thereafter. Thus, female/male ratios in agricultural EAN were, according to population censuses, around 0.2 over 1877–1900 and ranged between 0.05 and 0.1 during the first half of twentieth century (Nicolau 2005).
6. The exclusion of females working in agriculture from the total working population is usual in Spanish historical literature (Nicolau 2005; Erdozáin and Mikelarena 1999; Pérez Moreda 1999: 55). Carré et al. (1975: 89) followed a similar strategy to one proposed here for the French case.
7. Pre-1930 figures for rural population come from Gómez Mendoza and Luna Rodrigo (1986) and EAN from Pérez Moreda (1999), for 1860 and 1877, and Nicolau (2005), thereafter. Not everyone living in rural districts worked in agriculture, as some proportion, however small it might be, must have been employed in the provision of services and processed goods. It is often alleged that, at least in the south of the Iberian peninsula, there were agglomerations of fairly expansive populations that had no urban characteristics until the mid-1900s, as their inhabitants continued to carry out agricultural tasks. However, in these population centres a significant portion of the working population provided services and non-agricultural goods to the rest of the inhabitants. Thus, I have made the reasonable conjecture that those persons employed in agriculture but living in urban centres would tend to balance out with the population of industrial and service sector workers

living in rural population centres. Moreover, as income levels increase, both the rural population and the overall population of agricultural workers will decrease, although the latter does so at a faster rate, as there always exists some part of the population that opts to live in the countryside despite not being employed primarily in either agriculture or the raising of livestock (Prados de la Escosura 2007).
8. Thus, the percentage share of agriculture in EAN for 1887 (65.3), 1900 (66.3), 1910 (66.0), and 1920 (57.2) became 62.7, 60.75, 58.0, and 54.5%, respectively. Original shares come from Nicolau (2005).
9. Yearly estimates of population aged 15–64 for 1858–1960 were derived through interpolation between age cohorts at census benchmarks by David Reher, who kindly supply them to me. I extended the estimates back to 1850.
10. Soto Carmona (1989: 608) pointed out that, on average, the number of days worked per occupied up to 1919 ranged between 240 and 270. Vandellós (1925) reckoned that, in 1914, the average number of days worked per year in mining was 250. Doménech (2007: 472), in turn, provides a figure of 291 days per year for textile industry workers in the early twentieth century.
11. Gómez Mendoza (1982: 101) emphasized the seasonal nature of late nineteenth-century employment and estimated that, on average, a farm labourer worked 210 days out of 275–300 working days per year. This figure is not far from Bairoch (1965) estimate of 196 days for nineteenth-century Europe. Simpson (1992) obtained even a lower Fig. (108 to 130 days per worker-year) from labour requirements in Andalusia's agriculture between 1886 and 1930. García Sanz (1979–1980: 63) provided a higher figure, 242 days per year, for day labourers in mid-nineteenth-century Spain.
12. The implication is that the assumed female/male ratio, in equivalent work effort, would range between 0.125 and 0.286, depending on whether male employees in agriculture are assumed to work 240 or 210 days per year, respectively.
13. The figure for the 1950s was obtained by dividing the figure for yearly hours, which was kindly provided by Teresa Sanchis (private communication), by the number of working days per year.

References

Bairoch, P. 1965. Niveaux de développement économique de 1810 à 1910. *Annales ESC* 20 (6): 1091–1117.
Caballero, F. 1864. *Memoria sobre el fomento de la población rural*. Madrid: Imprenta del Colegio de Sordo-mudos y de Ciegos.
Carré, J.-J., Dubois, P. and E. Malinvaud. 1976. *French Economic Growth*, Stanford, CA: Stanford University Press.
Doménech Felíu, J. 2007. Working Hours in the European Periphery. The Length of the Working Day in Spain, 1880–1920. *Explorations in Economic History* 44 (3): 469–486.
Erdozáin Azpilicueta, P., and F. Mikelarena Peña. 1999. Las cifras de activos agrarios de los censos de población española del período 1877–1991. Un análisis crítico. *Boletín de la Asociación de Demografía Histórica XVII* 1: 89–113.
García-Perea, P. and R. Gómez. 1994. Elaboración de series históricas de empleo a partir de la encuesta de población activa (1964–1992). Banco de España, Servicio de Estudios, Documento de Trabajo 9409.
García Sanz, A. 1979–1980. Jornales agrícolas y presupuesto familiar campesino en España a mediados del siglo XIX. *Anales del CUNEF* 49–71.
Gomez Mendoza, A. 1982. *Ferrocarriles y cambio económico en España, 1855–1913*. Madrid: Alianza.
Gomez Mendoza, A. 1986. La industria de la construcción residencial: Madrid, 1820–1935. *Moneda y Crédito* 117: 53–81.
Huberman, M. 2005. Working Hours of the World Unite? New International Evidence of Worktime, 1870–1913. *Journal of Economic History* 64 (4): 964–1001.
Instituto de Estudios Fiscales. 1969. *La Contabilidad Nacional de España. Años 1954 a 1964*. Madrid: Ministerio de Hacienda.
Maluquer de Motes, J. and M. Llonch. 2005. Trabajo y relaciones laborales. In *Estadísticas Históricas de España, siglos XIX y XX*, eds. A. Carreras and X. Tafunell, 1154–1245. Bilbao: Fundación BBVA, III.
Ministerio de Trabajo. 1964–1978. *Salarios*. Madrid: Ministerio de Trabajo.
Nicolau, R. 2005. Población, salud y actividad. In *Estadísticas Históricas de España. Siglos XIX-XX*, 3 vols., I, eds. A. Carreras and X. Tafunell, 77–154. Bilbao: Fundación BBVA.
OECD. 2006. *The Labor Force Statistics Database*. Paris: OECD.

Prados de la Escosura, L. 2007. European Patterns of Development in Historical Perspective. *Scandinavian Economic History Review* 55 (3): 187–221.

Prados de la Escosura, L. and J.R. Rosés. 2010. Human Capital and Economic Growth in Spain, 1850–2000. *Explorations in Economic History* 47 (4): 520–532.

Pérez Moreda, V. 1999. Población y economía en la España de los siglos XIX y XX. In *Historia Económica de España*, ed. G. Anes, 7–62. Galaxia Gutemberg/Círculo de Lectores: Siglos XIX y XX, Barcelona.

Silvestre, J. 2003. Migraciones interiores y mercado de trabajo en España, 1877–1936. Unpublished PhD dissertation, Universidad de Zaragoza.

Simpson, J. 1992. Technical Change, Labor Absorption, and Living Standards in Andalucia 1886–1936. *Agricultural History* 66 (3): 1–24.

Soto Carmona, A. 1989. *El trabajo industrial en la España contemporánea: (1874–1936)*. Rubí: Anthropos.

Vandellós, J.A. 1925. La richesse et le revenu de la Péninsule Ibérique. *Metron* V (4): 151–186.

Open Access This chapter is licensed under the terms of the Creative Commons Attribution 4.0 International License (http://creativecommons.org/licenses/by/4.0/), which permits use, sharing, adaptation, distribution and reproduction in any medium or format, as long as you give appropriate credit to the original author(s) and the source, provide a link to the Creative Commons license and indicate if changes were made.

The images or other third party material in this chapter are included in the chapter's Creative Commons license, unless indicated otherwise in a credit line to the material. If material is not included in the chapter's Creative Commons license and your intended use is not permitted by statutory regulation or exceeds the permitted use, you will need to obtain permission directly from the copyright holder.

Appendices

Appendix. Final Output and Gross Value Added in Agriculture, 1850–1958

See Tables A.1, A.2 and A.3.

Table A.1 Ratios of final output to total production for main crops

	Up to 1929	1929–1950s	1960–1964
Wheat	0.860	0.860	0.929
Barley	0.344	0.255	0.255
Oats	0.200	0.200	0.200
Rye	0.774	0.722	0.464
Maize	0.570	0.470[a]	0.155
Rice	0.990	0.990	0.992
Chickpeas	0.870	0.870	0.874
Broad beans	0.430	0.430	0.347
Beans	0.890	0.890	0.852
Potatoes	0.765	0.765	0.896
Sugar Beet	0.970	0.970	0.970

[a]0.37 in the 1950s

Sources Simpson (1994); Federico (1992); Ministerio de Agricultura (1979b)

Table A.2 Conversion coefficients applied to livestock numbers to derive meat, wool and milk output, 1891–1924

	1865	1891/1924
Meat (dressed carcass) (Kilograms per livestock unit[a])		
Cattle	22.226	37.090
Sheep	2.432	3.675
Goat	11.327	3.626
Pigs	43.681	51.550
Horse		6.360
Wool (greasy[a,b])	1.660	1.660
Milk (less animal consumption) (litres per livestock unit[c])		
Cow	175	363
Sheep	4.196	3.660
Goat	77.07	63.70

[a]Kilograms per unit of total livestock (not just slaughtered livestock), *1865*. The share of livestock slaughtered comes from García Sanz (1994), but for cattle the share has been raised from 6.36%, the figure provided by García Sanz, to 11.36% in order to include slaughtered young animals. Such proportion is obtained as follows: in the 1933 cattle census, adult animals slaughtered represented 15.68% of its total. However, according to Simpson (1994), when young animals are considered, the percentage increases to 28%. A similar correction for 1865 would result in 11.36% of livestock slaughtered [28 * 6.36/15.68 = 11.36]. Lack of information led me to accept dressed carcass weights for 1920 from Flores de Lemus (1926), 38.472 kg per livestock unit and 3.753 kg per sheep and goat unit, *1891/1924*. For sheep and pigs, coefficients provided by Simpson (1994) and Comín (1985) were applied. Simpson (1994) assumes, following the 1929 Census, that 37.5% of sheep and 59.6% of pigs were slaughtered annually. Comín (1985) provides dressed carcass weight per unit, 9.8 kg per sheep and 86.5 kg per pig. For cattle and goats, total dressed carcass weight/livestock number ratios for 1925–1935 were accepted, while for horsemeat it was the 1950 ratio, all from Ministerio de Agricultura (1979a). If, alternatively, Simpson (1994) approach, which assumes that 28% and 38.3% of cattle and goats were sacrificed each year, was used, and average dressed carcass weight of 137.4 kg and 9.8 kg, respectively, from Comín (1985) was applied, the resulting conversion coefficients would be slightly higher than those adopted here

[b]Simpson (1994), Comín (1985), Carreras (1983) and Prados de la Escosura (1983) accept this figure. Alternatively, Parejo (1989) suggests 2 kg

[c]Litres per unit of total livestock (not per females), *1865*. He aplicado los rendimientos que proporciona Simpson (1994) yields 700 l per milking cow-year, being milking 45% of all cows that, in turn, represented 59% of total cattle. I have adjusted this figure (186 l per cattle unit) downwards with the ratio between milk production derived by me and by Simpson for 1891/1924 (363/387). In the cases of sheep and goat, female represented 69.5% and 73.4% of the total, respectively, and I have accepted the milking female/total female ratio for 1929/33, *1891–1924*.

(continued)

(continued)

1925–1935 average milk/livestock unit ratios were accepted from Ministerio de Agricultura (1979a). Simpson (1994) estimates for 1929/33 are very close. For cows, Simpson assumed that females represented 75% of cattle, from which 45% were milked, yielding 1,146 l per head per year. For sheep, the corresponding figures were 62.7%, 23.4% and 25.8 l and for goats, 65.2%, 60% and 175 l

Sources Carreras (1983); Comín (1985); Simpson (1994); Ministerio de Agricultura (1979a)

Table A.3 Coverage of the sample of products included in the annual index for each agricultural group at benchmarks (%) (current prices)

	c.1890	c.1900	1909/13	1929/3	3 1950	1960/64
Cereals[a]	99.05	99.25	99.50	99.38	99.83	99.79
Pulses[b]	94.22	93.80	92.87	90.18	90.91	87.61
Vegetables[c]	–	35.83	41.79	52.23	51.40	43.67
Raw materials[d]	41.70	70.30	70.60	81.91	84.53	94.90
Fruits and nuts[e]	44.63	48.30	61.20	68.14	69.15	69.34
Wine (must)	100.00	100.00	100.00	100.00	100.00	100.00
Olive oil[f]	98.44	98.42	95.34	98.03	79.88	95.30
Meat[g]	92.87	92.87	92.87	92.89	98.98	94.70
Poultry and eggs	–	–	100.00	100.00	100.00	100.00
Milk and honey[h]	98.30	98.30	98.32	98.30	98.28	98.40
Total	77.48	79.88	86.40	86.13	86.50	85.14

[a]Wheat, barley, rye, oats, maize, rice
[b]Chickpeas, broad beans, beans
[c]Potatoes, onions
[d]Sugar beet, sugar cane, wool, silk cocoons, cotton (since 1950), tobacco (since 1950)
[e]Almonds, oranges, carobs, apples, chestnuts, lemons, bananas (only almonds and oranges before 1910)
[f]Olive oil, no olives and sub products included
[g]Beef and veal, lamb and mouton, goat, pork, horsemeat (since 1950)
[h]Milk only
Sources See the text

References

Carreras, A. 1983. La producció industrial espanyola i italiana des de mitjan segle XIX fins l'actualitat. Universitat Autònoma de Barcelona, 3 vols., unpublished Ph.D. dissertation.

Comín, F. 1985. Cálculos para la estimación de la producción agraria entre 1900 y 1950. Memoria del Banco de España (mimeo).

Federico, G. 1992. Il valore aggiunto dell'agricoltura italiana in 1911. In *I conti economici dell'Italia II. Una stima del valore aggiunto per il 1911*, ed. G.M. Rey, 3–103. Roma: Laterza.

Flores de Lemus, A. 1926. Sobre una dirección fundamental de la producción rural española. *El Financiero*, 5 April 1926. Reprinted in (1976), *Hacienda Pública Española* 42–43: 471–485.

García Sanz, A. 1994. La ganadería española entre 1750 y 1865: los efectos de la reforma agraria liberal. *Agricultura y Sociedad* 72: 81–119.

Ministerio de Agricultura. 1979a. *Anuario de estadística agraria 1978*. Madrid: Secretaría General Técnica del Ministerio de Agricultura.

Ministerio de Agricultura. 1979b. *Cuentas del sector agrario nº 4*. Secretaría General Técnica del Ministerio de Agricultura.

Parejo Barranco, A. 1989. Producción y consumo industrial de lana en España (1849–1900). *Revista de Historia Económica* VII (3): 589–618.

Prados de la Escosura, L. 1983. Producción y consumo de tejidos en España, 1800-1913: primeros resultados. In *Historia económica y pensamiento social. Ensayos en homenaje a Diego Mateo del Peral*, ed. G. Anes, L.A. Rojo and P. Tedde, 455–471. Madrid: Alianza.

Simpson, J. 1994. La producción y la productividad agraria españolas, 1890–1936. *Revista de Historia Económica* XII 1: 43–84.

Statistical Appendix: Spain's Historical National Accounts: Expenditure and Output, 1850–2015

See Tables S1, S2, S3, S4, S5, S6, S7, S8, S9, S10, S11, S12, S13, S14, S15, S16, S17, S18, S19, S20, S21, S22, S23, S24, S25, S26, S27 and S28.

Table S1 Gross domestic product and its expenditure components, 1850–2015 (million Euro)

	Final consumption expenditure of NPISHs and Households (million Euro)	Final consumption expenditure by government (million Euro)	Gross fixed capital formation (million Euro)	Changes in inventories and acquisitions less disposals of valuables (million Euro)	Exports of goods and services (million Euro)	Imports of goods and services (million Euro)	Gross domestic product at market prices (million Euro)
1850	21.8	2.5	1.2	0.2	1.0	1.1	25.6
1851	22.3	2.6	1.3	0.2	0.9	1.2	26.1
1852	22.4	2.5	1.6	0.2	0.9	1.3	26.3
1853	26.8	2.6	1.6	0.2	1.2	1.3	31.0
1854	27.9	2.6	1.3	0.2	1.5	1.5	32.1
1855	29.9	2.4	1.2	0.2	2.0	1.7	34.0
1856	29.3	2.6	1.6	0.2	2.0	2.1	33.6
1857	27.5	3.2	2.0	0.2	2.0	2.5	32.4
1858	26.5	3.3	2.9	0.2	1.2	2.5	31.6
1859	27.6	3.4	3.1	0.2	1.5	2.1	33.7
1860	27.9	4.3	3.7	0.2	2.0	2.2	35.8
1861	29.5	3.9	3.4	0.1	1.9	2.3	36.6
1862	30.9	3.8	3.7	0.1	1.5	2.5	37.6
1863	33.4	4.0	3.6	0.1	1.6	3.1	39.6
1864	33.5	4.2	3.2	0.1	1.5	3.0	39.5
1865	31.1	4.3	2.7	0.1	1.6	2.7	37.2
1866	34.1	3.8	2.7	0.1	1.7	2.6	39.8
1867	35.6	3.7	2.8	0.1	2.3	2.1	42.4
1868	30.8	3.5	1.6	0.1	2.4	2.5	35.9
1869	27.7	3.2	1.4	0.1	2.7	2.1	33.1
1870	30.9	3.3	1.7	0.2	2.1	2.3	35.9
1871	32.9	3.3	2.0	0.3	2.8	2.6	38.5
1872	38.1	3.7	2.2	0.3	3.1	3.3	44.1
1873	39.5	4.4	1.9	0.3	3.7	2.8	47.1

(continued)

Table S1 (continued)

	Final consumption expenditure of NPISHs and Households (million Euro)	Final consumption expenditure by government (million Euro)	Gross fixed capital formation (million Euro)	Changes in inventories and acquisitions less disposals of valuables (million Euro)	Exports of goods and services (million Euro)	Imports of goods and services (million Euro)	Gross domestic product at market prices (million Euro)
1874	38.7	5.7	2.2	0.3	3.2	3.4	46.8
1875	36.9	6.4	2.2	0.4	3.4	2.9	46.3
1876	41.2	4.4	2.8	0.4	2.9	3.6	48.1
1877	44.8	4.6	2.8	0.3	3.6	3.2	53.0
1878	43.8	4.5	3.4	0.3	3.4	3.0	52.4
1879	43.9	4.3	2.6	0.3	3.4	3.5	51.1
1880	45.0	4.5	3.3	0.3	4.7	3.5	54.2
1881	48.5	4.6	2.8	0.2	4.8	4.0	56.8
1882	50.1	5.6	3.5	0.2	4.9	4.2	60.1
1883	51.3	4.8	4.2	0.1	5.2	4.5	61.0
1884	49.1	4.8	4.1	0.0	4.5	3.9	58.6
1885	49.0	5.1	3.0	0.0	4.8	3.9	58.0
1886	50.0	5.1	2.7	−0.1	5.2	4.0	59.0
1887	46.1	4.6	2.6	−0.1	4.8	3.9	54.1
1888	48.9	4.5	2.4	−0.1	5.2	4.3	56.5
1889	44.8	4.5	2.7	−0.1	5.4	4.8	52.4
1890	45.1	4.3	3.0	−0.1	5.5	4.8	53.1
1891	45.8	4.2	2.9	−0.1	5.9	4.6	54.2
1892	44.7	4.6	3.0	0.0	5.9	4.5	53.7
1893	43.7	4.6	2.9	0.0	5.6	4.5	52.3
1894	42.8	4.4	2.8	0.1	5.7	4.6	51.2
1895	42.4	4.5	3.0	0.1	5.5	3.9	51.6
1896	39.3	4.6	3.0	0.2	6.8	4.4	49.4

(continued)

Appendices 207

Table S1 (continued)

	Final consumption expenditure of NPISHs and Households (million Euro)	Final consumption expenditure by government (million Euro)	Gross fixed capital formation (million Euro)	Changes in inventories and acquisitions less disposals of valuables (million Euro)	Exports of goods and services (million Euro)	Imports of goods and services (million Euro)	Gross domestic product at market prices (million Euro)
1897	42.6	5.1	3.1	0.2	7.2	4.7	53.6
1898	45.3	5.4	3.3	0.3	8.1	4.8	57.5
1899	47.3	4.9	5.0	0.3	6.9	6.2	58.4
1900	48.6	5.0	6.6	0.3	7.9	6.8	61.7
1901	54.2	5.0	5.0	0.3	7.2	6.9	64.8
1902	52.4	5.0	4.3	0.3	7.2	6.6	62.6
1903	56.6	5.0	4.8	0.3	7.5	7.1	67.0
1904	59.3	5.3	5.2	0.3	7.9	7.2	70.7
1905	57.1	5.1	4.6	0.3	8.7	7.6	68.1
1906	56.9	5.4	4.8	0.3	8.5	6.5	69.5
1907	58.3	5.6	5.6	0.3	9.0	6.4	72.3
1908	59.6	5.6	5.2	0.4	7.3	6.3	71.8
1909	59.4	6.4	5.6	0.5	7.2	5.8	73.4
1910	55.1	6.6	6.3	0.6	8.0	6.4	70.2
1911	60.0	7.0	6.7	0.8	8.9	7.5	75.8
1912	59.2	7.4	8.0	1.0	9.7	8.1	77.2
1913	64.0	8.0	8.9	1.3	10.0	9.2	82.9
1914	63.8	8.4	7.9	1.5	7.5	6.6	82.5
1915	67.1	11.7	6.7	1.8	9.4	5.9	90.8
1916	82.2	9.8	7.6	2.0	11.1	8.0	105
1917	87.1	9.8	8.7	2.2	13.9	7.6	114
1918	109	11.8	10.6	2.3	11.3	6.9	138
1919	112	14.0	11.0	2.3	22.0	12.3	149

(continued)

208 Appendices

Table S1 (continued)

	Final consumption expenditure of NPISHs and Households (million Euro)	Final consumption expenditure by government (million Euro)	Gross fixed capital formation (million Euro)	Changes in inventories and acquisitions less disposals of valuables (million Euro)	Exports of goods and services (million Euro)	Imports of goods and services (million Euro)	Gross domestic product at market prices (million Euro)
1920	145	19.4	14.5	2.2	19.0	23.6	177
1921	123	23.2	17.4	2.0	13.1	16.0	163
1922	132	19.9	16.8	1.8	9.9	15.8	165
1923	136	18.4	17.3	1.6	11.9	20.2	165
1924	143	21.9	21.7	1.3	12.6	19.5	181
1925	154	21.3	20.8	1.1	14.1	19.0	192
1926	143	20.8	24.3	0.9	12.6	13.7	188
1927	157	20.0	26.1	0.6	13.1	15.9	201
1928	150	20.5	31.4	0.4	12.7	18.0	197
1929	161	20.5	35.8	0.2	14.7	20.9	212
1930	160	20.3	35.3	0.0	15.8	20.0	212
1931	163	20.2	24.5	−0.1	15.5	15.9	208
1932	167	21.5	21.0	−0.1	14.9	16.8	208
1933	154	23.3	23.7	0.0	9.9	12.4	198
1934	173	24.4	23.8	0.3	9.5	12.7	219
1935	178	25.6	25.0	0.8	9.0	12.0	226
1936	116	44.6	21.3	1.4	9.3	9.6	183
1937	121	51.0	17.3	2.4	10.0	9.8	192
1938	148	52.1	17.3	3.5	7.6	10.8	218
1939	170	60.5	18.1	4.7	7.4	9.6	251
1940	231	51.8	25.4	6.0	7.1	8.5	313
1941	237	57.9	39.4	7.4	10.1	5.6	346
1942	286	64.4	50.2	8.9	12.0	5.0	417

(continued)

Table S1 (continued)

	Final consumption expenditure of NPISHs and Households (million Euro)	Final consumption expenditure by government (million Euro)	Gross fixed capital formation (million Euro)	Changes in inventories and acquisitions less disposals of valuables (million Euro)	Exports of goods and services (million Euro)	Imports of goods and services (million Euro)	Gross domestic product at market prices (million Euro)
1943	284	100	52.5	10.5	13.5	12.6	449
1944	353	92	52.5	12.4	20.1	12.2	518
1945	343	98	56.6	14.6	15.7	13.3	514
1946	479	85	70.8	17.2	17.2	19.7	650
1947	544	96	95.9	20.1	24.0	24.3	756
1948	558	103	134	23.5	24.5	26.7	816
1949	608	111	135	27.3	31.4	37.7	874
1950	773	120	160	31.7	41.7	48.1	1079
1951	1063	137	156	36.6	84.4	103.8	1373
1952	1144	153	194	42.0	95.1	118.2	1510
1953	1213	166	222	48.3	123.7	141.2	1632
1954	1337	191	317	55.7	135	148	1888
1955	1418	202	408	64.3	144	198	2039
1956	1690	245	579	74.0	161	227	2523
1957	2026	274	639	84.7	183	263	2944
1958	2464	282	730	97	223	297	3497
1959	2746	312	692	−3	190	268	3669
1960	2759	320	724	−9	301	277	3818
1961	3195	355	863	89	308	411	4399
1962	3750	403	1018	203	351	582	5143
1963	4584	488	1215	237	351	733	6142
1964	5249	527	1465	192	446	855	7024
1965	6233	628	1811	253	482	1147	8260

(continued)

Table S1 (continued)

	Final consumption expenditure of NPISHs and Households (million Euro)	Final consumption expenditure by government (million Euro)	Gross fixed capital formation (million Euro)	Changes in inventories and acquisitions less disposals of valuables (million Euro)	Exports of goods and services (million Euro)	Imports of goods and services (million Euro)	Gross domestic product at market prices (million Euro)
1966	7147	756	2117	288	607	1373	9541
1967	7916	925	2409	150	661	1366	10694
1968	8765	1010	2757	94	922	1637	11910
1969	9680	1161	3182	349	1133	1956	13548
1970	10672	1328	3464	199	1373	2200	14836
1971	12118	1546	3634	231	1670	2329	16871
1972	14239	1816	4649	275	2123	2961	20141
1973	17116	2216	6089	243	2668	3826	24507
1974	20919	2829	8011	996	3663	5993	30424
1975	24636	3547	9063	1101	4078	6364	36061
1976	29959	4588	10388	1224	5487	8070	43577
1977	37948	6001	12903	655	7348	9370	55486
1978	46042	7698	15239	−160	9569	10034	68355
1979	53437	9485	17145	459	11658	11997	80186
1980	63050	11768	20850	1116	14637	17107	94315
1981	70815	14465	23113	−1	18486	21095	105785
1982	81225	17003	26465	721	22075	24942	122547
1983	91843	20049	29124	967	28389	30272	140100
1984	102722	22303	29741	1586	35691	33238	158806
1985	114114	25410	33707	88	39013	36601	175730
1986	129230	29031	39294	1016	39091	35838	201824
1987	144871	33864	47499	1625	42562	43422	226999
1988	159988	37323	58100	2669	46025	50282	253822

(continued)

Table S1 (continued)

	Final consumption expenditure of NPISHs and Households (million Euro)	Final consumption expenditure by government (million Euro)	Gross fixed capital formation (million Euro)	Changes in inventories and acquisitions less disposals of valuables (million Euro)	Exports of goods and services (million Euro)	Imports of goods and services (million Euro)	Gross domestic product at market prices (million Euro)
1989	180679	43648	70380	2875	49457	60361	286677
1990	199867	50640	80394	2976	51846	64381	321343
1991	219332	58375	86739	2839	56949	70021	354213
1992	239167	67278	86627	3198	62984	75920	383334
1993	247497	72341	82335	−27	71478	76737	396886
1994	262551	75170	88592	944	87070	90382	423945
1995	279946	81083	101154	1594	100741	105181	459337
1996	295071	85609	106422	1337	112816	113263	487992
1997	312004	88456	115320	1154	133417	132302	518049
1998	331147	93793	129667	2193	145066	147824	554042
1999	354683	100080	147833	3271	156883	168434	594316
2000	385790	108113	168958	2812	184932	204355	646250
2001	414178	115901	183497	2389	194904	211341	699528
2002	438364	124561	199489	2074	198390	213590	749288
2003	463042	134688	222197	1356	204462	222273	803472
2004	499125	147817	245709	1974	216896	250101	861420
2005	536684	161090	278162	1154	229550	276074	930566
2006	577213	174929	313006	2451	250703	310328	1007974
2007	615840	191042	335552	3124	277851	342602	1080807
2008	633540	209521	326064	4288	282589	339795	1116207
2009	605346	221028	262499	2574	244658	257071	1079034
2010	618755	221715	248987	5562	275847	289953	1080913

(continued)

Table S1 (continued)

	Final consumption expenditure of NPISHs and Households (million Euro)	Final consumption expenditure by government (million Euro)	Gross fixed capital formation (million Euro)	Changes in inventories and acquisitions less disposals of valuables (million Euro)	Exports of goods and services (million Euro)	Imports of goods and services (million Euro)	Gross domestic product at market prices (million Euro)
2011	618865	219673	229884	4623	309575	312207	1070413
2012	611349	205236	205839	2061	319223	303950	1039758
2013	598482	201840	192371	−450	330453	297062	1025634
2014	608945	201974	198335	2700	338769	313698	1037025
2015	625035	208489	212069	3700	356873	330527	1075639

Sources Please cite the database as: Leandro Prados de la Escosura (2017), Spanish Economic Growth, 1850–2015

Appendices 213

Table S2 Gross domestic product, gross and net national income, 1850–2015 (million Euro)

	Gross domestic product at market prices (million Euro)	Net primary income from the rest of the world (million Euro)	Gross national income (million Euro)	Consumption of fixed capital (million Euro)	Net national income (million Euro)	Net current transfers from the rest of the world (million Euro)	Net national disposable income (million Euro)
1850	25.6	−0.3	25.2	0.5	24.7	0.0	24.8
1851	26.1	−0.3	25.8	0.5	25.3	0.0	25.3
1852	26.3	−0.3	26.0	0.5	25.5	0.0	25.5
1853	31.0	−0.3	30.7	0.5	30.2	0.0	30.2
1854	32.1	−0.3	31.8	0.6	31.2	0.0	31.2
1855	34.0	−0.3	33.8	0.5	33.2	0.0	33.3
1856	33.6	−0.3	33.4	0.6	32.8	0.0	32.8
1857	32.4	−0.2	32.2	0.6	31.5	0.0	31.6
1858	31.6	−0.3	31.3	0.6	30.7	0.0	30.7
1859	33.7	−0.3	33.4	0.8	32.6	0.1	32.7
1860	35.8	−0.3	35.5	0.8	34.7	0.1	34.8
1861	36.6	−0.3	36.3	0.9	35.4	0.1	35.5
1862	37.6	−0.3	37.3	0.9	36.3	0.1	36.4
1863	39.6	−0.3	39.2	1.0	38.2	0.1	38.3
1864	39.5	−0.4	39.1	1.1	37.9	0.1	38.0
1865	37.2	−0.3	36.9	1.2	35.7	0.1	35.8
1866	39.8	−0.4	39.4	1.3	38.1	0.1	38.2
1867	42.4	−0.4	42.1	1.3	40.7	0.1	40.8
1868	35.9	−0.5	35.4	1.3	34.1	0.1	34.1
1869	33.1	−0.7	32.4	1.3	31.1	0.1	31.2
1870	35.9	−0.7	35.2	1.4	33.8	0.1	33.9

(continued)

Table S2 (continued)

	Gross domestic product at market prices (million Euro)	Net primary income from the rest of the world (million Euro)	Gross national income (million Euro)	Consumption of fixed capital (million Euro)	Net national income (million Euro)	Net current transfers from the rest of the world (million Euro)	Net national disposable income (million Euro)
1871	38.5	−0.8	37.8	1.5	36.3	0.1	36.4
1872	44.1	−0.8	43.3	1.5	41.8	0.1	41.9
1873	47.1	−0.8	46.3	1.8	44.5	0.1	44.6
1874	46.8	−1.1	45.6	1.8	43.8	0.2	44.0
1875	46.3	−1.1	45.1	1.9	43.3	0.2	43.4
1876	48.1	−0.7	47.4	1.6	45.8	0.2	46.0
1877	53.0	−0.7	52.3	1.6	50.7	0.2	50.9
1878	52.4	−0.7	51.7	1.7	50.0	0.2	50.1
1879	51.1	−0.7	50.3	1.6	48.7	0.2	48.9
1880	54.2	−0.8	53.4	1.7	51.7	0.2	51.8
1881	56.8	−1.0	55.8	1.7	54.1	0.1	54.3
1882	60.1	−1.1	59.0	1.8	57.2	0.2	57.4
1883	61.0	−1.2	59.8	1.8	58.0	0.2	58.2
1884	58.6	−1.1	57.5	2.0	55.5	0.2	55.7
1885	58.0	−1.2	56.8	1.9	54.9	0.2	55.1
1886	59.0	−1.2	57.8	1.8	56.0	0.2	56.3
1887	54.1	−1.1	52.9	1.8	51.2	0.3	51.5
1888	56.5	−1.3	55.3	1.8	53.4	0.4	53.8
1889	52.4	−1.3	51.1	1.9	49.2	0.5	49.7
1890	53.1	−1.3	51.8	2.0	49.8	0.4	50.2
1891	54.2	−1.3	52.9	2.0	50.9	0.5	51.4

(continued)

Table S2 (continued)

	Gross domestic product at market prices (million Euro)	Net primary income from the rest of the world (million Euro)	Gross national income (million Euro)	Consumption of fixed capital (million Euro)	Net national income (million Euro)	Net current transfers from the rest of the world (million Euro)	Net national disposable income (million Euro)
1892	53.7	−1.2	52.5	2.1	50.5	0.6	51.0
1893	52.3	−1.2	51.1	2.2	48.9	0.6	49.6
1894	51.2	−1.2	50.0	2.2	47.8	0.5	48.3
1895	51.6	−1.1	50.5	2.2	48.4	0.4	48.8
1896	49.4	−1.3	48.1	2.3	45.9	0.5	46.4
1897	53.6	−1.4	52.1	2.4	49.7	0.5	50.3
1898	57.5	−1.8	55.8	2.8	53.0	0.6	53.6
1899	58.4	−2.0	56.4	2.8	53.6	0.6	54.1
1900	61.7	−2.1	59.6	3.2	56.4	0.6	57.0
1901	64.8	−1.7	63.1	3.0	60.1	0.7	60.7
1902	62.6	−1.7	60.9	3.1	57.9	0.6	58.4
1903	67.0	−1.8	65.3	3.3	61.9	0.7	62.6
1904	70.7	−1.8	68.8	3.4	65.4	0.9	66.3
1905	68.1	−1.8	66.3	3.2	63.1	1.1	64.1
1906	69.5	−2.2	67.3	3.3	64.1	1.2	65.3
1907	72.3	−2.4	69.9	3.6	66.3	1.3	67.7
1908	71.8	−1.8	70.0	3.4	66.5	1.7	68.2
1909	73.4	−1.9	71.5	3.6	67.9	1.7	69.6
1910	70.2	−1.9	68.4	3.7	64.6	2.0	66.6
1911	75.8	−1.6	74.2	3.9	70.3	2.0	72.4
1912	77.2	−1.8	75.3	4.0	71.4	2.4	73.8

(continued)

Table S2 (continued)

	Gross domestic product at market prices (million Euro)	Net primary income from the rest of the world (million Euro)	Gross national income (million Euro)	Consumption of fixed capital (million Euro)	Net national income (million Euro)	Net current transfers from the rest of the world (million Euro)	Net national disposable income (million Euro)
1913	82.9	−2.2	80.7	4.3	76.4	2.2	78.6
1914	82.5	−0.8	81.7	4.2	77.5	1.9	79.3
1915	90.8	−0.8	90.0	4.9	85.1	1.6	86.6
1916	104.8	−1.1	103.8	5.7	98.1	1.5	99.6
1917	114.1	−0.7	113.4	7.3	106.1	1.4	107.4
1918	138.4	−0.6	137.8	9.4	128.4	1.2	129.5
1919	149.2	−0.5	148.6	9.0	139.7	1.8	141.5
1920	176.6	−0.6	176.0	11.9	164.1	3.0	167.1
1921	162.7	−0.5	162.2	12.4	149.8	3.3	153.1
1922	165.1	−0.5	164.6	12.1	152.5	2.2	154.7
1923	165.4	−0.7	164.7	11.5	153.2	2.7	156.0
1924	181.1	−0.9	180.3	12.6	167.7	2.9	170.6
1925	192.2	−1.2	191.0	12.5	178.5	2.3	180.8
1926	187.7	−1.1	186.6	12.9	173.7	2.0	175.6
1927	201.2	−0.8	200.4	13.4	187.0	1.7	188.8
1928	196.5	−0.8	195.8	13.8	181.9	1.6	183.5
1929	211.6	−0.9	210.7	14.7	196.0	1.8	197.8
1930	211.7	−0.8	210.9	15.4	195.5	1.9	197.4
1931	207.8	−0.1	207.7	16.3	191.3	2.3	193.6
1932	207.9	−0.4	207.6	16.7	190.9	2.8	193.7
1933	198.4	−0.4	198.1	17.7	180.3	2.1	182.5

(continued)

Table S2 (continued)

	Gross domestic product at market prices (million Euro)	Net primary income from the rest of the world (million Euro)	Gross national income (million Euro)	Consumption of fixed capital (million Euro)	Net national income (million Euro)	Net current transfers from the rest of the world (million Euro)	Net national disposable income (million Euro)
1934	218.6	−0.4	218.2	18.5	199.7	1.7	201.3
1935	226.0	−0.3	225.6	19.2	206.4	0.7	207.1
1936	183.4	−0.3	183.1	−4.5	187.7	0.6	188.3
1937	192.2	−0.3	191.9	−4.5	196.4	1.0	197.4
1938	218.1	−0.3	217.7	−4.3	222.1	0.8	222.9
1939	251.4	−0.3	251.0	−3.8	254.8	0.7	255.5
1940	312.9	−0.1	312.8	25.1	287.7	0.5	288.2
1941	345.8	0.6	346.4	29.2	317.1	0.4	317.5
1942	416.7	0.1	416.8	32.3	384.5	0.3	384.8
1943	448.5	0.0	448.6	35.7	412.9	0.4	413.3
1944	518.0	0.0	518.0	37.4	480.6	0.8	481.4
1945	514.0	0.0	513.9	39.3	474.7	0.8	475.5
1946	650.2	0.3	650.5	49.6	600.8	1.2	602.1
1947	755.5	−0.1	755.4	63.2	692.2	1.4	693.6
1948	815.5	−0.3	815.2	68.6	746.6	1.0	747.7
1949	874.2	−0.5	873.7	70.4	803.3	0.8	804.1
1950	1078.7	−0.9	1077.9	86.8	991.1	0.4	991.5
1951	1373.1	−0.7	1372.4	96.1	1276.2	1.2	1277.4
1952	1509.8	−0.7	1509.0	100.8	1408.2	1.0	1409.3
1953	1631.9	−0.9	1631.0	105.9	1525.0	2.5	1527.5
1954	1888	0.1	1888	145.7	1742	6.8	1749

(continued)

Table S2 (continued)

	Gross domestic product at market prices (million Euro)	Net primary income from the rest of the world (million Euro)	Gross national income (million Euro)	Consumption of fixed capital (million Euro)	Net national income (million Euro)	Net current transfers from the rest of the world (million Euro)	Net national disposable income (million Euro)
1955	2039	−1.5	2038	154.5	1883	14.4	1898
1956	2523	−1.4	2522	212.3	2309	14.3	2324
1957	2944	−3.2	2941	255.1	2686	15.1	2701
1958	3497	−3.5	3494	234	3259	22.3	3281
1959	3669	−1.3	3668	281	3387	25	3412
1960	3818	−4.0	3814	318	3496	36	3532
1961	4399	−4.8	4394	386	4008	66	4073
1962	5143	−5.6	5137	468	4669	63	4732
1963	6142	−8.6	6134	575	5559	86	5645
1964	7024	−13.1	7010	712	6298	109	6407
1965	8260	−23	8237	791	7447	122	7569
1966	9541	−42	9499	874	8625	144	8768
1967	10694	−49	10645	942	9703	150	9853
1968	11910	−62	11848	1115	10733	173	10907
1969	13548	−94	13454	1258	12196	213	12410
1970	14836	−99	14737	1440	13296	259	13556
1971	16871	−91	16779	1635	15144	301	15445
1972	20141	−96	20045	1845	18200	316	18516
1973	24507	−70	24437	2203	22234	417	22651
1974	30424	−6	30418	2833	27585	319	27904
1975	36061	−117	35944	3502	32442	311	32753

(continued)

Table S2 (continued)

	Gross domestic product at market prices (million Euro)	Net primary income from the rest of the world (million Euro)	Gross national income (million Euro)	Consumption of fixed capital (million Euro)	Net national income (million Euro)	Net current transfers from the rest of the world (million Euro)	Net national disposable income (million Euro)
1976	43577	−253	43323	4268	39055	314	39369
1977	55486	−394	55092	5480	49612	314	49926
1978	68355	−558	67796	6760	61036	379	61415
1979	80186	−514	79672	8329	71343	234	71577
1980	94315	−742	93573	10057	83516	390	83905
1981	105785	−1402	104382	12825	91558	437	91994
1982	122547	−1677	120869	14993	105876	488	106364
1983	140100	−2120	137981	17574	120407	440	120846
1984	158806	−2344	156462	20213	136249	453	136702
1985	175730	−1917	173814	22484	151329	419	151749
1986	201824	−1678	200146	24228	175918	−24	175894
1987	226999	−1550	225448	26814	198634	621	199255
1988	253822	−2000	251822	30168	221654	1270	222924
1989	286677	−1557	285120	33767	251353	710	252063
1990	321343	−1660	319682	38031	281652	−394	281258
1991	354213	−1948	352264	42228	310037	−721	309316
1992	383334	−2552	380781	46204	334578	−1681	332896
1993	396886	−1016	395870	50785	345084	−1812	343272
1994	423945	−4869	419076	55066	364011	−2619	361392
1995	459337	−517	458820	60289	398530	−685	397845
1996	487992	490	488482	63410	425072	−1593	423480

(continued)

Table S2 (continued)

	Gross domestic product at market prices (million Euro)	Net primary income from the rest of the world (million Euro)	Gross national income (million Euro)	Consumption of fixed capital (million Euro)	Net national income (million Euro)	Net current transfers from the rest of the world (million Euro)	Net national disposable income (million Euro)
1997	518049	4919	522968	67443	455525	−1917	453608
1998	554042	7706	561748	71314	490434	−2441	487993
1999	594316	−3419	590897	79094	511803	−2326	509477
2000	646250	−2401	643849	88002	555847	−4514	551333
2001	699528	−7401	692127	95485	596642	−5235	591407
2002	749288	−8320	740968	103616	637352	−5226	632126
2003	803472	−6494	796978	112835	684143	−7720	676423
2004	861420	−7912	853508	124682	728826	−7866	720960
2005	930566	−13458	917108	137514	779594	−10403	769191
2006	1007974	−17550	990424	151151	839273	−14030	825243
2007	1080807	−26134	1054673	163764	890909	−13283	877626
2008	1116207	−29956	1086251	174258	911993	−15696	896297
2009	1079034	−19793	1059241	177000	882241	−14268	867973
2010	1080913	−15155	1065758	182025	883733	−12718	871015
2011	1070413	−18559	1051854	185764	866090	−14142	851948
2012	1039758	−7325	1032433	186405	846028	−12583	833445
2013	1025634	−5327	1020307	182948	837359	−13078	824281
2014	1037025	−3335	1033690	184773	848917	−11361	837556
2015	1075639	−780	1074859	189807	885052	−11286	873766

Sources Please cite the database as: Leandro Prados de la Escosura (2017), Spanish Economic Growth, 1850–2015

Table S3 Absolute and per capita gross domestic product, gross and net domestic income, 1850–2015 (million Euro and Euro)

	Gross domestic product at market prices (million Euro)	Gross national income (million Euro)	Net national income (million Euro)	Net national disposable income (million Euro)	Population (million)	Per capita GDP at market prices (Euro)	Gross national income Per Capita (Euro)	Net national income Per Capita (Euro)	Net national disposable income per capita (Euro)
1850	25.6	25.2	24.7	24.8	14.8	1.7	1.7	1.7	1.7
1851	26.1	25.8	25.3	25.3	14.9	1.8	1.7	1.7	1.7
1852	26.3	26.0	25.5	25.5	15.0	1.8	1.7	1.7	1.7
1853	31.0	30.7	30.2	30.2	15.1	2.1	2.0	2.0	2.0
1854	32.1	31.8	31.2	31.2	15.2	2.1	2.1	2.1	2.1
1855	34.0	33.8	33.2	33.3	15.2	2.2	2.2	2.2	2.2
1856	33.6	33.4	32.8	32.8	15.3	2.2	2.2	2.1	2.1
1857	32.4	32.2	31.5	31.6	15.5	2.1	2.1	2.0	2.0
1858	31.6	31.3	30.7	30.7	15.5	2.0	2.0	2.0	2.0
1859	33.7	33.4	32.6	32.7	15.5	2.2	2.1	2.1	2.1
1860	35.8	35.5	34.7	34.8	15.6	2.3	2.3	2.2	2.2
1861	36.6	36.3	35.4	35.5	15.8	2.3	2.3	2.2	2.3
1862	37.6	37.3	36.3	36.4	15.9	2.4	2.3	2.3	2.3
1863	39.6	39.2	38.2	38.3	16.0	2.5	2.5	2.4	2.4
1864	39.5	39.1	37.9	38.0	16.1	2.5	2.4	2.4	2.4
1865	37.2	36.9	35.7	35.8	16.1	2.3	2.3	2.2	2.2
1866	39.8	39.4	38.1	38.2	16.2	2.5	2.4	2.4	2.4
1867	42.4	42.1	40.7	40.8	16.3	2.6	2.6	2.5	2.5
1868	35.9	35.4	34.1	34.1	16.3	2.2	2.2	2.1	2.1
1869	33.1	32.4	31.1	31.2	16.3	2.0	2.0	1.9	1.9

(continued)

Table S3 (continued)

	Gross domestic product at market prices (million Euro)	Gross national income (million Euro)	Net national income (million Euro)	Net national disposable income (million Euro)	Population (million)	Per capita GDP at market prices (Euro)	Gross national income Per Capita (Euro)	Net national income Per Capita (Euro)	Net national disposable income per capita (Euro)
1870	35.9	35.2	33.8	33.9	16.3	2.2	2.2	2.1	2.1
1871	38.5	37.8	36.3	36.4	16.4	2.4	2.3	2.2	2.2
1872	44.1	43.3	41.8	41.9	16.4	2.7	2.6	2.5	2.6
1873	47.1	46.3	44.5	44.6	16.5	2.9	2.8	2.7	2.7
1874	46.8	45.6	43.8	44.0	16.5	2.8	2.8	2.7	2.7
1875	46.3	45.1	43.3	43.4	16.5	2.8	2.7	2.6	2.6
1876	48.1	47.4	45.8	46.0	16.6	2.9	2.9	2.8	2.8
1877	53.0	52.3	50.7	50.9	16.6	3.2	3.1	3.0	3.1
1878	52.4	51.7	50.0	50.1	16.7	3.1	3.1	3.0	3.0
1879	51.1	50.3	48.7	48.9	16.8	3.0	3.0	2.9	2.9
1880	54.2	53.4	51.7	51.8	17.0	3.2	3.1	3.0	3.1
1881	56.8	55.8	54.1	54.3	17.1	3.3	3.3	3.2	3.2
1882	60.1	59.0	57.2	57.4	17.2	3.5	3.4	3.3	3.3
1883	61.0	59.8	58.0	58.2	17.3	3.5	3.5	3.4	3.4
1884	58.6	57.5	55.5	55.7	17.3	3.4	3.3	3.2	3.2
1885	58.0	56.8	54.9	55.1	17.4	3.3	3.3	3.2	3.2
1886	59.0	57.8	56.0	56.3	17.4	3.4	3.3	3.2	3.2
1887	54.1	52.9	51.2	51.5	17.5	3.1	3.0	2.9	2.9
1888	56.5	55.3	53.4	53.8	17.6	3.2	3.1	3.0	3.1
1889	52.4	51.1	49.2	49.7	17.6	3.0	2.9	2.8	2.8
1890	53.1	51.8	49.8	50.2	17.6	3.0	2.9	2.8	2.9

(continued)

Appendices 223

Table S3 (continued)

	Gross domestic product at market prices (million Euro)	Gross national income (million Euro)	Net national income (million Euro)	Net national disposable income (million Euro)	Population (million)	Per capita GDP at market prices (Euro)	Gross national income Per Capita (Euro)	Net national income Per Capita (Euro)	Net national disposable income per capita (Euro)
1891	54.2	52.9	50.9	51.4	17.6	3.1	3.0	2.9	2.9
1892	53.7	52.5	50.5	51.0	17.7	3.0	3.0	2.9	2.9
1893	52.3	51.1	48.9	49.6	17.7	3.0	2.9	2.8	2.8
1894	51.2	50.0	47.8	48.3	17.8	2.9	2.8	2.7	2.7
1895	51.6	50.5	48.4	48.8	17.8	2.9	2.8	2.7	2.7
1896	49.4	48.1	45.9	46.4	17.9	2.8	2.7	2.6	2.6
1897	53.6	52.1	49.7	50.3	18.1	3.0	2.9	2.8	2.8
1898	57.5	55.8	53.0	53.6	18.3	3.2	3.1	2.9	2.9
1899	58.4	56.4	53.6	54.1	18.4	3.2	3.1	2.9	2.9
1900	61.7	59.6	56.4	57.0	18.6	3.3	3.2	3.0	3.1
1901	64.8	63.1	60.1	60.7	18.7	3.5	3.4	3.2	3.2
1902	62.6	60.9	57.9	58.4	18.9	3.3	3.2	3.1	3.1
1903	67.0	65.3	61.9	62.6	19.1	3.5	3.4	3.2	3.3
1904	70.7	68.8	65.4	66.3	19.3	3.7	3.6	3.4	3.4
1905	68.1	66.3	63.1	64.1	19.4	3.5	3.4	3.3	3.3
1906	69.5	67.3	64.1	65.3	19.5	3.6	3.5	3.3	3.4
1907	72.3	69.9	66.3	67.7	19.6	3.7	3.6	3.4	3.5
1908	71.8	70.0	66.5	68.2	19.7	3.6	3.6	3.4	3.5
1909	73.4	71.5	67.9	69.6	19.8	3.7	3.6	3.4	3.5
1910	70.2	68.4	64.6	66.6	19.9	3.5	3.4	3.2	3.3
1911	75.8	74.2	70.3	72.4	20.0	3.8	3.7	3.5	3.6

(continued)

Appendices

Table S3 (continued)

	Gross domestic product at market prices (million Euro)	Gross national income (million Euro)	Net national income (million Euro)	Net national disposable income (million Euro)	Population (million)	Per capita GDP at market prices (Euro)	Gross national income Per Capita (Euro)	Net national income Per Capita (Euro)	Net national disposable income per capita (Euro)
1912	77.2	75.3	71.4	73.8	20.1	3.8	3.7	3.5	3.7
1913	82.9	80.7	76.4	78.6	20.3	4.1	4.0	3.8	3.9
1914	82.5	81.7	77.5	79.3	20.5	4.0	4.0	3.8	3.9
1915	90.8	90.0	85.1	86.6	20.7	4.4	4.3	4.1	4.2
1916	105	104	98	100	21.0	5.0	4.9	4.7	4.7
1917	114	113	106	107	21.2	5.4	5.4	5.0	5.1
1918	138	138	128	130	21.2	6.5	6.5	6.1	6.1
1919	149	149	140	142	21.2	7.0	7.0	6.6	6.7
1920	177	176	164	167	21.4	8.3	8.2	7.7	7.8
1921	163	162	150	153	21.5	7.6	7.5	7.0	7.1
1922	165	165	153	155	21.8	7.6	7.6	7.0	7.1
1923	165	165	153	156	21.9	7.5	7.5	7.0	7.1
1924	181	180	168	171	22.1	8.2	8.2	7.6	7.7
1925	192	191	179	181	22.3	8.6	8.6	8.0	8.1
1926	188	187	174	176	22.5	8.3	8.3	7.7	7.8
1927	201	200	187	189	22.8	8.8	8.8	8.2	8.3
1928	197	196	182	183	23.0	8.5	8.5	7.9	8.0
1929	212	211	196	198	23.3	9.1	9.1	8.4	8.5
1930	212	211	196	197	23.6	9.0	8.9	8.3	8.4
1931	208	208	191	194	24.0	8.7	8.7	8.0	8.1
1932	208	208	191	194	24.4	8.5	8.5	7.8	7.9

(continued)

Table S3 (continued)

	Gross domestic product at market prices (million Euro)	Gross national income (million Euro)	Net national income (million Euro)	Net national disposable income (million Euro)	Population (million)	Per capita GDP at market prices (Euro)	Gross national income Per Capita (Euro)	Net national income Per Capita (Euro)	Net national disposable income per capita (Euro)
1933	198	198	180	182	24.8	8.0	8.0	7.3	7.4
1934	219	218	200	201	25.2	8.7	8.7	7.9	8.0
1935	226	226	206	207	25.5	8.8	8.8	8.1	8.1
1936	183	183	188	188	25.9	7.1	7.1	7.3	7.3
1937	192	192	196	197	26.0	7.4	7.4	7.5	7.6
1938	218	218	222	223	26.1	8.3	8.3	8.5	8.5
1939	251	251	255	255	25.9	9.7	9.7	9.8	9.9
1940	313	313	288	288	25.7	12.2	12.2	11.2	11.2
1941	346	346	317	318	25.7	13.5	13.5	12.4	12.4
1942	417	417	385	385	25.6	16.3	16.3	15.0	15.0
1943	449	449	413	413	25.8	17.4	17.4	16.0	16.0
1944	518	518	481	481	26.0	19.9	19.9	18.5	18.5
1945	514	514	475	475	26.3	19.5	19.5	18.1	18.1
1946	650	650	601	602	26.6	24.5	24.5	22.6	22.7
1947	756	755	692	694	26.8	28.2	28.1	25.8	25.8
1948	816	815	747	748	27.2	29.9	29.9	27.4	27.4
1949	874	874	803	804	27.7	31.5	31.5	29.0	29.0
1950	1079	1078	991	991	28.0	38.5	38.5	35.4	35.4
1951	1373	1372	1276	1277	28.2	48.8	48.7	45.3	45.4
1952	1510	1509	1408	1409	28.3	53.3	53.2	49.7	49.7
1953	1632	1631	1525	1528	28.6	57.1	57.1	53.4	53.5

(continued)

Table S3 (continued)

	Gross domestic product at market prices (million Euro)	Gross national income (million Euro)	Net national income (million Euro)	Net national disposable income (million Euro)	Population (million)	Per capita GDP at market prices (Euro)	Gross national income Per Capita (Euro)	Net national income Per Capita (Euro)	Net national disposable income per capita (Euro)
1954	1888	1888	1742	1749	28.8	65.5	65.5	60.5	60.7
1955	2039	2038	1883	1898	29.0	70.2	70.2	64.9	65.4
1956	2523	2522	2309	2324	29.3	86.2	86.2	78.9	79.4
1957	2944	2941	2686	2701	29.5	99.8	99.7	91.0	91.6
1958	3497	3494	3259	3281	29.8	117	117	109	110
1959	3669	3668	3387	3412	30.1	122	122	113	113
1960	3818	3814	3496	3532	30.4	125	125	115	116
1961	4399	4394	4008	4073	30.8	143	143	130	132
1962	5143	5137	4669	4732	31.1	166	165	150	152
1963	6142	6134	5559	5645	31.3	196	196	177	180
1964	7024	7010	6298	6407	31.6	222	222	199	203
1965	8260	8237	7447	7569	31.9	259	258	233	237
1966	9541	9499	8625	8768	32.4	295	294	267	271
1967	10694	10645	9703	9853	32.8	326	325	296	300
1968	11910	11848	10733	10907	33.2	359	357	323	329
1969	13548	13454	12196	12410	33.6	404	401	364	370
1970	14836	14737	13296	13556	33.9	438	435	393	400
1971	16871	16779	15144	15445	34.2	493	490	443	451
1972	20141	20045	18200	18516	34.6	582	579	526	535
1973	24507	24437	22234	22651	35.0	701	699	636	648
1974	30424	30418	27585	27904	35.4	860	860	780	789

(continued)

Appendices 227

Table S3 (continued)

	Gross domestic product at market prices (million Euro)	Gross national income (million Euro)	Net national income (million Euro)	Net national disposable income (million Euro)	Population (million)	Per capita GDP at market prices (Euro)	Gross national income Per Capita (Euro)	Net national income Per Capita (Euro)	Net national disposable income per capita (Euro)
1975	36061	35944	32442	32753	35.8	1009	1005	908	916
1976	43577	43323	39055	39369	36.1	1206	1199	1081	1090
1977	55486	55092	49612	49926	36.5	1520	1509	1359	1368
1978	68355	67796	61036	61415	36.9	1854	1839	1656	1666
1979	80186	79672	71343	71577	37.2	2156	2142	1918	1924
1980	94315	93573	83516	83905	37.5	2516	2496	2228	2238
1981	105785	104382	91558	91994	37.8	2801	2764	2424	2436
1982	122547	120869	105876	106364	38.0	3226	3182	2787	2800
1983	140100	137981	120407	120846	38.2	3671	3616	3155	3167
1984	158806	156462	136249	136702	38.3	4144	4083	3555	3567
1985	175730	173814	151329	151749	38.5	4568	4519	3934	3945
1986	201824	200146	175918	175894	38.6	5232	5189	4561	4560
1987	226999	225448	198634	199255	38.7	5868	5828	5135	5151
1988	253822	251822	221654	222924	38.8	6548	6496	5718	5751
1989	286677	285120	251353	252063	38.8	7385	7344	6475	6493
1990	321343	319682	281652	281258	38.9	8269	8226	7248	7238
1991	354213	352264	310037	309316	38.9	9096	9046	7962	7943
1992	383334	380781	334578	332896	39.1	9792	9727	8547	8504
1993	396886	395870	345084	343272	39.4	10085	10059	8768	8722
1994	423945	419076	364011	361392	39.5	10720	10597	9204	9138
1995	459337	458820	398530	397845	39.7	11565	11552	10034	10017

(continued)

Table S3 (continued)

	Gross domestic product at market prices (million Euro)	Gross national income (million Euro)	Net national income (million Euro)	Net national disposable income (million Euro)	Population (million)	Per capita GDP at market prices (Euro)	Gross national income Per Capita (Euro)	Net national income Per Capita (Euro)	Net national disposable income per capita (Euro)
1996	487992	488482	425072	423480	39.9	12235	12248	10658	10618
1997	518049	522968	455525	453608	40.0	12935	13058	11374	11326
1998	554042	561748	490434	487993	40.2	13777	13969	12196	12135
1999	594316	590897	511803	509477	40.4	14722	14637	12678	12620
2000	646250	643849	555847	551333	40.6	15935	15876	13706	13595
2001	699528	692127	596642	591407	40.8	17160	16978	14636	14507
2002	749288	740968	637352	632126	41.4	18089	17888	15386	15260
2003	803472	796978	684143	676423	42.2	19041	18887	16213	16030
2004	861420	853508	728826	720960	42.9	20099	19914	17005	16822
2005	930566	917108	779594	769191	43.7	21313	21004	17855	17617
2006	1007974	990424	839273	825243	44.4	22722	22327	18919	18603
2007	1080807	1054673	890909	877626	45.2	23893	23315	19695	19401
2008	1116207	1086251	911993	896297	46.0	24274	23623	19833	19492
2009	1079034	1059241	882241	867973	46.4	23271	22844	19027	18719
2010	1080913	1065758	883733	871015	46.6	23214	22889	18980	18706
2011	1070413	1051854	866090	851948	46.7	22903	22506	18531	18229
2012	1039758	1032433	846028	833445	46.8	22233	22076	18091	17821
2013	1025634	1020307	837359	824281	46.6	22013	21899	17972	17692
2014	1037025	1033690	848917	837556	46.5	22323	22251	18274	18029
2015	1075639	1074859	885052	873766	46.4	23178	23161	19071	18828

Sources Please cite the database as: Leandro Prados de la Escosura (2017), Spanish Economic Growth, 1850–2015

Table S4 Volume indices of absolute and per capita gross domestic product, gross and net national income, 1850–2015 (2010 = 100)

	Gross domestic product at market prices (2010 = 100)	Gross national income (2010 = 100)	Net national income (2010 = 100)	Net national disposable income (2010 = 100)	Per capita GDP (2010 = 100)	gross national income per capita (2010 = 100)	Net national income per capita (2010 = 100)	Net national disposable income per capita (2010 = 100)
1850	2.0	2.0	2.4	2.4	6.3	6.3	7.6	7.7
1851	2.0	2.0	2.4	2.5	6.4	6.4	7.6	7.8
1852	2.1	2.1	2.6	2.6	6.6	6.7	7.9	8.1
1853	2.1	2.2	2.6	2.6	6.6	6.7	7.9	8.1
1854	2.2	2.2	2.6	2.7	6.7	6.7	8.0	8.1
1855	2.3	2.3	2.7	2.8	7.0	7.1	8.4	8.5
1856	2.2	2.2	2.6	2.7	6.6	6.7	8.0	8.1
1857	2.1	2.2	2.6	2.6	6.4	6.5	7.7	7.8
1858	2.2	2.2	2.6	2.7	6.6	6.6	7.9	8.0
1859	2.3	2.3	2.8	2.8	6.9	6.9	8.2	8.4
1860	2.4	2.4	2.9	2.9	7.1	7.2	8.5	8.7
1861	2.4	2.4	2.9	2.9	7.1	7.2	8.5	8.7
1862	2.4	2.5	2.9	3.0	7.1	7.2	8.5	8.7
1863	2.5	2.5	3.0	3.0	7.2	7.3	8.6	8.8
1864	2.5	2.5	3.0	3.0	7.2	7.2	8.6	8.7
1865	2.4	2.4	2.8	2.9	6.9	7.0	8.2	8.3
1866	2.5	2.6	3.0	3.1	7.3	7.4	8.7	8.8
1867	2.5	2.5	3.0	3.0	7.2	7.3	8.5	8.6
1868	2.2	2.2	2.6	2.6	6.3	6.3	7.4	7.5
1869	2.3	2.3	2.7	2.7	6.5	6.5	7.6	7.7

(continued)

230 Appendices

Table S4 (continued)

	Gross domestic product at market prices (2010 = 100)	Gross national income (2010 = 100)	Net national income (2010 = 100)	Net national disposable income (2010 = 100)	Per capita GDP (2010 = 100)	gross national income per capita (2010 = 100)	Net national income per capita (2010 = 100)	Net national disposable income per capita (2010 = 100)
1870	2.3	2.4	2.7	2.8	6.7	6.7	7.8	8.0
1871	2.5	2.5	3.0	3.0	7.2	7.2	8.4	8.6
1872	2.9	2.9	3.4	3.5	8.3	8.3	9.8	9.9
1873	3.2	3.2	3.7	3.8	9.0	9.0	10.5	10.7
1874	2.9	2.9	3.4	3.5	8.2	8.2	9.6	9.7
1875	3.0	3.0	3.5	3.5	8.4	8.4	9.8	10.0
1876	3.1	3.1	3.6	3.7	8.7	8.7	10.2	10.4
1877	3.4	3.5	4.1	4.1	9.6	9.7	11.4	11.6
1878	3.3	3.3	3.9	4.0	9.2	9.3	10.9	11.0
1879	3.1	3.1	3.6	3.7	8.6	8.6	10.0	10.2
1880	3.4	3.4	4.0	4.1	9.3	9.3	10.9	11.1
1881	3.4	3.4	4.0	4.1	9.4	9.4	11.0	11.2
1882	3.5	3.5	4.1	4.1	9.4	9.4	11.0	11.2
1883	3.5	3.5	4.1	4.2	9.5	9.5	11.1	11.3
1884	3.6	3.6	4.2	4.2	9.6	9.6	11.2	11.4
1885	3.4	3.4	4.0	4.1	9.2	9.2	10.7	10.9
1886	3.4	3.4	3.9	4.0	9.0	9.0	10.4	10.6
1887	3.3	3.3	3.8	3.9	8.8	8.8	10.2	10.4
1888	3.4	3.4	4.0	4.1	9.1	9.1	10.6	10.8
1889	3.4	3.4	4.0	4.1	9.1	9.1	10.6	10.8
1890	3.4	3.4	4.0	4.1	9.1	9.1	10.5	10.7

(continued)

Table S4 (continued)

	Gross domestic product at market prices (2010 = 100)	Gross national income (2010 = 100)	Net national income (2010 = 100)	Net national disposable income (2010 = 100)	Per capita GDP (2010 = 100)	gross national income per capita (2010 = 100)	Net national income per capita (2010 = 100)	Net national disposable income per capita (2010 = 100)
1891	3.5	3.5	4.1	4.1	9.3	9.3	10.7	11.0
1892	3.8	3.8	4.4	4.5	10.0	10.1	11.7	11.9
1893	3.7	3.7	4.2	4.3	9.6	9.6	11.2	11.4
1894	3.7	3.7	4.3	4.4	9.7	9.7	11.3	11.5
1895	3.7	3.7	4.2	4.3	9.6	9.6	11.1	11.3
1896	3.3	3.3	3.8	3.9	8.6	8.6	9.9	10.1
1897	3.5	3.5	4.1	4.2	9.1	9.1	10.5	10.7
1898	3.8	3.8	4.4	4.5	9.7	9.7	11.2	11.4
1899	3.9	3.8	4.4	4.5	9.7	9.7	11.2	11.4
1900	3.9	3.9	4.5	4.6	9.9	9.9	11.4	11.6
1901	4.3	4.3	5.0	5.1	10.7	10.7	12.3	12.6
1902	4.1	4.1	4.7	4.8	10.1	10.1	11.7	11.9
1903	4.1	4.1	4.7	4.8	10.0	10.0	11.5	11.8
1904	4.1	4.1	4.7	4.8	9.8	9.8	11.3	11.6
1905	4.0	4.0	4.6	4.7	9.7	9.7	11.1	11.4
1906	4.3	4.3	4.9	5.0	10.2	10.2	11.7	12.1
1907	4.4	4.4	5.0	5.2	10.4	10.4	12.0	12.3
1908	4.6	4.6	5.3	5.4	10.8	10.8	12.4	12.8
1909	4.7	4.7	5.4	5.5	11.0	11.0	12.7	13.0
1910	4.5	4.5	5.1	5.3	10.4	10.4	12.0	12.4
1911	4.8	4.8	5.6	5.7	11.2	11.2	12.9	13.3

(continued)

Table S4 (continued)

	Gross domestic product at market prices	Gross national income	Net national income	Net national disposable income	Per capita GDP	gross national income per capita	Net national income per capita	Net national disposable income per capita
	(2010 = 100)	(2010 = 100)	(2010 = 100)	(2010 = 100)	(2010 = 100)	(2010 = 100)	(2010 = 100)	(2010 = 100)
1912	4.7	4.7	5.3	5.5	10.8	10.8	12.4	12.8
1913	4.9	4.9	5.7	5.8	11.3	11.3	13.0	13.4
1914	4.8	4.8	5.6	5.7	10.9	11.0	12.6	13.0
1915	4.9	4.9	5.7	5.8	11.0	11.1	12.7	13.0
1916	5.1	5.2	5.9	6.1	11.4	11.5	13.2	13.5
1917	5.1	5.1	5.8	6.0	11.1	11.3	12.9	13.1
1918	5.0	5.1	5.8	5.9	11.0	11.1	12.7	13.0
1919	5.1	5.2	5.9	6.0	11.2	11.3	12.9	13.2
1920	5.5	5.6	6.3	6.5	12.0	12.1	13.8	14.1
1921	5.7	5.7	6.6	6.7	12.3	12.4	14.2	14.5
1922	5.9	6.0	6.8	7.0	12.7	12.8	14.6	14.9
1923	6.0	6.0	6.9	7.1	12.7	12.8	14.7	15.0
1924	6.2	6.2	7.1	7.3	13.0	13.1	15.0	15.3
1925	6.6	6.7	7.6	7.8	13.8	13.9	15.9	16.3
1926	6.5	6.6	7.5	7.7	13.5	13.6	15.5	15.9
1927	7.2	7.2	8.3	8.5	14.6	14.8	16.9	17.3
1928	7.1	7.2	8.2	8.4	14.4	14.6	16.7	17.0
1929	7.7	7.8	8.9	9.1	15.4	15.6	17.8	18.2
1930	7.3	7.4	8.4	8.6	14.5	14.7	16.7	17.0
1931	7.2	7.3	8.3	8.4	14.0	14.2	16.1	16.4
1932	7.5	7.6	8.6	8.7	14.2	14.4	16.3	16.7

(continued)

Table S4 (continued)

	Gross domestic product at market prices (2010 = 100)	Gross national income (2010 = 100)	Net national income (2010 = 100)	Net national disposable income (2010 = 100)	Per capita GDP (2010 = 100)	gross national income per capita (2010 = 100)	Net national income per capita (2010 = 100)	Net national disposable income per capita (2010 = 100)
1933	7.3	7.4	8.3	8.5	13.6	13.8	15.6	15.9
1934	7.6	7.6	8.6	8.8	14.0	14.1	16.0	16.3
1935	7.7	7.8	8.8	9.0	14.1	14.2	16.1	16.4
1936	5.9	6.0	7.3	7.5	10.6	10.8	13.2	13.4
1937	5.5	5.6	6.8	6.9	9.8	9.9	12.2	12.4
1938	5.5	5.5	6.8	6.9	9.7	9.9	12.1	12.3
1939	5.9	6.0	7.3	7.5	10.7	10.8	13.2	13.4
1940	6.5	6.6	7.4	7.5	11.7	11.9	13.3	13.6
1941	6.5	6.6	7.4	7.5	11.8	12.0	13.5	13.7
1942	6.9	7.0	7.9	8.0	12.5	12.7	14.3	14.6
1943	7.3	7.4	8.3	8.4	13.1	13.3	15.0	15.2
1944	7.6	7.7	8.7	8.8	13.6	13.8	15.6	15.8
1945	7.0	7.1	8.0	8.1	12.4	12.6	14.1	14.3
1946	7.3	7.4	8.4	8.5	12.8	13.0	14.6	14.9
1947	7.5	7.6	8.6	8.7	13.0	13.2	14.8	15.1
1948	7.5	7.6	8.6	8.7	12.8	13.0	14.7	14.9
1949	7.5	7.7	8.6	8.8	12.7	12.9	14.5	14.7
1950	7.7	7.8	8.8	8.9	12.8	13.0	14.6	14.8
1951	8.5	8.6	9.7	9.9	14.0	14.2	16.1	16.3
1952	9.2	9.4	10.7	10.8	15.2	15.4	17.5	17.8
1953	9.2	9.3	10.6	10.8	15.0	15.2	17.3	17.6

(continued)

Table S4 (continued)

	Gross domestic product at market prices	Gross national income	Net national income	Net national disposable income	Per capita GDP	gross national income per capita	Net national income per capita	Net national disposable income per capita
	(2010 = 100)	(2010 = 100)	(2010 = 100)	(2010 = 100)	(2010 = 100)	(2010 = 100)	(2010 = 100)	(2010 = 100)
1954	9.9	10.0	11.4	11.6	16.0	16.2	18.5	18.8
1955	10.2	10.4	11.8	12.0	16.4	16.6	19.0	19.3
1956	11.1	11.2	12.8	13.0	17.6	17.9	20.4	20.7
1957	11.5	11.6	13.3	13.5	18.1	18.3	20.9	21.3
1958	12.2	12.4	14.3	14.5	19.1	19.4	22.3	22.7
1959	12.1	12.3	14.0	14.3	18.8	19.0	21.7	22.1
1960	12.2	12.3	13.9	14.2	18.6	18.9	21.3	21.7
1961	13.6	13.8	15.5	15.9	20.6	20.9	23.5	24.0
1962	15.0	15.2	17.0	17.4	22.5	22.8	25.5	26.0
1963	16.5	16.7	18.7	19.1	24.5	24.8	27.7	28.3
1964	17.4	17.6	19.5	20.0	25.6	26.0	28.7	29.4
1965	18.8	19.0	21.1	21.6	27.4	27.7	30.7	31.4
1966	20.2	20.5	22.7	23.2	29.1	29.4	32.6	33.4
1967	21.4	21.6	24.0	24.6	30.3	30.7	34.1	34.9
1968	22.7	22.9	25.3	25.9	31.8	32.1	35.5	36.3
1969	24.8	25.0	27.6	28.3	34.4	34.7	38.4	39.3
1970	25.6	25.8	28.4	29.2	35.1	35.5	39.1	40.1
1971	26.8	27.1	29.8	30.6	36.5	36.9	40.6	41.7
1972	29.6	29.9	33.0	33.9	39.9	40.3	44.5	45.6
1973	32.3	32.7	36.2	37.1	43.0	43.5	48.1	49.4
1974	34.7	35.2	39.0	39.8	45.7	46.4	51.3	52.4

(continued)

Table S4 (continued)

	Gross domestic product at market prices (2010 = 100)	Gross national income (2010 = 100)	Net national income (2010 = 100)	Net national disposable income (2010 = 100)	Per capita GDP (2010 = 100)	gross national income per capita (2010 = 100)	Net national income per capita (2010 = 100)	Net national disposable income per capita (2010 = 100)
1975	35.8	36.2	39.9	40.7	46.6	47.2	52.0	53.0
1976	37.4	37.8	41.5	42.3	48.2	48.7	53.5	54.6
1977	38.6	39.0	42.8	43.6	49.3	49.8	54.6	55.6
1978	39.7	40.0	43.9	44.7	50.1	50.6	55.4	56.5
1979	40.4	40.8	44.5	45.2	50.5	51.0	55.7	56.6
1980	41.6	42.1	45.9	46.7	51.7	52.2	57.0	58.0
1981	41.6	41.9	45.2	46.0	51.3	51.7	55.8	56.7
1982	42.3	42.6	45.8	46.6	51.9	52.3	56.2	57.1
1983	43.1	43.4	46.5	47.3	52.6	53.0	56.8	57.7
1984	43.5	43.8	46.7	47.5	52.8	53.2	56.8	57.7
1985	44.8	45.2	48.2	48.9	54.2	54.7	58.3	59.2
1986	46.6	47.0	50.3	51.0	56.3	56.8	60.7	61.5
1987	49.9	50.4	53.9	54.8	60.1	60.7	64.9	66.0
1988	53.1	53.6	57.4	58.4	63.8	64.3	68.9	70.2
1989	56.5	57.1	61.2	62.2	67.8	68.5	73.4	74.6
1990	59.2	59.8	64.0	64.8	71.0	71.7	76.7	77.7
1991	61.1	61.7	65.8	66.7	73.1	73.8	78.7	79.7
1992	62.1	62.6	66.4	67.1	73.9	74.5	79.0	79.8
1993	61.1	61.8	65.0	65.7	72.3	73.2	76.9	77.7
1994	62.8	63.1	66.1	66.6	73.9	74.3	77.8	78.5
1995	65.1	66.0	69.1	70.0	76.4	77.4	81.0	82.0

(continued)

Table S4 (continued)

	Gross domestic product at market prices (2010 = 100)	Gross national income (2010 = 100)	Net national income (2010 = 100)	Net national disposable income (2010 = 100)	Per capita GDP (2010 = 100)	gross national income per capita (2010 = 100)	Net national income per capita (2010 = 100)	Net national disposable income per capita (2010 = 100)
1996	66.9	67.9	71.1	71.9	78.1	79.3	83.0	83.9
1997	69.4	70.9	74.4	75.2	80.7	82.5	86.5	87.5
1998	72.6	74.5	78.3	79.1	84.1	86.3	90.6	91.6
1999	76.1	76.8	80.2	81.0	87.8	88.6	92.5	93.5
2000	80.1	81.0	84.7	85.4	92.0	93.0	97.3	98.0
2001	83.3	83.8	87.4	88.0	95.2	95.7	99.8	100.5
2002	85.8	86.1	89.7	90.3	96.4	96.8	100.8	101.5
2003	88.6	89.1	92.6	93.0	97.7	98.4	102.2	102.6
2004	91.4	91.9	95.2	95.6	99.3	99.8	103.4	103.8
2005	94.8	94.8	98.0	98.1	101.1	101.1	104.5	104.6
2006	98.7	98.4	101.5	101.3	103.6	103.3	106.6	106.4
2007	102.5	101.4	104.2	104.2	105.5	104.4	107.3	107.2
2008	103.7	102.4	104.5	104.2	105.0	103.7	105.8	105.5
2009	100.0	99.5	100.0	99.7	100.4	99.9	100.4	100.1
2010	100.0	100.0	100.0	100.0	100.0	100.0	100.0	100.0
2011	99.0	98.8	98.0	97.9	98.6	98.4	97.6	97.5
2012	95.9	96.7	94.9	95.0	95.5	96.3	94.5	94.6
2013	94.2	95.1	92.7	92.7	94.2	95.1	92.6	92.6
2014	95.6	96.7	94.3	94.5	95.9	96.9	94.5	94.7
2015	98.8	100.1	98.0	98.2	99.1	100.5	98.3	98.5

Sources Please cite the database as: Leandro Prados de la Escosura (2017), Spanish Economic Growth, 1850–2015

Table S5 Shares of expenditure components in gross domestic product, 1850–2015 (percentage)

	Final consumption expenditure		Gross capital formation			
	Final consumption expenditure of NPISHs and households (%)	Final consumption expenditure by government (%)	Gross fixed capital formation (%)	Changes inventories and acquisitions less disposals of valuables (%)	Exports of goods and services (%)	Imports of goods and services (%)
1850	85.28	9.63	4.63	0.84	4.00	4.38
1851	85.37	9.82	5.08	0.87	3.48	4.63
1852	85.30	9.47	5.90	0.90	3.28	4.86
1853	86.23	8.36	5.04	0.78	3.85	4.26
1854	87.05	8.05	4.21	0.75	4.61	4.66
1855	87.77	7.10	3.40	0.67	5.97	4.91
1856	86.94	7.79	4.81	0.63	6.07	6.23
1857	84.77	9.72	6.26	0.60	6.31	7.66
1858	83.81	10.55	9.18	0.58	3.78	7.90
1859	81.94	10.10	9.12	0.52	4.50	6.18
1860	77.89	11.94	10.32	0.46	5.45	6.05
1861	80.61	10.73	9.26	0.41	5.19	6.20
1862	82.30	10.24	9.76	0.35	4.08	6.72
1863	84.51	9.99	9.11	0.28	3.93	7.82
1864	84.75	10.71	8.12	0.22	3.85	7.66
1865	83.73	11.49	7.32	0.20	4.41	7.15
1866	85.79	9.57	6.76	0.18	4.35	6.65
1867	83.97	8.64	6.65	0.18	5.48	4.93
1868	85.82	9.74	4.33	0.27	6.67	6.84
1869	83.74	9.76	4.38	0.42	8.20	6.50
1870	86.02	9.07	4.70	0.55	5.95	6.29

(continued)

Table S5 (continued)

	Final consumption expenditure		Gross capital formation			
	Final consumption expenditure of NPISHs and households (%)	Final consumption expenditure by government (%)	Gross fixed capital formation (%)	Changes inventories and acquisitions less disposals of valuables (%)	Exports of goods and services (%)	Imports of goods and services (%)
1871	85.31	8.58	5.07	0.66	7.26	6.87
1872	86.28	8.43	4.95	0.68	7.12	7.46
1873	83.86	9.41	4.07	0.70	7.86	5.90
1874	82.77	12.23	4.70	0.74	6.88	7.32
1875	79.67	13.77	4.75	0.76	7.33	6.28
1876	85.62	9.24	5.84	0.74	6.00	7.43
1877	84.53	8.65	5.38	0.66	6.76	5.97
1878	83.59	8.49	6.57	0.63	6.46	5.76
1879	85.97	8.41	5.05	0.60	6.74	6.76
1880	83.12	8.22	6.09	0.51	8.59	6.54
1881	85.28	8.03	4.91	0.41	8.44	7.08
1882	83.45	9.37	5.83	0.30	8.11	7.06
1883	83.98	7.80	6.83	0.19	8.50	7.29
1884	83.85	8.13	6.91	0.08	7.70	6.67
1885	84.58	8.84	5.10	−0.02	8.25	6.76
1886	84.82	8.69	4.62	−0.10	8.75	6.78
1887	85.19	8.49	4.85	−0.17	8.86	7.23
1888	86.43	8.00	4.30	−0.20	9.13	7.67
1889	85.48	8.52	5.25	−0.22	10.23	9.26
1890	84.93	8.10	5.72	−0.19	10.42	8.98
1891	84.49	7.77	5.39	−0.15	10.92	8.44

(continued)

Table S5 (continued)

	Final consumption expenditure		Gross capital formation		Exports of goods and services (%)	Imports of goods and services (%)
	Final consumption expenditure of NPISHs and households (%)	Final consumption expenditure by government (%)	Gross fixed capital formation (%)	Changes inventories and acquisitions less disposals of valuables (%)		
1892	83.25	8.64	5.52	−0.09	11.01	8.34
1893	83.53	8.76	5.54	−0.01	10.73	8.55
1894	83.60	8.52	5.51	0.10	11.20	8.94
1895	82.13	8.66	5.87	0.22	10.59	7.47
1896	79.44	9.27	6.00	0.37	13.75	8.83
1897	79.57	9.44	5.87	0.46	13.46	8.81
1898	78.75	9.35	5.74	0.52	14.02	8.38
1899	81.07	8.47	8.64	0.56	11.82	10.55
1900	78.90	8.08	10.66	0.55	12.78	10.97
1901	83.64	7.72	7.77	0.51	11.05	10.69
1902	83.59	7.99	6.92	0.50	11.52	10.51
1903	84.37	7.44	7.13	0.44	11.26	10.64
1904	83.86	7.54	7.32	0.38	11.11	10.22
1905	83.77	7.48	6.76	0.37	12.73	11.11
1906	81.93	7.84	6.97	0.37	12.26	9.38
1907	80.57	7.78	7.73	0.41	12.39	8.88
1908	83.03	7.81	7.28	0.50	10.20	8.81
1909	80.99	8.72	7.69	0.63	9.82	7.84
1910	78.50	9.34	8.93	0.87	11.42	9.07
1911	79.09	9.24	8.82	1.05	11.75	9.94
1912	76.66	9.53	10.31	1.32	12.62	10.44

(continued)

Table S5 (continued)

	Final consumption expenditure		Gross capital formation		Exports of goods and services (%)	Imports of goods and services (%)
	Final consumption expenditure of NPISHs and households (%)	Final consumption expenditure by government (%)	Gross fixed capital formation (%)	Changes inventories and acquisitions less disposals of valuables (%)		
1913	77.24	9.65	10.69	1.52	12.04	11.15
1914	77.39	10.16	9.54	1.85	9.07	8.00
1915	73.88	12.91	7.40	1.97	10.35	6.50
1916	78.43	9.39	7.26	1.93	10.59	7.59
1917	76.39	8.56	7.63	1.92	12.15	6.66
1918	79.01	8.50	7.63	1.66	8.17	4.95
1919	75.21	9.39	7.37	1.53	14.73	8.23
1920	82.17	10.99	8.20	1.23	10.75	13.34
1921	75.52	14.28	10.72	1.21	8.06	9.81
1922	80.21	12.07	10.20	1.07	6.01	9.56
1923	82.47	11.14	10.46	0.94	7.19	12.20
1924	79.01	12.08	11.97	0.74	6.98	10.78
1925	80.08	11.08	10.83	0.58	7.35	9.91
1926	76.10	11.07	12.97	0.46	6.73	7.32
1927	78.18	9.93	12.98	0.31	6.51	7.91
1928	76.10	10.41	15.96	0.20	6.47	9.15
1929	76.24	9.68	16.90	0.09	6.96	9.88
1930	75.72	9.58	16.67	0.00	7.47	9.44
1931	78.68	9.74	11.80	−0.05	7.48	7.64
1932	80.53	10.33	10.12	−0.05	7.16	8.09
1933	77.55	11.74	11.96	0.01	4.99	6.25

(continued)

Table S5 (continued)

	Final consumption expenditure		Gross capital formation				
	Final consumption expenditure of NPISHs and households (%)	Final consumption expenditure by government (%)	Gross fixed capital formation (%)	Changes inventories and acquisitions less disposals of valuables (%)	Exports of goods and services (%)	Imports of goods and services (%)
1934	79.22	11.17	10.90	0.14	4.37	5.81
1935	78.59	11.34	11.08	0.35	3.96	5.31
1936	63.48	24.29	11.60	0.79	5.08	5.25
1937	63.10	26.53	9.00	1.23	5.20	5.07
1938	68.04	23.89	7.94	1.59	3.49	4.96
1939	67.78	24.05	7.18	1.87	2.95	3.83
1940	73.84	16.57	8.12	1.93	2.26	2.71
1941	68.44	16.74	11.39	2.14	2.91	1.62
1942	68.66	15.47	12.06	2.14	2.88	1.20
1943	63.36	22.39	11.71	2.35	3.01	2.82
1944	68.18	17.75	10.14	2.40	3.88	2.35
1945	66.67	19.00	11.01	2.85	3.05	2.58
1946	73.69	13.14	10.90	2.65	2.65	3.03
1947	71.96	12.71	12.69	2.67	3.18	3.21
1948	68.37	12.63	16.40	2.88	3.00	3.28
1949	69.52	12.69	15.40	3.13	3.59	4.32
1950	71.69	11.16	14.80	2.94	3.87	4.46
1951	77.43	9.98	11.33	2.67	6.15	7.56
1952	75.76	10.16	12.83	2.78	6.30	7.83
1953	74.33	10.19	13.59	2.96	7.58	8.65
1954	70.83	10.12	16.80	2.95	7.17	7.86

(continued)

Table S5 (continued)

	Final consumption expenditure		Gross capital formation		Exports of goods and services (%)	Imports of goods and services (%)
	Final consumption expenditure of NPISHs and households (%)	Final consumption expenditure by government (%)	Gross fixed capital formation (%)	Changes inventories and acquisitions less disposals of valuables (%)		
1955	69.53	9.91	20.03	3.15	7.06	9.69
1956	66.97	9.72	22.97	2.93	6.40	8.98
1957	68.80	9.29	21.72	2.88	6.23	8.92
1958	70.45	8.05	20.87	2.76	6.36	8.50
1959	74.83	8.50	18.86	−0.08	5.19	7.30
1960	72.27	8.39	18.96	−0.24	7.88	7.27
1961	72.64	8.06	19.63	2.02	7.00	9.35
1962	72.91	7.83	19.80	3.94	6.83	11.32
1963	74.63	7.95	19.79	3.86	5.71	11.93
1964	74.73	7.50	20.86	2.73	6.35	12.17
1965	75.46	7.60	21.93	3.07	5.83	13.88
1966	74.90	7.92	22.19	3.02	6.36	14.39
1967	74.02	8.65	22.52	1.40	6.18	12.77
1968	73.59	8.48	23.15	0.79	7.74	13.75
1969	71.45	8.57	23.49	2.57	8.36	14.44
1970	71.93	8.95	23.35	1.34	9.26	14.83
1971	71.83	9.16	21.54	1.37	9.90	13.80
1972	70.69	9.02	23.08	1.37	10.54	14.70
1973	69.84	9.04	24.85	0.99	10.89	15.61
1974	68.76	9.30	26.33	3.27	12.04	19.70
1975	68.32	9.84	25.13	3.05	11.31	17.65

(continued)

Table S5 (continued)

	Final consumption expenditure		Gross capital formation		Exports of goods and services (%)	Imports of goods and services (%)
	Final consumption expenditure of NPISHs and households (%)	Final consumption expenditure by government (%)	Gross fixed capital formation (%)	Changes inventories and acquisitions less disposals of valuables (%)		
1976	68.75	10.53	23.84	2.81	12.59	18.52
1977	68.39	10.82	23.26	1.18	13.24	16.89
1978	67.36	11.26	22.29	−0.23	14.00	14.68
1979	66.64	11.83	21.38	0.57	14.54	14.96
1980	66.85	12.48	22.11	1.18	15.52	18.14
1981	66.94	13.67	21.85	0.00	17.48	19.94
1982	66.28	13.87	21.60	0.59	18.01	20.35
1983	65.56	14.31	20.79	0.69	20.26	21.61
1984	64.68	14.04	18.73	1.00	22.47	20.93
1985	64.94	14.46	19.18	0.05	22.20	20.83
1986	64.03	14.38	19.47	0.50	19.37	17.76
1987	63.82	14.92	20.92	0.72	18.75	19.13
1988	63.03	14.70	22.89	1.05	18.13	19.81
1989	63.03	15.23	24.55	1.00	17.25	21.06
1990	62.20	15.76	25.02	0.93	16.13	20.03
1991	61.92	16.48	24.49	0.80	16.08	19.77
1992	62.39	17.55	22.60	0.83	16.43	19.81
1993	62.36	18.23	20.75	−0.01	18.01	19.33
1994	61.93	17.73	20.90	0.22	20.54	21.32
1995	60.95	17.65	22.02	0.35	21.93	22.90
1996	60.47	17.54	21.81	0.27	23.12	23.21

(continued)

Table S5 (continued)

	Final consumption expenditure		Gross capital formation		Exports of goods and services (%)	Imports of goods and services (%)
	Final consumption expenditure of NPISHs and households (%)	Final consumption expenditure by government (%)	Gross fixed capital formation (%)	Changes inventories and acquisitions less disposals of valuables (%)		
1997	60.23	17.07	22.26	0.22	25.75	25.54
1998	59.77	16.93	23.40	0.40	26.18	26.68
1999	59.68	16.84	24.87	0.55	26.40	28.34
2000	59.70	16.73	26.14	0.44	28.62	31.62
2001	59.21	16.57	26.23	0.34	27.86	30.21
2002	58.50	16.62	26.62	0.28	26.48	28.51
2003	57.63	16.76	27.65	0.17	25.45	27.66
2004	57.94	17.16	28.52	0.23	25.18	29.03
2005	57.67	17.31	29.89	0.12	24.67	29.67
2006	57.26	17.35	31.05	0.24	24.87	30.79
2007	56.98	17.68	31.05	0.29	25.71	31.70
2008	56.76	18.77	29.21	0.38	25.32	30.44
2009	56.10	20.48	24.33	0.24	22.67	23.82
2010	57.24	20.51	23.03	0.51	25.52	26.82
2011	57.82	20.52	21.48	0.43	28.92	29.17
2012	58.80	19.74	19.80	0.20	30.70	29.23
2013	58.35	19.68	18.76	−0.04	32.22	28.96
2014	58.72	19.48	19.13	0.26	32.67	30.25
2015	58.11	19.38	19.72	0.34	33.18	30.73

Sources Please cite the database as: Leandro Prados de la Escosura (2017), Spanish Economic Growth, 1850–2015

Table S6 Volume indices of gross domestic product and its expenditure components, 1850–2015 (2010 = 100)

	Final consumption expenditure		Gross capital formation		Exports of goods and services	Imports of goods and services	Gross domestic product at market price
	Final consumption expenditure of NPISHs and households (%)	Final consumption expenditure by government (%)	Gross fixed domestic capital formation	Gross domestic capital formation			
	(2010 = 100)	(2010 = 100)	(2010 = 100)	(2010 = 100)	(2010 = 100)	(2010 = 100)	(2010 = 100)
1850	3.0	1.3	0.2	0.3	0.2	0.1	2.0
1851	3.1	1.3	0.3	0.3	0.2	0.2	2.0
1852	3.3	1.3	0.3	0.3	0.2	0.2	2.1
1853	3.2	1.3	0.3	0.4	0.2	0.2	2.1
1854	3.3	1.3	0.2	0.3	0.3	0.2	2.2
1855	3.4	1.2	0.2	0.3	0.3	0.2	2.3
1856	3.3	1.1	0.3	0.3	0.3	0.2	2.2
1857	3.2	1.3	0.4	0.4	0.3	0.3	2.1
1858	3.2	1.5	0.6	0.7	0.3	0.3	2.2
1859	3.3	1.6	0.6	0.7	0.2	0.2	2.3
1860	3.3	1.9	0.8	0.8	0.3	0.3	2.4
1861	3.4	1.7	0.7	0.7	0.3	0.3	2.4
1862	3.5	1.6	0.8	0.8	0.3	0.3	2.4
1863	3.7	1.6	0.8	0.8	0.2	0.4	2.5
1864	3.7	1.7	0.7	0.7	0.2	0.3	2.5
1865	3.5	1.8	0.6	0.6	0.3	0.3	2.4
1866	3.8	1.5	0.6	0.6	0.3	0.3	2.5
1867	3.6	1.5	0.6	0.6	0.4	0.3	2.5
1868	3.3	1.4	0.4	0.4	0.4	0.3	2.2

(continued)

Table S6 (continued)

	Final consumption expenditure		Gross capital formation					
	Final consumption expenditure of NPISHs and households (%)	Final consumption expenditure by government (%)	Gross fixed domestic capital formation	Gross domestic capital formation	Exports of goods and services	Imports of goods and services	Gross domestic product at market price
	(2010 = 100)	(2010 = 100)	(2010 = 100)	(2010 = 100)	(2010 = 100)	(2010 = 100)	(2010 = 100)
1869	3.3	1.5	0.3	0.4	0.4	0.3	2.3
1870	3.5	1.4	0.4	0.4	0.4	0.3	2.3
1871	3.8	1.5	0.5	0.5	0.4	0.4	2.5
1872	4.4	1.8	0.5	0.6	0.5	0.4	2.9
1873	4.6	2.1	0.4	0.5	0.5	0.3	3.2
1874	4.2	2.6	0.4	0.5	0.5	0.4	2.9
1875	4.2	2.9	0.5	0.5	0.5	0.4	3.0
1876	4.7	2.0	0.6	0.7	0.4	0.5	3.1
1877	5.1	2.1	0.7	0.7	0.5	0.5	3.4
1878	4.8	2.0	0.8	0.9	0.5	0.5	3.3
1879	4.5	1.9	0.7	0.7	0.6	0.5	3.1
1880	4.7	2.0	0.8	0.9	0.8	0.5	3.4
1881	4.9	2.0	0.7	0.8	0.8	0.6	3.4
1882	4.8	2.4	0.9	0.9	0.8	0.6	3.5
1883	4.9	2.1	1.1	1.1	0.9	0.7	3.5
1884	5.0	2.1	1.0	1.0	0.8	0.6	3.6
1885	4.7	2.3	0.8	0.8	0.9	0.6	3.4
1886	4.7	2.3	0.8	0.8	0.9	0.7	3.4
1887	4.5	2.1	0.8	0.7	1.0	0.7	3.3

(continued)

Appendices 247

Table S6 (continued)

	Final consumption expenditure		Gross capital formation		Exports of goods and services	Imports of goods and services	Gross domestic product at market price
	Final consumption expenditure of NPISHs and households (%)	Final consumption expenditure by government (%)	Gross fixed domestic capital formation	Gross domestic capital formation			
	(2010 = 100)	(2010 = 100)	(2010 = 100)	(2010 = 100)	(2010 = 100)	(2010 = 100)	(2010 = 100)
1888	4.9	2.1	0.7	0.7	1.0	0.7	3.4
1889	4.8	2.0	0.8	0.7	1.0	0.8	3.4
1890	4.8	2.0	0.9	0.8	1.0	0.7	3.4
1891	4.8	2.0	0.8	0.8	1.1	0.7	3.5
1892	5.3	2.2	0.8	0.8	1.1	0.7	3.8
1893	5.1	2.1	0.8	0.8	1.0	0.7	3.7
1894	5.2	2.1	0.8	0.8	1.1	0.7	3.7
1895	5.0	2.2	0.9	0.9	1.1	0.7	3.7
1896	4.2	2.1	0.9	0.9	1.3	0.7	3.3
1897	4.5	2.4	0.9	0.9	1.2	0.7	3.5
1898	5.0	2.5	0.8	0.9	1.1	0.6	3.8
1899	5.1	2.3	1.2	1.3	1.2	0.8	3.9
1900	5.1	2.1	1.5	1.5	1.2	0.8	3.9
1901	6.1	2.1	1.2	1.3	1.0	0.8	4.3
1902	5.7	2.1	1.1	1.1	1.1	0.8	4.1
1903	5.7	2.1	1.1	1.2	1.2	0.9	4.1
1904	5.5	2.2	1.2	1.2	1.2	0.9	4.1
1905	5.4	2.1	1.1	1.2	1.4	0.9	4.0
1906	5.8	2.3	1.2	1.2	1.4	0.9	4.3

(continued)

248 Appendices

Table S6 (continued)

	Final consumption expenditure		Gross capital formation		Exports of goods and services	Imports of goods and services	Gross domestic product at market price
	Final consumption expenditure of NPISHs and households (%)	Final consumption expenditure by government (%)	Gross fixed domestic capital formation	Gross domestic capital formation			
	(2010 = 100)	(2010 = 100)	(2010 = 100)	(2010 = 100)	(2010 = 100)	(2010 = 100)	(2010 = 100)
1907	5.8	2.2	1.3	1.3	1.4	0.9	4.4
1908	6.2	2.3	1.3	1.3	1.3	0.9	4.6
1909	6.2	2.7	1.4	1.4	1.3	0.8	4.7
1910	5.7	2.8	1.5	1.6	1.4	0.9	4.5
1911	6.2	3.0	1.6	1.7	1.5	1.0	4.8
1912	5.5	3.1	1.9	2.1	1.7	1.1	4.7
1913	6.0	3.3	2.0	2.2	1.6	1.2	4.9
1914	5.8	3.3	1.9	2.2	1.4	0.9	4.8
1915	5.2	4.5	1.4	1.7	1.9	0.7	4.9
1916	5.9	3.4	1.4	1.7	2.0	0.8	5.1
1917	6.0	2.9	1.4	1.6	1.8	0.7	5.1
1918	6.5	2.8	1.3	1.4	1.3	0.5	5.0
1919	6.1	3.1	1.5	1.6	1.8	0.7	5.1
1920	7.1	4.0	1.6	1.8	1.6	1.2	5.5
1921	7.0	5.5	1.9	2.0	1.4	0.9	5.7
1922	8.1	4.9	1.9	2.1	1.0	1.1	5.9
1923	8.2	4.5	2.1	2.2	1.3	1.3	6.0
1924	8.1	5.0	2.5	2.6	1.2	1.2	6.2
1925	8.8	4.8	2.4	2.5	1.4	1.3	6.6

(continued)

Table S6 (continued)

	Final consumption expenditure		Gross capital formation		Exports of goods and services	Imports of goods and services	Gross domestic product at market price
	Final consumption expenditure of NPISHs and households (%)	Final consumption expenditure by government (%)	Gross fixed domestic capital formation	Gross domestic capital formation			
	(2010 = 100)	(2010 = 100)	(2010 = 100)	(2010 = 100)	(2010 = 100)	(2010 = 100)	(2010 = 100)
1926	8.4	4.8	2.9	2.9	1.3	1.1	6.5
1927	9.9	4.7	3.1	3.1	1.2	1.4	7.2
1928	9.3	5.1	3.8	3.7	1.3	1.4	7.1
1929	10.0	5.1	4.2	4.2	1.5	1.6	7.7
1930	8.9	4.9	4.2	4.1	1.6	1.2	7.3
1931	9.3	4.8	2.9	2.8	1.6	1.0	7.2
1932	9.9	5.2	2.5	2.4	1.7	1.1	7.5
1933	9.6	5.8	2.7	2.7	1.2	0.9	7.3
1934	10.2	5.9	2.7	2.7	1.2	1.0	7.6
1935	10.4	6.1	2.8	2.8	1.1	1.0	7.7
1936	6.2	10.5	2.2	2.3	1.1	0.7	5.9
1937	5.5	10.7	1.6	1.8	1.0	0.3	5.5
1938	6.0	9.5	1.5	1.8	0.7	0.3	5.5
1939	6.9	9.6	1.5	1.9	0.6	0.3	5.9
1940	8.5	7.1	1.9	2.3	0.4	0.5	6.5
1941	8.1	6.3	2.6	2.9	0.4	0.2	6.5
1942	8.4	6.5	3.0	3.4	0.4	0.1	6.9
1943	8.2	9.9	2.9	3.4	0.7	0.3	7.3
1944	9.0	8.7	2.8	3.3	0.8	0.3	7.6

(continued)

Table S6 (continued)

	Final consumption expenditure		Gross capital formation					
	Final consumption expenditure of NPISHs and households (%)	Final consumption expenditure by government (%)	Gross fixed domestic capital formation	Gross domestic capital formation	Exports of goods and services	Imports of goods and services	Gross domestic product at market price
	(2010 = 100)	(2010 = 100)	(2010 = 100)	(2010 = 100)	(2010 = 100)	(2010 = 100)	(2010 = 100)
1945	7.9	8.5	3.0	3.5	0.6	0.3	7.0
1946	9.6	5.8	3.0	3.5	0.5	0.5	7.3
1947	9.5	5.6	3.2	3.7	0.6	0.4	7.5
1948	8.9	5.6	4.1	4.6	0.7	0.4	7.5
1949	8.9	5.7	4.1	4.7	0.7	0.4	7.5
1950	9.4	5.5	4.0	4.6	0.7	0.6	7.7
1951	10.8	5.5	3.6	4.1	1.3	0.8	8.5
1952	11.4	6.2	4.3	4.8	1.4	0.9	9.2
1953	11.0	6.5	4.8	5.4	1.6	1.2	9.2
1954	11.5	7.4	5.1	5.9	1.8	1.2	9.9
1955	12.0	7.6	6.4	7.2	1.5	1.5	10.2
1956	13.0	8.6	7.0	7.8	1.6	1.6	11.1
1957	14.0	8.5	6.7	7.6	1.3	1.5	11.5
1958	15.3	7.8	7.6	8.4	1.2	1.8	12.2
1959	15.7	8.2	7.1	6.9	1.0	1.5	12.1
1960	15.1	8.4	7.6	7.4	1.7	1.5	12.2
1961	16.9	8.9	9.0	9.7	1.7	2.1	13.6
1962	18.4	9.5	10.0	11.7	1.9	2.8	15.0
1963	20.5	10.5	11.2	13.1	1.8	3.4	16.5

(continued)

Table S6 (continued)

	Final consumption expenditure		Gross capital formation			Exports of goods and services	Imports of goods and services	Gross domestic product at market price
	Final consumption expenditure of NPISHs and households (%)	Final consumption expenditure by government (%)	Gross fixed domestic capital formation	Gross domestic capital formation				
	(2010 = 100)	(2010 = 100)	(2010 = 100)	(2010 = 100)		(2010 = 100)	(2010 = 100)	(2010 = 100)
1964	21.5	10.7	12.9	14.2		2.3	3.8	17.4
1965	23.2	11.1	15.2	17.0		2.4	5.1	18.8
1966	24.9	11.3	17.3	19.3		2.9	6.1	20.2
1967	26.6	11.5	18.7	19.6		3.0	5.9	21.4
1968	28.1	11.7	20.6	21.1		3.7	6.4	22.7
1969	30.1	12.2	22.7	24.8		4.6	7.4	24.8
1970	31.4	12.9	23.1	24.2		5.4	8.0	25.6
1971	33.1	13.6	22.8	24.1		6.3	8.0	26.8
1972	36.0	14.5	27.5	28.9		7.6	10.1	29.6
1973	38.9	15.6	32.1	33.1		8.6	11.8	32.3
1974	40.9	17.1	35.2	37.5		9.6	12.9	34.7
1975	42.4	18.1	34.8	37.0		9.8	12.8	35.8
1976	44.6	19.3	34.9	37.2		11.5	14.2	37.4
1977	45.9	20.3	35.4	36.1		13.0	13.5	38.6
1978	47.2	21.6	35.1	34.3		14.8	13.4	39.7
1979	47.7	22.7	34.2	34.4		17.0	15.0	40.4
1980	48.6	24.0	35.2	36.1		17.8	15.5	41.6
1981	48.1	25.8	34.3	33.4		19.0	14.7	41.6
1982	48.2	27.1	35.0	34.9		20.0	15.5	42.3

(continued)

Table S6 (continued)

	Final consumption expenditure		Gross capital formation					
	Final consumption expenditure of NPISHs and households (%)	Final consumption expenditure by government (%)	Gross fixed domestic capital formation		Gross domestic capital formation	Exports of goods and services	Imports of goods and services	Gross domestic product at market price
	(2010 = 100)	(2010 = 100)	(2010 = 100)	(2010 = 100)	(2010 = 100)	(2010 = 100)	(2010 = 100)	(2010 = 100)
1983	48.4	28.2	34.2		34.6	22.0	15.4	43.1
1984	48.4	28.9	31.9		32.6	24.6	15.2	43.5
1985	50.2	30.5	33.8		33.1	25.2	16.4	44.8
1986	51.9	32.1	37.2		37.2	25.7	18.8	46.6
1987	55.1	35.4	42.9		43.3	27.3	22.6	49.9
1988	57.9	37.3	49.4		50.5	28.6	25.8	53.1
1989	61.3	41.0	56.8		57.8	29.5	30.3	56.5
1990	63.7	44.3	61.3		62.3	30.4	32.7	59.2
1991	65.7	47.4	63.0		63.7	32.7	35.6	61.1
1992	67.3	50.0	60.9		61.9	35.1	38.1	62.1
1993	66.0	51.9	55.2		53.9	38.0	36.2	61.1
1994	66.8	52.4	57.3		56.6	44.3	40.3	62.8
1995	68.0	54.1	62.7		62.4	48.7	44.8	65.1
1996	69.7	54.8	64.3		63.7	53.5	48.1	66.9
1997	71.7	56.2	67.7		66.9	61.3	54.3	69.4
1998	74.8	58.1	75.0		74.6	66.3	61.9	72.6
1999	78.5	60.4	82.4		82.5	71.6	70.5	76.1
2000	82.1	63.0	88.6		88.2	79.1	77.2	80.1
2001	85.1	65.4	92.9		92.1	82.0	79.9	83.3

(continued)

Table S6 (continued)

	Final consumption expenditure		Gross capital formation		Exports of goods and services	Imports of goods and services	Gross domestic product at market price
	Final consumption expenditure of NPISHs and households (%)	Final consumption expenditure by government (%)	Gross fixed domestic capital formation	Gross domestic capital formation			
	(2010 = 100)	(2010 = 100)	(2010 = 100)	(2010 = 100)	(2010 = 100)	(2010 = 100)	(2010 = 100)
2002	87.7	68.0	97.2	96.2	83.1	82.8	85.8
2003	89.8	71.3	104.0	102.4	85.9	87.7	88.6
2004	93.4	75.9	109.3	107.9	89.6	96.5	91.4
2005	97.2	80.1	117.5	115.5	91.2	103.3	94.8
2006	100.8	84.1	126.1	124.5	95.7	111.7	98.7
2007	104.2	89.3	131.6	130.1	103.6	121.3	102.5
2008	103.5	94.6	126.4	125.5	102.7	114.5	103.7
2009	99.8	98.5	105.1	103.9	91.4	93.5	100.0
2010	100.0	100.0	100.0	100.0	100.0	100.0	100.0
2011	97.6	99.7	93.1	92.8	107.4	99.2	99.0
2012	94.1	95.0	85.1	83.9	108.5	92.9	95.9
2013	91.2	93.0	82.1	80.0	113.2	92.4	94.2
2014	92.6	92.7	85.2	84.4	118.0	98.4	95.6
2015	95.3	94.5	90.4	89.9	123.7	103.9	98.8

Sources Please cite the database as: Leandro Prados de la Escosura (2017), Spanish Economic Growth, 1850–2015

Appendices

Table S7 Deflators of gross domestic product and its expenditure components, 1850–2015 (2010 = 100)

	Final consumption expenditure		Gross capital formation		Exports	Imports	Gross domestic product at market price	Gross national income	Net national income	Net national disposable income
	Final consumption expenditure of NPISHs and households	Final consumption expenditure by government	Gross fixed capital formation	Capital formation						
	(2010 = 100)	(2010 = 100)	(2010 = 100)	(2010 = 100)	(2010 = 100)	(2010 = 100)	(2010 = 100)	(2010 = 100)	(2010 = 100)	(2010 = 100)
1850	0.1	0.1	0.2	0.2	0.2	0.3	0.1	0.1	0.1	0.1
1851	0.1	0.1	0.2	0.2	0.2	0.3	0.1	0.1	0.1	0.1
1852	0.1	0.1	0.2	0.2	0.2	0.3	0.1	0.1	0.1	0.1
1853	0.1	0.1	0.2	0.2	0.2	0.3	0.1	0.1	0.1	0.1
1854	0.1	0.1	0.2	0.2	0.2	0.3	0.1	0.1	0.1	0.1
1855	0.1	0.1	0.2	0.2	0.2	0.3	0.1	0.1	0.1	0.1
1856	0.1	0.1	0.2	0.2	0.2	0.3	0.1	0.1	0.1	0.1
1857	0.1	0.1	0.2	0.2	0.3	0.3	0.1	0.1	0.1	0.1
1858	0.1	0.1	0.2	0.2	0.3	0.3	0.1	0.1	0.1	0.1
1859	0.1	0.1	0.2	0.2	0.2	0.3	0.1	0.1	0.1	0.1
1860	0.1	0.1	0.2	0.2	0.2	0.3	0.1	0.1	0.1	0.1
1861	0.1	0.1	0.2	0.2	0.2	0.3	0.1	0.1	0.1	0.1
1862	0.1	0.1	0.2	0.2	0.2	0.3	0.1	0.1	0.1	0.1
1863	0.1	0.1	0.2	0.2	0.2	0.3	0.1	0.1	0.1	0.1
1864	0.1	0.1	0.2	0.2	0.2	0.3	0.1	0.1	0.1	0.1
1865	0.1	0.1	0.2	0.2	0.2	0.3	0.1	0.1	0.1	0.1
1866	0.1	0.1	0.2	0.2	0.2	0.3	0.1	0.1	0.1	0.1
1867	0.2	0.1	0.2	0.2	0.2	0.3	0.2	0.2	0.2	0.2
1868	0.2	0.1	0.2	0.2	0.2	0.3	0.2	0.1	0.1	0.1
1869	0.1	0.1	0.2	0.2	0.2	0.3	0.1	0.1	0.1	0.1
1870	0.1	0.1	0.2	0.2	0.2	0.3	0.1	0.1	0.1	0.1
1871	0.1	0.1	0.2	0.2	0.2	0.3	0.1	0.1	0.1	0.1
1872	0.1	0.1	0.2	0.2	0.2	0.3	0.1	0.1	0.1	0.1
1873	0.1	0.1	0.2	0.2	0.2	0.3	0.1	0.1	0.1	0.1
1874	0.1	0.1	0.2	0.2	0.3	0.3	0.1	0.1	0.1	0.1
1875	0.1	0.1	0.2	0.2	0.3	0.3	0.1	0.1	0.1	0.1

(continued)

Table S7 (continued)

	Final consumption expenditure		Gross capital formation							
	Final consumption expenditure of NPISHs and households	Final consumption expenditure by government	Gross fixed capital formation	Capital formation	Exports	Imports	Gross domestic product at market price	Gross national income	Net national income	Net national disposable income
	(2010 = 100)	(2010 = 100)	(2010 = 100)	(2010 = 100)	(2010 = 100)	(2010 = 100)	(2010 = 100)	(2010 = 100)	(2010 = 100)	(2010 = 100)
1876	0.1	0.1	0.2	0.2	0.2	0.2	0.1	0.1	0.1	0.1
1877	0.1	0.1	0.2	0.2	0.2	0.2	0.1	0.1	0.1	0.1
1878	0.1	0.1	0.2	0.2	0.2	0.2	0.1	0.1	0.1	0.1
1879	0.2	0.1	0.2	0.2	0.2	0.2	0.2	0.2	0.2	0.2
1880	0.2	0.1	0.2	0.2	0.2	0.2	0.1	0.1	0.1	0.1
1881	0.2	0.1	0.2	0.2	0.2	0.2	0.2	0.2	0.2	0.2
1882	0.2	0.1	0.2	0.2	0.2	0.2	0.2	0.2	0.2	0.2
1883	0.2	0.1	0.2	0.2	0.2	0.2	0.2	0.2	0.2	0.2
1884	0.2	0.1	0.2	0.2	0.2	0.2	0.2	0.2	0.2	0.2
1885	0.2	0.1	0.1	0.1	0.2	0.2	0.2	0.2	0.2	0.2
1886	0.2	0.1	0.1	0.1	0.2	0.2	0.2	0.2	0.2	0.2
1887	0.2	0.1	0.1	0.1	0.2	0.2	0.2	0.2	0.2	0.2
1888	0.2	0.1	0.1	0.1	0.2	0.2	0.2	0.2	0.2	0.2
1889	0.1	0.1	0.1	0.1	0.2	0.2	0.1	0.1	0.1	0.1
1890	0.2	0.1	0.1	0.1	0.2	0.2	0.1	0.1	0.1	0.1
1891	0.2	0.1	0.1	0.1	0.2	0.2	0.1	0.1	0.1	0.1
1892	0.1	0.1	0.1	0.1	0.2	0.2	0.1	0.1	0.1	0.1
1893	0.1	0.1	0.1	0.1	0.2	0.2	0.1	0.1	0.1	0.1
1894	0.1	0.1	0.1	0.1	0.2	0.2	0.1	0.1	0.1	0.1
1895	0.1	0.1	0.1	0.1	0.2	0.2	0.1	0.1	0.1	0.1
1896	0.2	0.1	0.1	0.1	0.2	0.2	0.1	0.1	0.1	0.1
1897	0.2	0.1	0.1	0.1	0.2	0.2	0.1	0.1	0.1	0.1
1898	0.1	0.1	0.2	0.2	0.3	0.3	0.1	0.1	0.1	0.1
1899	0.1	0.1	0.2	0.2	0.2	0.3	0.1	0.1	0.1	0.1
1900	0.2	0.1	0.2	0.2	0.2	0.3	0.1	0.1	0.1	0.1
1901	0.1	0.1	0.2	0.2	0.3	0.3	0.1	0.1	0.1	0.1

(continued)

Table S7 (continued)

	Final consumption expenditure		Gross capital formation		Exports	Imports	Gross domestic product at market price	Gross national income	Net national income	Net national disposable income
	Final consumption expenditure of NPISHs and households	Final consumption expenditure by government	Gross fixed capital formation	Capital formation						
	(2010 = 100)	(2010 = 100)	(2010 = 100)	(2010 = 100)	(2010 = 100)	(2010 = 100)	(2010 = 100)	(2010 = 100)	(2010 = 100)	(2010 = 100)
1902	0.1	0.1	0.2	0.2	0.2	0.3	0.1	0.1	0.1	0.1
1903	0.2	0.1	0.2	0.2	0.2	0.3	0.2	0.1	0.1	0.1
1904	0.2	0.1	0.2	0.2	0.2	0.3	0.2	0.2	0.2	0.2
1905	0.2	0.1	0.2	0.2	0.2	0.3	0.2	0.2	0.2	0.2
1906	0.2	0.1	0.2	0.2	0.2	0.2	0.2	0.1	0.1	0.1
1907	0.2	0.1	0.2	0.2	0.2	0.3	0.2	0.2	0.2	0.2
1908	0.2	0.1	0.2	0.2	0.2	0.3	0.1	0.1	0.1	0.1
1909	0.2	0.1	0.2	0.2	0.2	0.2	0.1	0.1	0.1	0.1
1910	0.2	0.1	0.2	0.2	0.2	0.3	0.1	0.1	0.1	0.1
1911	0.2	0.1	0.2	0.2	0.2	0.3	0.1	0.1	0.1	0.1
1912	0.2	0.1	0.2	0.2	0.2	0.3	0.2	0.2	0.2	0.2
1913	0.2	0.1	0.2	0.2	0.2	0.3	0.2	0.2	0.2	0.2
1914	0.2	0.1	0.2	0.2	0.2	0.3	0.2	0.2	0.2	0.2
1915	0.2	0.1	0.2	0.2	0.2	0.3	0.2	0.2	0.2	0.2
1916	0.2	0.1	0.2	0.2	0.2	0.3	0.2	0.2	0.2	0.2
1917	0.2	0.2	0.3	0.3	0.3	0.4	0.2	0.2	0.2	0.2
1918	0.3	0.2	0.3	0.3	0.3	0.5	0.3	0.3	0.3	0.3
1919	0.3	0.2	0.3	0.3	0.4	0.6	0.3	0.3	0.3	0.3
1920	0.3	0.2	0.4	0.4	0.4	0.7	0.3	0.3	0.3	0.3
1921	0.3	0.2	0.4	0.4	0.3	0.6	0.3	0.3	0.3	0.3
1922	0.3	0.2	0.4	0.4	0.4	0.5	0.3	0.3	0.3	0.3
1923	0.3	0.2	0.3	0.3	0.3	0.5	0.3	0.3	0.3	0.3
1924	0.3	0.2	0.3	0.3	0.4	0.6	0.3	0.3	0.3	0.3
1925	0.3	0.2	0.3	0.3	0.4	0.5	0.3	0.3	0.3	0.3
1926	0.3	0.2	0.3	0.3	0.4	0.5	0.3	0.3	0.3	0.3
1927	0.3	0.2	0.3	0.3	0.4	0.4	0.3	0.3	0.3	0.3

(continued)

Table S7 (continued)

	Final consumption expenditure		Gross capital formation		Exports		Imports		Gross domestic product at market price		Gross national income		Net national income		Net national disposable income	
	Final consumption expenditure of NPISHs and households	Final consumption expenditure by government	Gross fixed capital formation	Capital formation												
	(2010 = 100)	(2010 = 100)	(2010 = 100)	(2010 = 100)		(2010 = 100)		(2010 = 100)		(2010 = 100)		(2010 = 100)		(2010 = 100)		(2010 = 100)
1928	0.3	0.2	0.3	0.3	0.3	0.3	0.4	0.4	0.3	0.3	0.3	0.3	0.2	0.2	0.3	0.3
1929	0.3	0.2	0.3	0.3	0.4	0.4	0.4	0.4	0.3	0.3	0.3	0.3	0.2	0.2	0.2	0.2
1930	0.3	0.2	0.3	0.3	0.3	0.3	0.6	0.6	0.3	0.3	0.3	0.3	0.3	0.3	0.3	0.3
1931	0.3	0.2	0.3	0.3	0.4	0.4	0.5	0.5	0.3	0.3	0.3	0.3	0.3	0.3	0.3	0.3
1932	0.3	0.2	0.3	0.3	0.3	0.3	0.5	0.5	0.3	0.3	0.3	0.3	0.3	0.3	0.3	0.3
1933	0.3	0.2	0.3	0.3	0.3	0.3	0.5	0.5	0.3	0.3	0.3	0.3	0.3	0.3	0.3	0.3
1934	0.3	0.2	0.4	0.4	0.3	0.3	0.4	0.4	0.3	0.3	0.3	0.3	0.2	0.2	0.2	0.2
1935	0.3	0.2	0.4	0.4	0.3	0.3	0.4	0.4	0.3	0.3	0.3	0.3	0.3	0.3	0.3	0.3
1936	0.3	0.2	0.4	0.4	0.3	0.3	0.5	0.5	0.3	0.3	0.3	0.3	0.3	0.3	0.3	0.3
1937	0.4	0.2	0.4	0.4	0.4	0.4	1.0	1.0	0.3	0.3	0.3	0.3	0.3	0.3	0.3	0.3
1938	0.4	0.2	0.5	0.5	0.4	0.4	1.1	1.1	0.4	0.4	0.4	0.4	0.4	0.4	0.4	0.4
1939	0.4	0.3	0.5	0.5	0.5	0.5	1.0	1.0	0.4	0.4	0.4	0.4	0.4	0.4	0.4	0.4
1940	0.4	0.3	0.5	0.5	0.6	0.6	0.6	0.6	0.4	0.4	0.4	0.4	0.4	0.4	0.4	0.4
1941	0.5	0.4	0.6	0.6	0.9	0.9	1.1	1.1	0.5	0.5	0.5	0.5	0.5	0.5	0.5	0.5
1942	0.6	0.4	0.7	0.7	1.0	1.0	1.4	1.4	0.6	0.6	0.6	0.6	0.6	0.6	0.6	0.6
1943	0.6	0.5	0.7	0.7	0.7	0.7	1.3	1.3	0.6	0.6	0.6	0.6	0.6	0.6	0.6	0.6
1944	0.6	0.5	0.7	0.8	0.9	0.9	1.3	1.3	0.6	0.6	0.6	0.6	0.6	0.6	0.6	0.6
1945	0.7	0.5	0.7	0.8	0.9	0.9	1.8	1.8	0.7	0.7	0.7	0.7	0.7	0.7	0.7	0.7
1946	0.8	0.7	0.8	1.0	1.4	1.4	1.3	1.3	0.8	0.8	0.8	0.8	0.8	0.8	0.8	0.8
1947	0.9	0.8	0.9	1.0	1.5	1.5	2.0	2.0	0.9	0.9	0.9	0.9	0.9	0.9	0.9	0.9
1948	1.0	0.8	1.2	1.3	1.3	1.3	2.5	2.5	1.0	1.0	1.0	1.0	1.0	1.0	1.0	1.0
1949	1.1	0.9	1.3	1.4	1.6	1.6	2.9	2.9	1.1	1.1	1.1	1.1	1.1	1.1	1.1	1.1
1950	1.3	1.0	1.6	1.6	2.1	2.1	3.0	3.0	1.3	1.3	1.3	1.3	1.3	1.3	1.3	1.3
1951	1.6	1.1	1.8	1.9	2.4	2.4	4.3	4.3	1.5	1.5	1.5	1.5	1.5	1.5	1.5	1.5
1952	1.6	1.1	1.8	1.9	2.4	2.4	4.6	4.6	1.5	1.5	1.5	1.5	1.5	1.5	1.5	1.5
1953	1.8	1.1	1.9	2.0	2.8	2.8	4.2	4.2	1.6	1.6	1.6	1.6	1.6	1.6	1.6	1.6

(continued)

258 Appendices

Table S7 (continued)

	Final consumption expenditure		Gross capital formation				Exports		Imports		Gross domestic product at market price		Gross national income		Net national income		Net national disposable income	
	Final consumption expenditure of NPISHs and households	Final consumption expenditure by government	Gross fixed capital formation		Capital formation													
	(2010 = 100)	(2010 = 100)	(2010 = 100)		(2010 = 100)			(2010 = 100)		(2010 = 100)		(2010 = 100)		(2010 = 100)		(2010 = 100)		(2010 = 100)
1954	1.9	1.2	2.5		2.5		2.7		4.2		1.8		1.8		1.7		1.7	
1955	1.9	1.2	2.6		2.6		3.4		4.5		1.8		1.8		1.8		1.8	
1956	2.1	1.3	3.3		3.3		3.8		4.7		2.1		2.1		2.0		2.0	
1957	2.3	1.4	3.8		3.8		5.2		5.9		2.4		2.4		2.3		2.3	
1958	2.6	1.6	3.9		3.9		6.6		5.8		2.6		2.6		2.6		2.6	
1959	2.8	1.7	3.9		3.9		6.7		6.2		2.8		2.8		2.7		2.7	
1960	2.9	1.7	3.8		3.8		6.6		6.6		2.9		2.9		2.8		2.9	
1961	3.1	1.8	3.8		3.9		6.6		6.8		3.0		3.0		2.9		2.9	
1962	3.3	1.9	4.1		4.1		6.8		7.1		3.2		3.2		3.1		3.1	
1963	3.6	2.1	4.4		4.4		7.0		7.4		3.4		3.4		3.4		3.4	
1964	3.9	2.2	4.6		4.6		6.9		7.7		3.7		3.7		3.7		3.7	
1965	4.3	2.6	4.8		4.8		7.2		7.7		4.1		4.1		4.0		4.0	
1966	4.6	3.0	4.9		4.9		7.5		7.7		4.4		4.4		4.3		4.3	
1967	4.8	3.6	5.2		5.1		8.1		7.9		4.6		4.6		4.6		4.6	
1968	5.0	3.9	5.4		5.3		8.9		8.8		4.9		4.9		4.8		4.8	
1969	5.2	4.3	5.6		5.6		8.9		9.1		5.1		5.0		5.0		5.0	
1970	5.5	4.7	6.0		5.9		9.2		9.5		5.4		5.4		5.3		5.3	
1971	5.9	5.1	6.4		6.3		9.6		10.0		5.8		5.8		5.7		5.8	
1972	6.4	5.7	6.8		6.7		10.1		10.2		6.3		6.3		6.2		6.3	
1973	7.1	6.4	7.6		7.5		11.2		11.2		7.0		7.0		7.0		7.0	
1974	8.3	7.5	9.1		9.4		13.9		16.1		8.1		8.1		8.0		8.1	
1975	9.4	8.8	10.5		10.8		15.1		17.2		9.3		9.3		9.2		9.2	
1976	10.9	10.7	11.9		12.3		17.3		19.6		10.8		10.8		10.6		10.7	
1977	13.4	13.4	14.7		14.8		20.5		24.0		13.3		13.2		13.1		13.1	
1978	15.8	16.1	17.4		17.3		23.5		25.8		15.9		15.9		15.7		15.8	
1979	18.1	18.8	20.1		20.1		24.9		27.7		18.4		18.3		18.2		18.2	

(continued)

Appendices 259

Table S7 (continued)

	Final consumption expenditure		Gross capital formation			Exports	(2010 = 100)	Imports	(2010 = 100)	Gross domestic product at market price	(2010 = 100)	Gross national income	(2010 = 100)	Net national income	(2010 = 100)	Net national disposable income	(2010 = 100)
	Final consumption expenditure of NPISHs and households	Final consumption expenditure by government	Gross fixed capital formation	Capital formation													
	(2010 = 100)	(2010 = 100)	(2010 = 100)	(2010 = 100)													
1980	20.9	22.2	23.8	23.9		29.8	38.1		20.9		20.9		20.6		20.6	
1981	23.8	25.3	27.1	27.2		35.2	49.3		23.5		23.4		22.9		23.0	
1982	27.3	28.3	30.4	30.6		40.1	55.6		26.8		26.6		26.1		26.2	
1983	30.7	32.1	34.2	34.2		46.8	67.6		30.1		29.8		29.3		29.3	
1984	34.3	34.8	37.5	37.8		52.7	75.6		33.8		33.5		33.0		33.1	
1985	36.8	37.6	40.0	40.1		56.1	77.0		36.3		36.1		35.5		35.6	
1986	40.2	40.8	42.4	42.5		55.1	65.9		40.1		39.9		39.6		39.6	
1987	42.5	43.1	44.5	44.6		56.5	66.4		42.1		42.0		41.7		41.7	
1988	44.6	45.1	47.2	47.2		58.3	67.2		44.2		44.1		43.7		43.8	
1989	47.6	48.0	49.7	49.8		60.9	68.7		46.9		46.8		46.5		46.5	
1990	50.7	51.6	52.7	52.6		61.9	67.9		50.2		50.1		49.8		49.8	
1991	53.9	55.5	55.3	55.2		63.1	67.7		53.6		53.5		53.3		53.3	
1992	57.4	60.7	57.1	57.0		65.1	68.7		57.1		57.0		57.0		57.0	
1993	60.6	62.9	59.9	60.0		68.2	73.2		60.1		60.1		60.1		60.0	
1994	63.6	64.7	62.1	62.2		71.2	77.3		62.5		62.3		62.3		62.3	
1995	66.5	67.6	64.8	64.7		75.0	81.0		65.2		65.2		65.3		65.3	
1996	68.5	70.5	66.5	66.5		76.4	81.3		67.5		67.5		67.7		67.6	
1997	70.4	70.9	68.4	68.4		78.8	84.1		69.1		69.2		69.3		69.2	
1998	71.5	72.8	69.5	69.4		79.4	82.3		70.6		70.7		70.9		70.8	
1999	73.0	74.7	72.0	72.0		79.5	82.4		72.2		72.2		72.2		72.2	
2000	76.0	77.4	76.6	76.5		84.8	91.3		74.6		74.6		74.2		74.1	
2001	78.6	79.9	79.3	79.2		86.2	91.2		77.7		77.5		77.2		77.1	
2002	80.8	82.6	82.4	82.3		86.5	89.0		80.8		80.7		80.4		80.4	
2003	83.3	85.2	85.8	85.7		86.2	87.4		83.9		83.9		83.6		83.5	
2004	86.4	87.9	90.3	90.2		87.8	89.4		87.2		87.2		86.6		86.6	
2005	89.2	90.7	95.1	95.0		91.3	92.2		90.8		90.8		90.0		90.0	

(continued)

Table S7 (continued)

	Final consumption expenditure		Gross capital formation		Exports	Imports	Gross domestic product at market price	Gross national income	Net national income	Net national disposable income
	Final consumption expenditure of NPISHs and households	Final consumption expenditure by government	Gross fixed capital formation	Capital formation						
	(2010 = 100)	(2010 = 100)	(2010 = 100)	(2010 = 100)	(2010 = 100)	(2010 = 100)	(2010 = 100)	(2010 = 100)	(2010 = 100)	(2010 = 100)
2006	92.5	93.8	99.7	99.5	95.0	95.8	94.4	94.4	93.5	93.5
2007	95.5	96.5	102.4	102.3	97.2	97.4	97.6	97.6	96.7	96.7
2008	98.9	99.9	103.6	103.4	99.7	102.4	99.6	99.5	98.8	98.7
2009	98.1	101.2	100.3	100.2	97.1	94.8	99.8	99.9	99.8	99.9
2010	100.0	100.0	100.0	100.0	100.0	100.0	100.0	100.0	100.0	100.0
2011	102.4	99.4	99.2	99.3	104.5	108.5	100.0	99.9	100.1	99.9
2012	104.9	97.4	97.2	97.3	106.6	112.8	100.3	100.2	100.9	100.7
2013	106.1	97.9	94.1	94.2	105.8	110.9	100.7	100.7	102.2	102.1
2014	106.3	98.3	93.5	93.6	104.1	110.0	100.3	100.3	101.9	101.8
2015	106.0	99.5	94.3	94.3	104.6	109.7	100.7	100.7	102.2	102.2

Sources Please cite the database as: Leandro Prados de la Escosura (2017), Spanish Economic Growth, 1850–2015

Table S8 Gross domestic fixed capital formation, 1850–2014 (million Euro)

	Dwellings (million Euro)	Other construction (million Euro)	Machinery and equipment* (million Euro)	Transport equipment (million Euro)	Gross fixed capital formation (million Euro)
1850	0.6	0.4	0.05	0.1	1.2
1851	0.7	0.5	0.1	0.1	1.3
1852	0.9	0.5	0.1	0.1	1.6
1853	0.7	0.6	0.1	0.2	1.6
1854	0.6	0.5	0.1	0.1	1.3
1855	0.5	0.5	0.1	0.1	1.2
1856	0.6	0.6	0.1	0.3	1.6
1857	0.8	0.7	0.1	0.3	2.0
1858	1.1	0.9	0.1	0.8	2.9
1859	1.5	1.0	0.2	0.5	3.1
1860	1.7	1.6	0.1	0.3	3.7
1861	1.2	1.6	0.1	0.5	3.4
1862	1.3	1.6	0.2	0.6	3.7
1863	1.3	1.5	0.2	0.6	3.6
1864	1.1	1.3	0.2	0.6	3.2
1865	0.9	0.9	0.2	0.8	2.7
1866	0.8	0.8	0.1	0.9	2.7
1867	0.8	0.9	0.1	1.0	2.8
1868	0.6	0.7	0.1	0.1	1.6
1869	0.5	0.6	0.1	0.2	1.4
1870	0.6	0.6	0.1	0.4	1.7
1871	0.8	0.7	0.1	0.4	2.0
1872	0.8	0.8	0.2	0.4	2.2
1873	0.8	0.7	0.2	0.2	1.9
1874	0.8	0.8	0.2	0.5	2.2
1875	1.0	0.9	0.2	0.2	2.2
1876	1.1	1.0	0.2	0.5	2.8
1877	1.2	1.1	0.2	0.3	2.8
1878	1.0	0.9	0.2	1.2	3.4
1879	0.9	1.0	0.3	0.4	2.6
1880	1.0	1.1	0.4	0.9	3.3
1881	1.0	1.1	0.4	0.3	2.8
1882	1.1	1.3	0.4	0.6	3.5
1883	1.3	1.4	0.4	1.1	4.2
1884	1.2	1.3	0.4	1.2	4.1
1885	0.9	1.1	0.4	0.6	3.0
1886	0.8	1.1	0.3	0.5	2.7
1887	0.8	1.1	0.3	0.4	2.6
1888	0.7	1.2	0.3	0.2	2.4
1889	0.8	1.0	0.4	0.5	2.7
1890	0.9	1.2	0.5	0.4	3.0
1891	0.9	1.2	0.5	0.3	2.9
1892	1.0	1.2	0.5	0.2	3.0

(continued)

Appendices

Table S8 (continued)

	Dwellings (million Euro)	Other construction (million Euro)	Machinery and equipment* (million Euro)	Transport equipment (million Euro)	Gross fixed capital formation (million Euro)
1893	1.1	1.2	0.4	0.3	2.9
1894	1.1	1.1	0.5	0.2	2.8
1895	1.1	1.2	0.5	0.3	3.0
1896	1.1	1.1	0.5	0.2	3.0
1897	1.1	1.1	0.6	0.3	3.1
1898	1.2	1.2	0.6	0.3	3.3
1899	1.5	1.4	0.7	1.5	5.0
1900	2.0	1.8	1.0	1.7	6.6
1901	1.6	1.5	0.9	1.1	5.0
1902	1.5	1.5	0.9	0.5	4.3
1903	1.7	1.6	1.0	0.5	4.8
1904	1.9	1.7	1.0	0.6	5.2
1905	1.5	1.5	0.9	0.7	4.6
1906	1.4	1.6	1.1	0.8	4.8
1907	1.7	1.8	1.1	0.9	5.6
1908	1.8	1.8	1.2	0.4	5.2
1909	2.0	1.9	1.1	0.7	5.6
1910	2.0	2.5	1.2	0.6	6.3
1911	2.3	2.6	1.2	0.6	6.7
1912	2.3	2.8	1.5	1.3	8.0
1913	2.5	2.8	1.8	1.7	8.9
1914	2.5	2.8	1.4	1.2	7.9
1915	2.2	2.7	1.3	0.5	6.7
1916	2.0	2.6	2.0	0.9	7.6
1917	1.8	2.6	2.1	2.1	8.7
1918	1.8	2.6	2.7	3.4	10.6
1919	2.2	3.3	2.2	3.3	11.0
1920	3.5	4.5	2.5	3.9	14.5
1921	4.1	5.9	3.6	3.9	17.4
1922	4.7	6.5	2.4	3.4	16.8
1923	5.7	6.4	3.3	1.9	17.3
1924	6.1	6.7	3.6	5.4	21.7
1925	6.8	7.8	4.2	2.0	20.8
1926	7.2	8.2	4.3	4.7	24.3
1927	7.8	8.3	5.2	4.8	26.1
1928	8.7	8.5	6.3	7.8	31.4
1929	9.8	10.0	8.0	7.9	35.8
1930	10.0	10.3	9.7	5.4	35.3
1931	4.0	8.4	8.7	3.4	24.5
1932	3.6	7.3	8.1	2.1	21.0
1933	3.5	8.8	7.8	3.6	23.7
1934	3.4	8.3	7.8	4.3	23.8
1935	3.6	8.8	8.4	4.3	25.0

(continued)

Table S8 (continued)

	Dwellings (million Euro)	Other construction (million Euro)	Machinery and equipment* (million Euro)	Transport equipment (million Euro)	Gross fixed capital formation (million Euro)
1936	3.0	7.4	8.5	2.3	21.3
1937	2.3	6.9	7.8	0.3	17.3
1938	2.5	6.9	7.7	0.3	17.3
1939	2.7	6.1	8.2	1.2	18.1
1940	3.2	9.4	9.8	2.9	25.4
1941	11.4	12.5	11.7	3.7	39.4
1942	13.1	15.9	12.1	9.2	50.2
1943	15.6	18.7	13.9	4.4	52.5
1944	14.3	21.4	13.9	2.9	52.5
1945	14.8	18.7	18.9	4.3	56.6
1946	19.1	22.4	22.2	7.2	70.8
1947	33.9	29.3	27.4	5.3	95.9
1948	53.5	39.2	31.3	9.9	134
1949	45.1	40.4	38.2	10.9	135
1950	50.5	47.8	47.3	14.1	160
1951	44.0	47.6	49.5	14.5	156
1952	51.1	58.8	66.3	17.4	194
1953	58.9	61.3	83.6	17.9	222
1954	102	84	102	29	317
1955	133	113	120	43	408
1956	195	152	173	59	579
1957	191	161	209	79	639
1958	228	182	223	96	730
1959	230	165	196	101	692
1960	219	168	233	104	724
1961	262	179	303	119	863
1962	317	256	328	117	1018
1963	389	354	330	143	1215
1964	496	450	348	172	1465
1965	533	554	514	210	1811
1966	559	666	658	234	2117
1967	569	871	675	294	2409
1968	687	989	760	321	2757
1969	776	1109	931	366	3182
1970	807	1241	1019	398	3464
1971	854	1349	1063	368	3634
1972	1047	1673	1401	528	4649
1973	1450	2093	1807	739	6089
1974	1923	2746	2334	1008	8011
1975	2250	3056	2632	1125	9063
1976	2690	3460	3123	1115	10388
1977	3363	4280	3821	1439	12903

(continued)

Table S8 (continued)

	Dwellings (million Euro)	Other construction (million Euro)	Machinery and equipment* (million Euro)	Transport equipment (million Euro)	Gross fixed capital formation (million Euro)
1978	3976	5117	4510	1636	15239
1979	4648	5945	4784	1767	17145
1980	5448	7358	5895	2150	20850
1981	6135	7743	6494	2741	23113
1982	6783	8955	7265	3462	26465
1983	6855	10399	8498	3372	29124
1984	6845	10852	9279	2766	29741
1985	7130	12525	10888	3163	33707
1986	8172	14666	12715	3741	39294
1987	9876	16842	15826	4956	47499
1988	12644	20153	19227	6077	58100
1989	14782	25882	22609	7107	70380
1990	17934	31121	24009	7331	80394
1991	19448	35228	24623	7440	86739
1992	20395	34592	24458	7182	86627
1993	21437	32900	21859	6139	82335
1994	23389	34717	23641	6845	88592
1995	27784	37967	27629	7774	101154
1996	30602	36368	31167	8285	106422
1997	32305	38444	34469	10102	115320
1998	36359	41838	39405	12065	129667
1999	42677	47422	43396	14338	147833
2000	56596	47764	47943	16655	168958
2001	63708	53513	49709	16567	183497
2002	72114	59638	51577	16160	199489
2003	83124	65833	55401	17839	222197
2004	93976	73208	58849	19676	245709
2005	107292	83450	65171	22249	278162
2006	121774	94563	72177	24492	313006
2007	126927	100930	81108	26587	335552
2008	115946	101632	84311	24175	326064
2009	87224	87164	73703	14408	262499
2010	74677	79868	78360	16082	248987
2011	61433	72617	78933	16901	229884
2012	51612	61647	76649	15931	205839
2013	43800	55768	76186	16617	192371
2014	43649	56510	78165	20011	198335
2015	45743	60620	82224	23482	212069

Sources Please cite the database as: Leandro Prados de la Escosura (2017), Spanish Economic Growth, 1850–2015
*includes other concepts such as "agriculture" and "other". The latter including intellectual property since 1995

Table S9 Composition of gross domestic fixed capital formation, 1850–2015 (percentages)

	Dwellings (%)	Other construction (%)	Machinery & equipment*	Transport equipment (%)
1850	53.44	36.50	4.20	5.85
1851	55.81	34.30	4.68	5.21
1852	55.75	34.08	4.40	5.77
1853	46.50	35.61	5.62	12.27
1854	46.31	36.07	7.69	9.93
1855	44.27	38.94	7.35	9.44
1856	39.43	34.28	6.62	19.67
1857	41.89	36.37	5.66	16.08
1858	39.29	29.43	5.17	26.12
1859	47.41	32.09	5.10	15.41
1860	45.46	44.07	3.35	7.12
1861	34.13	47.22	4.39	14.26
1862	36.35	43.37	4.79	15.49
1863	35.86	41.85	5.58	16.70
1864	35.53	39.19	5.79	19.48
1865	31.70	34.17	6.18	27.95
1866	29.90	30.88	5.24	33.98
1867	28.57	30.17	4.57	36.69
1868	39.40	44.92	7.66	8.01
1869	35.97	44.26	7.33	12.44
1870	36.93	33.72	7.99	21.36
1871	38.43	35.32	7.67	18.59
1872	38.59	34.50	8.17	18.75
1873	42.98	37.18	9.17	10.67
1874	38.03	34.19	7.05	20.73
1875	44.63	40.41	8.10	6.86
1876	38.50	36.38	7.28	17.84
1877	42.65	40.16	8.24	8.96
1878	30.29	27.50	6.49	35.73
1879	35.90	37.38	10.51	16.20
1880	29.27	33.60	11.11	26.03
1881	35.81	40.85	13.97	9.37
1882	32.47	36.35	12.64	18.55
1883	30.85	32.72	10.11	26.32
1884	28.75	31.98	10.70	28.58
1885	31.98	36.89	12.20	18.94
1886	29.65	40.08	12.47	17.80
1887	30.23	43.52	11.84	14.41
1888	30.84	48.28	12.22	8.66
1889	30.31	37.75	14.66	17.27

(continued)

Table S9 (continued)

	Dwellings (%)	Other construction (%)	Machinery & equipment* (%)	Transport equipment (%)
1890	30.98	39.96	16.42	12.64
1891	32.36	40.90	17.11	9.63
1892	34.75	41.46	18.42	5.37
1893	36.49	40.07	13.74	9.70
1894	38.84	39.02	16.07	6.08
1895	36.43	38.89	15.96	8.72
1896	36.73	37.78	17.78	7.71
1897	35.90	34.78	18.44	10.87
1898	36.71	36.40	17.87	9.02
1899	29.46	27.12	14.68	28.74
1900	29.97	27.71	15.74	26.58
1901	30.92	30.32	17.65	21.12
1902	34.03	33.51	20.44	12.02
1903	34.66	34.14	19.88	11.32
1904	36.50	33.22	19.64	10.63
1905	33.07	32.58	19.86	14.49
1906	28.80	32.30	21.99	16.90
1907	30.91	32.87	19.90	16.32
1908	34.84	35.01	22.13	8.02
1909	34.67	33.22	20.36	11.74
1910	32.29	39.37	18.97	9.37
1911	34.50	38.19	18.23	9.08
1912	29.41	35.76	18.43	16.40
1913	28.54	31.54	20.60	19.33
1914	31.63	35.50	17.73	15.14
1915	32.82	39.73	19.44	8.01
1916	26.75	34.14	26.69	12.42
1917	20.90	30.33	24.13	24.64
1918	17.38	24.80	25.54	32.29
1919	19.82	29.93	20.45	29.80
1920	24.49	30.96	17.51	27.03
1921	23.77	33.61	20.46	22.16
1922	27.74	38.31	14.06	19.89
1923	32.76	37.10	19.11	11.03
1924	27.93	30.74	16.55	24.77
1925	32.65	37.71	20.08	9.55
1926	29.57	33.50	17.78	19.15
1927	29.79	31.95	19.72	18.54
1928	27.67	27.25	20.10	24.98
1929	27.49	27.83	22.46	22.23

(continued)

Table S9 (continued)

	Dwellings (%)	Other construction (%)	Machinery & equipment* (%)	Transport equipment (%)
1930	28.22	29.05	27.37	15.36
1931	16.42	34.28	35.51	13.79
1932	17.04	34.61	38.43	9.92
1933	14.77	36.97	33.07	15.20
1934	14.26	34.76	32.81	18.17
1935	14.40	34.98	33.60	17.01
1936	14.29	34.93	39.75	11.04
1937	13.36	40.12	45.00	1.52
1938	14.40	39.92	44.19	1.49
1939	14.73	33.68	45.19	6.39
1940	12.68	37.18	38.61	11.53
1941	29.02	31.66	29.82	9.50
1942	25.98	31.58	24.15	18.29
1943	29.62	35.55	26.49	8.34
1944	27.21	40.72	26.46	5.60
1945	26.07	33.09	33.32	7.52
1946	26.98	31.59	31.32	10.11
1947	35.38	30.58	28.55	5.48
1948	39.98	29.28	23.38	7.37
1949	33.48	30.02	28.40	8.11
1950	31.61	29.96	29.62	8.81
1951	28.28	30.60	31.79	9.33
1952	26.39	30.36	34.25	9.00
1953	26.56	27.65	37.70	8.09
1954	32.31	26.40	32.06	9.23
1955	32.46	27.63	29.43	10.48
1956	33.61	26.28	29.93	10.18
1957	29.90	25.11	32.65	12.34
1958	31.23	24.99	30.57	13.20
1959	33.31	23.83	28.29	14.57
1960	30.30	23.15	32.19	14.36
1961	30.36	20.69	35.15	13.79
1962	31.12	25.18	32.19	11.51
1963	31.99	29.11	27.17	11.74
1964	33.87	30.69	23.73	11.71
1965	29.43	30.61	28.38	11.58
1966	26.41	31.46	31.09	11.04
1967	23.62	36.18	28.01	12.19
1968	24.92	35.88	27.56	11.64
1969	24.39	34.85	29.24	11.51
1970	23.28	35.83	29.41	11.48

(continued)

Table S9 (continued)

	Dwellings (%)	Other construction (%)	Machinery & equipment*	Transport equipment (%)
1971	23.51	37.12	29.26	10.11
1972	22.53	35.98	30.13	11.36
1973	23.82	34.36	29.68	12.14
1974	24.00	34.28	29.14	12.59
1975	24.82	33.72	29.04	12.42
1976	25.89	33.31	30.06	10.73
1977	26.06	33.17	29.61	11.15
1978	26.09	33.58	29.59	10.73
1979	27.11	34.67	27.91	10.31
1980	26.13	35.29	28.27	10.31
1981	26.55	33.50	28.10	11.86
1982	25.63	33.84	27.45	13.08
1983	23.54	35.71	29.18	11.58
1984	23.02	36.49	31.20	9.30
1985	21.15	37.16	32.30	9.39
1986	20.80	37.32	32.36	9.52
1987	20.79	35.46	33.32	10.43
1988	21.76	34.69	33.09	10.46
1989	21.00	36.77	32.12	10.10
1990	22.31	38.71	29.86	9.12
1991	22.42	40.61	28.39	8.58
1992	23.54	39.93	28.23	8.29
1993	26.04	39.96	26.55	7.46
1994	26.40	39.19	26.68	7.73
1995	27.47	37.53	27.31	7.69
1996	28.76	34.17	29.29	7.79
1997	28.01	33.34	29.89	8.76
1998	28.04	32.27	30.39	9.30
1999	28.87	32.08	29.35	9.70
2000	33.50	28.27	28.38	9.86
2001	34.72	29.16	27.09	9.03
2002	36.15	29.90	25.85	8.10
2003	37.41	29.63	24.93	8.03
2004	38.25	29.79	23.95	8.01
2005	38.57	30.00	23.43	8.00
2006	38.90	30.21	23.06	7.82
2007	37.83	30.08	24.17	7.92
2008	35.56	31.17	25.86	7.41
2009	33.23	33.21	28.08	5.49
2010	29.99	32.08	31.47	6.46
2011	26.72	31.59	34.34	7.35

(continued)

Table S9 (continued)

	Dwellings (%)	Other construction (%)	Machinery & equipment*	Transport equipment (%)
2012	25.07	29.95	37.24	7.74
2013	22.77	28.99	39.60	8.64
2014	22.01	28.49	39.41	10.09
2015	21.57	28.59	38.77	11.07

Sources Please cite the database as: Leandro Prados de la Escosura (2017), Spanish Economic Growth, 1850–2015
*includes other concepts such as "agriculture" and "other". The latter including intellectual property since 1995

Table S10 Volume indices of gross domestic fixed capital formation, 1850–2015 (2010 = 100)

	Dwellings	Other construction	Machinery & equipment*	Transport equipment	Gross fixed capital formation
	(2010 = 100)	(2010 = 100)	(2010 = 100)	(2010 = 100)	(2010 = 100)
1850	0.7	0.3	0.02	0.1	0.2
1851	0.8	0.3	0.02	0.1	0.3
1852	1.0	0.3	0.02	0.1	0.3
1853	0.9	0.3	0.03	0.2	0.3
1854	0.7	0.3	0.03	0.1	0.2
1855	0.7	0.3	0.02	0.1	0.2
1856	0.8	0.3	0.03	0.3	0.3
1857	1.1	0.5	0.03	0.3	0.4
1858	1.7	0.6	0.04	0.8	0.6
1859	1.9	0.6	0.04	0.5	0.6
1860	2.1	1.2	0.03	0.3	0.8
1861	1.5	1.2	0.04	0.5	0.7
1862	1.7	1.2	0.05	0.7	0.8
1863	1.6	1.1	0.05	0.7	0.8
1864	1.5	0.9	0.05	0.7	0.7
1865	1.2	0.7	0.05	0.8	0.6
1866	1.1	0.6	0.04	1.0	0.6
1867	1.1	0.6	0.04	1.1	0.6
1868	0.9	0.5	0.04	0.1	0.4
1869	0.8	0.5	0.03	0.2	0.3
1870	0.9	0.4	0.04	0.4	0.4
1871	1.1	0.5	0.05	0.3	0.5
1872	1.3	0.6	0.05	0.4	0.5
1873	1.2	0.5	0.05	0.1	0.4
1874	1.1	0.5	0.04	0.4	0.4
1875	1.3	0.6	0.04	0.1	0.5
1876	1.5	0.7	0.05	0.7	0.6
1877	1.8	0.9	0.07	0.4	0.7
1878	1.6	0.7	0.07	1.5	0.8
1879	1.5	0.8	0.08	0.6	0.7
1880	1.5	0.9	0.11	1.1	0.8
1881	1.7	1.0	0.12	0.4	0.7
1882	1.9	1.1	0.13	0.8	0.9
1883	2.1	1.1	0.13	1.7	1.1
1884	2.0	1.2	0.13	1.2	1.0
1885	1.6	1.0	0.12	0.8	0.8
1886	1.4	1.1	0.12	0.8	0.8
1887	1.4	1.2	0.11	0.7	0.8
1888	1.4	1.3	0.10	0.3	0.7
1889	1.5	1.1	0.13	0.6	0.8
1890	1.6	1.3	0.2	0.5	0.9

(continued)

Table S10 (continued)

	Dwellings	Other construction	Machinery & equipment*	Transport equipment	Gross fixed capital formation
	(2010 = 100)	(2010 = 100)	(2010 = 100)	(2010 = 100)	(2010 = 100)
1891	1.7	1.3	0.2	0.4	0.8
1892	1.8	1.3	0.2	0.2	0.8
1893	1.8	1.1	0.1	0.4	0.8
1894	1.9	1.1	0.1	0.3	0.8
1895	2.0	1.2	0.2	0.5	0.9
1896	1.9	1.2	0.2	0.4	0.9
1897	2.0	1.1	0.2	0.5	0.9
1898	1.9	1.1	0.2	0.4	0.8
1899	2.3	1.2	0.2	1.7	1.2
1900	2.9	1.5	0.3	1.9	1.5
1901	2.5	1.4	0.2	1.3	1.2
1902	2.4	1.4	0.2	0.6	1.1
1903	2.5	1.4	0.2	0.7	1.1
1904	2.7	1.4	0.2	0.7	1.2
1905	2.4	1.3	0.2	0.9	1.1
1906	2.2	1.4	0.3	1.2	1.2
1907	2.5	1.5	0.3	1.4	1.3
1908	2.7	1.6	0.3	0.6	1.3
1909	2.8	1.6	0.3	1.1	1.4
1910	2.9	2.1	0.3	0.9	1.5
1911	3.3	2.1	0.3	0.9	1.6
1912	3.4	2.4	0.4	2.0	1.9
1913	3.6	2.3	0.5	2.2	2.0
1914	3.5	2.3	0.4	2.0	1.9
1915	3.0	2.0	0.3	0.7	1.4
1916	2.5	1.8	0.4	1.1	1.4
1917	2.1	1.4	0.3	2.1	1.4
1918	1.7	1.1	0.3	2.3	1.3
1919	1.9	1.4	0.3	2.7	1.5
1920	2.6	1.8	0.3	2.3	1.6
1921	2.7	2.4	0.4	2.3	1.9
1922	3.0	2.5	0.3	2.4	1.9
1923	3.7	2.7	0.5	1.8	2.1
1924	4.0	2.6	0.5	3.6	2.5
1925	4.5	3.3	0.6	1.5	2.4
1926	4.9	3.4	0.7	3.2	2.9
1927	5.3	3.5	0.8	3.3	3.1
1928	5.9	3.5	1.0	5.5	3.8
1929	6.6	4.1	1.2	5.7	4.2
1930	6.6	4.4	1.5	3.9	4.2
1931	2.5	3.6	1.3	2.5	2.9
1932	2.2	3.2	1.3	1.6	2.5
1933	2.1	3.6	1.2	2.6	2.7

(continued)

Appendices

Table S10 (continued)

	Dwellings	Other construction	Machinery & equipment*	Transport equipment	Gross fixed capital formation
	(2010 = 100)	(2010 = 100)	(2010 = 100)	(2010 = 100)	(2010 = 100)
1934	2.0	3.3	1.2	2.9	2.7
1935	2.1	3.5	1.3	2.9	2.8
1936	1.7	2.9	1.2	1.4	2.2
1937	1.2	2.5	1.0	0.1	1.6
1938	1.2	2.3	0.9	0.1	1.5
1939	1.2	2.0	0.9	0.6	1.5
1940	1.2	2.8	1.0	1.2	1.9
1941	4.0	2.9	1.1	1.3	2.6
1942	4.3	3.4	1.1	2.7	3.0
1943	4.9	3.8	1.1	1.2	2.9
1944	4.3	4.3	1.1	0.9	2.8
1945	4.2	3.6	1.5	1.1	3.0
1946	4.6	3.5	1.3	1.6	3.0
1947	6.0	3.7	1.3	1.0	3.2
1948	8.5	4.5	1.4	1.8	4.1
1949	7.6	4.7	1.7	1.8	4.1
1950	7.3	4.6	1.6	1.7	4.0
1951	5.9	3.9	1.6	1.7	3.6
1952	6.5	4.6	2.1	1.9	4.3
1953	6.9	4.6	2.7	2.0	4.8
1954	8.9	4.8	2.5	2.5	5.1
1955	11.5	6.3	2.8	3.6	6.4
1956	12.5	6.7	3.0	4.0	7.0
1957	11.1	6.3	3.1	4.4	6.7
1958	13.3	7.0	3.3	5.2	7.6
1959	12.9	6.1	2.9	5.9	7.1
1960	13.2	6.6	3.5	6.4	7.6
1961	16.3	7.3	4.4	6.4	9.0
1962	17.4	9.2	4.7	6.1	10.0
1963	18.8	11.3	4.7	7.3	11.2
1964	22.0	13.3	4.7	8.6	12.9
1965	23.5	16.2	7.2	10.8	15.2
1966	24.6	19.4	9.4	12.2	17.3
1967	23.4	24.3	9.4	15.0	18.7
1968	26.6	26.2	10.1	16.0	20.6
1969	29.1	28.1	12.0	18.3	22.7
1970	28.3	29.4	12.6	19.2	23.1
1971	27.4	29.7	12.5	17.8	22.8
1972	32.2	35.2	15.8	23.9	27.5
1973	37.2	39.9	19.0	32.3	32.1
1974	39.8	43.2	21.8	38.9	35.2
1975	38.1	43.8	21.1	41.7	34.8
1976	38.5	43.4	21.5	42.1	34.9

(continued)

Table S10 (continued)

	Dwellings	Other construction	Machinery & equipment*	Transport equipment	Gross fixed capital formation
	(2010 = 100)	(2010 = 100)	(2010 = 100)	(2010 = 100)	(2010 = 100)
1977	38.3	43.7	22.0	45.5	35.4
1978	36.6	44.3	22.5	43.8	35.1
1979	34.4	44.1	22.2	42.5	34.2
1980	34.4	44.9	24.3	43.9	35.2
1981	36.7	39.8	23.7	46.7	34.3
1982	36.2	41.5	24.0	50.9	35.0
1983	34.0	42.1	24.4	43.9	34.2
1984	31.4	39.8	24.0	32.8	31.9
1985	31.6	42.5	26.9	34.7	33.8
1986	32.4	47.8	30.6	38.9	37.2
1987	36.5	53.4	37.0	49.8	42.9
1988	42.8	59.7	43.3	59.2	49.4
1989	46.7	72.2	48.7	66.9	56.8
1990	52.0	79.9	50.1	66.5	61.3
1991	52.8	84.8	50.0	65.4	63.0
1992	53.3	79.9	48.8	61.1	60.9
1993	53.2	72.3	40.8	50.0	55.2
1994	56.4	73.5	42.0	55.4	57.3
1995	64.1	77.1	47.0	62.1	62.7
1996	68.8	72.2	51.8	64.7	64.3
1997	70.9	74.5	55.9	76.4	67.7
1998	78.5	80.3	63.1	90.3	75.0
1999	87.0	87.6	68.1	105.5	82.4
2000	106.4	82.0	72.4	117.0	88.6
2001	113.2	88.1	73.9	114.9	92.9
2002	120.4	94.1	75.8	109.3	97.2
2003	130.2	99.8	80.2	118.3	104.0
2004	136.6	105.1	83.7	127.7	109.3
2005	145.6	112.9	90.3	141.6	117.5
2006	155.1	121.0	97.8	154.3	126.1
2007	157.0	125.4	106.7	166.2	131.6
2008	142.2	123.8	109.2	150.8	126.4
2009	113.2	109.5	96.0	90.2	105.1
2010	100.0	100.0	100.0	100.0	100.0
2011	86.7	89.8	100.1	104.5	93.1
2012	78.4	76.6	96.9	99.7	85.1
2013	71.8	70.2	98.9	107.6	82.1
2014	71.9	71.8	102.6	129.2	85.2
2015	73.5	77.1	107.7	149.8	90.4

Sources Please cite the database as: Leandro Prados de la Escosura (2017), Spanish Economic Growth, 1850–2015
*includes other concepts such as "agriculture" and "other". The latter including intellectual property since 1995

Table S11 Deflators of gross domestic fixed capital formation, 1850–2015 (2000 = 100)

	Dwellings	Other construction	Machinery & equipment*	Transport equipment	Gross fixed capital formation
	(2010 = 100)	(2010 = 100)	(2010 = 100)	(2010 = 100)	(2010 = 100)
1850	0.1	0.2	0.4	0.5	0.2
1851	0.1	0.2	0.4	0.5	0.2
1852	0.1	0.2	0.4	0.5	0.2
1853	0.1	0.2	0.4	0.6	0.2
1854	0.1	0.2	0.5	0.7	0.2
1855	0.1	0.2	0.5	0.7	0.2
1856	0.1	0.2	0.5	0.7	0.2
1857	0.1	0.2	0.5	0.7	0.2
1858	0.1	0.2	0.5	0.6	0.2
1859	0.1	0.2	0.5	0.6	0.2
1860	0.1	0.2	0.5	0.5	0.2
1861	0.1	0.2	0.5	0.6	0.2
1862	0.1	0.2	0.5	0.5	0.2
1863	0.1	0.2	0.5	0.5	0.2
1864	0.1	0.2	0.5	0.6	0.2
1865	0.1	0.2	0.5	0.6	0.2
1866	0.1	0.2	0.5	0.6	0.2
1867	0.1	0.2	0.4	0.6	0.2
1868	0.1	0.2	0.4	0.6	0.2
1869	0.1	0.2	0.4	0.5	0.2
1870	0.1	0.2	0.4	0.6	0.2
1871	0.1	0.2	0.4	0.7	0.2
1872	0.1	0.2	0.4	0.6	0.2
1873	0.1	0.2	0.5	0.9	0.2
1874	0.1	0.2	0.5	0.7	0.2
1875	0.1	0.2	0.5	0.7	0.2
1876	0.1	0.2	0.5	0.4	0.2
1877	0.1	0.2	0.5	0.4	0.2
1878	0.1	0.2	0.4	0.5	0.2
1879	0.1	0.1	0.4	0.4	0.2
1880	0.1	0.1	0.4	0.5	0.2
1881	0.1	0.1	0.4	0.4	0.2
1882	0.1	0.1	0.4	0.5	0.2
1883	0.1	0.1	0.4	0.4	0.2
1884	0.1	0.1	0.4	0.6	0.2
1885	0.1	0.1	0.4	0.4	0.1
1886	0.1	0.1	0.4	0.4	0.1
1887	0.1	0.1	0.4	0.3	0.1
1888	0.1	0.1	0.4	0.4	0.1
1889	0.1	0.1	0.4	0.5	0.1
1890	0.1	0.1	0.4	0.4	0.1

(continued)

Table S11 (continued)

	Dwellings	Other construction	Machinery & equipment*	Transport equipment	Gross fixed capital formation
	(2010 = 100)	(2010 = 100)	(2010 = 100)	(2010 = 100)	(2010 = 100)
1891	0.1	0.1	0.4	0.4	0.1
1892	0.1	0.1	0.4	0.4	0.1
1893	0.1	0.1	0.4	0.4	0.1
1894	0.1	0.1	0.4	0.4	0.1
1895	0.1	0.1	0.4	0.4	0.1
1896	0.1	0.1	0.4	0.4	0.1
1897	0.1	0.1	0.4	0.4	0.1
1898	0.1	0.1	0.5	0.5	0.2
1899	0.1	0.1	0.5	0.5	0.2
1900	0.1	0.2	0.5	0.6	0.2
1901	0.1	0.1	0.5	0.5	0.2
1902	0.1	0.1	0.5	0.5	0.2
1903	0.1	0.1	0.5	0.5	0.2
1904	0.1	0.2	0.5	0.5	0.2
1905	0.1	0.1	0.5	0.4	0.2
1906	0.1	0.1	0.5	0.4	0.2
1907	0.1	0.2	0.5	0.4	0.2
1908	0.1	0.1	0.5	0.4	0.2
1909	0.1	0.1	0.4	0.4	0.2
1910	0.1	0.1	0.5	0.4	0.2
1911	0.1	0.1	0.5	0.4	0.2
1912	0.1	0.1	0.5	0.4	0.2
1913	0.1	0.2	0.5	0.5	0.2
1914	0.1	0.2	0.5	0.4	0.2
1915	0.1	0.2	0.5	0.5	0.2
1916	0.1	0.2	0.7	0.5	0.2
1917	0.1	0.2	0.9	0.6	0.3
1918	0.1	0.3	1.1	0.9	0.3
1919	0.2	0.3	0.9	0.7	0.3
1920	0.2	0.3	1.0	1.1	0.4
1921	0.2	0.3	1.0	1.1	0.4
1922	0.2	0.3	1.0	0.9	0.4
1923	0.2	0.3	0.9	0.7	0.3
1924	0.2	0.3	0.9	0.9	0.3
1925	0.2	0.3	0.9	0.8	0.3
1926	0.2	0.3	0.8	0.9	0.3
1927	0.2	0.3	0.8	0.9	0.3
1928	0.2	0.3	0.8	0.9	0.3
1929	0.2	0.3	0.8	0.9	0.3
1930	0.2	0.3	0.8	0.9	0.3
1931	0.2	0.3	0.8	0.8	0.3
1932	0.2	0.3	0.8	0.8	0.3
1933	0.2	0.3	0.8	0.9	0.4

(continued)

Table S11 (continued)

	Dwellings	Other construction	Machinery & equipment*	Transport equipment	Gross fixed capital formation
	(2010 = 100)	(2010 = 100)	(2010 = 100)	(2010 = 100)	(2010 = 100)
1934	0.2	0.3	0.8	0.9	0.4
1935	0.2	0.3	0.9	0.9	0.4
1936	0.2	0.3	0.9	1.0	0.4
1937	0.3	0.3	1.0	1.1	0.4
1938	0.3	0.4	1.1	1.2	0.5
1939	0.3	0.4	1.1	1.3	0.5
1940	0.3	0.4	1.2	1.5	0.5
1941	0.4	0.5	1.3	1.8	0.6
1942	0.4	0.6	1.4	2.1	0.7
1943	0.4	0.6	1.6	2.2	0.7
1944	0.4	0.6	1.7	2.1	0.7
1945	0.5	0.6	1.6	2.5	0.8
1946	0.6	0.8	2.2	2.9	0.9
1947	0.8	1.0	2.7	3.4	1.2
1948	0.8	1.1	2.8	3.4	1.3
1949	0.8	1.1	2.9	3.8	1.3
1950	0.9	1.3	3.7	5.1	1.6
1951	1.0	1.5	4.0	5.4	1.8
1952	1.1	1.6	4.0	5.6	1.8
1953	1.1	1.7	3.9	5.5	1.9
1954	1.5	2.2	5.3	7.2	2.5
1955	1.5	2.2	5.5	7.4	2.6
1956	2.1	2.8	7.4	9.1	3.3
1957	2.3	3.2	8.5	11.2	3.8
1958	2.3	3.3	8.7	11.5	3.9
1959	2.4	3.4	8.5	10.6	3.9
1960	2.2	3.2	8.4	10.0	3.8
1961	2.1	3.1	8.9	11.7	3.8
1962	2.4	3.5	8.8	11.9	4.1
1963	2.8	3.9	9.0	12.2	4.4
1964	3.0	4.2	9.3	12.5	4.6
1965	3.0	4.3	9.1	12.1	4.8
1966	3.0	4.3	8.9	11.9	4.9
1967	3.3	4.5	9.1	12.2	5.2
1968	3.5	4.7	9.6	12.5	5.4
1969	3.6	4.9	9.9	12.4	5.6
1970	3.8	5.3	10.4	12.9	6.0
1971	4.2	5.7	10.9	12.8	6.4
1972	4.4	5.9	11.3	13.7	6.8
1973	5.2	6.6	12.1	14.2	7.6
1974	6.5	8.0	13.6	16.1	9.1
1975	7.9	8.7	15.9	16.8	10.5
1976	9.4	10.0	18.5	16.5	11.9

(continued)

Table S11 (continued)

	Dwellings	Other construction	Machinery & equipment*	Transport equipment	Gross fixed capital formation
	(2010 = 100)	(2010 = 100)	(2010 = 100)	(2010 = 100)	(2010 = 100)
1977	11.8	12.3	22.2	19.7	14.7
1978	14.5	14.5	25.6	23.2	17.4
1979	18.1	16.9	27.6	25.8	20.1
1980	21.2	20.5	30.9	30.4	23.8
1981	22.4	24.3	35.0	36.5	27.1
1982	25.1	27.0	38.6	42.3	30.4
1983	27.0	30.9	44.5	47.8	34.2
1984	29.2	34.1	49.4	52.5	37.5
1985	30.2	36.9	51.7	56.7	40.0
1986	33.8	38.4	53.1	59.7	42.4
1987	36.3	39.5	54.6	61.8	44.5
1988	39.5	42.2	56.7	63.8	47.2
1989	42.4	44.9	59.2	66.0	49.7
1990	46.1	48.8	61.1	68.5	52.7
1991	49.3	52.0	62.8	70.8	55.3
1992	51.3	54.2	63.9	73.0	57.1
1993	54.0	57.0	68.4	76.4	59.9
1994	55.6	59.2	71.9	76.8	62.1
1995	58.1	61.7	75.0	77.8	64.8
1996	59.5	63.1	76.7	79.7	66.5
1997	61.0	64.6	78.6	82.2	68.4
1998	62.1	65.3	79.7	83.1	69.5
1999	65.7	67.8	81.3	84.5	72.0
2000	71.2	72.9	84.5	88.6	76.6
2001	75.4	76.0	85.9	89.6	79.3
2002	80.2	79.4	86.9	91.9	82.4
2003	85.5	82.6	88.1	93.8	85.8
2004	92.1	87.2	89.7	95.8	90.3
2005	98.7	92.5	92.1	97.7	95.1
2006	105.1	97.8	94.1	98.7	99.7
2007	108.3	100.8	97.0	99.4	102.4
2008	109.2	102.8	98.6	99.7	103.6
2009	103.1	99.7	98.0	99.3	100.3
2010	100.0	100.0	100.0	100.0	100.0
2011	94.9	101.3	100.6	100.5	99.2
2012	88.1	100.7	100.9	99.4	97.2
2013	81.7	99.5	98.3	96.0	94.1
2014	81.3	98.5	97.3	96.3	93.5
2015	83.3	98.4	97.4	97.5	94.3

Sources Please cite the database as: Leandro Prados de la Escosura (2017), Spanish Economic Growth, 1850–2015
*includes other concepts such as "agriculture" and "other". The latter including intellectual property since 1995

278 Appendices

Table S12 Gross domestic product and its output components, 1850–2015 (million Euro)

	Agriculture, forestry and fishing (million Euro)	Manufacturing, extractive industries, and utilities (million Euro)	Construction (million Euro)	Service activities (million Euro)	Gross value added (million Euro)	Taxes less subsidies on products (million Euro)	Gross domestic product at market prices (million Euro)
1850	9.3	3.4	0.9	11.3	24.8	0.8	25.6
1851	9.4	3.7	0.9	11.4	25.3	0.8	26.1
1852	9.0	4.0	1.0	11.5	25.4	0.9	26.3
1853	13.4	3.8	1.0	12.0	30.2	0.8	31.0
1854	13.6	4.1	0.9	12.7	31.3	0.8	32.1
1855	16.3	4.3	0.8	12.2	33.6	0.4	34.0
1856	13.8	5.2	1.0	13.2	33.2	0.4	33.6
1857	12.3	5.1	1.1	13.1	31.6	0.9	32.4
1858	11.7	5.3	1.2	12.7	30.8	0.8	31.6
1859	12.9	5.4	1.4	13.1	32.8	0.9	33.7
1860	13.7	5.4	1.7	14.0	34.8	1.0	35.8
1861	14.1	5.8	1.5	14.1	35.5	1.1	36.6
1862	14.3	6.3	1.6	14.4	36.5	1.1	37.6
1863	15.1	6.9	1.5	15.0	38.5	1.1	39.6
1864	14.4	7.1	1.4	15.5	38.4	1.1	39.5
1865	13.8	6.6	1.1	14.5	36.1	1.0	37.2
1866	15.4	7.0	1.1	15.3	38.8	1.0	39.8
1867	17.5	7.2	1.1	15.7	41.4	1.0	42.4
1868	12.6	6.6	0.9	15.1	35.2	0.7	35.9
1869	10.9	6.6	0.9	14.1	32.5	0.6	33.1
1870	13.5	6.5	0.9	14.4	35.3	0.6	35.9
1871	14.8	7.1	0.9	15.0	37.9	0.6	38.5

(continued)

Table S12 (continued)

	Agriculture, forestry and fishing (million Euro)	Manufacturing, extractive industries, and utilities (million Euro)	Construction (million Euro)	Service activities (million Euro)	Gross value added (million Euro)	Taxes less subsidies on products (million Euro)	Gross domestic product at market prices (million Euro)
1872	18.4	8.1	1.0	16.1	43.5	0.6	44.1
1873	18.7	9.4	1.0	17.3	46.4	0.7	47.1
1874	17.5	8.4	1.0	18.3	45.3	1.5	46.8
1875	16.5	8.6	1.1	18.6	44.9	1.4	46.3
1876	18.8	8.6	1.2	17.9	46.5	1.6	48.1
1877	21.7	9.9	1.3	18.4	51.3	1.7	53.0
1878	21.5	9.6	1.2	18.4	50.7	1.7	52.4
1879	20.0	10.0	1.1	18.0	49.2	1.8	51.1
1880	20.6	11.6	1.3	18.7	52.2	2.0	54.2
1881	21.2	13.2	1.2	19.3	54.9	1.9	56.8
1882	22.5	14.1	1.3	20.1	58.0	2.1	60.1
1883	22.5	14.5	1.4	20.6	59.1	1.9	61.0
1884	21.9	13.2	1.3	20.4	56.7	1.9	58.6
1885	21.4	13.3	1.2	20.1	56.0	1.9	58.0
1886	22.8	12.9	1.2	20.1	57.0	2.0	59.0
1887	18.7	12.4	1.1	19.9	52.1	2.0	54.1
1888	20.5	13.5	1.1	19.7	54.8	1.8	56.5
1889	17.3	12.2	1.2	19.7	50.3	2.1	52.4
1890	17.1	13.0	1.3	19.6	51.0	2.2	53.1
1891	17.3	13.9	1.2	19.6	52.0	2.2	54.2
1892	17.2	13.2	1.3	19.9	51.6	2.1	53.7
1893	15.5	13.3	1.3	19.8	49.9	2.4	52.3

(continued)

Table S12 (continued)

	Agriculture, forestry and fishing (million Euro)	Manufacturing, extractive industries, and utilities (million Euro)	Construction (million Euro)	Service activities (million Euro)	Gross value added (million Euro)	Taxes less subsidies on products (million Euro)	Gross domestic product at market prices (million Euro)
1894	15.5	12.7	1.3	19.5	48.9	2.2	51.2
1895	16.1	12.7	1.3	19.3	49.5	2.2	51.6
1896	14.4	12.0	1.3	19.5	47.2	2.2	49.4
1897	18.2	12.0	1.3	20.0	51.5	2.1	53.6
1898	18.1	13.8	1.4	22.0	55.3	2.2	57.5
1899	16.9	14.7	1.5	22.6	55.7	2.7	58.4
1900	17.6	16.0	1.8	23.5	58.9	2.7	61.7
1901	20.6	16.4	1.6	23.4	62.0	2.8	64.8
1902	18.8	15.4	1.6	24.3	60.0	2.6	62.6
1903	20.6	16.9	1.7	25.2	64.3	2.7	67.0
1904	21.6	18.2	1.9	26.3	67.9	2.7	70.7
1905	21.0	16.7	1.7	26.0	65.3	2.8	68.1
1906	21.0	17.6	1.6	26.2	66.4	3.1	69.5
1907	22.9	19.1	1.9	25.5	69.4	3.0	72.3
1908	21.0	18.8	1.9	27.3	69.0	2.8	71.8
1909	23.1	18.1	2.0	27.4	70.6	2.8	73.4
1910	18.7	18.3	2.3	27.8	67.1	3.1	70.2
1911	22.7	18.8	2.4	29.0	72.9	2.9	75.8
1912	20.0	21.0	2.6	30.7	74.3	2.8	77.2
1913	23.1	21.5	2.7	32.0	79.3	3.6	82.9
1914	22.0	21.2	2.7	33.6	79.5	3.0	82.5
1915	29.2	22.7	2.6	33.9	88.4	2.4	90.8

(continued)

Appendices 281

Table S12 (continued)

	Agriculture, forestry and fishing (million Euro)	Manufacturing, extractive industries, and utilities (million Euro)	Construction (million Euro)	Service activities (million Euro)	Gross value added (million Euro)	Taxes less subsidies on products (million Euro)	Gross domestic product at market prices (million Euro)
1916	33	29	3	38	102	3	105
1917	33	32	3	44	111	3	114
1918	41	39	3	53	136	2	138
1919	47	38	3	57	146	4	149
1920	55	47	4	65	171	5	177
1921	45	42	5	64	156	7	163
1922	47	41	6	65	159	6	165
1923	41	44	6	67	158	7	165
1924	46	49	6	72	172	9	181
1925	51	50	7	76	183	9	192
1926	44	51	7	77	179	9	188
1927	55	55	7	75	192	9	201
1928	44	56	8	78	186	10	197
1929	53	58	8	82	202	10	212
1930	46	57	9	91	203	9	212
1931	48	51	7	94	200	8	208
1932	53	50	6	90	199	9	208
1933	42	49	7	92	190	9	198
1934	52	51	7	101	210	8	219
1935	50	53	7	107	217	9	226
1936	32	38	6	102	177	6	183
1937	40	37	5	102	186	7	192

(continued)

Table S12 (continued)

	Agriculture, forestry and fishing (million Euro)	Manufacturing, extractive industries, and utilities (million Euro)	Construction (million Euro)	Service activities (million Euro)	Gross value added (million Euro)	Taxes less subsidies on products (million Euro)	Gross domestic product at market prices (million Euro)
1938	44	48	5	114	211	7	218
1939	64	53	4	121	243	9	251
1940	81	64	7	152	304	9	313
1941	83	64	12	170	329	17	346
1942	107	85	13	190	394	22	417
1943	113	84	16	207	419	29	449
1944	152	97	18	219	487	31	518
1945	128	103	17	238	486	28	514
1946	187	140	20	272	619	32	650
1947	196	165	28	327	716	40	756
1948	193	190	38	351	771	44	816
1949	230	175	35	379	821	54	874
1950	294	235	42	454	1025	54	1079
1951	378	351	43	538	1310	63	1373
1952	382	398	46	605	1431	79	1510
1953	387	461	51	646	1545	87	1632
1954	428	527	75	767	1798	90	1888
1955	460	575	100	820	1956	83	2039
1956	547	722	131	1023	2423	100	2523
1957	647	869	135	1173	2825	119	2944
1958	768	1028	155	1340	3291	206	3497
1959	807	1055	152	1419	3433	236	3669

(continued)

Table S12 (continued)

	Agriculture, forestry and fishing (million Euro)	Manufacturing, extractive industries, and utilities (million Euro)	Construction (million Euro)	Service activities (million Euro)	Gross value added (million Euro)	Taxes less subsidies on products (million Euro)	Gross domestic product at market prices (million Euro)
1960	832	1090	139	1477	3539	279	3818
1961	932	1281	151	1718	4082	317	4399
1962	1081	1456	197	2046	4781	362	5143
1963	1266	1703	256	2476	5702	441	6142
1964	1162	2014	305	3028	6509	514	7024
1965	1269	2405	389	3574	7637	623	8260
1966	1422	2713	470	4174	8780	761	9541
1967	1458	2937	568	4882	9845	849	10694
1968	1559	3246	662	5543	11011	900	11910
1969	1650	3765	777	6247	12439	1109	13548
1970	1607	3964	889	7163	13623	1213	14836
1971	1914	4456	1012	8262	15643	1227	16871
1972	2114	5702	1267	9649	18732	1410	20141
1973	2470	7041	1746	11540	22797	1709	24507
1974	2860	8963	2470	14437	28730	1694	30424
1975	3310	10388	3063	17608	34369	1692	36061
1976	3769	12664	3649	21692	41775	1802	43577
1977	4672	15925	4720	28078	53395	2091	55486
1978	5646	19536	5967	35514	66663	1692	68355
1979	5816	22518	7335	42487	78157	2029	80186
1980	6293	27195	8756	49819	92063	2252	94315
1981	6042	29770	9015	56344	101172	4613	105785

(continued)

Table S12 (continued)

	Agriculture, forestry and fishing (million Euro)	Manufacturing, extractive industries, and utilities (million Euro)	Construction (million Euro)	Service activities (million Euro)	Gross value added (million Euro)	Taxes less subsidies on products (million Euro)	Gross domestic product at market prices (million Euro)
1982	7033	33541	10386	65557	116517	6030	122547
1983	7752	38275	11165	75672	132865	7235	140100
1984	9179	43546	11231	86065	150020	8786	158806
1985	9730	50879	13304	97232	171144	4586	175730
1986	10570	55586	14845	108264	189264	12560	201824
1987	11951	59992	17503	121266	210712	16287	226999
1988	13458	64153	21205	136178	234994	18828	253822
1989	14359	69872	26334	153985	264549	22128	286677
1990	15948	73842	31903	175841	297535	23808	321343
1991	16253	78285	35444	197578	327560	26653	354213
1992	15431	80520	35034	221533	352518	30816	383334
1993	16799	80244	34275	237489	368808	28078	396886
1994	17502	84404	35547	254971	392423	31522	423945
1995	17869	90824	39458	276621	424772	34565	459337
1996	21436	96521	40522	291542	450021	37971	487992
1997	22276	102885	42298	307842	475301	42748	518049
1998	23021	107876	46401	328276	505574	48468	554042
1999	22670	113373	52167	350728	538938	55378	594316
2000	24160	121042	59165	381954	586321	59929	646250
2001	25533	128511	66633	416147	636824	62704	699528
2002	25891	134460	73631	448398	682380	66908	749288
2003	27171	140977	79692	479845	727685	75787	803472

(continued)

Table S12 (continued)

	Agriculture, forestry and fishing (million Euro)	Manufacturing, extractive industries, and utilities (million Euro)	Construction (million Euro)	Service activities (million Euro)	Gross value added (million Euro)	Taxes less subsidies on products (million Euro)	Gross domestic product at market prices (million Euro)
2004	26478	147531	85986	516198	776193	85227	861420
2005	25238	157280	96620	555109	834247	96319	930566
2006	23748	167380	105326	603638	900092	107882	1007974
2007	26376	176905	109192	660382	972855	107952	1080807
2008	25561	183870	113190	703051	1025672	90535	1116207
2009	23549	167465	106503	708605	1006122	72912	1079034
2010	25253	169978	87526	707156	989913	91000	1080913
2011	24391	171651	73980	713699	983721	86692	1070413
2012	24019	165568	63521	700918	954026	85732	1039758
2013	25749	163944	53948	692014	935655	89979	1025634
2014	23560	165978	53524	700717	943779	93246	1037025
2015	25004	176102	54554	720135	975795	99844	1075639

Sources Please cite the database as: Leandro Prados de la Escosura (2017), Spanish Economic Growth, 1850–2015

Table S13 Absolute and per capita gross value added and gross domestic product at market prices, 1850–2015 (million Euro and Euro)

	Gross value added (million Euro)	Gross domestic product at market prices (million Euro)	Population (million)	Per capita gross value added (Euro)	Gross domestic product at market prices per person (Euro)
1850	25	26	14.8	1.7	1.7
1851	25	26	14.9	1.7	1.8
1852	25	26	15.0	1.7	1.8
1853	30	31	15.1	2.0	2.1
1854	31	32	15.2	2.1	2.1
1855	34	34	15.2	2.2	2.2
1856	33	34	15.3	2.2	2.2
1857	32	32	15.5	2.0	2.1
1858	31	32	15.5	2.0	2.0
1859	33	34	15.5	2.1	2.2
1860	35	36	15.6	2.2	2.3
1861	36	37	15.8	2.3	2.3
1862	37	38	15.9	2.3	2.4
1863	38	40	16.0	2.4	2.5
1864	38	39	16.1	2.4	2.5
1865	36	37	16.1	2.2	2.3
1866	39	40	16.2	2.4	2.5
1867	41	42	16.3	2.5	2.6
1868	35	36	16.3	2.2	2.2
1869	33	33	16.3	2.0	2.0
1870	35	36	16.3	2.2	2.2
1871	38	39	16.4	2.3	2.4
1872	43	44	16.4	2.6	2.7
1873	46	47	16.5	2.8	2.9
1874	45	47	16.5	2.7	2.8
1875	45	46	16.5	2.7	2.8
1876	46	48	16.6	2.8	2.9
1877	51	53	16.6	3.1	3.2
1878	51	52	16.7	3.0	3.1
1879	49	51	16.8	2.9	3.0
1880	52	54	17.0	3.1	3.2
1881	55	57	17.1	3.2	3.3
1882	58	60	17.2	3.4	3.5
1883	59	61	17.3	3.4	3.5
1884	57	59	17.3	3.3	3.4

(continued)

Table S13 (continued)

	Gross value added (million Euro)	Gross domestic product at market prices (million Euro)	Population (million)	Per capita gross value added (Euro)	Gross domestic product at market prices per person (Euro)
1885	56	58	17.4	3.2	3.3
1886	57	59	17.4	3.3	3.4
1887	52	54	17.5	3.0	3.1
1888	55	57	17.6	3.1	3.2
1889	50	52	17.6	2.9	3.0
1890	51	53	17.6	2.9	3.0
1891	52	54	17.6	3.0	3.1
1892	52	54	17.7	2.9	3.0
1893	50	52	17.7	2.8	3.0
1894	49	51	17.8	2.8	2.9
1895	49	52	17.8	2.8	2.9
1896	47	49	17.9	2.6	2.8
1897	51	54	18.1	2.8	3.0
1898	55	58	18.3	3.0	3.2
1899	56	58	18.4	3.0	3.2
1900	59	62	18.6	3.2	3.3
1901	62	65	18.7	3.3	3.5
1902	60	63	18.9	3.2	3.3
1903	64	67	19.1	3.4	3.5
1904	68	71	19.3	3.5	3.7
1905	65	68	19.4	3.4	3.5
1906	66	70	19.5	3.4	3.6
1907	69	72	19.6	3.5	3.7
1908	69	72	19.7	3.5	3.6
1909	71	73	19.8	3.6	3.7
1910	67	70	19.9	3.4	3.5
1911	73	76	20.0	3.6	3.8
1912	74	77	20.1	3.7	3.8
1913	79	83	20.3	3.9	4.1
1914	79	83	20.5	3.9	4.0
1915	88	91	20.7	4.3	4.4
1916	102	105	21.0	4.9	5.0
1917	111	114	21.2	5.3	5.4
1918	136	138	21.2	6.4	6.5
1919	146	149	21.2	6.9	7.0
1920	171	177	21.4	8.0	8.3

(continued)

Table S13 (continued)

	Gross value added (million Euro)	Gross domestic product at market prices (million Euro)	Population (million)	Per capita gross value added (Euro)	Gross domestic product at market prices per person (Euro)
1921	156	163	21.5	7.2	7.6
1922	159	165	21.8	7.3	7.6
1923	158	165	21.9	7.2	7.5
1924	172	181	22.1	7.8	8.2
1925	183	192	22.3	8.2	8.6
1926	179	188	22.5	7.9	8.3
1927	192	201	22.8	8.4	8.8
1928	186	197	23.0	8.1	8.5
1929	202	212	23.3	8.7	9.1
1930	203	212	23.6	8.6	9.0
1931	200	208	24.0	8.3	8.7
1932	199	208	24.4	8.2	8.5
1933	190	198	24.8	7.7	8.0
1934	210	219	25.2	8.4	8.7
1935	217	226	25.5	8.5	8.8
1936	177	183	25.9	6.8	7.1
1937	186	192	26.0	7.1	7.4
1938	211	218	26.1	8.1	8.3
1939	243	251	25.9	9.4	9.7
1940	304	313	25.7	11.8	12.2
1941	329	346	25.7	12.8	13.5
1942	394	417	25.6	15.4	16.3
1943	419	449	25.8	16.3	17.4
1944	487	518	26.0	18.7	19.9
1945	486	514	26.3	18.5	19.5
1946	619	650	26.6	23.3	24.5
1947	716	756	26.8	26.7	28.2
1948	771	816	27.2	28.3	29.9
1949	821	874	27.7	29.6	31.5
1950	1025	1079	28.0	36.6	38.5
1951	1310	1373	28.2	46.5	48.8
1952	1431	1510	28.3	50.5	53.3
1953	1545	1632	28.6	54.1	57.1
1954	1798	1888	28.8	62.4	65.5
1955	1956	2039	29.0	67.4	70.2
1956	2423	2523	29.3	82.8	86.2

(continued)

Table S13 (continued)

	Gross value added (million Euro)	Gross domestic product at market prices (million Euro)	Population (million)	Per capita gross value added (Euro)	Gross domestic product at market prices per person (Euro)
1957	2825	2944	29.5	95.8	99.8
1958	3291	3497	29.8	110	117
1959	3433	3669	30.1	114	122
1960	3539	3818	30.4	116	125
1961	4082	4399	30.8	133	143
1962	4781	5143	31.1	154	166
1963	5702	6142	31.3	182	196
1964	6509	7024	31.6	206	222
1965	7637	8260	31.9	239	259
1966	8780	9541	32.4	271	295
1967	9845	10694	32.8	300	326
1968	11011	11910	33.2	332	359
1969	12439	13548	33.6	371	404
1970	13623	14836	33.9	402	438
1971	15643	16871	34.2	457	493
1972	18732	20141	34.6	541	582
1973	22797	24507	35.0	652	701
1974	28730	30424	35.4	812	860
1975	34369	36061	35.8	961	1009
1976	41775	43577	36.1	1156	1206
1977	53395	55486	36.5	1463	1520
1978	66663	68355	36.9	1808	1854
1979	78157	80186	37.2	2101	2156
1980	92063	94315	37.5	2455	2516
1981	101172	105785	37.8	2679	2801
1982	116517	122547	38.0	3067	3226
1983	132865	140100	38.2	3482	3671
1984	150020	158806	38.3	3914	4144
1985	171144	175730	38.5	4449	4568
1986	189264	201824	38.6	4907	5232
1987	210712	226999	38.7	5447	5868
1988	234994	253822	38.8	6062	6548
1989	264549	286677	38.8	6815	7385
1990	297535	321343	38.9	7656	8269
1991	327560	354213	38.9	8412	9096
1992	352518	383334	39.1	9005	9792

(continued)

Table S13 (continued)

	Gross value added (million Euro)	Gross domestic product at market prices (million Euro)	Population (million)	Per capita gross value added (Euro)	Gross domestic product at market prices per person (Euro)
1993	368808	396886	39.4	9371	10084
1994	392423	423945	39.5	9923	10720
1995	424772	459337	39.7	10694	11565
1996	450021	487992	39.9	11283	12235
1997	475301	518049	40.0	11868	12935
1998	505574	554042	40.2	12572	13777
1999	538938	594316	40.4	13350	14722
2000	586321	646250	40.6	14458	15935
2001	636824	699528	40.8	15621	17160
2002	682380	749288	41.4	16473	18088
2003	727685	803472	42.2	17245	19041
2004	776193	861420	42.9	18110	20099
2005	834247	930566	43.7	19107	21313
2006	900092	1007974	44.4	20290	22722
2007	972855	1080807	45.2	21506	23893
2008	1025672	1116207	46.0	22305	24274
2009	1006122	1079034	46.4	21699	23271
2010	989913	1080913	46.6	21260	23214
2011	983721	1070413	46.7	21048	22903
2012	954026	1039758	46.8	20400	22233
2013	935655	1025634	46.6	20082	22013
2014	943779	1037025	46.5	20316	22323
2015	975795	1075639	46.4	21027	23178

Sources Please cite the database as: Leandro Prados de la Escosura (2017), Spanish Economic Growth, 1850–2015

Table S14 Volume indices of absolute and per capita gross domestic product at market prices and gross value added, 1850–2015 (2010 = 100)

	Gross value added	Gross domestic product at market prices	Per Capita gross value added	Gross domestic product at market prices per person
	(2010 = 100)	(2010 = 100)	(2010 = 100)	(2010 = 100)
1850	2.0	2.0	6.4	6.3
1851	2.1	2.0	6.5	6.4
1852	2.1	2.1	6.7	6.6
1853	2.2	2.1	6.7	6.6
1854	2.2	2.2	6.8	6.7
1855	2.4	2.3	7.2	7.0
1856	2.3	2.2	6.9	6.6
1857	2.2	2.1	6.6	6.4
1858	2.2	2.2	6.7	6.6
1859	2.3	2.3	7.0	6.9
1860	2.4	2.4	7.2	7.1
1861	2.5	2.4	7.2	7.1
1862	2.5	2.4	7.3	7.1
1863	2.5	2.5	7.4	7.2
1864	2.5	2.5	7.3	7.2
1865	2.4	2.4	7.0	6.9
1866	2.6	2.5	7.4	7.3
1867	2.6	2.5	7.3	7.2
1868	2.3	2.2	6.5	6.3
1869	2.3	2.3	6.7	6.5
1870	2.4	2.3	6.9	6.7
1871	2.6	2.5	7.4	7.2
1872	3.0	2.9	8.6	8.3
1873	3.3	3.2	9.2	9.0
1874	2.9	2.9	8.3	8.2
1875	3.0	3.0	8.5	8.4
1876	3.1	3.1	8.8	8.7
1877	3.5	3.4	9.7	9.6
1878	3.4	3.3	9.3	9.2
1879	3.1	3.1	8.6	8.6
1880	3.4	3.4	9.4	9.3
1881	3.5	3.4	9.5	9.4
1882	3.5	3.5	9.5	9.4
1883	3.6	3.5	9.7	9.5
1884	3.6	3.6	9.7	9.6
1885	3.5	3.4	9.3	9.2

(continued)

Table S14 (continued)

	Gross value added	Gross domestic product at market prices	Per Capita gross value added	Gross domestic product at market prices per person
	(2010 = 100)	(2010 = 100)	(2010 = 100)	(2010 = 100)
1886	3.4	3.4	9.1	9.0
1887	3.3	3.3	8.9	8.8
1888	3.5	3.4	9.3	9.1
1889	3.5	3.4	9.2	9.1
1890	3.4	3.4	9.1	9.1
1891	3.5	3.5	9.3	9.3
1892	3.8	3.8	10.1	10.0
1893	3.7	3.7	9.6	9.6
1894	3.7	3.7	9.7	9.7
1895	3.7	3.7	9.6	9.6
1896	3.3	3.3	8.6	8.6
1897	3.6	3.5	9.2	9.1
1898	3.8	3.8	9.8	9.7
1899	3.8	3.9	9.7	9.7
1900	3.9	3.9	9.9	9.9
1901	4.3	4.3	10.7	10.7
1902	4.1	4.1	10.1	10.1
1903	4.1	4.1	10.1	10.0
1904	4.1	4.1	9.9	9.8
1905	4.0	4.0	9.7	9.7
1906	4.3	4.3	10.2	10.2
1907	4.4	4.4	10.5	10.4
1908	4.6	4.6	10.8	10.8
1909	4.7	4.7	11.1	11.0
1910	4.5	4.5	10.4	10.4
1911	4.8	4.8	11.2	11.2
1912	4.7	4.7	10.8	10.8
1913	4.9	4.9	11.3	11.3
1914	4.8	4.8	11.0	10.9
1915	5.0	4.9	11.2	11.0
1916	5.2	5.1	11.6	11.4
1917	5.2	5.1	11.4	11.1
1918	5.1	5.0	11.3	11.0
1919	5.2	5.1	11.4	11.2
1920	5.6	5.5	12.2	12.0
1921	5.7	5.7	12.3	12.3
1922	6.0	5.9	12.7	12.7

(continued)

Table S14 (continued)

	Gross value added (2010 = 100)	Gross domestic product at market prices (2010 = 100)	Per Capita gross value added (2010 = 100)	Gross domestic product at market prices per person (2010 = 100)
1923	6.0	6.0	12.7	12.7
1924	6.1	6.2	12.9	13.0
1925	6.6	6.6	13.7	13.8
1926	6.5	6.5	13.4	13.5
1927	7.1	7.2	14.6	14.6
1928	7.1	7.1	14.3	14.4
1929	7.7	7.7	15.4	15.4
1930	7.4	7.3	14.5	14.5
1931	7.2	7.2	14.1	14.0
1932	7.5	7.5	14.2	14.2
1933	7.3	7.3	13.6	13.6
1934	7.6	7.6	14.1	14.0
1935	7.7	7.7	14.1	14.1
1936	6.0	5.9	10.7	10.6
1937	5.5	5.5	9.9	9.8
1938	5.5	5.5	9.8	9.7
1939	6.0	5.9	10.8	10.7
1940	6.6	6.5	11.9	11.7
1941	6.5	6.5	11.7	11.8
1942	6.8	6.9	12.4	12.5
1943	7.1	7.3	12.8	13.1
1944	7.5	7.6	13.4	13.6
1945	6.9	7.0	12.3	12.4
1946	7.3	7.3	12.8	12.8
1947	7.4	7.5	12.9	13.0
1948	7.4	7.5	12.7	12.8
1949	7.4	7.5	12.5	12.7
1950	7.6	7.7	12.7	12.8
1951	8.5	8.5	14.0	14.0
1952	9.1	9.2	15.0	15.2
1953	9.1	9.2	14.9	15.0
1954	9.9	9.9	15.9	16.0
1955	10.3	10.2	16.5	16.4
1956	11.1	11.1	17.7	17.6
1957	11.5	11.5	18.2	18.1
1958	12.0	12.2	18.8	19.1
1959	11.7	12.1	18.0	18.8

(continued)

Table S14 (continued)

	Gross value added (2010 = 100)	Gross domestic product at market prices (2010 = 100)	Per Capita gross value added (2010 = 100)	Gross domestic product at market prices per person (2010 = 100)
1960	11.8	12.2	18.0	18.6
1961	13.2	13.6	20.0	20.6
1962	14.7	15.0	22.0	22.5
1963	16.1	16.5	23.9	24.5
1964	17.8	17.4	26.2	25.6
1965	19.0	18.8	27.7	27.4
1966	20.5	20.2	29.5	29.1
1967	22.0	21.4	31.2	30.3
1968	23.3	22.7	32.7	31.8
1969	25.5	24.8	35.3	34.4
1970	26.7	25.6	36.7	35.1
1971	28.2	26.8	38.4	36.5
1972	31.0	29.6	41.7	39.9
1973	34.0	32.3	45.2	43.0
1974	36.6	34.7	48.2	45.7
1975	38.0	35.8	49.6	46.6
1976	39.7	37.4	51.2	48.2
1977	41.5	38.6	52.9	49.3
1978	42.9	39.7	54.2	50.1
1979	43.7	40.4	54.8	50.5
1980	44.8	41.6	55.6	51.7
1981	43.7	41.6	53.9	51.3
1982	44.5	42.3	54.5	51.9
1983	45.4	43.1	55.4	52.6
1984	45.9	43.5	55.8	52.8
1985	47.1	44.8	57.0	54.2
1986	48.9	46.6	59.0	56.3
1987	51.6	49.9	62.1	60.1
1988	54.5	53.1	65.5	63.8
1989	57.6	56.5	69.1	67.8
1990	60.3	59.2	72.3	71.0
1991	62.0	61.1	74.1	73.1
1992	62.5	62.1	74.3	73.9
1993	62.2	61.1	73.6	72.3
1994	64.0	62.8	75.3	73.9
1995	66.2	65.1	77.6	76.4
1996	67.6	66.9	78.9	78.1

(continued)

Table S14 (continued)

	Gross value added	Gross domestic product at market prices	Per Capita gross value added	Gross domestic product at market prices per person
	(2010 = 100)	(2010 = 100)	(2010 = 100)	(2010 = 100)
1997	69.8	69.4	81.2	80.7
1998	72.6	72.6	84.1	84.1
1999	75.8	76.1	87.4	87.8
2000	79.9	80.1	91.7	92.0
2001	83.2	83.3	95.0	95.2
2002	85.6	85.8	96.2	96.4
2003	88.0	88.6	97.1	97.7
2004	90.6	91.4	98.4	99.3
2005	93.8	94.8	100.1	101.1
2006	97.9	98.7	102.8	103.6
2007	102.0	102.5	105.0	105.5
2008	103.4	103.7	104.7	105.0
2009	100.0	100.0	100.4	100.4
2010	100.0	100.0	100.0	100.0
2011	99.4	99.0	99.0	98.6
2012	96.6	95.9	96.1	95.5
2013	95.1	94.2	95.0	94.2
2014	96.2	95.6	96.5	95.9
2015	98.9	98.8	99.3	99.1

Sources Please cite the database as: Leandro Prados de la Escosura (2017), Spanish Economic Growth, 1850–2015

Table S15 Shares of output components in gross value added, 1850–2015 (percentage)

	Agriculture, forestry and fishing (%)	Manufacturing, extractive industries, and utilities (%)	Construction (%)	Service activities (%)
1850	37.4	13.6	3.6	45.4
1851	37.0	14.6	3.7	44.8
1852	35.3	15.5	4.0	45.2
1853	44.5	12.5	3.3	39.8
1854	43.4	13.0	3.0	40.5
1855	48.5	12.7	2.4	36.4
1856	41.7	15.6	2.9	39.8
1857	38.8	16.2	3.5	41.5
1858	38.1	17.1	3.8	41.1
1859	39.3	16.6	4.2	39.8
1860	39.5	15.5	5.0	40.1
1861	39.6	16.4	4.3	39.7
1862	39.1	17.1	4.3	39.5
1863	39.2	17.9	4.0	38.9
1864	37.6	18.5	3.7	40.3
1865	38.3	18.4	3.2	40.1
1866	39.6	18.0	2.8	39.5
1867	42.2	17.5	2.6	37.8
1868	35.7	18.8	2.6	42.9
1869	33.6	20.2	2.7	43.5
1870	38.3	18.4	2.5	40.8
1871	39.0	18.9	2.4	39.7
1872	42.3	18.5	2.3	36.9
1873	40.3	20.3	2.1	37.2
1874	38.6	18.6	2.3	40.5
1875	36.8	19.2	2.5	41.4
1876	40.3	18.5	2.6	38.6
1877	42.4	19.3	2.5	35.8
1878	42.4	19.0	2.3	36.3
1879	40.7	20.4	2.3	36.7
1880	39.4	22.3	2.4	35.9
1881	38.5	24.1	2.3	35.1
1882	38.7	24.3	2.3	34.7
1883	38.1	24.6	2.4	34.9
1884	38.6	23.2	2.4	35.9
1885	38.3	23.7	2.2	35.9
1886	40.0	22.6	2.1	35.3
1887	35.8	23.8	2.2	38.1

(continued)

Table S15 (continued)

	Agriculture, forestry and fishing (%)	Manufacturing, extractive industries, and utilities (%)	Construction (%)	Service activities (%)
1888	37.4	24.6	2.0	35.9
1889	34.3	24.2	2.3	39.2
1890	33.6	25.5	2.5	38.4
1891	33.3	26.7	2.3	37.7
1892	33.4	25.6	2.5	38.5
1893	31.1	26.6	2.6	39.7
1894	31.6	25.9	2.7	39.9
1895	32.6	25.7	2.6	39.1
1896	30.5	25.5	2.8	41.2
1897	35.3	23.3	2.6	38.9
1898	32.8	24.9	2.6	39.8
1899	30.4	26.4	2.7	40.5
1900	29.9	27.2	3.1	39.8
1901	33.2	26.4	2.6	37.8
1902	31.3	25.7	2.6	40.4
1903	32.0	26.2	2.7	39.1
1904	31.7	26.8	2.7	38.8
1905	32.1	25.6	2.6	39.7
1906	31.6	26.4	2.5	39.5
1907	33.0	27.5	2.7	36.8
1908	30.4	27.3	2.8	39.5
1909	32.7	25.6	2.9	38.9
1910	27.8	27.3	3.4	41.4
1911	31.1	25.8	3.3	39.8
1912	26.9	28.3	3.5	41.3
1913	29.1	27.1	3.4	40.4
1914	27.7	26.7	3.4	42.3
1915	33.0	25.7	3.0	38.4
1916	32.0	28.2	2.5	37.3
1917	29.5	28.7	2.2	39.6
1918	30.3	28.4	2.0	39.3
1919	32.1	26.2	2.3	39.4
1920	31.9	27.7	2.5	37.9
1921	28.9	26.8	3.2	41.1
1922	29.4	25.8	3.6	41.1
1923	25.9	27.9	3.7	42.5
1924	26.5	28.4	3.4	41.7
1925	27.5	27.2	3.6	41.7
1926	24.5	28.7	3.9	42.9

(continued)

Table S15 (continued)

	Agriculture, forestry and fishing (%)	Manufacturing, extractive industries, and utilities (%)	Construction (%)	Service activities (%)
1927	28.6	28.6	3.7	39.1
1928	23.7	30.1	4.1	42.2
1929	26.4	28.7	4.1	40.8
1930	22.8	27.9	4.3	45.0
1931	24.2	25.6	3.4	46.8
1932	26.6	25.2	2.9	45.3
1933	22.3	25.8	3.6	48.2
1934	24.6	24.2	3.1	48.2
1935	23.0	24.3	3.2	49.5
1936	17.8	21.5	3.4	57.3
1937	21.7	20.2	2.9	55.2
1938	21.1	22.6	2.4	53.9
1939	26.2	21.9	1.8	50.0
1940	26.8	21.0	2.2	49.9
1941	25.4	19.3	3.6	51.7
1942	27.0	21.5	3.4	48.1
1943	26.9	19.9	3.8	49.3
1944	31.3	20.0	3.7	45.1
1945	26.4	21.2	3.5	48.9
1946	30.2	22.6	3.2	44.0
1947	27.4	23.0	4.0	45.6
1948	25.0	24.6	4.9	45.5
1949	28.1	21.4	4.3	46.2
1950	28.7	23.0	4.1	44.3
1951	28.9	26.8	3.2	41.1
1952	26.7	27.8	3.3	42.3
1953	25.0	29.9	3.3	41.8
1954	23.8	29.3	4.2	42.6
1955	23.5	29.4	5.1	41.9
1956	22.6	29.8	5.4	42.2
1957	22.9	30.8	4.8	41.5
1958	23.3	31.2	4.7	40.7
1959	23.5	30.7	4.4	41.3
1960	23.5	30.8	3.9	41.7
1961	22.8	31.4	3.7	42.1
1962	22.6	30.4	4.1	42.8
1963	22.2	29.9	4.5	43.4
1964	17.9	30.9	4.7	46.5
1965	16.6	31.5	5.1	46.8

(continued)

Table S15 (continued)

	Agriculture, forestry and fishing (%)	Manufacturing, extractive industries, and utilities (%)	Construction (%)	Service activities (%)
1966	16.2	30.9	5.4	47.5
1967	14.8	29.8	5.8	49.6
1968	14.2	29.5	6.0	50.3
1969	13.3	30.3	6.2	50.2
1970	11.8	29.1	6.5	52.6
1971	12.2	28.5	6.5	52.8
1972	11.3	30.4	6.8	51.5
1973	10.8	30.9	7.7	50.6
1974	10.0	31.2	8.6	50.3
1975	9.6	30.2	8.9	51.2
1976	9.0	30.3	8.7	51.9
1977	8.8	29.8	8.8	52.6
1978	8.5	29.3	9.0	53.3
1979	7.4	28.8	9.4	54.4
1980	6.8	29.5	9.5	54.1
1981	6.0	29.4	8.9	55.7
1982	6.0	28.8	8.9	56.3
1983	5.8	28.8	8.4	57.0
1984	6.1	29.0	7.5	57.4
1985	5.7	29.7	7.8	56.8
1986	5.6	29.4	7.8	57.2
1987	5.7	28.5	8.3	57.6
1988	5.7	27.3	9.0	57.9
1989	5.4	26.4	10.0	58.2
1990	5.4	24.8	10.7	59.1
1991	5.0	23.9	10.8	60.3
1992	4.4	22.8	9.9	62.8
1993	4.6	21.8	9.3	64.4
1994	4.5	21.5	9.1	65.0
1995	4.2	21.4	9.3	65.1
1996	4.8	21.4	9.0	64.8
1997	4.7	21.6	8.9	64.8
1998	4.6	21.3	9.2	64.9
1999	4.2	21.0	9.7	65.1
2000	4.1	20.6	10.1	65.1
2001	4.0	20.2	10.5	65.3
2002	3.8	19.7	10.8	65.7
2003	3.7	19.4	11.0	65.9
2004	3.4	19.0	11.1	66.5

(continued)

Table S15 (continued)

	Agriculture, forestry and fishing (%)	Manufacturing, extractive industries, and utilities (%)	Construction (%)	Service activities (%)
2005	3.0	18.9	11.6	66.5
2006	2.6	18.6	11.7	67.1
2007	2.7	18.2	11.2	67.9
2008	2.5	17.9	11.0	68.5
2009	2.3	16.6	10.6	70.4
2010	2.6	17.2	8.8	71.4
2011	2.5	17.4	7.5	72.6
2012	2.5	17.4	6.7	73.5
2013	2.8	17.5	5.8	74.0
2014	2.5	17.6	5.7	74.2
2015	2.6	18.0	5.6	73.8

Sources Please cite the database as: Leandro Prados de la Escosura (2017), Spanish Economic Growth, 1850–2015

Table S16 Volume indices of gross value added and its output components, 1850–2015 (2010 = 100)

	Agriculture, forestry and fishing	Manufacturing, extractive industries, and utilities	Construction	Service activities	Gross value added
	(2010 = 100)	(2010 = 100)	(2010 = 100)	(2010 = 100)	(2010 = 100)
1850	13.4	0.7	1.2	1.5	2.0
1851	13.7	0.7	1.2	1.5	2.1
1852	14.0	0.8	1.4	1.5	2.1
1853	14.5	0.7	1.4	1.6	2.2
1854	15.0	0.7	1.3	1.6	2.2
1855	16.4	0.8	1.3	1.6	2.4
1856	14.7	0.9	1.4	1.6	2.3
1857	13.3	0.9	1.7	1.6	2.2
1858	13.5	1.0	2.0	1.6	2.2
1859	14.3	1.0	2.1	1.7	2.3
1860	15.0	1.0	2.6	1.7	2.4
1861	15.0	1.1	2.4	1.7	2.5
1862	15.3	1.0	2.5	1.7	2.5
1863	15.6	1.1	2.4	1.8	2.5
1864	15.7	1.1	2.2	1.8	2.5
1865	14.7	1.1	1.9	1.8	2.4
1866	16.7	1.1	1.8	1.8	2.6
1867	16.2	1.1	1.8	1.8	2.6
1868	13.1	1.1	1.6	1.7	2.3
1869	13.9	1.1	1.5	1.7	2.3
1870	14.5	1.1	1.5	1.8	2.4
1871	15.7	1.3	1.6	1.9	2.6
1872	19.5	1.4	1.7	2.0	3.0
1873	20.8	1.6	1.7	2.2	3.3
1874	17.4	1.5	1.6	2.2	2.9
1875	18.1	1.5	1.8	2.2	3.0
1876	19.2	1.6	1.9	2.2	3.1
1877	22.2	1.7	2.2	2.2	3.5
1878	20.6	1.7	2.1	2.3	3.4
1879	18.0	1.8	2.1	2.2	3.1
1880	20.2	2.0	2.3	2.3	3.4
1881	19.7	2.2	2.4	2.3	3.5
1882	19.5	2.3	2.6	2.4	3.5
1883	19.7	2.4	2.7	2.4	3.6
1884	20.2	2.3	2.7	2.5	3.6

(continued)

Appendices

Table S16 (continued)

	Agriculture, forestry and fishing	Manufacturing, extractive industries, and utilities	Construction	Service activities	Gross value added
	(2010 = 100)	(2010 = 100)	(2010 = 100)	(2010 = 100)	(2010 = 100)
1885	18.7	2.3	2.5	2.5	3.5
1886	18.4	2.1	2.5	2.5	3.4
1887	17.4	2.2	2.5	2.5	3.3
1888	19.0	2.2	2.5	2.5	3.5
1889	18.1	2.3	2.6	2.5	3.5
1890	17.5	2.4	2.7	2.5	3.4
1891	17.7	2.5	2.6	2.6	3.5
1892	20.5	2.7	2.8	2.6	3.8
1893	18.4	2.7	2.7	2.6	3.7
1894	19.3	2.6	2.7	2.6	3.7
1895	18.8	2.6	2.8	2.7	3.7
1896	15.2	2.5	2.8	2.6	3.3
1897	18.4	2.4	2.8	2.6	3.6
1898	19.7	2.6	2.7	2.8	3.8
1899	18.7	2.8	2.9	2.9	3.8
1900	19.3	2.9	3.2	2.9	3.9
1901	22.9	3.0	3.2	2.9	4.3
1902	20.9	2.8	3.1	3.1	4.1
1903	20.6	2.9	3.2	3.1	4.1
1904	19.9	3.0	3.2	3.1	4.1
1905	19.9	2.8	3.1	3.1	4.0
1906	22.2	2.9	3.0	3.1	4.3
1907	22.4	3.1	3.2	3.2	4.4
1908	23.1	3.3	3.4	3.3	4.6
1909	25.2	3.1	3.6	3.4	4.7
1910	21.3	3.1	4.0	3.4	4.5
1911	24.7	3.2	4.1	3.6	4.8
1912	20.7	3.6	4.6	3.7	4.7
1913	23.4	3.6	4.6	3.8	4.9
1914	22.0	3.6	4.6	3.8	4.8
1915	24.3	3.5	4.1	3.8	5.0
1916	25.7	3.8	3.6	3.9	5.2
1917	25.7	3.7	3.1	3.9	5.2
1918	25.8	3.7	2.7	3.9	5.1
1919	26.0	3.5	3.2	4.1	5.2
1920	27.4	3.8	3.8	4.4	5.6

(continued)

Table S16 (continued)

	Agriculture, forestry and fishing	Manufacturing, extractive industries, and utilities	Construction	Service activities	Gross value added
	(2010 = 100)	(2010 = 100)	(2010 = 100)	(2010 = 100)	(2010 = 100)
1921	26.8	3.8	4.0	4.7	5.7
1922	27.6	4.1	4.6	4.9	6.0
1923	25.9	4.4	4.7	5.1	6.0
1924	25.9	4.6	4.7	5.3	6.1
1925	28.6	4.9	5.3	5.5	6.6
1926	26.0	5.1	5.7	5.6	6.5
1927	30.2	5.6	5.8	5.9	7.1
1928	26.0	5.9	6.3	6.3	7.1
1929	31.4	6.0	6.8	6.5	7.7
1930	27.1	6.0	7.1	6.6	7.4
1931	29.0	5.4	5.2	6.6	7.2
1932	32.2	5.3	4.4	6.7	7.5
1933	28.8	5.3	5.2	6.8	7.3
1934	32.2	5.3	4.8	6.9	7.6
1935	31.9	5.5	5.0	7.2	7.7
1936	21.3	3.9	4.1	6.4	6.0
1937	22.7	3.5	3.4	5.5	5.5
1938	21.4	3.7	2.9	5.6	5.5
1939	24.7	4.1	2.4	5.9	6.0
1940	25.4	4.5	3.4	6.6	6.6
1941	24.0	4.3	4.9	6.6	6.5
1942	25.1	4.9	5.1	6.8	6.8
1943	26.3	4.9	5.9	7.1	7.1
1944	28.5	5.2	6.3	7.2	7.5
1945	23.2	5.0	5.7	7.3	6.9
1946	26.4	5.5	5.6	7.1	7.3
1947	26.6	5.6	6.1	7.2	7.4
1948	25.2	5.7	7.3	7.4	7.4
1949	25.6	5.4	7.1	7.5	7.4
1950	25.2	6.0	7.0	7.6	7.6
1951	32.1	6.4	6.2	8.0	8.5
1952	32.6	7.5	6.5	8.6	9.1
1953	30.2	7.6	6.7	8.9	9.1
1954	33.8	8.2	7.5	9.4	9.9
1955	32.9	8.8	9.9	9.8	10.3
1956	34.9	9.8	9.8	10.6	11.1

(continued)

Table S16 (continued)

	Agriculture, forestry and fishing	Manufacturing, extractive industries, and utilities	Construction	Service activities	Gross value added
	(2010 = 100)	(2010 = 100)	(2010 = 100)	(2010 = 100)	(2010 = 100)
1957	34.8	10.7	9.1	11.0	11.5
1958	33.7	11.7	10.4	11.5	12.0
1959	34.1	11.3	9.9	11.2	11.7
1960	34.8	11.2	9.7	11.3	11.8
1961	38.1	12.3	11.0	12.9	13.2
1962	41.7	12.9	13.3	14.3	14.7
1963	46.2	13.8	15.6	15.6	16.1
1964	41.6	14.9	17.7	17.6	17.8
1965	39.3	17.1	21.0	18.5	19.0
1966	41.5	19.1	24.4	19.6	20.5
1967	43.1	20.9	28.7	20.6	22.0
1968	43.1	22.7	31.1	21.8	23.3
1969	43.8	26.1	33.5	23.7	25.5
1970	43.4	27.0	35.7	24.9	26.7
1971	48.0	29.3	37.2	26.2	28.2
1972	48.1	36.2	41.5	27.9	31.0
1973	49.8	40.9	49.3	29.8	34.0
1974	53.4	45.8	55.3	31.5	36.6
1975	53.3	48.3	57.0	32.7	38.0
1976	55.6	52.1	57.6	34.0	39.7
1977	53.2	55.8	59.4	35.4	41.5
1978	56.7	59.3	59.5	36.5	42.9
1979	54.4	61.5	60.4	37.0	43.7
1980	59.2	64.7	61.5	37.4	44.8
1981	53.6	59.4	58.3	37.7	43.7
1982	52.7	58.4	60.2	38.9	44.5
1983	56.0	59.9	60.7	39.6	45.4
1984	60.7	59.6	57.3	40.7	45.9
1985	62.6	61.5	58.9	41.6	47.1
1986	56.9	64.4	62.7	43.1	48.9
1987	66.2	66.9	67.8	45.4	51.6
1988	71.2	69.4	74.4	47.8	54.5
1989	69.4	71.4	84.3	50.6	57.6
1990	74.5	72.3	92.6	52.9	60.3
1991	77.4	72.7	95.1	54.7	62.0
1992	79.6	72.1	89.7	56.2	62.5

(continued)

Table S16 (continued)

	Agriculture, forestry and fishing	Manufacturing, extractive industries, and utilities	Construction	Service activities	Gross value added
	(2010 = 100)	(2010 = 100)	(2010 = 100)	(2010 = 100)	(2010 = 100)
1993	82.7	69.6	84.5	56.9	62.2
1994	78.0	71.5	85.8	58.9	64.0
1995	73.3	73.8	91.1	61.0	66.2
1996	88.7	75.9	90.4	62.0	67.6
1997	94.7	79.9	91.7	63.8	69.8
1998	97.7	83.8	96.1	66.1	72.6
1999	97.0	87.9	101.9	68.9	75.8
2000	104.1	92.1	107.0	72.7	79.9
2001	102.5	95.7	113.8	75.7	83.2
2002	103.4	97.0	117.5	78.3	85.6
2003	102.6	99.6	119.2	80.8	88.0
2004	100.0	101.0	119.8	84.1	90.6
2005	92.0	103.1	123.3	88.0	93.8
2006	97.5	106.2	125.7	92.5	97.9
2007	104.4	108.1	126.3	97.5	102.0
2008	101.6	107.2	126.6	99.7	103.4
2009	97.9	96.5	117.0	98.7	100.0
2010	100.0	100.0	100.0	100.0	100.0
2011	104.4	99.8	87.2	100.7	99.4
2012	94.3	94.9	79.5	99.2	96.6
2013	107.1	91.2	71.1	98.6	95.1
2014	105.4	92.9	70.3	99.9	96.2
2015	102.4	97.9	70.4	102.6	98.9

Sources Please cite the database as: Leandro Prados de la Escosura (2017), Spanish Economic Growth, 1850–2015

Appendices

Table S17 Deflators of gross value added and its output components, 1850–2015 (2010 = 100)

	Agriculture, forestry and fishing	Manufacturing, extractive industries, and utilities	Construction	Service activities	Gross value added
	(2010 = 100)	(2010 = 100)	(2010 = 100)	(2010 = 100)	(2010 = 100)
1850	0.3	0.3	0.1	0.1	0.1
1851	0.3	0.3	0.1	0.1	0.1
1852	0.3	0.3	0.1	0.1	0.1
1853	0.4	0.3	0.1	0.1	0.1
1854	0.4	0.3	0.1	0.1	0.1
1855	0.4	0.3	0.1	0.1	0.1
1856	0.4	0.3	0.1	0.1	0.1
1857	0.4	0.3	0.1	0.1	0.1
1858	0.3	0.3	0.1	0.1	0.1
1859	0.4	0.3	0.1	0.1	0.1
1860	0.4	0.3	0.1	0.1	0.1
1861	0.4	0.3	0.1	0.1	0.1
1862	0.4	0.4	0.1	0.1	0.1
1863	0.4	0.4	0.1	0.1	0.2
1864	0.4	0.4	0.1	0.1	0.2
1865	0.4	0.4	0.1	0.1	0.2
1866	0.4	0.4	0.1	0.1	0.2
1867	0.4	0.4	0.1	0.1	0.2
1868	0.4	0.4	0.1	0.1	0.2
1869	0.3	0.3	0.1	0.1	0.1
1870	0.4	0.3	0.1	0.1	0.1
1871	0.4	0.3	0.1	0.1	0.1
1872	0.4	0.3	0.1	0.1	0.1
1873	0.4	0.3	0.1	0.1	0.1
1874	0.4	0.3	0.1	0.1	0.2
1875	0.4	0.3	0.1	0.1	0.1
1876	0.4	0.3	0.1	0.1	0.2
1877	0.4	0.3	0.1	0.1	0.1
1878	0.4	0.3	0.1	0.1	0.2
1879	0.4	0.3	0.1	0.1	0.2
1880	0.4	0.3	0.1	0.1	0.2
1881	0.4	0.4	0.1	0.1	0.2
1882	0.5	0.4	0.1	0.1	0.2
1883	0.5	0.4	0.1	0.1	0.2
1884	0.4	0.3	0.1	0.1	0.2

(continued)

Table S17 (continued)

	Agriculture, forestry and fishing	Manufacturing, extractive industries, and utilities	Construction	Service activities	Gross value added
	(2010 = 100)	(2010 = 100)	(2010 = 100)	(2010 = 100)	(2010 = 100)
1885	0.5	0.3	0.1	0.1	0.2
1886	0.5	0.4	0.1	0.1	0.2
1887	0.4	0.3	0.1	0.1	0.2
1888	0.4	0.4	0.1	0.1	0.2
1889	0.4	0.3	0.1	0.1	0.1
1890	0.4	0.3	0.1	0.1	0.1
1891	0.4	0.3	0.1	0.1	0.1
1892	0.3	0.3	0.1	0.1	0.1
1893	0.3	0.3	0.1	0.1	0.1
1894	0.3	0.3	0.1	0.1	0.1
1895	0.3	0.3	0.1	0.1	0.1
1896	0.4	0.3	0.1	0.1	0.1
1897	0.4	0.3	0.1	0.1	0.1
1898	0.4	0.3	0.1	0.1	0.1
1899	0.4	0.3	0.1	0.1	0.1
1900	0.4	0.3	0.1	0.1	0.2
1901	0.4	0.3	0.1	0.1	0.1
1902	0.4	0.3	0.1	0.1	0.1
1903	0.4	0.3	0.1	0.1	0.2
1904	0.4	0.4	0.1	0.1	0.2
1905	0.4	0.3	0.1	0.1	0.2
1906	0.4	0.4	0.1	0.1	0.2
1907	0.4	0.4	0.1	0.1	0.2
1908	0.4	0.3	0.1	0.1	0.2
1909	0.4	0.3	0.1	0.1	0.2
1910	0.3	0.3	0.1	0.1	0.2
1911	0.4	0.3	0.1	0.1	0.2
1912	0.4	0.3	0.1	0.1	0.2
1913	0.4	0.4	0.1	0.1	0.2
1914	0.4	0.3	0.1	0.1	0.2
1915	0.5	0.4	0.1	0.1	0.2
1916	0.5	0.4	0.1	0.1	0.2
1917	0.5	0.5	0.1	0.2	0.2
1918	0.6	0.6	0.1	0.2	0.3
1919	0.7	0.6	0.1	0.2	0.3
1920	0.8	0.7	0.1	0.2	0.3

(continued)

Table S17 (continued)

	Agriculture, forestry and fishing	Manufacturing, extractive industries, and utilities	Construction	Service activities	Gross value added
	(2010 = 100)	(2010 = 100)	(2010 = 100)	(2010 = 100)	(2010 = 100)
1921	0.7	0.6	0.1	0.2	0.3
1922	0.7	0.6	0.1	0.2	0.3
1923	0.6	0.6	0.1	0.2	0.3
1924	0.7	0.6	0.1	0.2	0.3
1925	0.7	0.6	0.1	0.2	0.3
1926	0.7	0.6	0.1	0.2	0.3
1927	0.7	0.6	0.1	0.2	0.3
1928	0.7	0.6	0.1	0.2	0.3
1929	0.7	0.6	0.1	0.2	0.3
1930	0.7	0.6	0.1	0.2	0.3
1931	0.7	0.6	0.1	0.2	0.3
1932	0.7	0.6	0.2	0.2	0.3
1933	0.6	0.5	0.2	0.2	0.3
1934	0.6	0.6	0.2	0.2	0.3
1935	0.6	0.6	0.2	0.2	0.3
1936	0.6	0.6	0.2	0.2	0.3
1937	0.7	0.6	0.2	0.3	0.3
1938	0.8	0.8	0.2	0.3	0.4
1939	1.0	0.8	0.2	0.3	0.4
1940	1.3	0.8	0.2	0.3	0.5
1941	1.4	0.9	0.3	0.4	0.5
1942	1.7	1.0	0.3	0.4	0.6
1943	1.7	1.0	0.3	0.4	0.6
1944	2.1	1.1	0.3	0.4	0.7
1945	2.2	1.2	0.3	0.5	0.7
1946	2.8	1.5	0.4	0.5	0.9
1947	2.9	1.7	0.5	0.6	1.0
1948	3.0	2.0	0.6	0.7	1.0
1949	3.6	1.9	0.6	0.7	1.1
1950	4.6	2.3	0.7	0.8	1.4
1951	4.7	3.2	0.8	1.0	1.6
1952	4.6	3.1	0.8	1.0	1.6
1953	5.1	3.6	0.9	1.0	1.7
1954	5.0	3.8	1.1	1.2	1.8
1955	5.5	3.8	1.2	1.2	1.9
1956	6.2	4.3	1.5	1.4	2.2

(continued)

Table S17 (continued)

	Agriculture, forestry and fishing	Manufacturing, extractive industries, and utilities	Construction	Service activities	Gross value added
	(2010 = 100)	(2010 = 100)	(2010 = 100)	(2010 = 100)	(2010 = 100)
1957	7.4	4.8	1.7	1.5	2.5
1958	9.0	5.2	1.7	1.6	2.8
1959	9.4	5.5	1.8	1.8	3.0
1960	9.5	5.7	1.6	1.8	3.0
1961	9.7	6.2	1.6	1.9	3.1
1962	10.3	6.6	1.7	2.0	3.3
1963	10.8	7.3	1.9	2.2	3.6
1964	11.1	7.9	2.0	2.4	3.7
1965	12.8	8.3	2.1	2.7	4.1
1966	13.6	8.3	2.2	3.0	4.3
1967	13.4	8.3	2.3	3.3	4.5
1968	14.3	8.4	2.4	3.6	4.8
1969	14.9	8.5	2.7	3.7	4.9
1970	14.7	8.6	2.8	4.1	5.2
1971	15.8	8.9	3.1	4.5	5.6
1972	17.4	9.3	3.5	4.9	6.1
1973	19.6	10.1	4.0	5.5	6.8
1974	21.2	11.5	5.1	6.5	7.9
1975	24.6	12.7	6.1	7.6	9.1
1976	26.8	14.3	7.2	9.0	10.6
1977	34.8	16.8	9.1	11.2	13.0
1978	39.4	19.4	11.4	13.8	15.7
1979	42.4	21.5	13.9	16.2	18.1
1980	42.1	24.7	16.3	18.8	20.8
1981	44.7	29.5	17.7	21.1	23.4
1982	52.8	33.8	19.7	23.8	26.5
1983	54.9	37.6	21.0	27.0	29.6
1984	59.8	43.0	22.4	29.9	33.0
1985	61.6	48.7	25.8	33.0	36.7
1986	73.6	50.8	27.0	35.5	39.1
1987	71.5	52.7	29.5	37.8	41.2
1988	74.8	54.4	32.5	40.2	43.6
1989	82.0	57.6	35.7	43.0	46.4
1990	84.8	60.1	39.4	47.0	49.8
1991	83.1	63.3	42.6	51.1	53.4
1992	76.8	65.7	44.6	55.7	57.0

(continued)

Table S17 (continued)

	Agriculture, forestry and fishing	Manufacturing, extractive industries, and utilities	Construction	Service activities	Gross value added
	(2010 = 100)	(2010 = 100)	(2010 = 100)	(2010 = 100)	(2010 = 100)
1993	80.4	67.8	46.4	59.0	59.9
1994	88.8	69.4	47.4	61.2	62.0
1995	96.5	72.4	49.5	64.2	64.9
1996	95.7	74.8	51.2	66.4	67.2
1997	93.2	75.8	52.7	68.2	68.8
1998	93.3	75.7	55.2	70.2	70.3
1999	92.6	75.9	58.5	72.0	71.9
2000	91.9	77.3	63.2	74.3	74.2
2001	98.6	79.0	66.9	77.7	77.3
2002	99.1	81.5	71.6	81.0	80.5
2003	104.8	83.3	76.4	83.9	83.5
2004	104.8	86.0	82.0	86.8	86.6
2005	108.6	89.7	89.5	89.2	89.8
2006	96.5	92.7	95.7	92.3	92.9
2007	100.0	96.3	98.8	95.8	96.3
2008	99.6	100.9	102.2	99.7	100.2
2009	95.2	102.1	104.0	101.5	101.7
2010	100.0	100.0	100.0	100.0	100.0
2011	92.5	101.2	96.9	100.3	100.0
2012	100.8	102.6	91.3	100.0	99.8
2013	95.2	105.8	86.6	99.3	99.4
2014	88.5	105.1	87.0	99.1	99.1
2015	96.7	105.8	88.6	99.3	99.6

Sources Please cite the database as: Leandro Prados de la Escosura (2017), Spanish Economic Growth, 1850–2015

Table S18 Employment (full-time equivalent), 1850–2015 (million)

	Agriculture, forestry and fishing (million)	Manufacturing, extractive industries, and utilities (million)	Construction (million)	Service activities (million)	Total (million)
1850	3.317	0.636	0.225	1.061	5.239
1851	3.345	0.639	0.226	1.071	5.281
1852	3.374	0.643	0.227	1.080	5.324
1853	3.403	0.646	0.228	1.090	5.367
1854	3.433	0.649	0.229	1.100	5.411
1855	3.433	0.646	0.228	1.101	5.409
1856	3.459	0.649	0.229	1.110	5.448
1857	3.509	0.656	0.232	1.127	5.523
1858	3.526	0.657	0.232	1.133	5.547
1859	3.546	0.658	0.232	1.140	5.576
1860	3.573	0.660	0.233	1.149	5.616
1861	3.613	0.665	0.235	1.163	5.676
1862	3.657	0.671	0.237	1.177	5.742
1863	3.694	0.675	0.238	1.190	5.798
1864	3.726	0.679	0.240	1.201	5.844
1865	3.750	0.680	0.240	1.209	5.879
1866	3.776	0.683	0.241	1.218	5.919
1867	3.810	0.686	0.242	1.230	5.969
1868	3.830	0.687	0.243	1.237	5.998
1869	3.840	0.687	0.242	1.241	6.010
1870	3.856	0.687	0.243	1.247	6.032
1871	3.877	0.688	0.243	1.254	6.062
1872	3.899	0.689	0.243	1.262	6.094
1873	3.920	0.691	0.244	1.270	6.124
1874	3.940	0.692	0.244	1.277	6.153
1875	3.961	0.693	0.245	1.284	6.182
1876	3.982	0.694	0.245	1.292	6.212
1877	4.008	0.696	0.246	1.301	6.251
1878	4.002	0.705	0.249	1.296	6.252
1879	3.996	0.714	0.252	1.292	6.254
1880	3.990	0.724	0.256	1.288	6.258
1881	3.986	0.734	0.259	1.284	6.263
1882	3.977	0.743	0.263	1.279	6.262
1883	3.958	0.751	0.265	1.270	6.244
1884	3.941	0.759	0.268	1.262	6.230
1885	3.917	0.765	0.270	1.252	6.204
1886	3.896	0.773	0.273	1.243	6.185
1887	3.882	0.781	0.276	1.236	6.176

(continued)

Table S18 (continued)

	Agriculture, forestry and fishing (million)	Manufacturing, extractive industries, and utilities (million)	Construction (million)	Service activities (million)	Total (million)
1888	3.885	0.784	0.277	1.249	6.195
1889	3.885	0.786	0.278	1.262	6.211
1890	3.879	0.787	0.278	1.272	6.216
1891	3.878	0.789	0.279	1.284	6.229
1892	3.882	0.792	0.280	1.298	6.252
1893	3.890	0.796	0.281	1.314	6.281
1894	3.897	0.799	0.282	1.329	6.308
1895	3.906	0.803	0.284	1.345	6.338
1896	3.920	0.808	0.285	1.363	6.376
1897	3.943	0.815	0.288	1.384	6.431
1898	3.977	0.825	0.291	1.410	6.502
1899	4.011	0.834	0.294	1.436	6.575
1900	4.037	0.841	0.297	1.459	6.634
1901	4.052	0.854	0.299	1.485	6.690
1902	4.071	0.868	0.301	1.511	6.751
1903	4.097	0.883	0.304	1.542	6.825
1904	4.115	0.897	0.306	1.569	6.887
1905	4.131	0.911	0.307	1.596	6.945
1906	4.119	0.919	0.307	1.613	6.958
1907	4.122	0.930	0.308	1.636	6.995
1908	4.127	0.941	0.309	1.660	7.038
1909	4.134	0.954	0.310	1.685	7.083
1910	4.140	0.966	0.312	1.710	7.127
1911	4.130	0.990	0.314	1.714	7.148
1912	4.122	1.016	0.316	1.719	7.173
1913	4.119	1.044	0.318	1.726	7.207
1914	4.131	1.076	0.322	1.740	7.269
1915	4.157	1.113	0.327	1.759	7.356
1916	4.174	1.149	0.331	1.775	7.430
1917	4.178	1.182	0.334	1.786	7.480
1918	4.157	1.209	0.335	1.785	7.487
1919	4.136	1.237	0.337	1.785	7.494
1920	4.131	1.270	0.339	1.791	7.532
1921	4.102	1.297	0.351	1.854	7.604
1922	4.075	1.325	0.364	1.919	7.683
1923	4.039	1.351	0.376	1.983	7.749
1924	4.001	1.377	0.389	2.047	7.814
1925	3.969	1.404	0.402	2.116	7.891

(continued)

Table S18 (continued)

	Agriculture, forestry and fishing (million)	Manufacturing, extractive industries, and utilities (million)	Construction (million)	Service activities (million)	Total (million)
1926	3.944	1.435	0.417	2.191	7.987
1927	3.921	1.468	0.432	2.271	8.092
1928	3.898	1.501	0.448	2.352	8.199
1929	3.874	1.534	0.464	2.437	8.309
1930	3.859	1.572	0.482	2.530	8.443
1931	3.857	1.616	0.503	2.635	8.611
1932	3.861	1.664	0.525	2.749	8.798
1933	3.863	1.712	0.547	2.867	8.990
1934	3.861	1.760	0.570	2.986	9.176
1935	3.854	1.807	0.594	3.106	9.360
1936	4.027	1.718	0.582	3.036	9.362
1937	4.181	1.623	0.566	2.948	9.318
1938	4.325	1.527	0.549	2.853	9.254
1939	4.428	1.422	0.527	2.732	9.110
1940	4.527	1.323	0.506	2.613	8.968
1941	4.520	1.350	0.521	2.610	9.002
1942	4.519	1.380	0.537	2.611	9.048
1943	4.552	1.421	0.558	2.632	9.163
1944	4.599	1.467	0.582	2.660	9.308
1945	4.648	1.516	0.607	2.690	9.461
1946	4.699	1.567	0.633	2.721	9.619
1947	4.753	1.620	0.660	2.753	9.786
1948	4.830	1.682	0.692	2.799	10.004
1949	4.916	1.750	0.727	2.850	10.244
1950	4.972	1.810	0.758	2.884	10.424
1951	4.871	1.850	0.763	2.974	10.459
1952	4.773	1.892	0.768	3.067	10.500
1953	4.686	1.938	0.774	3.169	10.567
1954	4.602	1.986	0.781	3.276	10.645
1955	4.562	2.061	0.811	3.348	10.782
1956	4.519	2.148	0.846	3.433	10.947
1957	4.475	2.227	0.877	3.531	11.109
1958	4.428	2.325	0.916	3.650	11.319
1959	4.375	2.325	0.916	3.568	11.184
1960	4.313	2.295	0.905	3.547	11.059
1961	4.246	2.372	0.936	3.691	11.245
1962	4.160	2.484	0.980	3.813	11.437
1963	4.070	2.583	1.020	3.962	11.635

(continued)

Table S18 (continued)

	Agriculture, forestry and fishing (million)	Manufacturing, extractive industries, and utilities (million)	Construction (million)	Service activities (million)	Total (million)
1964	3.845	2.709	1.070	4.090	11.715
1965	3.979	2.692	1.143	4.373	12.187
1966	3.989	2.708	1.187	4.326	12.210
1967	3.848	2.761	1.231	4.478	12.318
1968	3.767	2.773	1.263	4.611	12.414
1969	3.597	2.844	1.280	4.705	12.427
1970	3.420	2.883	1.286	4.905	12.494
1971	3.285	2.935	1.315	5.133	12.667
1972	3.161	3.042	1.330	5.393	12.926
1973	3.073	3.164	1.367	5.681	13.286
1974	2.923	3.203	1.391	5.802	13.319
1975	2.647	3.232	1.350	5.755	12.985
1976	2.483	3.290	1.346	5.799	12.918
1977	2.387	3.292	1.418	5.852	12.948
1978	2.287	3.207	1.329	5.806	12.629
1979	2.180	3.089	1.250	5.915	12.434
1980	2.044	2.974	1.148	5.812	11.978
1981	1.915	2.798	1.061	5.912	11.686
1982	1.860	2.674	1.045	6.006	11.586
1983	1.843	2.620	1.015	6.070	11.548
1984	1.767	2.557	0.883	6.080	11.287
1985	1.701	2.486	0.840	6.148	11.175
1986	1.579	2.523	0.902	6.440	11.444
1987	1.535	2.604	1.009	6.856	12.005
1988	1.511	2.649	1.112	7.166	12.438
1989	1.406	2.727	1.236	7.536	12.905
1990	1.352	2.810	1.334	7.917	13.413
1991	1.218	2.772	1.392	8.212	13.594
1992	1.127	2.680	1.307	8.307	13.422
1993	1.065	2.535	1.190	8.264	13.055
1994	1.017	2.482	1.158	8.357	13.014
1995	0.966	2.521	1.224	8.573	13.285
1996	0.993	2.610	1.234	8.613	13.450
1997	0.979	2.729	1.331	8.889	13.928
1998	0.982	2.833	1.441	9.261	14.517
1999	0.956	2.931	1.613	9.687	15.187
2000	0.942	3.027	1.847	10.108	15.924
2001	0.949	3.033	1.978	10.521	16.482

(continued)

Table S18 (continued)

	Agriculture, forestry and fishing (million)	Manufacturing, extractive industries, and utilities (million)	Construction (million)	Service activities (million)	Total (million)
2002	0.938	3.011	2.051	10.893	16.894
2003	0.927	3.027	2.141	11.285	17.379
2004	0.897	3.021	2.224	11.728	17.869
2005	0.872	3.014	2.380	12.248	18.513
2006	0.824	2.968	2.520	12.881	19.193
2007	0.805	2.923	2.649	13.436	19.812
2008	0.775	2.894	2.336	13.844	19.850
2009	0.742	2.562	1.830	13.508	18.642
2010	0.747	2.486	1.574	13.341	18.148
2011	0.720	2.400	1.334	13.193	17.647
2012	0.696	2.234	1.093	12.773	16.797
2013	0.686	2.133	0.954	12.453	16.226
2014	0.691	2.106	0.924	12.679	16.401
2015	0.700	2.140	0.985	13.060	16.885

Sources Please cite the database as: Leandro Prados de la Escosura (2017), Spanish Economic Growth, 1850–2015

Table S19 Sector shares in employment (full-time equivalent), 1850–2015 (percentage)

	Agriculture, forestry and fishing (%)	Manufacturing, extractive industries, and utilities (%)	Construction (%)	Service activities (%)
1850	63.3	12.1	4.3	20.2
1851	63.3	12.1	4.3	20.3
1852	63.4	12.1	4.3	20.3
1853	63.4	12.0	4.2	20.3
1854	63.4	12.0	4.2	20.3
1855	63.5	12.0	4.2	20.4
1856	63.5	11.9	4.2	20.4
1857	63.5	11.9	4.2	20.4
1858	63.6	11.8	4.2	20.4
1859	63.6	11.8	4.2	20.4
1860	63.6	11.8	4.2	20.5
1861	63.7	11.7	4.1	20.5
1862	63.7	11.7	4.1	20.5
1863	63.7	11.6	4.1	20.5
1864	63.7	11.6	4.1	20.5
1865	63.8	11.6	4.1	20.6
1866	63.8	11.5	4.1	20.6
1867	63.8	11.5	4.1	20.6
1868	63.9	11.5	4.0	20.6
1869	63.9	11.4	4.0	20.6
1870	63.9	11.4	4.0	20.7
1871	64.0	11.4	4.0	20.7
1872	64.0	11.3	4.0	20.7
1873	64.0	11.3	4.0	20.7
1874	64.0	11.2	4.0	20.8
1875	64.1	11.2	4.0	20.8
1876	64.1	11.2	3.9	20.8
1877	64.1	11.1	3.9	20.8
1878	64.0	11.3	4.0	20.7
1879	63.9	11.4	4.0	20.7
1880	63.8	11.6	4.1	20.6
1881	63.6	11.7	4.1	20.5
1882	63.5	11.9	4.2	20.4
1883	63.4	12.0	4.2	20.3
1884	63.3	12.2	4.3	20.3
1885	63.1	12.3	4.4	20.2
1886	63.0	12.5	4.4	20.1
1887	62.9	12.7	4.5	20.0

(continued)

Table S19 (continued)

	Agriculture, forestry and fishing (%)	Manufacturing, extractive industries, and utilities (%)	Construction (%)	Service activities (%)
1888	62.7	12.7	4.5	20.2
1889	62.6	12.7	4.5	20.3
1890	62.4	12.7	4.5	20.5
1891	62.2	12.7	4.5	20.6
1892	62.1	12.7	4.5	20.8
1893	61.9	12.7	4.5	20.9
1894	61.8	12.7	4.5	21.1
1895	61.6	12.7	4.5	21.2
1896	61.5	12.7	4.5	21.4
1897	61.3	12.7	4.5	21.5
1898	61.2	12.7	4.5	21.7
1899	61.0	12.7	4.5	21.8
1900	60.8	12.7	4.5	22.0
1901	60.6	12.8	4.5	22.2
1902	60.3	12.9	4.5	22.4
1903	60.0	12.9	4.4	22.6
1904	59.8	13.0	4.4	22.8
1905	59.5	13.1	4.4	23.0
1906	59.2	13.2	4.4	23.2
1907	58.9	13.3	4.4	23.4
1908	58.6	13.4	4.4	23.6
1909	58.4	13.5	4.4	23.8
1910	58.1	13.5	4.4	24.0
1911	57.8	13.9	4.4	24.0
1912	57.5	14.2	4.4	24.0
1913	57.1	14.5	4.4	24.0
1914	56.8	14.8	4.4	23.9
1915	56.5	15.1	4.4	23.9
1916	56.2	15.5	4.5	23.9
1917	55.9	15.8	4.5	23.9
1918	55.5	16.2	4.5	23.8
1919	55.2	16.5	4.5	23.8
1920	54.9	16.9	4.5	23.8
1921	53.9	17.1	4.6	24.4
1922	53.0	17.2	4.7	25.0
1923	52.1	17.4	4.9	25.6
1924	51.2	17.6	5.0	26.2
1925	50.3	17.8	5.1	26.8
1926	49.4	18.0	5.2	27.4

(continued)

Appendices

Table S19 (continued)

	Agriculture, forestry and fishing (%)	Manufacturing, extractive industries, and utilities (%)	Construction (%)	Service activities (%)
1927	48.5	18.1	5.3	28.1
1928	47.5	18.3	5.5	28.7
1929	46.6	18.5	5.6	29.3
1930	45.7	18.6	5.7	30.0
1931	44.8	18.8	5.8	30.6
1932	43.9	18.9	6.0	31.2
1933	43.0	19.0	6.1	31.9
1934	42.1	19.2	6.2	32.5
1935	41.2	19.3	6.3	33.2
1936	43.0	18.3	6.2	32.4
1937	44.9	17.4	6.1	31.6
1938	46.7	16.5	5.9	30.8
1939	48.6	15.6	5.8	30.0
1940	50.5	14.8	5.6	29.1
1941	50.2	15.0	5.8	29.0
1942	49.9	15.3	5.9	28.9
1943	49.7	15.5	6.1	28.7
1944	49.4	15.8	6.3	28.6
1945	49.1	16.0	6.4	28.4
1946	48.9	16.3	6.6	28.3
1947	48.6	16.6	6.7	28.1
1948	48.3	16.8	6.9	28.0
1949	48.0	17.1	7.1	27.8
1950	47.7	17.4	7.3	27.7
1951	46.6	17.7	7.3	28.4
1952	45.5	18.0	7.3	29.2
1953	44.3	18.3	7.3	30.0
1954	43.2	18.7	7.3	30.8
1955	42.3	19.1	7.5	31.1
1956	41.3	19.6	7.7	31.4
1957	40.3	20.0	7.9	31.8
1958	39.1	20.5	8.1	32.2
1959	39.1	20.8	8.2	31.9
1960	39.0	20.7	8.2	32.1
1961	37.8	21.1	8.3	32.8
1962	36.4	21.7	8.6	33.3
1963	35.0	22.2	8.8	34.1
1964	32.8	23.1	9.1	34.9
1965	32.7	22.1	9.4	35.9

(continued)

Table S19 (continued)

	Agriculture, forestry and fishing (%)	Manufacturing, extractive industries, and utilities (%)	Construction (%)	Service activities (%)
1966	32.7	22.2	9.7	35.4
1967	31.2	22.4	10.0	36.4
1968	30.3	22.3	10.2	37.1
1969	28.9	22.9	10.3	37.9
1970	27.4	23.1	10.3	39.3
1971	25.9	23.2	10.4	40.5
1972	24.5	23.5	10.3	41.7
1973	23.1	23.8	10.3	42.8
1974	21.9	24.0	10.4	43.6
1975	20.4	24.9	10.4	44.3
1976	19.2	25.5	10.4	44.9
1977	18.4	25.4	10.9	45.2
1978	18.1	25.4	10.5	46.0
1979	17.5	24.8	10.1	47.6
1980	17.1	24.8	9.6	48.5
1981	16.4	23.9	9.1	50.6
1982	16.1	23.1	9.0	51.8
1983	16.0	22.7	8.8	52.6
1984	15.7	22.7	7.8	53.9
1985	15.2	22.2	7.5	55.0
1986	13.8	22.0	7.9	56.3
1987	12.8	21.7	8.4	57.1
1988	12.1	21.3	8.9	57.6
1989	10.9	21.1	9.6	58.4
1990	10.1	21.0	9.9	59.0
1991	9.0	20.4	10.2	60.4
1992	8.4	20.0	9.7	61.9
1993	8.2	19.4	9.1	63.3
1994	7.8	19.1	8.9	64.2
1995	7.3	19.0	9.2	64.5
1996	7.4	19.4	9.2	64.0
1997	7.0	19.6	9.6	63.8
1998	6.8	19.5	9.9	63.8
1999	6.3	19.3	10.6	63.8
2000	5.9	19.0	11.6	63.5
2001	5.8	18.4	12.0	63.8
2002	5.6	17.8	12.1	64.5
2003	5.3	17.4	12.3	64.9
2004	5.0	16.9	12.4	65.6

(continued)

Table S19 (continued)

	Agriculture, forestry and fishing (%)	Manufacturing, extractive industries, and utilities (%)	Construction (%)	Service activities (%)
2005	4.7	16.3	12.9	66.2
2006	4.3	15.5	13.1	67.1
2007	4.1	14.8	13.4	67.8
2008	3.9	14.6	11.8	69.7
2009	4.0	13.7	9.8	72.5
2010	4.1	13.7	8.7	73.5
2011	4.1	13.6	7.6	74.8
2012	4.1	13.3	6.5	76.0
2013	4.2	13.1	5.9	76.7
2014	4.2	12.8	5.6	77.3
2015	4.1	12.7	5.8	77.3

Sources Please cite the database as: Leandro Prados de la Escosura (2017), Spanish Economic Growth, 1850–2015

Table S20 Relative sector labour productivity (full-time equivalent employment), 1850–2015 (Average productivity = 1)

	Agriculture, forestry and fishing	Manufacturing, extractive industries, and utilities	Construction	Service activities
1850	0.59	1.12	0.83	2.24
1851	0.58	1.20	0.86	2.21
1852	0.56	1.29	0.94	2.23
1853	0.70	1.04	0.77	1.96
1854	0.68	1.09	0.72	1.99
1855	0.76	1.06	0.57	1.79
1856	0.66	1.31	0.69	1.95
1857	0.61	1.37	0.83	2.03
1858	0.60	1.44	0.91	2.01
1859	0.62	1.41	1.02	1.95
1860	0.62	1.32	1.20	1.96
1861	0.62	1.40	1.03	1.94
1862	0.61	1.47	1.04	1.93
1863	0.61	1.54	0.98	1.89
1864	0.59	1.59	0.89	1.96
1865	0.60	1.59	0.78	1.95
1866	0.62	1.56	0.69	1.92
1867	0.66	1.52	0.63	1.84
1868	0.56	1.64	0.65	2.08
1869	0.53	1.77	0.67	2.11
1870	0.60	1.62	0.61	1.98
1871	0.61	1.66	0.60	1.92
1872	0.66	1.64	0.57	1.78
1873	0.63	1.80	0.54	1.80
1874	0.60	1.65	0.58	1.95
1875	0.57	1.72	0.64	1.99
1876	0.63	1.66	0.65	1.85
1877	0.66	1.74	0.63	1.72
1878	0.66	1.68	0.58	1.75
1879	0.64	1.78	0.56	1.78
1880	0.62	1.93	0.59	1.74
1881	0.61	2.06	0.55	1.71
1882	0.61	2.05	0.55	1.70
1883	0.60	2.04	0.57	1.72
1884	0.61	1.90	0.55	1.77
1885	0.61	1.92	0.51	1.78
1886	0.64	1.81	0.47	1.76
1887	0.57	1.88	0.49	1.91

(continued)

Table S20 (continued)

	Agriculture, forestry and fishing	Manufacturing, extractive industries, and utilities	Construction	Service activities
1888	0.60	1.95	0.46	1.78
1889	0.55	1.91	0.51	1.93
1890	0.54	2.01	0.56	1.88
1891	0.53	2.11	0.52	1.83
1892	0.54	2.02	0.56	1.86
1893	0.50	2.10	0.58	1.90
1894	0.51	2.04	0.60	1.89
1895	0.53	2.03	0.59	1.84
1896	0.50	2.01	0.62	1.93
1897	0.58	1.83	0.57	1.81
1898	0.54	1.96	0.57	1.83
1899	0.50	2.08	0.61	1.85
1900	0.49	2.15	0.68	1.81
1901	0.55	2.07	0.58	1.70
1902	0.52	2.00	0.58	1.80
1903	0.53	2.02	0.61	1.73
1904	0.53	2.06	0.62	1.70
1905	0.54	1.95	0.58	1.73
1906	0.53	2.00	0.56	1.70
1907	0.56	2.07	0.62	1.57
1908	0.52	2.04	0.63	1.68
1909	0.56	1.90	0.66	1.63
1910	0.48	2.01	0.79	1.73
1911	0.54	1.87	0.74	1.66
1912	0.47	2.00	0.80	1.72
1913	0.51	1.87	0.77	1.69
1914	0.49	1.80	0.76	1.77
1915	0.58	1.70	0.66	1.60
1916	0.57	1.82	0.56	1.56
1917	0.53	1.81	0.50	1.66
1918	0.55	1.76	0.45	1.65
1919	0.58	1.59	0.51	1.65
1920	0.58	1.64	0.55	1.59
1921	0.54	1.57	0.68	1.69
1922	0.56	1.50	0.77	1.65
1923	0.50	1.60	0.76	1.66
1924	0.52	1.61	0.68	1.59
1925	0.55	1.53	0.70	1.55
1926	0.50	1.59	0.75	1.56

(continued)

Table S20 (continued)

	Agriculture, forestry and fishing	Manufacturing, extractive industries, and utilities	Construction	Service activities
1927	0.59	1.58	0.70	1.39
1928	0.50	1.64	0.75	1.47
1929	0.57	1.56	0.74	1.39
1930	0.50	1.50	0.76	1.50
1931	0.54	1.37	0.58	1.53
1932	0.61	1.33	0.48	1.45
1933	0.52	1.35	0.60	1.51
1934	0.58	1.26	0.50	1.48
1935	0.56	1.26	0.51	1.49
1936	0.41	1.17	0.55	1.77
1937	0.48	1.16	0.48	1.74
1938	0.45	1.37	0.40	1.75
1939	0.54	1.41	0.31	1.67
1940	0.53	1.43	0.40	1.71
1941	0.51	1.29	0.62	1.78
1942	0.54	1.41	0.56	1.67
1943	0.54	1.29	0.63	1.72
1944	0.63	1.27	0.59	1.58
1945	0.54	1.32	0.54	1.72
1946	0.62	1.39	0.49	1.55
1947	0.56	1.39	0.59	1.62
1948	0.52	1.46	0.71	1.63
1949	0.59	1.25	0.61	1.66
1950	0.60	1.32	0.56	1.60
1951	0.62	1.52	0.45	1.44
1952	0.59	1.54	0.44	1.45
1953	0.56	1.63	0.45	1.39
1954	0.55	1.57	0.57	1.39
1955	0.56	1.54	0.68	1.35
1956	0.55	1.52	0.70	1.35
1957	0.57	1.53	0.61	1.31
1958	0.60	1.52	0.58	1.26
1959	0.60	1.48	0.54	1.30
1960	0.60	1.49	0.48	1.30
1961	0.60	1.49	0.44	1.28
1962	0.62	1.40	0.48	1.28
1963	0.63	1.35	0.51	1.28
1964	0.54	1.34	0.51	1.33
1965	0.51	1.43	0.54	1.30

(continued)

Table S20 (continued)

	Agriculture, forestry and fishing	Manufacturing, extractive industries, and utilities	Construction	Service activities
1966	0.50	1.39	0.55	1.34
1967	0.47	1.33	0.58	1.36
1968	0.47	1.32	0.59	1.36
1969	0.46	1.32	0.61	1.33
1970	0.43	1.26	0.63	1.34
1971	0.47	1.23	0.62	1.30
1972	0.46	1.29	0.66	1.23
1973	0.47	1.30	0.74	1.18
1974	0.45	1.30	0.82	1.15
1975	0.47	1.21	0.86	1.16
1976	0.47	1.19	0.84	1.16
1977	0.47	1.17	0.81	1.16
1978	0.47	1.15	0.85	1.16
1979	0.42	1.16	0.93	1.14
1980	0.40	1.19	0.99	1.12
1981	0.36	1.23	0.98	1.10
1982	0.38	1.25	0.99	1.09
1983	0.37	1.27	0.96	1.08
1984	0.39	1.28	0.96	1.06
1985	0.37	1.34	1.03	1.03
1986	0.40	1.33	0.99	1.02
1987	0.44	1.31	0.99	1.01
1988	0.47	1.28	1.01	1.01
1989	0.50	1.25	1.04	1.00
1990	0.53	1.18	1.08	1.00
1991	0.55	1.17	1.06	1.00
1992	0.52	1.14	1.02	1.02
1993	0.56	1.12	1.02	1.02
1994	0.57	1.13	1.02	1.01
1995	0.58	1.13	1.01	1.01
1996	0.64	1.11	0.98	1.01
1997	0.67	1.10	0.93	1.01
1998	0.67	1.09	0.92	1.02
1999	0.67	1.09	0.91	1.02
2000	0.70	1.09	0.87	1.03
2001	0.70	1.10	0.87	1.02
2002	0.68	1.11	0.89	1.02
2003	0.70	1.11	0.89	1.02
2004	0.68	1.12	0.89	1.01

(continued)

Table S20 (continued)

	Agriculture, forestry and fishing	Manufacturing, extractive industries, and utilities	Construction	Service activities
2005	0.64	1.16	0.90	1.01
2006	0.61	1.20	0.89	1.00
2007	0.67	1.23	0.84	1.00
2008	0.64	1.23	0.94	0.98
2009	0.59	1.21	1.08	0.97
2010	0.62	1.25	1.02	0.97
2011	0.61	1.28	0.99	0.97
2012	0.61	1.30	1.02	0.97
2013	0.65	1.33	0.98	0.96
2014	0.59	1.37	1.01	0.96
2015	0.62	1.42	0.96	0.95

Sources Please cite the database as: Leandro Prados de la Escosura (2017), Spanish Economic Growth, 1850–2015

Table S21 Labour productivity indices (gross value added per full-time equivalent occupied), 1850–2015 (2010 = 100)

	Agriculture, forestry and fishing	Manufacturing, extractive industries, and utilities	Construction	Service activities	Gross Value Added
	(2010 = 100)	(2010 = 100)	(2010 = 100)	(2010 = 100)	(2010 = 100)
1850	3.0	2.6	8.3	18.7	7.0
1851	3.1	2.7	8.7	18.5	7.1
1852	3.1	3.1	9.4	18.9	7.3
1853	3.2	2.8	9.5	19.0	7.4
1854	3.3	2.9	8.9	18.9	7.4
1855	3.6	2.9	9.2	19.2	7.9
1856	3.2	3.4	9.6	18.9	7.5
1857	2.8	3.5	11.6	18.8	7.1
1858	2.9	3.7	13.6	19.0	7.3
1859	3.0	3.8	14.4	19.4	7.6
1860	3.1	3.8	17.8	19.7	7.9
1861	3.1	4.0	15.9	19.7	7.8
1862	3.1	3.8	16.6	19.7	7.8
1863	3.2	4.0	15.9	19.8	7.9
1864	3.1	3.9	14.3	19.9	7.9
1865	2.9	3.9	12.2	19.7	7.5
1866	3.3	3.9	11.6	19.5	7.9
1867	3.2	4.1	11.5	19.5	7.8
1868	2.6	3.9	10.4	18.7	6.9
1869	2.7	4.1	9.8	18.8	7.1
1870	2.8	4.1	9.9	19.0	7.3
1871	3.0	4.7	10.5	19.8	7.8
1872	3.7	5.0	11.1	21.1	9.0
1873	4.0	5.9	10.9	22.6	9.7
1874	3.3	5.3	10.6	22.8	8.7
1875	3.4	5.4	11.4	23.0	8.9
1876	3.6	5.6	12.3	22.3	9.1
1877	4.1	6.2	13.8	22.9	10.1
1878	3.8	6.1	13.4	23.3	9.7
1879	3.4	6.2	13.2	22.8	9.1
1880	3.8	6.8	14.3	23.8	9.9
1881	3.7	7.5	14.7	24.4	10.1
1882	3.7	7.6	15.6	24.9	10.2
1883	3.7	7.8	15.9	25.6	10.4
1884	3.8	7.4	15.9	26.1	10.5

(continued)

Table S21 (continued)

	Agriculture, forestry and fishing	Manufacturing, extractive industries, and utilities	Construction	Service activities	Gross Value Added
	(2010 = 100)	(2010 = 100)	(2010 = 100)	(2010 = 100)	(2010 = 100)
1885	3.6	7.5	14.3	26.2	10.2
1886	3.5	6.9	14.5	26.4	10.0
1887	3.3	6.9	14.0	26.7	9.8
1888	3.6	7.1	14.1	26.7	10.2
1889	3.5	7.4	14.5	26.6	10.1
1890	3.4	7.5	15.3	26.7	10.1
1891	3.4	8.0	14.9	26.5	10.3
1892	4.0	8.4	15.7	26.9	11.1
1893	3.5	8.3	15.1	26.7	10.5
1894	3.7	8.1	15.0	26.5	10.7
1895	3.6	8.0	15.7	26.3	10.5
1896	2.9	7.7	15.4	25.3	9.4
1897	3.5	7.2	15.4	25.3	10.0
1898	3.7	7.9	14.7	26.4	10.7
1899	3.5	8.5	15.7	26.7	10.6
1900	3.6	8.6	17.2	26.4	10.8
1901	4.2	8.6	16.7	26.5	11.6
1902	3.8	8.1	16.3	27.0	11.1
1903	3.8	8.2	16.4	26.5	11.0
1904	3.6	8.2	16.6	26.2	10.8
1905	3.6	7.7	16.0	25.6	10.6
1906	4.0	7.9	15.5	26.0	11.2
1907	4.1	8.4	16.2	26.1	11.4
1908	4.2	8.7	17.5	26.5	11.8
1909	4.5	8.0	18.0	26.6	12.1
1910	3.9	8.1	20.2	26.8	11.4
1911	4.5	8.1	20.7	27.7	12.3
1912	3.8	8.8	22.7	28.4	11.9
1913	4.2	8.5	22.8	29.0	12.4
1914	4.0	8.3	22.3	29.0	12.1
1915	4.4	7.9	19.6	28.7	12.3
1916	4.6	8.3	17.3	29.3	12.8
1917	4.6	7.8	14.5	29.3	12.5
1918	4.6	7.6	12.9	29.3	12.5
1919	4.7	7.0	15.2	30.6	12.6
1920	5.0	7.5	17.5	32.7	13.4

(continued)

Table S21 (continued)

	Agriculture, forestry and fishing	Manufacturing, extractive industries, and utilities	Construction	Service activities	Gross Value Added
	(2010 = 100)	(2010 = 100)	(2010 = 100)	(2010 = 100)	(2010 = 100)
1921	4.9	7.4	18.0	34.0	13.6
1922	5.1	7.7	19.8	34.0	14.1
1923	4.8	8.1	19.8	34.1	14.0
1924	4.8	8.4	19.0	34.4	14.3
1925	5.4	8.6	20.7	34.7	15.1
1926	4.9	8.9	21.7	34.2	14.8
1927	5.8	9.4	21.2	34.7	16.0
1928	5.0	9.8	22.2	35.5	15.7
1929	6.1	9.7	22.9	35.7	16.8
1930	5.3	9.5	23.3	34.7	15.8
1931	5.6	8.3	16.3	33.4	15.2
1932	6.2	7.9	13.1	32.3	15.4
1933	5.6	7.6	14.8	31.8	14.7
1934	6.2	7.5	13.4	31.0	15.0
1935	6.2	7.5	13.4	31.0	15.0
1936	4.0	5.7	11.2	28.0	11.6
1937	4.1	5.3	9.5	25.0	10.8
1938	3.7	6.0	8.3	26.3	10.8
1939	4.2	7.2	7.1	28.6	11.9
1940	4.2	8.4	10.5	33.9	13.3
1941	4.0	8.0	14.7	33.8	13.0
1942	4.2	8.9	14.9	34.7	13.7
1943	4.3	8.6	16.5	35.9	14.1
1944	4.6	8.9	17.0	36.2	14.6
1945	3.7	8.2	14.8	36.0	13.3
1946	4.2	8.8	13.8	34.6	13.7
1947	4.2	8.6	14.5	35.1	13.8
1948	3.9	8.4	16.6	35.0	13.5
1949	3.9	7.6	15.4	34.9	13.1
1950	3.8	8.2	14.6	35.4	13.3
1951	4.9	8.6	12.9	35.9	14.7
1952	5.1	9.8	13.3	37.6	15.8
1953	4.8	9.8	13.6	37.6	15.7
1954	5.5	10.2	15.1	38.4	16.8
1955	5.4	10.7	19.2	38.9	17.3
1956	5.8	11.4	18.3	41.4	18.4

(continued)

Table S21 (continued)

	Agriculture, forestry and fishing	Manufacturing, extractive industries, and utilities	Construction	Service activities	Gross Value Added
	(2010 = 100)	(2010 = 100)	(2010 = 100)	(2010 = 100)	(2010 = 100)
1957	5.8	12.0	16.3	41.5	18.8
1958	5.7	12.5	17.9	42.2	19.3
1959	5.8	12.1	17.0	41.7	18.9
1960	6.0	12.2	16.8	42.7	19.3
1961	6.7	12.8	18.4	46.5	21.4
1962	7.5	12.9	21.4	50.1	23.3
1963	8.5	13.3	24.2	52.7	25.1
1964	8.1	13.7	26.1	57.4	27.5
1965	7.4	15.8	28.9	56.6	28.4
1966	7.8	17.6	32.4	60.4	30.5
1967	8.4	18.8	36.8	61.4	32.3
1968	8.5	20.3	38.8	63.1	34.1
1969	9.1	22.8	41.2	67.1	37.2
1970	9.5	23.3	43.7	67.8	38.8
1971	10.9	24.8	44.5	68.0	40.5
1972	11.4	29.6	49.0	68.9	43.5
1973	12.1	32.2	56.7	70.0	46.4
1974	13.6	35.5	62.6	72.4	49.9
1975	15.0	37.1	66.5	75.8	53.2
1976	16.7	39.4	67.4	78.2	55.8
1977	16.6	42.1	66.0	80.8	58.2
1978	18.5	46.0	70.5	83.8	61.7
1979	18.6	49.5	76.1	83.5	63.8
1980	21.6	54.1	84.3	85.9	67.9
1981	20.9	52.8	86.5	85.1	67.8
1982	21.2	54.3	90.7	86.4	69.7
1983	22.7	56.8	94.1	87.1	71.3
1984	25.7	57.9	102.1	89.2	73.8
1985	27.5	61.5	110.3	90.3	76.5
1986	26.9	63.5	109.5	89.4	77.5
1987	32.2	63.9	105.7	88.3	78.0
1988	35.2	65.1	105.3	89.1	79.5
1989	36.9	65.1	107.3	89.6	81.1
1990	41.2	63.9	109.3	89.2	81.6
1991	47.5	65.2	107.5	88.9	82.7
1992	52.8	66.9	108.0	90.3	84.5

(continued)

Table S21 (continued)

	Agriculture, forestry and fishing	Manufacturing, extractive industries, and utilities	Construction	Service activities	Gross Value Added
	(2010 = 100)	(2010 = 100)	(2010 = 100)	(2010 = 100)	(2010 = 100)
1993	58.0	68.3	111.7	91.9	86.5
1994	57.3	71.6	116.6	94.1	89.2
1995	56.7	72.8	117.2	94.9	90.4
1996	66.7	72.3	115.3	96.1	91.2
1997	72.3	72.7	108.4	95.8	91.0
1998	74.3	73.5	105.0	95.3	90.8
1999	75.8	74.5	99.4	94.8	90.5
2000	82.6	75.6	91.2	96.0	91.0
2001	80.7	78.4	90.6	96.0	91.6
2002	82.4	80.1	90.1	95.8	91.9
2003	82.7	81.8	87.7	95.6	91.9
2004	83.3	83.1	84.8	95.7	92.0
2005	78.8	85.0	81.5	95.9	92.0
2006	88.4	89.0	78.5	95.8	92.6
2007	96.9	91.9	75.1	96.8	93.5
2008	97.9	92.1	85.3	96.1	94.5
2009	98.6	93.6	100.6	97.5	97.3
2010	100.0	100.0	100.0	100.0	100.0
2011	108.4	103.4	102.9	101.8	102.2
2012	101.2	105.6	114.5	103.6	104.3
2013	116.6	106.3	117.4	105.6	106.4
2014	113.9	109.6	119.6	105.2	106.5
2015	109.3	113.7	112.4	104.8	106.3

Sources Please cite the database as: Leandro Prados de la Escosura (2017), Spanish Economic Growth, 1850–2015

Table S22 Hours worked, 1850–2015 (million)

	Agriculture, forestry and fishing (million)	Manufacturing, extractive industries, and utilities (million)	Construction (million)	Service activities (million)	Total (million)
1850	8961	1834	607	3310	14712
1851	9039	1823	610	3341	14812
1852	9117	1999	613	3371	15100
1853	9195	1759	616	3402	14972
1854	9275	1719	619	3433	15046
1855	9275	1646	617	3435	14973
1856	9347	1902	619	3464	15332
1857	9480	1981	626	3515	15602
1858	9526	2009	626	3534	15695
1859	9581	1993	628	3556	15758
1860	9654	1924	630	3586	15794
1861	9762	2044	635	3627	16068
1862	9881	1929	640	3674	16124
1863	9982	2002	644	3713	16341
1864	10066	1952	647	3746	16411
1865	10130	1970	649	3772	16521
1866	10203	1876	651	3801	16532
1867	10295	1957	655	3837	16744
1868	10349	1896	656	3860	16761
1869	10375	1879	655	3872	16780
1870	10417	1806	655	3889	16768
1871	10475	1979	656	3869	16980
1872	10534	1955	656	3885	17030
1873	10591	2172	656	3900	17318
1874	10645	1950	655	3914	17164
1875	10701	1911	655	3928	17195
1876	10758	1824	654	3943	17179
1877	10830	1907	655	3963	17355
1878	10812	1859	662	3942	17276
1879	10795	1892	669	3922	17279
1880	10781	2001	676	3902	17360
1881	10770	2184	684	3884	17522
1882	10746	2218	691	3862	17517
1883	10694	2256	697	3829	17476
1884	10648	2121	702	3799	17270
1885	10582	2164	707	3762	17214
1886	10527	2003	712	3729	16970
1887	10489	2043	718	3702	16952

(continued)

Table S22 (continued)

	Agriculture, forestry and fishing (million)	Manufacturing, extractive industries, and utilities (million)	Construction (million)	Service activities (million)	Total (million)
1888	10496	2025	719	3734	16973
1889	10497	2101	719	3764	17082
1890	10481	2124	718	3788	17111
1891	10476	2229	718	3818	17242
1892	10489	2238	719	3854	17300
1893	10511	2283	721	3893	17408
1894	10530	2171	723	3931	17355
1895	10554	2150	725	3972	17401
1896	10590	2191	727	4018	17527
1897	10654	1947	732	4075	17408
1898	10745	2151	738	4144	17778
1899	10837	2357	745	4214	18153
1900	11016	2251	752	4275	18294
1901	11059	2291	756	4323	18428
1902	11109	2332	761	4373	18576
1903	11180	2378	768	4433	18760
1904	11230	2421	773	4484	18908
1905	11272	2463	778	4533	19046
1906	11241	2489	777	4552	19059
1907	11248	2524	780	4587	19138
1908	11263	2561	782	4626	19232
1909	11281	2600	785	4666	19332
1910	11296	2628	788	4696	19407
1911	11294	2568	791	4640	19293
1912	11304	2706	795	4644	19449
1913	11324	2800	799	4655	19578
1914	11389	2975	807	4704	19875
1915	11491	2973	817	4714	19996
1916	11571	3039	826	4713	20149
1917	11613	3117	832	4695	20256
1918	11586	2987	833	4647	20052
1919	11559	3110	834	4552	20055
1920	11577	3176	839	4549	20141
1921	11450	3229	867	4696	20242
1922	11330	3284	896	4849	20359
1923	11187	3333	924	4996	20440
1924	11039	3381	952	5144	20516
1925	10906	3434	983	5302	20624

(continued)

Table S22 (continued)

	Agriculture, forestry and fishing (million)	Manufacturing, extractive industries, and utilities (million)	Construction (million)	Service activities (million)	Total (million)
1926	10795	3495	1016	5474	20780
1927	10692	3558	1051	5655	20956
1928	10587	3623	1087	5840	21137
1929	10482	3688	1124	6029	21324
1930	10401	3763	1165	6238	21567
1931	10395	3853	1212	6462	21922
1932	10403	3951	1262	6692	22308
1933	10408	4050	1314	6929	22701
1934	10399	4146	1366	7165	23076
1935	10379	4240	1419	7402	23440
1936	10733	4015	1387	7184	23319
1937	11151	3792	1350	6961	23254
1938	11541	3568	1310	6719	23139
1939	11823	3323	1257	6420	22823
1940	12093	3090	1205	6126	22514
1941	12086	3154	1242	6116	22598
1942	12095	3224	1281	6113	22713
1943	12193	3319	1331	6156	22999
1944	12330	3428	1387	6217	23362
1945	12472	3542	1446	6281	23742
1946	12620	3660	1508	6347	24135
1947	12775	3784	1574	6416	24550
1948	12994	3931	1650	6517	25092
1949	13237	4090	1733	6629	25688
1950	13399	4228	1808	6700	26135
1951	13128	4321	1917	6805	26172
1952	12864	4418	2035	6911	26228
1953	12629	4524	2165	7029	26347
1954	11991	4042	2525	8189	26748
1955	11799	4220	2827	8024	26870
1956	11581	4440	3019	8039	27080
1957	11366	4624	3177	8125	27292
1958	11102	4867	3379	8271	27619
1959	11152	4849	3376	7778	27156
1960	11152	4706	3337	7543	26738
1961	10974	4835	3309	7837	26954
1962	10704	5101	3365	8020	27190
1963	10421	5312	3403	8301	27438

(continued)

Table S22 (continued)

	Agriculture, forestry and fishing (million)	Manufacturing, extractive industries, and utilities (million)	Construction (million)	Service activities (million)	Total (million)
1964	8673	6229	3275	8841	27019
1965	8911	6484	3106	9498	28000
1966	8985	6216	3519	9352	28072
1967	8703	6323	3743	9676	28444
1968	8353	6283	3645	9853	28135
1969	7947	6431	3717	9952	28046
1970	7599	6504	3718	10490	28310
1971	7341	6617	3820	11072	28851
1972	7026	6797	3756	11585	29164
1973	6825	6982	3823	12175	29806
1974	6429	7010	3820	12283	29542
1975	5728	6967	3643	11958	28296
1976	5284	6983	3564	11833	27664
1977	4995	6877	3661	11723	27256
1978	4704	6593	3364	11417	26078
1979	4408	6246	3101	11416	25171
1980	4094	5959	2847	11121	24020
1981	3768	5504	2695	11112	23079
1982	3619	5203	2622	11168	22612
1983	3523	5010	2522	11097	22153
1984	3296	4771	2247	10852	21164
1985	3155	4613	2141	10919	20827
1986	2918	4661	2242	11404	21224
1987	2822	4787	2424	12095	22129
1988	2772	4861	2593	12625	22851
1989	2562	4970	2778	13188	23498
1990	2465	5125	2949	13879	24418
1991	2232	5078	3075	14464	24849
1992	2056	4887	2948	14555	24446
1993	1933	4602	2742	14423	23700
1994	1846	4506	2657	14617	23628
1995	2061	4411	2277	15324	24073
1996	2092	4605	2305	15439	24441
1997	2067	4851	2515	15955	25388
1998	2101	5072	2737	16720	26630
1999	2035	5292	3073	17523	27923
2000	1987	5476	3510	18282	29255
2001	2001	5510	3825	19063	30399

(continued)

Table S22 (continued)

	Agriculture, forestry and fishing (million)	Manufacturing, extractive industries, and utilities (million)	Construction (million)	Service activities (million)	Total (million)
2002	1974	5491	4026	19729	31220
2003	1933	5537	4206	20426	32102
2004	1878	5544	4379	21236	33037
2005	1819	5514	4695	22111	34139
2006	1722	5436	4971	23230	35358
2007	1674	5347	5212	24025	36259
2008	1608	5335	4627	24949	36519
2009	1538	4727	3622	24484	34371
2010	1530	4635	3128	24297	33591
2011	1495	4498	2668	24126	32788
2012	1461	4183	2152	23408	31204
2013	1429	3999	1884	22938	30250
2014	1426	3976	1838	23338	30579
2015	1424	4049	1979	23976	31428

Sources Please cite the database as: Leandro Prados de la Escosura (2017), Spanish Economic Growth, 1850–2015

Table S23 Sector shares in worked hours, 1850–2015 (percentage)

	Agriculture, forestry and fishing (%)	Manufacturing, extractive industries, and utilities (%)	Construction (%)	Service activities (%)
1850	60.9	12.5	4.1	22.5
1851	61.0	12.3	4.1	22.6
1852	60.4	13.2	4.1	22.3
1853	61.4	11.7	4.1	22.7
1854	61.6	11.4	4.1	22.8
1855	61.9	11.0	4.1	22.9
1856	61.0	12.4	4.0	22.6
1857	60.8	12.7	4.0	22.5
1858	60.7	12.8	4.0	22.5
1859	60.8	12.6	4.0	22.6
1860	61.1	12.2	4.0	22.7
1861	60.8	12.7	3.9	22.6
1862	61.3	12.0	4.0	22.8
1863	61.1	12.2	3.9	22.7
1864	61.3	11.9	3.9	22.8
1865	61.3	11.9	3.9	22.8
1866	61.7	11.3	3.9	23.0
1867	61.5	11.7	3.9	22.9
1868	61.7	11.3	3.9	23.0
1869	61.8	11.2	3.9	23.1
1870	62.1	10.8	3.9	23.2
1871	61.7	11.7	3.9	22.8
1872	61.9	11.5	3.9	22.8
1873	61.2	12.5	3.8	22.5
1874	62.0	11.4	3.8	22.8
1875	62.2	11.1	3.8	22.8
1876	62.6	10.6	3.8	23.0
1877	62.4	11.0	3.8	22.8
1878	62.6	10.8	3.8	22.8
1879	62.5	11.0	3.9	22.7
1880	62.1	11.5	3.9	22.5
1881	61.5	12.5	3.9	22.2
1882	61.3	12.7	3.9	22.0
1883	61.2	12.9	4.0	21.9
1884	61.7	12.3	4.1	22.0
1885	61.5	12.6	4.1	21.9
1886	62.0	11.8	4.2	22.0
1887	61.9	12.1	4.2	21.8
1888	61.8	11.9	4.2	22.0

(continued)

Table S23 (continued)

	Agriculture, forestry and fishing (%)	Manufacturing, extractive industries, and utilities (%)	Construction (%)	Service activities (%)
1889	61.5	12.3	4.2	22.0
1890	61.3	12.4	4.2	22.1
1891	60.8	12.9	4.2	22.1
1892	60.6	12.9	4.2	22.3
1893	60.4	13.1	4.1	22.4
1894	60.7	12.5	4.2	22.7
1895	60.7	12.4	4.2	22.8
1896	60.4	12.5	4.1	22.9
1897	61.2	11.2	4.2	23.4
1898	60.4	12.1	4.2	23.3
1899	59.7	13.0	4.1	23.2
1900	60.2	12.3	4.1	23.4
1901	60.0	12.4	4.1	23.5
1902	59.8	12.6	4.1	23.5
1903	59.6	12.7	4.1	23.6
1904	59.4	12.8	4.1	23.7
1905	59.2	12.9	4.1	23.8
1906	59.0	13.1	4.1	23.9
1907	58.8	13.2	4.1	24.0
1908	58.6	13.3	4.1	24.1
1909	58.4	13.4	4.1	24.1
1910	58.2	13.5	4.1	24.2
1911	58.5	13.3	4.1	24.1
1912	58.1	13.9	4.1	23.9
1913	57.8	14.3	4.1	23.8
1914	57.3	15.0	4.1	23.7
1915	57.5	14.9	4.1	23.6
1916	57.4	15.1	4.1	23.4
1917	57.3	15.4	4.1	23.2
1918	57.8	14.9	4.2	23.2
1919	57.6	15.5	4.2	22.7
1920	57.5	15.8	4.2	22.6
1921	56.6	16.0	4.3	23.2
1922	55.7	16.1	4.4	23.8
1923	54.7	16.3	4.5	24.4
1924	53.8	16.5	4.6	25.1
1925	52.9	16.7	4.8	25.7
1926	52.0	16.8	4.9	26.3
1927	51.0	17.0	5.0	27.0

(continued)

Table S23 (continued)

	Agriculture, forestry and fishing (%)	Manufacturing, extractive industries, and utilities (%)	Construction (%)	Service activities (%)
1928	50.1	17.1	5.1	27.6
1929	49.2	17.3	5.3	28.3
1930	48.2	17.4	5.4	28.9
1931	47.4	17.6	5.5	29.5
1932	46.6	17.7	5.7	30.0
1933	45.8	17.8	5.8	30.5
1934	45.1	18.0	5.9	31.0
1935	44.3	18.1	6.1	31.6
1936	46.0	17.2	5.9	30.8
1937	48.0	16.3	5.8	29.9
1938	49.9	15.4	5.7	29.0
1939	51.8	14.6	5.5	28.1
1940	53.7	13.7	5.4	27.2
1941	53.5	14.0	5.5	27.1
1942	53.3	14.2	5.6	26.9
1943	53.0	14.4	5.8	26.8
1944	52.8	14.7	5.9	26.6
1945	52.5	14.9	6.1	26.5
1946	52.3	15.2	6.3	26.3
1947	52.0	15.4	6.4	26.1
1948	51.8	15.7	6.6	26.0
1949	51.5	15.9	6.7	25.8
1950	51.3	16.2	6.9	25.6
1951	50.2	16.5	7.3	26.0
1952	49.0	16.8	7.8	26.3
1953	47.9	17.2	8.2	26.7
1954	44.8	15.1	9.4	30.6
1955	43.9	15.7	10.5	29.9
1956	42.8	16.4	11.2	29.7
1957	41.6	16.9	11.6	29.8
1958	40.2	17.6	12.2	29.9
1959	41.1	17.9	12.4	28.6
1960	41.7	17.6	12.5	28.2
1961	40.7	17.9	12.3	29.1
1962	39.4	18.8	12.4	29.5
1963	38.0	19.4	12.4	30.3
1964	32.1	23.1	12.1	32.7
1965	31.8	23.2	11.1	33.9
1966	32.0	22.1	12.5	33.3

(continued)

Table S23 (continued)

	Agriculture, forestry and fishing (%)	Manufacturing, extractive industries, and utilities (%)	Construction (%)	Service activities (%)
1967	30.6	22.2	13.2	34.0
1968	29.7	22.3	13.0	35.0
1969	28.3	22.9	13.3	35.5
1970	26.8	23.0	13.1	37.1
1971	25.4	22.9	13.2	38.4
1972	24.1	23.3	12.9	39.7
1973	22.9	23.4	12.8	40.8
1974	21.8	23.7	12.9	41.6
1975	20.2	24.6	12.9	42.3
1976	19.1	25.2	12.9	42.8
1977	18.3	25.2	13.4	43.0
1978	18.0	25.3	12.9	43.8
1979	17.5	24.8	12.3	45.4
1980	17.0	24.8	11.9	46.3
1981	16.3	23.8	11.7	48.1
1982	16.0	23.0	11.6	49.4
1983	15.9	22.6	11.4	50.1
1984	15.6	22.5	10.6	51.3
1985	15.1	22.1	10.3	52.4
1986	13.7	22.0	10.6	53.7
1987	12.8	21.6	11.0	54.7
1988	12.1	21.3	11.3	55.2
1989	10.9	21.2	11.8	56.1
1990	10.1	21.0	12.1	56.8
1991	9.0	20.4	12.4	58.2
1992	8.4	20.0	12.1	59.5
1993	8.2	19.4	11.6	60.9
1994	7.8	19.1	11.2	61.9
1995	8.6	18.3	9.5	63.7
1996	8.6	18.8	9.4	63.2
1997	8.1	19.1	9.9	62.8
1998	7.9	19.0	10.3	62.8
1999	7.3	19.0	11.0	62.8
2000	6.8	18.7	12.0	62.5
2001	6.6	18.1	12.6	62.7
2002	6.3	17.6	12.9	63.2
2003	6.0	17.2	13.1	63.6
2004	5.7	16.8	13.3	64.3
2005	5.3	16.2	13.8	64.8

(continued)

Table S23 (continued)

	Agriculture, forestry and fishing (%)	Manufacturing, extractive industries, and utilities (%)	Construction (%)	Service activities (%)
2006	4.9	15.4	14.1	65.7
2007	4.6	14.7	14.4	66.3
2008	4.4	14.6	12.7	68.3
2009	4.5	13.8	10.5	71.2
2010	4.6	13.8	9.3	72.3
2011	4.6	13.7	8.1	73.6
2012	4.7	13.4	6.9	75.0
2013	4.7	13.2	6.2	75.8
2014	4.7	13.0	6.0	76.3
2015	4.5	12.9	6.3	76.3

Sources Please cite the database as: Leandro Prados de la Escosura (2017), Spanish Economic Growth, 1850–2015

Table S24 Relative sector labour productivity (hours), 1850–2015

	Agriculture, forestry and fishing	Manufacturing, extractive industries, and utilities	Construction	Service activities
1850	0.61	1.09	0.87	2.02
1851	0.61	1.18	0.89	1.99
1852	0.58	1.17	0.98	2.02
1853	0.72	1.06	0.80	1.75
1854	0.70	1.14	0.74	1.78
1855	0.78	1.16	0.59	1.58
1856	0.68	1.26	0.72	1.76
1857	0.64	1.28	0.87	1.84
1858	0.63	1.33	0.95	1.82
1859	0.65	1.31	1.06	1.76
1860	0.65	1.27	1.24	1.77
1861	0.65	1.29	1.08	1.76
1862	0.64	1.43	1.08	1.73
1863	0.64	1.46	1.02	1.71
1864	0.61	1.56	0.93	1.76
1865	0.62	1.54	0.81	1.76
1866	0.64	1.59	0.71	1.72
1867	0.69	1.49	0.65	1.65
1868	0.58	1.66	0.68	1.86
1869	0.54	1.80	0.69	1.88
1870	0.62	1.71	0.63	1.76
1871	0.63	1.62	0.62	1.74
1872	0.68	1.61	0.59	1.62
1873	0.66	1.62	0.57	1.65
1874	0.62	1.63	0.61	1.78
1875	0.59	1.73	0.66	1.81
1876	0.64	1.75	0.67	1.68
1877	0.68	1.76	0.65	1.57
1878	0.68	1.76	0.60	1.59
1879	0.65	1.86	0.58	1.62
1880	0.63	1.94	0.62	1.60
1881	0.63	1.93	0.58	1.58
1882	0.63	1.92	0.58	1.57
1883	0.62	1.90	0.60	1.59
1884	0.63	1.89	0.58	1.63
1885	0.62	1.88	0.54	1.64
1886	0.65	1.91	0.50	1.61
1887	0.58	1.98	0.52	1.75
1888	0.60	2.07	0.48	1.63

(continued)

Appendices

Table S24 (continued)

	Agriculture, forestry and fishing	Manufacturing, extractive industries, and utilities	Construction	Service activities
1889	0.56	1.97	0.54	1.78
1890	0.55	2.05	0.60	1.73
1891	0.55	2.06	0.56	1.70
1892	0.55	1.98	0.61	1.73
1893	0.51	2.03	0.63	1.78
1894	0.52	2.07	0.64	1.76
1895	0.54	2.08	0.64	1.71
1896	0.51	2.04	0.66	1.80
1897	0.58	2.08	0.61	1.66
1898	0.54	2.06	0.62	1.71
1899	0.51	2.03	0.67	1.74
1900	0.50	2.21	0.74	1.70
1901	0.55	2.13	0.63	1.61
1902	0.52	2.05	0.64	1.72
1903	0.54	2.07	0.66	1.66
1904	0.53	2.09	0.67	1.63
1905	0.54	1.98	0.63	1.67
1906	0.54	2.02	0.60	1.65
1907	0.56	2.08	0.67	1.54
1908	0.52	2.05	0.68	1.64
1909	0.56	1.90	0.71	1.61
1910	0.48	2.02	0.85	1.71
1911	0.53	1.94	0.79	1.65
1912	0.46	2.03	0.86	1.73
1913	0.50	1.90	0.83	1.70
1914	0.48	1.78	0.83	1.79
1915	0.57	1.73	0.72	1.63
1916	0.56	1.87	0.61	1.60
1917	0.51	1.86	0.55	1.71
1918	0.52	1.91	0.48	1.70
1919	0.56	1.69	0.55	1.74
1920	0.56	1.76	0.60	1.68
1921	0.51	1.68	0.74	1.77
1922	0.53	1.60	0.83	1.73
1923	0.47	1.71	0.81	1.74
1924	0.49	1.72	0.72	1.66
1925	0.52	1.63	0.75	1.62
1926	0.47	1.70	0.80	1.63
1927	0.56	1.68	0.74	1.45

(continued)

Table S24 (continued)

	Agriculture, forestry and fishing	Manufacturing, extractive industries, and utilities	Construction	Service activities
1928	0.47	1.75	0.80	1.53
1929	0.54	1.66	0.78	1.44
1930	0.47	1.60	0.80	1.55
1931	0.51	1.46	0.61	1.59
1932	0.57	1.42	0.51	1.51
1933	0.49	1.45	0.63	1.58
1934	0.55	1.34	0.52	1.55
1935	0.52	1.34	0.53	1.57
1936	0.39	1.25	0.58	1.86
1937	0.45	1.24	0.51	1.84
1938	0.42	1.47	0.42	1.86
1939	0.51	1.51	0.33	1.78
1940	0.50	1.53	0.42	1.84
1941	0.47	1.38	0.66	1.91
1942	0.51	1.52	0.59	1.79
1943	0.51	1.38	0.66	1.84
1944	0.59	1.36	0.62	1.69
1945	0.50	1.42	0.57	1.85
1946	0.58	1.49	0.51	1.67
1947	0.53	1.49	0.62	1.75
1948	0.48	1.57	0.74	1.75
1949	0.55	1.34	0.64	1.79
1950	0.56	1.42	0.59	1.73
1951	0.58	1.62	0.44	1.58
1952	0.54	1.65	0.42	1.60
1953	0.52	1.74	0.40	1.57
1954	0.53	1.94	0.44	1.39
1955	0.54	1.87	0.49	1.40
1956	0.53	1.82	0.49	1.42
1957	0.55	1.82	0.41	1.40
1958	0.58	1.77	0.39	1.36
1959	0.57	1.72	0.36	1.44
1960	0.56	1.75	0.31	1.48
1961	0.56	1.75	0.30	1.45
1962	0.57	1.62	0.33	1.45
1963	0.58	1.54	0.36	1.44
1964	0.56	1.34	0.39	1.42
1965	0.52	1.36	0.46	1.38
1966	0.51	1.40	0.43	1.43

(continued)

Table S24 (continued)

	Agriculture, forestry and fishing	Manufacturing, extractive industries, and utilities	Construction	Service activities
1967	0.48	1.34	0.44	1.46
1968	0.48	1.32	0.46	1.44
1969	0.47	1.32	0.47	1.42
1970	0.44	1.27	0.50	1.42
1971	0.48	1.24	0.49	1.38
1972	0.47	1.31	0.53	1.30
1973	0.47	1.32	0.60	1.24
1974	0.46	1.31	0.66	1.21
1975	0.48	1.23	0.69	1.21
1976	0.47	1.20	0.68	1.21
1977	0.48	1.18	0.66	1.22
1978	0.47	1.16	0.69	1.22
1979	0.42	1.16	0.76	1.20
1980	0.40	1.19	0.80	1.17
1981	0.37	1.23	0.76	1.16
1982	0.38	1.25	0.77	1.14
1983	0.37	1.27	0.74	1.14
1984	0.39	1.29	0.71	1.12
1985	0.38	1.34	0.76	1.08
1986	0.41	1.34	0.74	1.06
1987	0.44	1.32	0.76	1.05
1988	0.47	1.28	0.80	1.05
1989	0.50	1.25	0.84	1.04
1990	0.53	1.18	0.89	1.04
1991	0.55	1.17	0.87	1.04
1992	0.52	1.14	0.82	1.06
1993	0.56	1.12	0.80	1.06
1994	0.57	1.13	0.81	1.05
1995	0.49	1.17	0.98	1.02
1996	0.56	1.14	0.95	1.03
1997	0.58	1.13	0.90	1.03
1998	0.58	1.12	0.89	1.03
1999	0.58	1.11	0.88	1.04
2000	0.61	1.10	0.84	1.04
2001	0.61	1.11	0.83	1.04
2002	0.60	1.12	0.84	1.04
2003	0.62	1.12	0.84	1.04
2004	0.60	1.13	0.84	1.03
2005	0.57	1.17	0.84	1.03

(continued)

Table S24 (continued)

	Agriculture, forestry and fishing	Manufacturing, extractive industries, and utilities	Construction	Service activities
2006	0.54	1.21	0.83	1.02
2007	0.59	1.23	0.78	1.02
2008	0.57	1.23	0.87	1.00
2009	0.52	1.21	1.00	0.99
2010	0.56	1.24	0.95	0.99
2011	0.54	1.27	0.92	0.99
2012	0.54	1.29	0.97	0.98
2013	0.58	1.33	0.93	0.98
2014	0.54	1.35	0.94	0.97
2015	0.57	1.40	0.89	0.97

Sources Please cite the database as: Leandro Prados de la Escosura (2017), Spanish Economic Growth, 1850–2015

Table S25 Labour productivity levels (per worked hour), 1850–2015 (2010 = 100)

	Agriculture, forestry and fishing	Manufacturing, extractive industries, and utilities	Construction	Service activities	Gross value added
	(2010 = 100)	(2010 = 100)	(2010 = 100)	(2010 = 100)	(2010 = 100)
1850	2.3	1.7	6.1	10.9	4.6
1851	2.3	1.8	6.4	10.8	4.7
1852	2.4	1.8	6.9	11.0	4.8
1853	2.4	1.9	7.0	11.1	4.9
1854	2.5	2.0	6.5	11.0	5.0
1855	2.7	2.1	6.8	11.2	5.3
1856	2.4	2.2	7.1	11.0	4.9
1857	2.1	2.2	8.5	11.0	4.7
1858	2.2	2.2	10.0	11.1	4.8
1859	2.3	2.3	10.6	11.3	5.0
1860	2.4	2.4	13.1	11.5	5.2
1861	2.3	2.4	11.7	11.5	5.1
1862	2.4	2.5	12.2	11.5	5.2
1863	2.4	2.5	11.7	11.6	5.2
1864	2.4	2.5	10.5	11.6	5.2
1865	2.2	2.5	9.0	11.5	4.9
1866	2.5	2.7	8.5	11.4	5.3
1867	2.4	2.7	8.4	11.4	5.2
1868	1.9	2.6	7.6	10.9	4.5
1869	2.1	2.8	7.2	11.0	4.7
1870	2.1	2.9	7.3	11.1	4.8
1871	2.3	3.1	7.7	11.7	5.2
1872	2.8	3.3	8.2	12.5	6.0
1873	3.0	3.5	8.1	13.4	6.3
1874	2.5	3.5	7.9	13.5	5.8
1875	2.6	3.7	8.5	13.7	5.9
1876	2.7	3.9	9.1	13.3	6.1
1877	3.1	4.2	10.3	13.7	6.7
1878	2.9	4.3	10.1	14.0	6.5
1879	2.6	4.3	9.9	13.7	6.1
1880	2.9	4.6	10.8	14.3	6.6
1881	2.8	4.7	11.0	14.7	6.7
1882	2.8	4.8	11.8	15.0	6.7
1883	2.8	4.9	12.1	15.5	6.9
1884	2.9	5.0	12.1	15.8	7.0
1885	2.7	4.9	10.9	15.9	6.8

(continued)

Table S25 (continued)

	Agriculture, forestry and fishing	Manufacturing, extractive industries, and utilities	Construction	Service activities	Gross value added
	(2010 = 100)	(2010 = 100)	(2010 = 100)	(2010 = 100)	(2010 = 100)
1886	2.7	5.0	11.1	16.1	6.7
1887	2.5	4.9	10.7	16.3	6.6
1888	2.8	5.1	10.8	16.2	6.9
1889	2.6	5.1	11.1	16.2	6.8
1890	2.6	5.2	11.7	16.3	6.8
1891	2.6	5.3	11.5	16.2	6.9
1892	3.0	5.5	12.2	16.5	7.4
1893	2.7	5.4	11.7	16.4	7.0
1894	2.8	5.6	11.6	16.3	7.2
1895	2.7	5.6	12.3	16.2	7.1
1896	2.2	5.3	12.0	15.6	6.4
1897	2.6	5.7	12.0	15.6	6.9
1898	2.8	5.7	11.5	16.4	7.2
1899	2.6	5.6	12.3	16.6	7.1
1900	2.7	6.0	13.5	16.4	7.2
1901	3.2	6.0	13.1	16.6	7.8
1902	2.9	5.6	12.8	17.0	7.4
1903	2.8	5.7	12.9	16.8	7.4
1904	2.7	5.7	13.1	16.7	7.3
1905	2.7	5.3	12.6	16.4	7.1
1906	3.0	5.4	12.2	16.8	7.6
1907	3.0	5.8	12.7	16.9	7.7
1908	3.1	6.0	13.8	17.3	8.0
1909	3.4	5.5	14.1	17.5	8.2
1910	2.9	5.5	15.8	17.7	7.7
1911	3.3	5.8	16.3	18.7	8.4
1912	2.8	6.2	17.9	19.1	8.1
1913	3.2	5.9	18.1	19.6	8.5
1914	3.0	5.6	17.7	19.5	8.2
1915	3.2	5.5	15.6	19.5	8.4
1916	3.4	5.8	13.7	20.1	8.7
1917	3.4	5.5	11.6	20.3	8.6
1918	3.4	5.7	10.3	20.5	8.6
1919	3.4	5.2	12.2	21.8	8.7
1920	3.6	5.6	14.1	23.4	9.3
1921	3.6	5.5	14.5	24.4	9.5

(continued)

Table S25 (continued)

	Agriculture, forestry and fishing	Manufacturing, extractive industries, and utilities	Construction	Service activities	Gross value added
	(2010 = 100)	(2010 = 100)	(2010 = 100)	(2010 = 100)	(2010 = 100)
1922	3.7	5.8	16.0	24.5	9.8
1923	3.5	6.1	16.0	24.6	9.8
1924	3.6	6.4	15.4	24.9	10.1
1925	4.0	6.6	16.8	25.2	10.7
1926	3.7	6.8	17.7	24.9	10.5
1927	4.3	7.3	17.3	25.4	11.4
1928	3.8	7.6	18.2	26.0	11.2
1929	4.6	7.6	18.8	26.3	12.1
1930	4.0	7.4	19.1	25.6	11.5
1931	4.3	6.5	13.4	24.8	11.1
1932	4.7	6.2	10.8	24.2	11.2
1933	4.2	6.0	12.3	23.9	10.8
1934	4.7	6.0	11.1	23.5	11.1
1935	4.7	6.0	11.1	23.7	11.1
1936	3.0	4.5	9.3	21.5	8.6
1937	3.1	4.3	7.9	19.3	8.0
1938	2.8	4.8	6.9	20.3	8.0
1939	3.2	5.7	5.9	22.2	8.8
1940	3.2	6.7	8.7	26.4	9.8
1941	3.0	6.4	12.3	26.3	9.6
1942	3.2	7.1	12.4	27.0	10.1
1943	3.3	6.9	13.8	28.0	10.4
1944	3.5	7.1	14.2	28.2	10.7
1945	2.8	6.5	12.3	28.1	9.8
1946	3.2	7.0	11.5	27.0	10.1
1947	3.2	6.8	12.1	27.4	10.1
1948	3.0	6.7	13.8	27.4	10.0
1949	3.0	6.1	12.8	27.3	9.7
1950	2.9	6.5	12.2	27.7	9.8
1951	3.7	6.8	10.2	28.6	10.8
1952	3.9	7.9	10.0	30.4	11.7
1953	3.7	7.8	9.6	30.8	11.6
1954	4.3	9.4	9.3	27.9	12.4
1955	4.3	9.7	10.9	29.6	12.8
1956	4.6	10.3	10.2	32.2	13.8
1957	4.7	10.8	9.0	32.9	14.2

(continued)

Table S25 (continued)

	Agriculture, forestry and fishing	Manufacturing, extractive industries, and utilities	Construction	Service activities	Gross value added
	(2010 = 100)	(2010 = 100)	(2010 = 100)	(2010 = 100)	(2010 = 100)
1958	4.6	11.2	9.7	33.9	14.6
1959	4.7	10.8	9.2	34.9	14.4
1960	4.8	11.1	9.1	36.5	14.8
1961	5.3	11.7	10.4	39.9	16.5
1962	6.0	11.7	12.4	43.4	18.2
1963	6.8	12.1	14.4	45.8	19.7
1964	7.3	11.1	16.9	48.4	22.1
1965	6.7	12.2	21.1	47.4	22.8
1966	7.1	14.3	21.7	50.9	24.5
1967	7.6	15.3	24.0	51.8	25.9
1968	7.9	16.7	26.7	53.8	27.9
1969	8.4	18.8	28.2	57.8	30.5
1970	8.7	19.2	30.1	57.7	31.7
1971	10.0	20.5	30.5	57.4	32.9
1972	10.5	24.7	34.5	58.4	35.7
1973	11.2	27.2	40.3	59.5	38.3
1974	12.7	30.3	45.3	62.3	41.6
1975	14.2	32.1	49.0	66.4	45.2
1976	16.1	34.6	50.6	69.8	48.2
1977	16.3	37.6	50.8	73.4	51.1
1978	18.4	41.7	55.4	77.6	55.3
1979	18.9	45.6	60.9	78.8	58.4
1980	22.1	50.3	67.6	81.8	62.6
1981	21.7	50.0	67.7	82.5	63.6
1982	22.3	52.0	71.9	84.6	66.1
1983	24.3	55.4	75.2	86.8	68.8
1984	28.2	57.9	79.7	91.1	72.8
1985	30.4	61.8	86.1	92.6	76.0
1986	29.8	64.0	87.6	91.9	77.4
1987	35.9	64.8	87.5	91.2	78.3
1988	39.3	66.2	89.8	92.1	80.1
1989	41.4	66.6	94.9	93.3	82.4
1990	46.3	65.4	98.2	92.7	83.0
1991	53.1	66.4	96.7	91.9	83.8
1992	59.3	68.4	95.2	93.8	85.9
1993	65.5	70.1	96.4	95.9	88.2

(continued)

Table S25 (continued)

	Agriculture, forestry and fishing	Manufacturing, extractive industries, and utilities	Construction	Service activities	Gross value added
	(2010 = 100)	(2010 = 100)	(2010 = 100)	(2010 = 100)	(2010 = 100)
1994	64.7	73.6	101.0	98.0	90.9
1995	54.5	77.5	125.2	96.7	92.3
1996	64.9	76.4	122.7	97.6	92.9
1997	70.1	76.3	114.0	97.2	92.4
1998	71.2	76.6	109.9	96.1	91.6
1999	72.9	77.0	103.7	95.5	91.1
2000	80.2	77.9	95.3	96.6	91.7
2001	78.4	80.5	93.1	96.5	91.9
2002	80.2	81.9	91.3	96.4	92.1
2003	81.2	83.4	88.7	96.2	92.1
2004	81.5	84.4	85.6	96.2	92.1
2005	77.4	86.7	82.1	96.7	92.3
2006	86.6	90.6	79.1	96.7	93.0
2007	95.4	93.7	75.8	98.6	94.5
2008	96.7	93.2	85.6	97.1	95.1
2009	97.4	94.6	101.1	98.0	97.7
2010	100.0	100.0	100.0	100.0	100.0
2011	106.9	102.8	102.2	101.4	101.9
2012	98.8	105.2	115.6	102.9	104.0
2013	114.7	105.7	118.2	104.4	105.6
2014	113.1	108.3	119.6	104.1	105.7
2015	110.0	112.1	111.2	104.0	105.7

Sources Please cite the database as: Leandro Prados de la Escosura (2017), Spanish Economic Growth, 1850–2015

Table S26 Hours worked per full-time equivalent occupied/year, 1850–2015

	Agriculture, forestry and fishing	Manufacturing, Extractive Industries, and Utilities	Construction	Service activities	Total
1850	2702	2881	2702	3120	2808
1851	2702	2850	2702	3120	2805
1852	2702	3111	2702	3120	2836
1853	2702	2724	2702	3120	2789
1854	2702	2650	2702	3120	2781
1855	2702	2546	2702	3120	2768
1856	2702	2931	2702	3120	2814
1857	2702	3021	2702	3120	2825
1858	2702	3060	2702	3120	2830
1859	2702	3029	2702	3120	2826
1860	2702	2914	2702	3120	2812
1861	2702	3073	2702	3120	2831
1862	2702	2876	2702	3120	2808
1863	2702	2964	2702	3120	2818
1864	2702	2876	2702	3120	2808
1865	2702	2895	2702	3120	2810
1866	2702	2748	2702	3120	2793
1867	2702	2852	2702	3120	2805
1868	2702	2759	2702	3120	2795
1869	2702	2736	2702	3120	2792
1870	2702	2630	2702	3120	2780
1871	2702	2877	2702	3085	2801
1872	2702	2835	2695	3078	2795
1873	2702	3145	2689	3072	2828
1874	2702	2820	2683	3065	2790
1875	2702	2759	2677	3059	2781
1876	2702	2630	2670	3053	2765
1877	2702	2741	2664	3046	2776
1878	2702	2637	2658	3041	2763
1879	2702	2649	2652	3036	2763
1880	2702	2763	2645	3031	2774
1881	2702	2975	2639	3025	2798
1882	2702	2984	2633	3020	2797
1883	2702	3005	2627	3015	2799
1884	2702	2795	2621	3010	2772
1885	2702	2828	2614	3005	2775
1886	2702	2592	2608	3000	2744
1887	2702	2614	2602	2995	2745

(continued)

Table S26 (continued)

	Agriculture, forestry and fishing	Manufacturing, Extractive Industries, and Utilities	Construction	Service activities	Total
1888	2702	2583	2596	2989	2740
1889	2702	2673	2590	2984	2750
1890	2702	2698	2584	2978	2753
1891	2702	2825	2578	2974	2768
1892	2702	2825	2572	2969	2767
1893	2702	2869	2566	2964	2772
1894	2702	2716	2560	2959	2751
1895	2702	2676	2554	2954	2745
1896	2702	2711	2548	2949	2749
1897	2702	2388	2542	2944	2707
1898	2702	2609	2536	2939	2734
1899	2702	2827	2530	2935	2761
1900	2729	2676	2530	2930	2758
1901	2729	2681	2530	2912	2755
1902	2729	2687	2530	2894	2752
1903	2729	2693	2530	2876	2749
1904	2729	2698	2530	2858	2745
1905	2729	2704	2530	2840	2742
1906	2729	2710	2530	2822	2739
1907	2729	2715	2530	2804	2736
1908	2729	2721	2530	2786	2733
1909	2729	2727	2530	2768	2729
1910	2729	2721	2530	2746	2723
1911	2735	2593	2524	2707	2699
1912	2742	2663	2518	2701	2711
1913	2750	2683	2513	2696	2717
1914	2757	2764	2507	2704	2734
1915	2764	2671	2501	2680	2718
1916	2772	2645	2496	2655	2712
1917	2779	2636	2490	2629	2708
1918	2787	2470	2484	2603	2678
1919	2795	2514	2478	2551	2676
1920	2802	2501	2473	2540	2674
1921	2791	2489	2467	2533	2662
1922	2780	2478	2462	2527	2650
1923	2770	2467	2456	2520	2638
1924	2759	2456	2450	2513	2626
1925	2748	2445	2445	2506	2614

(continued)

Table S26 (continued)

	Agriculture, forestry and fishing	Manufacturing, Extractive Industries, and Utilities	Construction	Service activities	Total
1926	2737	2434	2439	2498	2602
1927	2727	2424	2434	2490	2590
1928	2716	2414	2428	2482	2578
1929	2706	2404	2423	2474	2566
1930	2695	2394	2417	2466	2555
1931	2695	2384	2412	2452	2546
1932	2694	2375	2406	2434	2536
1933	2694	2365	2401	2417	2525
1934	2694	2356	2395	2400	2515
1935	2693	2347	2390	2383	2504
1936	2666	2337	2384	2367	2491
1937	2667	2337	2384	2361	2496
1938	2669	2337	2384	2355	2500
1939	2670	2336	2384	2350	2505
1940	2672	2336	2384	2344	2511
1941	2674	2336	2384	2343	2510
1942	2676	2336	2384	2341	2510
1943	2679	2336	2384	2339	2510
1944	2681	2336	2384	2337	2510
1945	2683	2336	2384	2335	2509
1946	2686	2336	2384	2333	2509
1947	2688	2336	2384	2331	2509
1948	2690	2336	2384	2328	2508
1949	2693	2336	2384	2326	2508
1950	2695	2336	2384	2323	2507
1951	2695	2336	2512	2288	2502
1952	2695	2335	2650	2253	2498
1953	2695	2334	2796	2218	2493
1954	2606	2035	3232	2500	2513
1955	2587	2048	3486	2396	2492
1956	2563	2067	3570	2342	2474
1957	2540	2076	3623	2301	2457
1958	2507	2094	3689	2266	2440
1959	2549	2086	3685	2180	2428
1960	2586	2051	3688	2126	2418
1961	2585	2038	3535	2123	2397
1962	2573	2054	3433	2103	2377
1963	2560	2057	3337	2095	2358

(continued)

Table S26 (continued)

	Agriculture, forestry and fishing	Manufacturing, Extractive Industries, and Utilities	Construction	Service activities	Total
1964	2256	2299	3061	2161	2306
1965	2240	2409	2718	2172	2298
1966	2252	2296	2964	2162	2299
1967	2262	2290	3041	2161	2309
1968	2217	2266	2885	2137	2266
1969	2209	2261	2903	2115	2257
1970	2222	2256	2892	2138	2266
1971	2235	2255	2906	2157	2278
1972	2223	2235	2823	2148	2256
1973	2221	2206	2796	2143	2243
1974	2199	2189	2747	2117	2218
1975	2164	2156	2697	2078	2179
1976	2128	2123	2648	2041	2142
1977	2093	2089	2583	2003	2105
1978	2057	2056	2531	1967	2065
1979	2022	2022	2481	1930	2024
1980	2003	2004	2479	1913	2005
1981	1968	1967	2539	1880	1975
1982	1946	1945	2509	1859	1952
1983	1912	1912	2485	1828	1918
1984	1865	1866	2544	1785	1875
1985	1855	1855	2547	1776	1864
1986	1847	1848	2485	1771	1855
1987	1838	1838	2402	1764	1843
1988	1835	1835	2331	1762	1837
1989	1822	1822	2248	1750	1821
1990	1824	1824	2210	1753	1820
1991	1832	1832	2209	1761	1828
1992	1824	1824	2255	1752	1821
1993	1815	1815	2303	1745	1815
1994	1815	1815	2295	1749	1815
1995	2132	1750	1860	1787	1812
1996	2106	1764	1868	1793	1817
1997	2112	1777	1890	1795	1823
1998	2139	1791	1899	1805	1834
1999	2129	1806	1905	1809	1839
2000	2110	1809	1901	1809	1837
2001	2108	1817	1934	1812	1844

(continued)

Table S26 (continued)

	Agriculture, forestry and fishing	Manufacturing, Extractive Industries, and Utilities	Construction	Service activities	Total
2002	2105	1824	1962	1811	1848
2003	2085	1829	1965	1810	1847
2004	2094	1835	1969	1811	1849
2005	2086	1829	1973	1805	1844
2006	2090	1831	1973	1803	1842
2007	2080	1829	1968	1788	1830
2008	2074	1843	1980	1802	1840
2009	2073	1845	1979	1813	1844
2010	2048	1865	1987	1821	1851
2011	2076	1874	2000	1829	1858
2012	2098	1872	1969	1833	1858
2013	2083	1875	1975	1842	1864
2014	2063	1888	1989	1841	1864
2015	2034	1892	2009	1836	1861

Sources Please cite the database as: Leandro Prados de la Escosura (2017), Spanish Economic Growth, 1850–2015

Table S27 Real per capita gross domestic product, 1850–2015 (EKS $2011)

	Spain	Italy	France	UK	USA	Germany
1850	2073	2733	2665	3402	2992	2728
1851	2091	2733	2616	3578	3114	2690
1852	2171	2664	2778	3622	3272	2725
1853	2171	2630	2633	3731	3496	2701
1854	2193	2459	2751	3800	3506	2758
1855	2299	2459	2699	3754	3429	2715
1856	2188	2494	2813	3986	3501	2927
1857	2118	2664	2969	4026	3424	3047
1858	2157	2767	3171	4004	3441	3008
1859	2263	2699	2960	4074	3534	2991
1860	2346	2699	3158	4132	3627	3133
1861	2348	2664	2953	4211	3552	3025
1862	2349	2699	3194	4205	3664	3144
1863	2381	2764	3293	4206	3900	3342
1864	2365	2768	3317	4286	4029	3402
1865	2266	2935	3211	4382	3820	3382
1866	2403	2930	3228	4414	3790	3385
1867	2366	2675	3026	4334	3915	3375
1868	2068	2730	3307	4434	3967	3557
1869	2140	2765	3349	4425	4072	3555
1870	2199	2833	3130	4658	3957	3515
1871	2368	2770	3170	4865	4051	3472
1872	2730	2708	3469	4846	4113	3691
1873	2950	2694	3208	4913	4215	3820
1874	2693	2834	3600	4945	4091	4059
1875	2768	2848	3704	5013	4206	4037

(continued)

Table S27 (continued)

	Spain	Italy	France	UK	USA	Germany
1876	2852	2779	3385	5008	4161	3957
1877	3162	2796	3551	5001	4201	3885
1878	3033	2866	3490	4968	4283	4019
1879	2816	2875	3260	4895	4709	3877
1880	3064	2919	3539	5077	5154	3806
1881	3085	3008	3661	5210	5205	3870
1882	3097	3045	3819	5319	5403	3907
1883	3140	3072	3818	5320	5404	4096
1884	3149	3026	3761	5288	5374	4163
1885	3031	3070	3684	5218	5293	4235
1886	2960	3138	3733	5256	5332	4226
1887	2895	3217	3754	5422	5452	4348
1888	3009	3200	3788	5620	5312	4473
1889	3001	3103	3876	5875	5525	4547
1890	2994	3105	3965	5853	5490	4640
1891	3050	3146	4059	5804	5612	4580
1892	3307	3150	4160	5616	6034	4719
1893	3164	3199	4231	5564	5630	4903
1894	3200	3217	4383	5883	5364	4964
1895	3146	3243	4288	6012	5899	5133
1896	2834	3292	4482	6203	5673	5236
1897	3001	3297	4405	6225	6102	5302
1898	3194	3284	4606	6465	6118	5442
1899	3204	3320	4859	6668	6558	5552
1900	3253	3408	4799	6558	6622	5704
1901	3507	3464	4717	6498	7226	5487

(continued)

Table S27 (continued)

	Spain	Italy	France	UK	USA	Germany
1902	3330	3519	4632	6607	7156	5530
1903	3297	3551	4724	6482	7366	5749
1904	3234	3613	4751	6465	7138	5893
1905	3187	3687	4830	6600	7514	5932
1906	3373	3812	4912	6762	8221	6024
1907	3437	3880	5124	6831	8198	6201
1908	3545	3962	5082	6496	7382	6219
1909	3620	3993	5285	6586	8122	6258
1910	3431	3997	4949	6732	8035	6398
1911	3680	4041	5423	6875	8167	6514
1912	3543	4045	5866	6953	8418	6734
1913	3728	4235	5816	7184	8580	6972
1914	3600	4004	5401	7193	7768	5847
1915	3613	3803	5421	7721	7874	5540
1916	3740	4116	5780	7862	8836	5608
1917	3664	4129	4972	7915	8494	5642
1918	3622	4025	3998	7971	9160	5701
1919	3677	3864	4692	7111	9195	4943
1920	3943	3956	5386	6640	8987	5343
1921	4038	3821	5131	6482	8616	5882
1922	4166	4100	6026	6770	8967	6366
1923	4173	4435	6264	6950	9978	5255
1924	4277	4514	6975	7185	10088	6113
1925	4528	4782	6953	7511	10169	6749
1926	4437	4778	7092	7207	10687	6889
1927	4813	4650	6933	7760	10645	7532

(continued)

Table S27 (continued)

	Spain	Italy	France	UK	USA	Germany
1928	4749	4899	7396	7822	10634	7816
1929	5074	5104	7861	8035	11167	7743
1930	4769	4834	7563	7944	10056	7593
1931	4603	4739	7068	7503	9212	6978
1932	4687	4805	6608	7517	7945	6424
1933	4486	4713	7075	7706	7732	6795
1934	4598	4663	6996	8187	8277	7373
1935	4628	4877	6819	8467	8849	7873
1936	3496	4668	7083	8812	10042	8506
1937	3225	5094	7488	9078	10408	8953
1938	3204	5200	7454	9150	9917	9543
1939	3507	5477	8000	9144	10620	10332
1940	3855	5323	6746	10010	11346	10325
1941	3879	5186	5523	10924	13282	10914
1942	4125	4866	4976	11153	15768	10969
1943	4317	4105	4773	11307	18644	11256
1944	4468	3302	4042	10813	19964	11626
1945	4081	2956	4294	10303	18952	8627
1946	4221	3972	6434	9849	14886	4237
1947	4271	4696	6906	9643	14384	4656
1948	4228	5026	7332	9849	14673	5415
1949	4176	5417	8255	10156	14477	6273
1950	4210	5828	8655	10132	15477	7417
1951	4608	6340	9114	10401	16375	8038
1952	4989	6594	9286	10353	16697	8700
1953	4944	7029	9486	10726	17178	9374

(continued)

Table S27 (continued)

	Spain	Italy	France	UK	USA	Germany
1954	5260	7242	9872	11125	16768	10027
1955	5400	7685	10345	11488	17638	11078
1956	5798	8011	10762	11577	17667	11804
1957	5956	8418	11285	11706	17676	12407
1958	6291	8841	11441	11631	17207	12874
1959	6182	9406	11647	12031	18178	13715
1960	6123	10004	12346	12623	18337	14725
1961	6792	10729	12882	12932	18456	15197
1962	7394	11374	13464	12944	19270	15713
1963	8070	11977	13957	13359	19816	16025
1964	8443	12336	14719	13970	20675	16860
1965	9019	12775	15297	14238	21720	17555
1966	9580	13520	15929	14433	22878	17940
1967	9986	14454	16535	14672	23196	17958
1968	10462	15400	17135	15200	24058	18852
1969	11314	16308	18167	15406	24570	19952
1970	11561	17196	19043	15722	24328	20714
1971	12026	17420	19769	15976	24773	21169
1972	13123	17986	20467	16490	25808	21941
1973	14147	19132	21403	17558	27015	22869
1974	15060	20054	21884	17315	26694	23053
1975	15343	19505	21625	17298	26358	23010
1976	15866	20784	22475	17689	27477	24240
1977	16217	21217	23220	18081	28434	24981
1978	16499	21820	23766	18730	29740	25714
1979	16630	23045	24424	19225	30414	26742

(continued)

Table S27 (continued)

	Spain	Italy	France	UK	USA	Germany
1980	17028	23776	24644	18881	30071	26973
1981	16891	23938	24767	18612	30521	27039
1982	17073	24018	25254	18915	29662	26831
1983	17308	24282	25443	19572	30626	27383
1984	17392	25064	25672	20033	32572	28252
1985	17857	25755	25919	20682	33535	28933
1986	18522	26487	26425	21524	34374	29562
1987	19776	27334	26967	22476	35267	30006
1988	20996	28473	28021	23522	36419	30883
1989	22318	29417	28872	23966	37325	31644
1990	23358	29997	29452	23989	37554	30441
1991	24067	30431	29581	23588	36959	31818
1992	24320	30650	29840	23556	37691	32279
1993	23801	30352	29484	24031	38266	31809
1994	24339	30994	30005	24994	39354	32541
1995	25135	31869	30478	25677	39880	33059
1996	25703	32218	30664	26346	40893	33291
1997	26564	32803	31193	27910	42206	33842
1998	27688	33246	32099	28799	43532	34455
1999	28898	33730	32997	29595	45112	35126
2000	30290	34967	34033	30729	46459	36202
2001	31337	35579	34460	31490	46498	36610
2002	31749	35720	34580	32134	46904	36579
2003	32174	35510	34696	33236	47684	36478
2004	32695	35701	35371	34030	48884	36853
2005	33294	35582	35799	34765	49923	37107

(continued)

Table S27 (continued)

	Spain	Italy	France	UK	USA	Germany
2006	34121	36128	36452	35459	50758	38299
2007	34728	36428	37054	36505	51239	39267
2008	34565	35652	36813	35921	50586	39753
2009	33064	33552	35455	34297	48396	37820
2010	32921	33821	35845	34717	49355	39486
2011	32467	33870	36391	35091	49782	40990
2012	31443	32800	36327	35127	50560	41228
2013	30999	32127	36253	35516	51270	41352
2014	31557	31890	36221	36318	52091	42094
2015	32629	32023	36349	36990	52853	42843

Sources Please cite the database as: Leandro Prados de la Escosura (2017), Spanish Economic Growth, 1850–2015. Spain, see the text; Italy, Baffigy (2011) completed with Conference Board for 2011–2015; France, UK, USA, and Germany, Maddison Project completed with Conference Board for 2011–2015

Table S28 Real per capita gross domestic product, 1850–2015 (Geary-Khamis $1990)

	Spain	Italy	France	UK	USA	Germany
1850	1155	1577	1597	2330	1849	1428
1851	1165	1577	1568	2451	1924	1408
1852	1210	1537	1664	2480	2022	1426
1853	1210	1517	1578	2555	2160	1413
1854	1222	1419	1648	2602	2166	1443
1855	1281	1419	1617	2571	2118	1420
1856	1219	1439	1686	2730	2163	1531
1857	1180	1537	1779	2757	2115	1594
1858	1202	1596	1900	2742	2126	1574
1859	1261	1557	1774	2790	2183	1565
1860	1307	1557	1892	2830	2241	1639
1861	1309	1537	1769	2884	2195	1583
1862	1309	1557	1914	2880	2263	1645
1863	1327	1595	1973	2881	2410	1749
1864	1318	1597	1988	2935	2489	1780
1865	1263	1693	1924	3001	2360	1770
1866	1339	1690	1934	3023	2342	1771
1867	1318	1543	1813	2968	2419	1766
1868	1152	1575	1982	3037	2451	1861
1869	1192	1595	2006	3031	2516	1860
1870	1225	1634	1876	3190	2445	1839
1871	1319	1598	1899	3332	2503	1817
1872	1521	1562	2078	3319	2541	1931
1873	1644	1554	1922	3365	2604	1999
1874	1501	1635	2157	3386	2527	2124
1875	1542	1643	2219	3434	2599	2112

(continued)

364 Appendices

Table S28 (continued)

	Spain	Italy	France	UK	USA	Germany
1876	1589	1603	2028	3430	2570	2071
1877	1762	1613	2127	3425	2595	2033
1878	1690	1654	2091	3403	2646	2103
1879	1569	1658	1953	3353	2909	2029
1880	1707	1684	2120	3477	3184	1991
1881	1719	1735	2194	3568	3215	2025
1882	1726	1756	2288	3643	3338	2044
1883	1750	1772	2288	3643	3339	2143
1884	1755	1746	2253	3622	3320	2178
1885	1689	1771	2207	3574	3270	2216
1886	1649	1810	2237	3600	3294	2211
1887	1613	1856	2249	3713	3368	2275
1888	1677	1846	2269	3849	3282	2341
1889	1672	1790	2322	4024	3413	2379
1890	1668	1791	2376	4009	3392	2428
1891	1700	1815	2432	3975	3467	2397
1892	1842	1817	2493	3846	3728	2469
1893	1763	1846	2535	3811	3478	2565
1894	1783	1856	2626	4029	3314	2598
1895	1753	1871	2569	4118	3644	2686
1896	1579	1899	2685	4249	3504	2740
1897	1672	1902	2639	4264	3769	2775
1898	1780	1894	2760	4428	3780	2848
1899	1785	1916	2911	4567	4051	2905
1900	1812	1966	2876	4492	4091	2985
1901	1954	1998	2826	4450	4464	2871

(continued)

Table S28 (continued)

	Spain	Italy	France	UK	USA	Germany
1902	1856	2030	2775	4525	4421	2893
1903	1837	2048	2831	4440	4551	3008
1904	1802	2084	2847	4428	4410	3083
1905	1776	2127	2894	4520	4642	3104
1906	1879	2199	2943	4631	5079	3152
1907	1915	2238	3070	4679	5065	3245
1908	1975	2286	3045	4449	4561	3254
1909	2017	2304	3167	4511	5017	3275
1910	1912	2306	2965	4611	4964	3348
1911	2051	2331	3250	4709	5046	3408
1912	1974	2334	3514	4762	5201	3524
1913	2078	2443	3485	4921	5301	3648
1914	2006	2310	3236	4927	4799	3059
1915	2013	2194	3248	5288	4864	2899
1916	2084	2375	3463	5384	5459	2935
1917	2041	2382	2979	5421	5248	2952
1918	2018	2322	2396	5459	5659	2983
1919	2049	2229	2811	4870	5680	2586
1920	2197	2282	3227	4548	5552	2796
1921	2250	2204	3075	4439	5323	3078
1922	2322	2365	3610	4637	5540	3331
1923	2325	2559	3754	4760	6164	2750
1924	2383	2604	4179	4921	6233	3199
1925	2523	2759	4166	5144	6282	3532
1926	2472	2756	4249	4936	6602	3605
1927	2682	2683	4154	5315	6576	3941

(continued)

Table S28 (continued)

	Spain	Italy	France	UK	USA	Germany
1928	2646	2826	4431	5357	6569	4090
1929	2827	2945	4710	5503	6899	4051
1930	2657	2789	4532	5441	6213	3973
1931	2565	2734	4235	5138	5691	3652
1932	2612	2772	3959	5148	4908	3362
1933	2500	2719	4239	5277	4777	3556
1934	2562	2690	4192	5608	5114	3858
1935	2579	2813	4086	5799	5467	4120
1936	1948	2693	4244	6035	6204	4451
1937	1797	2939	4487	6218	6430	4685
1938	1785	3000	4466	6266	6126	4994
1939	1954	3160	4793	6262	6561	5406
1940	2148	3071	4042	6856	7010	5403
1941	2162	2992	3309	7482	8206	5711
1942	2298	2807	2981	7639	9741	5740
1943	2405	2368	2860	7744	11518	5890
1944	2490	1905	2422	7405	12333	6084
1945	2274	1705	2573	7056	11709	4514
1946	2352	2291	3855	6745	9197	2217
1947	2380	2709	4138	6604	8886	2436
1948	2356	2899	4393	6746	9065	2834
1949	2327	3125	4946	6956	8944	3282
1950	2346	3362	5186	6939	9561	3881
1951	2568	3658	5461	7123	10116	4206
1952	2780	3804	5564	7091	10316	4553
1953	2755	4055	5684	7346	10613	4905

(continued)

Table S28 (continued)

	Spain	Italy	France	UK	USA	Germany
1954	2931	4178	5915	7619	10359	5247
1955	3009	4434	6199	7868	10897	5797
1956	3231	4622	6448	7929	10914	6177
1957	3319	4857	6762	8017	10920	6492
1958	3506	5100	6855	7966	10631	6737
1959	3445	5427	6979	8240	11230	7177
1960	3412	5771	7398	8645	11328	7705
1961	3785	6190	7718	8857	11402	7952
1962	4120	6562	8067	8865	11905	8222
1963	4497	6910	8363	9149	12242	8386
1964	4705	7117	8819	9568	12773	8822
1965	5026	7370	9165	9752	13419	9186
1966	5338	7800	9544	9885	14134	9388
1967	5564	8339	9907	10049	14330	9397
1968	5830	8884	10267	10410	14863	9864
1969	6304	9408	10886	10552	15179	10440
1970	6442	9921	11410	10767	15030	10839
1971	6701	10050	11845	10941	15304	11077
1972	7312	10376	12264	11294	15944	11481
1973	7883	11037	12824	12025	16689	11966
1974	8392	11569	13113	11859	16491	12063
1975	8549	11253	12957	11847	16284	12041
1976	8841	11990	13466	12115	16975	12684
1977	9037	12240	13913	12384	17567	13072
1978	9193	12588	14240	12828	18373	13455
1979	9267	13295	14634	13167	18789	13993

(continued)

368 Appendices

Table S28 (continued)

	Spain	Italy	France	UK	USA	Germany
1980	9488	13717	14766	12931	18577	14114
1981	9412	13810	14840	12747	18856	14149
1982	9514	13856	15132	12955	18325	14040
1983	9644	14009	15245	13404	18920	14329
1984	9691	14460	15382	13720	20123	14783
1985	9950	14858	15530	14165	20717	15140
1986	10321	15281	15833	14742	21236	15469
1987	11019	15769	16158	15393	21788	15701
1988	11699	16427	16790	16110	22499	16160
1989	12436	16971	17300	16414	23059	16558
1990	13015	17306	17647	16430	23201	15929
1991	13411	17556	17724	16155	22833	16650
1992	13551	17683	17880	16133	23285	16891
1993	13262	17511	17666	16458	23640	16645
1994	13562	17881	17978	17118	24313	17028
1995	14006	18386	18262	17586	24637	17299
1996	14322	18587	18373	18044	25263	17420
1997	14802	18924	18690	19115	26074	17709
1998	15428	19180	19233	19724	26893	18029
1999	16102	19459	19771	20269	27870	18380
2000	16878	20173	20392	21046	28702	18944
2001	17462	20526	20648	21567	28726	19157
2002	17691	20607	20720	22008	28977	19140
2003	17928	20486	20789	22763	29459	19088
2004	18218	20596	21193	23307	30200	19284
2005	18552	20528	21450	23810	30842	19417

(continued)

Table S28 (continued)

	Spain	Italy	France	UK	USA	Germany
2006	19013	20843	21842	24285	31358	20041
2007	19351	21016	22202	25002	31655	20547
2008	19260	20568	22057	24602	31251	20801
2009	18424	19357	21244	23489	29899	19790
2010	18344	19511	21477	23777	30491	20661
2011	18091	19540	21805	24033	30755	21449
2012	17521	18923	21766	24058	31235	21573
2013	17273	18534	21722	24324	31674	21638
2014	17584	18398	21703	24874	32181	22026
2015	18181	18474	21779	25334	32652	22418

Sources Please cite the database as: Leandro Prados de la Escosura (2017), Spanish Economic Growth, 1850–2015. Spain, see the text; Italy, Baffigy (2011) completed with Conference Board for 2011–2015; France, UK, USA, and Germany, Maddison Project completed with Conference Board for 2011–2015

Author Index

A

Acemoglu, D., 55
Alcaide Inchausti, J., 156, 159–161, 163
Almarcha, A., 88, 93, 99, 100
Alonso Alvarez, L., 133
Altinok, N., 55
Álvarez-Nogal, C., 45
Anand, S., 55
Andrews, D.,
Annual Statement Of Trade and Navigation, 136
Antolín, F., 94
Anuario(s) Estadístico(s) de España, 90
Arenales, M.C., 90, 91, 94
Ark, B. van, 184
Arrow, K.J., 184
Artola, M.,

B

Bacon, R., 161
Baffigi, A., 133, 142
Baiges, J.,
Bairoch, P., 161, 198
Bakker, G. den, 182
Balke, N.S., 86, 164
Ballesteros, E., 86, 90, 99, 140
Banco Central, 135, 137
Banco Urquijo, 130, 143, 162
Barciela López, C., 69, 88, 90, 91, 94, 134
Bardini, C., 164
Batista D., 93, 98, 142
Becker, G.S., 55
Beckerman, W., 112, 161
Bolt, J., 21
Bonhome L., 77, 95
Bordo, M.D., 18

Boskin, M.J., 182
Broadberry, S.N., 32, 37, 38, 164
Broder, A., 131, 143, 144
Bustinza, P., 77, 95

C

Caballero, F., 196
Cairncross, A.K., 95, 138
Calvo, A., 98
Calvo González, O., 20
Carreras, A., 69, 72–75, 88, 90–95, 98, 133, 135–137, 158–161, 164
Cassing, S., 162, 183
Castañeda, J., 163
Catalan, J., 23, 108
Chamorro, S., 142
Chenery, H.B., 9
Coll, S., 93, 94, 97
Comin, F., vii, 4, 79, 88, 90, 93, 96, 99, 116, 134
Comisaria del Plan de Desarrollo Economico y Social, 155
Consejo de Economia Nacional (CEN), 153, 154
Consejo Superior de la Emigración Española, 141
Cordero, R., 93, 136
Corrales, A., 86, 90, 171, 182, 185
Cortes-Conde, R., 98
Coyle, D., 54
Crafts, N.F.R., 161
Cucarella, V., 78, 182

D

David, P.A., 92, 183, 184
Deane, P., 132, 161
de la Fuente, A., 171, 181
Della Paolera, G., 143
Demeulemeester, J.L., 55
Deng, K., xxi
Diebolt, C.R., 55
Doménech Felíu, J., 198
Domínguez Martín, R., 89
Drelichman, M., 10

E

Edwards, S., 21
Engerman, S.L., xx
Eng, P. van der, 98, 142
Erdozáin Azpilicueta, P., 197
Escribano, A., 18
Escudero, A., 93, 94, 144
Estadística(s) de Comercio Exterior, 90, 137
Estadística(s) de fletes y seguros, 97
Eurostat, 51

F

Federico, G., 89
Feenstra, R.C.,
Feinstein, C.H., 77, 93, 122, 124, 132, 134–138, 145
Fenoaltea, S., 88, 92, 94, 183
Fernández Acha, 143
Fernández Fúster, L., 140

Fischer, S., 21
Fitoussi, L.P., xix
Flaxman, A.D., 55
Flores de Lemus, A., 89, 90
Forsyth, P.J., 10
Fraile Balbín, P., 18
Frax, E., 97, 99, 144
Freeman, M.K., 55
Fremdling, R., 92
Fuentes Quintana, E., 162
Fundación BBV, 96, 163

G

Gallego, D., 89, 91, 133, 134
Gandoy Juste, R., 92, 175–177, 184
Garcia Barbancho, A., 133, 164
García Delgado, J.L., 21
García López, J.R., 129, 142
García Sanz, A., 89, 90, 198
Garrués Irurzun, J., 94
General de la Emigración,
Giraldez, J., 91
Gomez Mendoza, A., 78, 79, 81, 82, 90, 91, 93, 95, 97, 98, 133, 135, 136, 138, 144, 197, 198
Gómez Villegas, J., 176, 184
Gordon, R.J., 86, 164
Grupo de Estudios de Historia Rural (GEHR), 66, 69, 87–91, 134
Guerreiro, A., 162

H

Hansen, B., 184
Hanushek, E.A., 55
Harley, C.K., 92

Hemberg, P., 91, 162
Heston, A., 86, 87, 92, 99, 126, 132, 139, 142
Higgs, R., xx
Hoffmann, W.G., 92
Holtfrerich, C.L., 92
Horlings, E., 133
Huberman, M., 196

I

Informacion Comercial Española, 157
Inklaar, R.,
Instituto de Estudios de Transportes y Comunicaciones, 97
Instituto de Estudios Fiscales, 86, 128, 193
Instituto Nacional de Estadística (INE), 189
Isserlis, L., 97
Ivanov, A., xx

J

Jáinaga, F., 127, 129, 131, 140, 142
Jefferys, J.B., 124, 132
Jerven, M., xxii
Johnson, S., 55
Jones, C.I., xx

K

Kakwani, N., 55
Kimko, D.D., 55
Kindleberger, C.P., 37
Klenow, P.J., xx

Krantz, O., 96, 98, 99, 184
Krugman, P., 50
Kuznets, S., xx, xxi

L

League Of Nations,
Lewis, W.A., 92, 93, 95, 98, 100, 138
Lindert, P.H., 55
Llordén, M., 128, 140, 141
Lluch, C., 164
Lopez, A.D., 55
López Carrillo, J.M., 97, 137
López García, S.M., 21

M

Maddison, A., 87, 96, 161, 183
Maddison project, 19, 21, 41, 45
Maluquer de Motes Bernet, J., 86, 93, 116, 133, 185, 189, 190, 196
Marolla, M., 140
Martin Aceña, P., 18, 99, 143
Martínez-Galarraga, J.,
Martínez Ruiz, E., 97, 125, 129, 138, 139
Martín Rodríguez, M., 90, 94, 133
Martins, C., 93, 98, 142
Masood, E., xix
Matilla, M.J., 99, 144
Matthews, R.C.O., 37
Melvin, J.R., 96
Menéndez, F., 93, 136

Miguel, A. de, 92
Mikelarena Peña, F., 197
Milanovic, B., 52
Ministerio de Agricultura, 66, 69, 86–88, 90, 91
Ministerio de Trabajo, 90, 94, 140–142, 196
Mitchell, B.R., 89, 98, 99, 144
Mohr, M.F., 184
Molto, M.L., 142, 182
Morales, R., 142
Morella, E., 75, 93, 94
Muñoz, J., 143, 144
Muñoz Rubio, M., 78, 81, 97, 136
Mulhall, M.G., 161, 162
Murray, C.J.L., 55

N

Nadal, J., 144
Naredo, J.M., 157, 160, 161, 163, 164
Nicholas, S.J., 10
Nicolau, R., 140, 189, 197, 198
Nordhaus, W.D., 50
North, D.C., 97, 126, 139
Núñez, C.E., 20, 99

O

O'Brien, P.K., vii
Odling-Smee, J.C., 37
OECD, 117, 155, 169, 171, 175, 196
Ojeda, A. de, 99, 115, 140

Organización Sindical Española,
Ortega, J.A., 20, 190
Oulton, N., xx

P

Parejo Barranco, A., 88
Paris Eguilaz, H., 90, 94
Peleah, M., xx
Pérez Moreda, V., 190, 197
Philipsen, D., xix
Philipson, T.J., 55
Pinheiro, M., 93, 98, 142
Pinilla, V., 88, 133
Piqueras, J., 90
Pla Brugat, D., 21
Pons, M.A., 143
Prados de la Escosura, L., 9, 12, 18, 20, 39, 45, 51, 56, 57, 80, 88, 92, 94, 97, 121, 125, 127, 132, 133, 138, 139, 141, 144, 161, 171, 175, 181, 183, 185, 196, 198
Pujol, J., 91

R

Reher, D.S., 86, 90, 99, 140, 198
Reis, J., 93, 98, 142
Rey, G.M., 162
Roccas, M., 140
Rockoff, H., 18
Roldán, S., 21, 144
Rooijen, R. van, 182

Rosés, J.R., 20, 92, 132, 175, 196

S

Salomon, J.A., 55
Sánchez Alonso, B., 18, 127, 141, 190
Sanchez-Albornoz, N., 90
Sanz-Villarroya, I., 20
Sardá, J., 86, 99, 141, 143
Schwartz, P., 98, 138, 142, 154, 158, 161, 162
Sen, A.K., 52–55
Serrano, A., 144
Shleifer, A., 23
Silvestre, J., 20, 190, 196
Simon, M., 126, 139, 140, 145
Simpson, J., 66, 69, 86–90, 198
Sims, C.A., 184
Smits, J.P., 98, 133, 138, 139
Soares, R.R., 55
Srinivasan, T.N., xxii
Stiglitz, J., 51
Sündbarg, G., 189, 190
Syrquin, M., 9

T

Tafunell, X., 94, 95
Taguas, D., 86, 90, 171, 182, 185
Tedde de Lorca, P., 130, 131, 143
Tena Junguito, A., 18, 125, 138–140, 142
Tobin, J., 50

Tortella, G., 99, 139, 163

U

United Nations Development Program (UNDP), 54, 55
Uriel, E., 142, 170, 181, 182, 185
Uriol Salcedo, J.I., 79

V

Valdaliso, J.M., 97, 126, 136, 139
Vandellos, J.A., 198
Vazquez, A., 128, 140–142
Velarde Fuertes, J., 19, 140, 142
Vilar, J.B., 141
Vitali, O., 133
Vos, T., 55

W

Walters, D., 124, 132
Wang, H., 55
Williamson, J.G., 142
World bank, 45

Y

Yáñez Gallardo, C., 141, 142
Young, A., 50

Z

Zanden, J.L. van, 21, 133

Subject Index

A

Agricultural census, 77
Agricultural final output, 65, 66, 69, 87, 90, 92
Agricultural volume indices, 70
Agriculture, 8, 10, 11, 13, 30, 32, 33, 64, 68, 70, 71, 85–87, 89–91, 93, 98, 111, 113, 124, 154–157, 163, 164, 176, 184, 194–198
Air transport, 83, 98

B

Backwardness, 19
Balance of payments, 125, 142, 145
Banco de España, 00
Bank deposits, 99
Banking, 84, 155
Banking and insurance, 81, 84

Base year, 64, 65, 72, 153, 162, 171, 182, 183
Basic prices, 181
Buildings, 95, 116–120, 124, 134, 135, 137, 138

C

Capital, 6, 8, 12, 18, 20, 21, 47, 94, 113, 117–124, 129–131, 134–137, 143, 144, 177
Capital formation, 6, 8, 117–120, 122–124, 128, 135, 138, 156, 176, 177
Capital goods, 19, 47, 73, 118, 159
Cereals, 67–69, 113
Civil war, 3, 4, 6, 9, 11, 12, 15, 19–21, 41, 42, 44, 50, 52, 53, 56, 69, 88, 91, 96, 99, 131, 134, 139, 142, 143, 154, 155, 157, 160, 190

Subject Index

Clothing, 112, 114, 158, 164, 197
Coal, 94, 97, 114, 126, 139
Commercialization, 67, 68, 88
Communications, 83, 115, 118, 120, 125, 155
Constant prices, 70, 73, 82, 128, 155, 156, 175, 179, 184
Construction, 7, 9, 27, 28, 47, 64, 65, 67, 73–81, 85, 88, 92, 94–96, 112, 117, 118, 119, 120, 122, 124, 131, 133–135, 139, 156–158, 162, 164, 170, 175–177, 184, 194–196
Consumer price index (CPI), 116, 164, 185
Consumption goods, 164
Consumption of goods and services, 111, 112
Cost of living, 84, 85, 99, 115, 117, 127, 134, 140, 156, 163
Crops, 65, 67, 68, 86, 90, 154
Cuba, 18, 128, 140, 142
Current prices, 64, 66, 69–71, 79, 80, 83–85, 117, 123, 124, 135, 136, 156, 157

D

Deflation, 65, 141, 177, 183, 184
Deflator, 64, 70, 71, 76–80, 83–87, 94–96, 99, 118–123, 128, 133, 134, 136, 145, 156, 164, 175, 179, 185
Demand, 3, 20, 37, 67, 69, 89, 111, 112, 118, 124, 128, 157, 159, 163, 164
Dependency rate, 37
Depreciation, 18, 47, 99, 130

Distribution, 11, 12, 51, 54, 57, 68, 83, 98, 128
Dividends, 129, 130, 143
Domestic trade, 111, 128
Double deflation, 162, 177, 184
Drink, 00
Dwellings, 77, 78, 84, 94, 95, 112, 114, 118, 123, 124, 134, 138, 156

E

Education, 55, 56, 81, 84, 99, 100, 112, 115
EKS $2011, 356
Electricity, 76, 94, 114, 119, 131, 135, 137, 143, 162
Emigrants, 127–129, 132, 141, 142, 145, 189
Emigration, 127, 128, 140, 142, 190
Employment, 10, 30, 32, 34, 81, 99, 115, 157, 163, 193–195, 198
Equipment, 74, 118, 122, 123, 138, 158
Exchange rate, 122, 129, 138
Exports, 7, 8, 71, 82, 89, 111, 125, 126, 128, 133, 139, 144, 156, 165
Exports of goods and services, 111, 125, 128
Extractive industries, 8, 64, 72, 76, 94

F

Fertilizers, 70, 91, 134
Finance, 99, 112, 115
Fiscal policy, 21

Subject Index 379

Fisher, 92
Fishing, 64, 71, 83, 91, 157, 164, 194
Foodstuffs, 112, 113, 133
Foreign trade, 18, 125, 126, 129
Forestry, 64, 70, 71, 91, 164, 194
Freight, 82, 97, 125, 126, 138, 139

G

Gas, 76, 94, 114, 119, 131
GDP at market prices, 64, 85, 86, 124, 156, 172, 176, 177, 184
GDP per head, 15, 18, 19, 21, 25, 27, 39, 40, 42–45, 47, 50, 53, 56, 57
Geary Khamis $1990, 363
General price index, 65
Gini coefficient, 51, 57
Gold standard, 18, 86, 139
Government, 18, 21, 78, 79, 84, 96, 99, 112, 116, 117, 119, 134, 156, 163, 164
Government consumption, 4, 49, 116, 117, 164
Great Depression, 19, 160
Great Recession, 3, 6, 9, 11, 15, 21, 27, 37, 42, 53, 180
Gross domestic capital formation, 118
Gross domestic fixed capital formation, 6, 117, 123, 124
Gross domestic product at market prices, 128, 132
Gross National Income, 3, 129, 132
Gross Value Added (GVA) per Hour Worked, 28

Gross Value Added, 11, 28, 63–65, 70, 71, 76–78, 80, 85, 86
Growth, 3, 8, 12, 18, 41, 44, 171, 175, 178, 180, 181, 183
Guerreiro, A., 162

H

Health, 54, 55, 84, 100, 115
Heating, 112, 114
Historical index of human development (HIHD), 55, 56
Hours worked per full-time equivalent occupied, 351
Hours worked, 10, 11, 25, 27, 28, 33, 34, 37, 193, 196
Hours worked per head, 34
Human Development, 54
Human development, 55
Hybrid linear interpolation, 179–181

I

II Republic, 52
Imports, 7, 8, 68, 82, 83, 89, 91, 97, 111, 113, 118, 122, 123, 125, 126, 128, 133, 138, 156, 165
Imports of goods and services, 124, 125, 128
Income distribution, 50–52
Income Inequality, xx, 51
Independence, 18
Industrial, 11, 73, 77, 92, 95, 154, 175, 184, 197
Industrial census, 11
Industrialization, 6, 12, 20, 35, 194
Industrial vehicles, 137

Subject Index

Industry, 8, 9, 11, 12, 30, 37, 64, 72, 73, 75, 77, 78, 80, 85, 94, 113, 123, 134, 154, 158, 160, 161, 163, 164, 175–177, 193, 195, 196
Inequality, 51, 52, 57
Inequality Extraction Ratio, 52
Input–output table, 63, 72, 84, 94, 96, 99, 114, 123, 137, 138, 158, 164, 182
Interest rate, 99, 130, 143
Interpolation, 43, 45, 78, 173, 174, 178–180, 193, 196
Interpolation Splicing, 178
Investmen in capital goods, 120
Investment in machinery, 123
Investment in trasport material, 123

L

Labour productivity, 11, 12, 25, 27, 99, 100, 163
Land transportation, 133
Laspeyres index, 133
Leisure, 81, 85, 100, 115
Life expectancy, 54, 55
Literacy, 55
Livestock, 65, 68, 69, 89, 90, 124, 154, 164, 198

M

Machinery, 6, 47, 118, 120, 122–124, 135, 156, 158
Manufacturing, 8, 34, 64, 72, 73, 75, 76, 79, 83, 92, 94, 124, 154, 184
Market prices, 64, 81, 144, 176

Merchant shipping, 121
Modified shift-share, 32
Monetary policy, 18, 126

N

National Accounts, 39, 43, 64, 71, 86, 94, 112, 114, 132, 142, 154, 157, 162, 171, 175, 180, 182, 185
Net exports of goods and services, 111, 126, 156, 177
Net National Disposable Income, 47, 52, 132, 142
Net National Income, 132
Non-residential construction, 6, 79, 80, 95, 96, 134
Non-residential investment, 124, 138, 156

O

Occupied, 114, 193, 196, 198
OECD, xix, 117, 155, 169, 171, 175, 196
Openness, 7, 18
Output, 25, 28, 32, 34, 63–65, 67–72, 76, 78, 79, 81, 82, 88, 90, 113, 120, 124, 133, 135, 164, 175, 184
Ownerhip of dwellings, 81, 84

P

Paasche, 65, 75
Per Capita GDP (GDP per head), 16, 19, 20, 27, 47, 49, 57
Per capita GDP, 43

Subject Index   381

Per hour worked, 34
Peseta, 18
Population, 15, 17, 50, 89, 189, 191, 194, 198
Population censuses, 100, 141, 162, 194, 197
Post, 7, 11
post, 7, 9, 11, 12, 18–20, 37, 40, 45, 50, 51, 56, 57, 68, 80, 88, 92, 94, 97, 98, 121, 124, 125, 127, 132, 133, 138, 139, 141, 144, 155, 160–164, 175, 178, 181, 183, 185, 196
Private consumption, 4, 19, 50, 111–114, 128
Productivity, 12, 27, 29, 30, 32
Public administration, 81, 84, 112, 156
Public consumption (government consumption), 112, 117, 134
Public investment, 156
Public works, 77, 79, 96, 158
Purchasing power parity, 39, 45

R

Railways, 78, 88, 119, 131, 143
Railways construction, 4
Raw materials, 19, 66, 67, 69, 76, 117, 175
Real per capita GDP, 28, 40, 42, 43, 45
Real per capita GDP and private consumption, 50
Real per capita NNDI, 51, 53
Relative labour productivity, 11
Rents, 114, 117
Residential and commercial construction, 78, 119
Residential investment, 156

Retropolation, 43, 44, 170, 173, 174, 185
Retropolation splicing, 45, 180
Roads, 79, 119
Rural dwellings, 95

S

Savings, 18, 84, 175
Schooling, 55, 84
Sea transport, 82, 98
Sen Welfare, 49, 52, 53, 54
Services, 8–10, 12, 27, 30, 50, 64, 70, 81, 83, 85, 95, 98, 99, 112, 114, 115, 125, 133, 154, 155, 158, 163, 164, 173, 184, 194, 196
Shift-share, 30, 32, 33
Shift-share analysis, 30, 33
Single deflation, 92, 175, 183, 184
Splicing, 43
Splicing national accounts, 44, 45, 179, 180
Standard of living, 54
State, 4, 121
Structural change, 9, 11, 28, 30, 33, 37, 171
Subsidies, 64, 86, 156, 176
Supply, 37, 94, 122, 135, 198

T

Tariff, 18, 19
Taxes, 64, 86, 156, 163, 176
Telegraph, 81, 83, 98
Telephone, 81, 83, 98, 119, 123, 137
Tobacco, 73, 75, 94, 112, 113, 133, 158
Tourism, 127, 140, 156
Transfers, 132, 142

Transport and communications, 81, 112, 115
Transport equipment, 6
Transport material, 20

U

Unemployment, 27, 37, 194, 196, 197
Urban dwellings, 95, 99
Urbanization, 6, 12, 35, 65, 90, 194
Utilities, 64, 72, 94, 130, 144, 162, 194

V

Value added, 63, 64, 70, 72, 73, 75–77, 80–84, 86, 91, 93, 96, 153, 158, 175, 176, 184
Variation in the stocks, 124

Vehicles, 82, 97, 120, 122, 156
Volume indices, 39, 43, 63, 65, 69, 71, 80, 85, 112, 123, 179

W

Wages, 68, 78, 79, 84, 95, 96, 99, 118, 129, 135, 138, 164
War, 18, 160, 190
Water, 83
Water supply, 76, 131
Welfare, 52–54
Wholesale and retail trade, 83
Wholesale trade, 100
Working age population, 34, 194
World War I, 4, 7, 12, 18, 33, 50, 52, 53, 127–130, 140, 159
World War II, 4, 7, 19–21, 41, 134, 190

© The Editor(s) (if applicable) and The Author(s) 2017

Open Access This book is licensed under the terms of the Creative Commons Attribution 4.0 International License (http://creativecommons.org/licenses/by/4.0/), which permits use, sharing, adaptation, distribution and reproduction in any medium or format, as long as you give appropriate credit to the original author(s) and the source, provide a link to the Creative Commons license and indicate if changes were made.

The images or other third party material in this book are included in the book's Creative Commons license, unless indicated otherwise in a credit line to the material. If material is not included in the book's Creative Commons license and your intended use is not permitted by statutory regulation or exceeds the permitted use, you will need to obtain permission directly from the copyright holder.

The manufacturer's authorised representative in the EU is Springer Nature Customer Service Centre GmbH, Europaplatz 3, 69115 Heidelberg, Germany. If you have any concerns regarding our products, please contact ProductSafety@springernature.com

Printed and bound by CPI Group (UK) Ltd, Croydon, CR0 4YY

23/03/2026

02076670-0008